HOW TO CHEAT

AT

Cleaning

HOW TO CHEAT
AT
Cleaning

**Time-Slashing Techniques to Cut Corners
and Restore Your Sanity**

JEFF BREDENBERG

The Taunton Press

The Taunton Press

The Taunton Press, Inc., 63 South Main Street, PO Box 5506, Newtown, CT 06470-5506
e-mail: tp@taunton.com

Editor: Pamela Hoenig/Erica Sanders-Foege
Cover design: Howard Grossman
Front cover: Photo by Jeffrey Krein
Illustrator: Joel Holland

How to Cheat at Cleaning is also published in paperback by The Taunton Press, Inc.

Library of Congress Cataloging-in-Publication Data
Bredenberg, Jeff.
   How to cheat at cleaning : time-slashing techniques to cut corners and restore your sanity /
Jeff Bredenberg.
      p. cm.
  Includes bibliographical references and index.
  ISBN-13: 978-1-56158-870-1 (alk. paper)
  ISBN-10: 1-56158-870-9 (alk. paper)
  ISBN-13 978-1-56158-994-4 hardcover
  ISBN-10 1-56158-994-2 hardcover
  1. House cleaning. I. Title.

TX324.B744 2007
648'.5--dc22

                                    2006023879

Printed in the United States of America
10 9 8 7 6 5 4 3 2 1

For Gladys Bredenberg.

Mom, maybe you shouldn't read any further.

Acknowledgments

The author is grateful for the invaluable expertise of the following sources:

Shannon Ackley
professional organizer,
Shelton, Connecticut

Jennifer Armentrout
test kitchen manager
and recipe editor for *Fine
Cooking* magazine,
Newtown, Connecticut

Alexander Barco
service technician, Computer
Medic, Dublin, Pennsylvania

Chris Barry
engineer for specialty glass
manufacturer Pilkington,
Toledo, Ohio

Sandra Beckwith
writer and speaker on gender
differences and male behavior,
author of *Why Can't a Man
Be More Like a Woman?*,
Fairport, New York

Steve Boorstein
a.k.a. The Clothing Doctor,
author of *The Ultimate Guide
to Shopping and Caring
for Clothing* and proprietor of
www.clothingdoctor.com,
Glen Echo, Maryland

Boy Scout Troop 320
in the suburbs of
Philadelphia, Pennsylvania

Pamela Brown, Ph.D
professor at the Texas
Cooperative Extension, Texas
A&M University, Lubbock, Texas

Cynthia Braun
professional organizer,
Lake Grove, New York

Dorothy Burling
retiree, Mishawaka, Indiana

C. Lee Cawley
professional organizer,
Alexandria, Virginia

Alan Cook
entrepreneur, inventor of
self-cleaning cat litter box,
Chicago, Illinois

Rashelle Cooper
product buyer for PetSmart,
Phoenix, Arizona

Pamela Dalton, Ph.D
odor scientist, Monell
Chemical Senses Center,
Philadelphia, Pennsylvania

Jeff Dross
product manager and trend
analyst for Kichler Lighting,
Cleveland, Ohio

Mary Findley
president, Mary Moppins Co.,
Eugene, Oregon

Evan Galen
architect, New York City

Charles Gerba, Ph.D
microbiologist at the
University of Arizona, Tucson

Joe Grant
owner, Computer Medic,
Dublin, Pennsylvania

Tom Gustin
product manager for Merry
Maids cleaning service,
Memphis, Tennessee

Elizabeth Hagen
professional organizer,
Sioux Falls, South Dakota

Rachel Hepner
spokesperson for specialty
glass manufacturer Pilkington,
Toledo, Ohio

Joni Hilton
creator of Holy Cow
cleaning products,
Sacramento, California

Roy Hinrichs
Internet technology manager,
Fort Worth, Texas

Jon Hoch
founder, Pressure Washers
Direct, Romeoville, Illinois

Ingrid Johnson
professor at the Fashion
Institute of Technology in
New York City

Kerul Kassel
productivity consultant,
Saint Cloud, Florida

Dana Korey
professional organizer,
Del Mar, California

Alexandra Krost
film crew worker,
Richmond, Virginia

Melissa Laiserin
dog behavior expert for
PetSmart, Phoenix, Arizona

Alisa LeSueur
executive director of the
American Association of Rain
Carrying System Installation
Specialists, San Antonio, Texas

Alexandria Lighty
owner, House Doctors Handyman Service, New York City

Robert R. Matheson, Ph.D.
technical manager for strategic
technology for DuPont Performance Coatings, Troy, Michigan

Janet Nelson
a Ross, Iowa-based spokesperson for The Maids Home Services

Susan Newman, Ph.D.
social psychologist at Rutgers University, author of *The Book of No: 250 Ways to Say It—and Mean It,* Metuchen, New Jersey

Lindsay Peroff
spokesperson for 1-800-GOT-JUNK?, Vancouver, British Columbia, Canada

Lisa Peterson
Newton, Connecticut-based spokesperson for the American Kennel Club

J. Winston Porter, Ph.D.
president of the Waste Policy Center consulting organization in Leesburg, Virginia, and former assistant administrator of the Environmental Protection Agency

Jay M. Portnoy, M.D.
chief of allergy, asthma, and immunology at the Children's Mercy Hospital, Kansas City, Missouri

Charlotte Reed
pet care expert, New York City

Philip Reed
senior consumer advice editor for Edmunds.com, Santa Monica, California

Trey Rogers, Ph.D.
professor of turf grass management, Michigan State University, East Lansing, Michigan.

Brian Sansoni
vice president of the Soap and Detergent Association, Washington, DC.

Victoria Scarborough, Ph.D.
director of research and development for Thompson's Water Seal, Olive Branch, Mississippi

Pat Schweitzer
senior home economist for Reynolds Consumer Products, Richmond, Virginia

Alissa Shanley
landscape and garden designer, Denver, Colorado.

Courtney Shaver
public relations coordinator, the Container Store, Coppell, Texas

Jen Singer
parenting writer and a stay-at-home mom, Kinnelon, New Jersey

Erik Sjogren
senior brand manager for Dixie Tabletop, Atlanta, Georgia.

Sarah Smock
spokesperson for Merry Maids cleaning service, Memphis, Tennessee

Judi Sturgeon
professional house cleaner and home health aid, Ambler, Pennsylvania

Brad Turner
plant manager for the Communications Factory, Mantua, Ohio

Lance Walheim
Exeter, California–based horticulturalist and garden expert for Bayer Advanced lawn care and pest control products company

Deborah Wiener
interior designer, Silver Spring, Maryland

Jeff Zbar
a.k.a. The Chief Home Officer, home office consultant, Coral Springs, Florida

*

The author would like to acknowledge the following print sources and those associated with them:

Consumer Reports, a valuable source of expert guidance about products.

Susan Strasser for her inspiring, scholarly history of American housework, *Never Done.*

Tim Vine of the newspaper *The Scotsman,* for his slightly less scholarly but nevertheless inspiring account of how to make your bed without getting out of it.

*

The author also is grateful for the contributions of executive editor Pam Hoenig, assistant editor Katie Benoit, the rest of the staff at The Taunton Press, and agent Linda Konner.

~ Contents ~

PERFECTIONISM IS SO OVERRATED

I'm the kind of person who's dying to dust the house with a leaf blower. I compile lists of things you can clean in the dishwasher—beside dishes. I'm a disciple of Erma Bombeck, the wry columnist who penned the words, "Housework, if you do it right, will kill you."

Do I want to be a slave to my house, working my fingers raw to create a shimmering show palace? No. Just give me an orderly, presentable, and sanitary environment. But don't make me work too hard for it—I have a career, you know, dinner to get on the table, and Little League games to attend. To heck with perfectionism. I'm gonna cheat.

What exactly do I mean by "cheating at cleaning"? If there's a faster way to clean, I'm going to adopt it. If corners can be cut, I'm going to cut them. If technology offers more cleaning power, automated cleaning, and easy-care materials, I'm there. And I'm going to set my own standards for cleanliness—goals that may be somewhat south of Martha Stewart's.

These actually are exciting times for people who hate to clean. Nanotech materials—that is, materials designed for specific purposes, molecule by molecule—have begun to reach the market. While few such products are in wide circulation yet, the science has given us miracle microfiber cleaning cloths, window glass that cleans itself, and light bulbs that destroy odor-causing particles. Self-cleaning garments aren't far behind. Personally, I'm hoping for dinner plates that scrape themselves off and jump into the dishwasher.

This talk of products leads me to a couple of crucial points about the writing of this book. First, many people who want to cheat at cleaning also hope to do so for minimal cost. Rest assured that for every innovative product I mention, there are 20 ways to cut corners that don't involve

extra expense at all. Second, it's impossible to give specific advice without the occasional mention of brand names. I want you to know that I accepted no freebies from manufacturers when I researched this book; I bought all of my own products for testing and I don't sell these products either.

Speaking of research, you'll notice that this book is written in a unique way. As I hunted for the cheatingest shortcuts possible, I spoke with scores of experts who were generous with advice. I name them in the text because I want to acknowledge them and because I want you to appreciate the authority of the information and the freshness of this research.

I also hope you find this book as fun to read as it was for me to write. The core of this book is specific advice on how to cheat at cleaning. However, along the way you'll also hear about the junk-removal company that had to dispose of 13 enormous Buddha statues. The guy who washed his socks in the dishwasher (honest, I don't do that). The couple who use their robotic vacuum cleaner to serve beer to guests. The researcher who bought dirty underwear from his students—all in the name of science.

My final point is an invitation to you. Not every person I quote has an impressive string of letters after his or her name. I'll be writing about home management for a long while, and I welcome tips and feedback from savvy readers such as yourself. Please feel free to write to me in care of this publisher, or stop in at www.jeffbredenberg.com and provide your input over the Internet. I may not put your name in lights, but I'll be happy to brand you as a first-class cheater.

—Jeff Bredenberg

REWRITING THE RULES YOUR MOTHER TAUGHT YOU

We all know what happened as two-career couples became the norm over the last several decades: Scores of new duties came rushing onto our to-do lists like a tsunami. In days of yore, Ozzie-and-Harriet families had one adult who went into the world to make money and another who managed the home front. Today, most families would collapse without two incomes.

With that as a backdrop, consider this interesting bit of research from the Soap and Detergent Association: 62 percent of women say they clean their homes pretty much the same way their mothers did. For goodness sake, corporations took a wrecking ball to the rules of business, but we're using the same old 1950s rules to manage our homes? No wonder we're overwhelmed. No wonder we're all going crazy.

It's time to rewrite the rules your mother taught you for housecleaning. Nothing less than your sanity is at stake.

One of the hardest things to set aside will be perfectionism. Why? Because we are inundated with images from movies, television, and magazines depicting homes with clutter-free, glimmering countertops—places where upholstery and dog hair never meet, where dust bunnies are extinct. Such homes are not achievable in the real world. Even when we work hard at house-cleaning, we feel guilty that we're not meeting unreachable goals. Let's wipe the slate clean and substitute a new set of priorities that meets the needs of modern families—a change that will restore your mental health.

GOAL 1: KEEP A SAFE AND HEALTHY HOME If you have to choose between killing germs and dusting your Hummels®, kill the germs. *How to Cheat at Cleaning* shows you how you can easily sanitize in all the right places.

GOAL 2: BE ABLE TO FIND YOUR POSSESSIONS WHEN YOU NEED THEM If your system's functional, it's fine. For those of you still in search of a semblance of order, this book provides scores of easy de-cluttering techniques.

GOAL 3: KEEP THE KIND OF HOME YOU ARE HAPPY WITH You are the one who has to be pleased with your surroundings, not your mother or your next-door neighbor.

NEW RULES FOR CLEANING

New goals require new pathways for reaching them and a new mind-set. Rather than perpetually marching toward perfection, we need real-world approaches—corner-cutting, time-saving, minimal-effort techniques for cleaning. Yes, we need ways of *cheating*.

The new rules for doing this are divided into two categories: mind-set, to get you properly focused, and procedures, to make sure you expend no more time or energy than absolutely necessary. These general principles will serve as valuable background as you proceed to all the specific corner-cutting advice in the coming chapters.

YOUR CHEATIN' HEART

Just what is it you spend so much time cleaning? Your material possessions. By redefining your whole approach to ownership, you can seriously reduce the time and effort you devote to cleaning. Here are some rules to put you into the cheat-at-cleaning frame of mind.

BE BRAVE ENOUGH TO THROW THINGS OUT Some of us actually have trouble throwing stuff away even when it's worn out, beyond repair, and has no conceivable value to anyone. I contend you should dispose of possessions that are in good repair, too, if you haven't used them within the last year. This goes for clothing, appliances, kitchenware, and more. Few of us have the extra physical and mental capacity to manage these unproductive items that clutter our homes.

BE WILLING TO SPEND MONEY IN EXCHANGE FOR CONVENIENCE Tolerance for spending varies from one individual to another, but remember that convenience items virtually allow you to "buy" time—often for a surprisingly small cost. Keep in mind also that any cleaning challenge is an invitation—I say *outright permission*—to buy cool gear.

ACQUIRE THE RIGHT STUFF, LITTLE BY LITTLE Your wardrobe is probably rife with clothes that stain easily, wrinkle readily, or require special care, such as hand washing and dry cleaning. Cumulatively, these clothes are an enormous hidden burden in your life. But no one expects you to toss them all out today. Just make sure that you replace worn-out clothes with stain- and wrinkle-resistant ones—items you can pull out of the dryer, hang, and wear without further care. This Materials On a Program (MOP) philosophy applies to virtually everything you own—not only clothing but also furniture, flooring, vehicles, appliances, building materials, and more. When it's time to buy something new, make easy care and easy cleaning priorities in your decision.

DON'T BUY THINGS THAT CAUSE YOU ANXIETY Do you have a car that's so pricey you feel compelled to wash and wax it

10 THINGS YOU CAN
QUIT CLEANING RIGHT NOW

1. **SNEAKERS.** Just buy dark-colored ones and wear them until they fall apart.

2. **GRILL GRATE.** When you're done grilling, leave the grill going. Close the cover over the grate and let any residue cook off for 15 minutes. Throw that wire brush away.

3. **SOCCER BALLS.** Everybody expects them to be marred and mud splotched. Think of it as a badge of honor.

4. **SHOWER CURTAIN LINER.** They're cheap. Throw your mildewed liner out and buy a new one every 6 months.

5. **PILLOW.** A washed pillow takes hours to dry. Throw it out and buy a new one every 6 to 8 months.

6. **STOVE DRIP PANS.** Use your grungy ones for everyday cooking, and keep a shiny new set to use when guests come.

7. **VENTILATION DUCTS.** Despite the advertising, regular professional duct cleaning is unnecessary.

8. **FIREPLACE WALLS.** Everybody expects a fireplace to have blackened walls. And you'll breathe even easier if you give up fires altogether.

9. **WAXING THE CAR.** The newer finishes are so tough cars don't need it anymore.

10. **MAKING THE BED.** Give it up—doctor's orders (see Chapter 6).

SPRING CLEANING: DON'T BE AN APRIL FOOL

Every spring you set aside two or three successive weekends on the calendar. You gather your cleaning armaments and warn your spouse that sudden out-of-town business trips will be viewed with deep suspicion. Then you tear through the house from attic to basement, a whirlwind of cleaning cloths, squirt bottles, brushes, and dusters.

If that doesn't sound like you, then at the very least you have the notion niggling at the back of your mind that you ought to perform spring cleaning every year. And you feel guilty about failing to.

If you feel good about doing a deep-down cleaning in your house once a year, go right ahead. But let's dispense with the guilt. The fact is, there is no reason for you to clean your house top to bottom all at once, and there is no reason to do this in the spring. The tradition of spring cleaning is a throwback to olden days when people shuttered their houses all winter and burned wood or coal for heat, spreading soot into every nook and cranny of the home. Come spring, those unfortunate souls couldn't wait to fling the windows open and start beating rugs, dusting lamps, and sweeping floors.

You don't have to do that—your heating system leaves the air clean. So free yourself of this dreaded ritual that wrecks your calendar or wracks you with guilt every April. A more reasonable approach: Manage the cleanliness of your home with a series of narrowly focused projects that are evenly distributed throughout the year.

every weekend? Furniture that's so fine you use it only for special occasions? A suit that's so delicate you're on tenterhooks every time you wear it? These possessions are Anxiety-Inducing Luxuries (AILments), and your own ego is making your life miserable. Gravitate toward modest, easy-care, functional possessions, even when you can afford the high-ticket stuff.

YOUR CHEATIN' HANDS

Now let's look at the rules of the game for cutting corners when you take that scrub brush in hand and actually attack some grime.

NARROW YOUR FOCUS With a schedule like yours, there's no time to clean the house from top to bottom. You'll get an appreciable amount of work done, however, if you attack mini cleaning projects throughout the week, 5 minutes here and 10 minutes there. This means taking a laser approach. You may not be able to clean the entire bathroom before you leave for work, but you *can* squirt cleaner on the tub and sponge it out.

BECOME A STORAGE NUT Make the best use of the storage in your home, and create new storage where none existed before. That's a key strategy to the easy elimination of clutter. This means mastering closets, shelving, boxes, bins, hooks, hangers, and more. Investment in storage gear pays off handsomely. See Chapter 3 for an in-depth discussion of clutter.

MAKE YOUR GEAR EASY TO GRAB The Accessibility Theorem goes like this: A cleaning task will be accomplished on a frequency that is inversely proportional to the distance between the object to be cleaned and the materials necessary to clean it. *Translation:* When it's hard to get to your cleaning tools, less cleaning gets done. At a minimum, keep a fully stocked cleaning station on each floor of the house.

ENGAGE THE BRAIN BEFORE CLEANING This is called the Thinking Wins Out (TWO) philosophy. Sure, it's tempting to let your mind wander while you're slogging through a cleaning chore. But the task will go more quickly and easily if you're ever alert for opportunities to cut corners: Set your plastic cutting board in the dishwasher rather than hand washing it; after brushing your teeth, touch up the mirror and several fixtures with one cleaning wipe; open your mail over a trash can and let all the junk fall into it. For every little labor-saving move you make, award yourself TWO points on your mental scoreboard.

BE WILLING TO REPLACE OLD GRUNGY ITEMS WITH FRESH NEW ONES Things like door mats, stovetop drip pans, shower curtains, and cookie sheets, for instance, are never really going to come clean. My advice is to run them into the ground, then replace them when they hit their inevitable irredeemably ragtag state.

A final note: I have no intention of becoming your new proverbial mother, looking over your shoulder as you clean. *You're* in charge. If you're not comfortable with instituting any particular piece of advice in this book, no problem—just slide on to the next item. Your mental health is more important than being a slave to someone else's ideas.

LET YOUR CLEANING TOOLS
DO THE WORK

The technology we use to clean our homes is always changing—sometimes ever so slowly, and sometimes in revolutionary ways. When we're right in the midst of them, the changes are difficult to appreciate. But look back to the beginning of the 20th century, when devices like the electric iron and the vacuum cleaner were first appearing in homes. Some folks were suspicious and even afraid of electrical devices. With booming industry drawing all of the servants away from household work, however, there was an enormous market for such cleaning "cheats."

The introduction of washing machines, dryers, easy-care fabrics, nonstick surfaces, self-cleaning ovens, and a nonstop parade of other labor-saving devices has had a radical effect on our lives. Cleaning tools are easy to take for granted as we slog through our daily chores, but the truth is that historically they have been one of the keys to human liberation. They have rescued us from the backbreaking, 24/7 task of managing a household. And the march of progress continues.

This brings up an intriguing question: What will be the next liberating device that historians will point to decades from now? Robotic vacuum cleaners? Windows that clean themselves? Automatic cat boxes? These gizmos—and scores of other innovative products—are available to you right now. You'll find them discussed in detail elsewhere in *How to Cheat at Cleaning*. The question is, Are you ready to incorporate such devices into your personal life?

Every individual has to answer that for himself or herself. Here's a quick set of questions to ask when you're considering adopting an innovative product. The BITE approach will help you decide whether to, uh, bite.

BETTER? Will this product actually perform the cleaning job better than my current method?

ILLUSION? Is there gimmickry involved? If it takes a half hour infomercial to sell this thing, could there be a reason it's not more popular?

TIME SAVING? Will this actually help me save time or cut corners?

ECONOMICAL? Is the extra convenience worth the cost of the item?

MANAGING YOUR TOOLS

If your only approach to cheating at cleaning is to not clean at all, well, you don't need a book to tell you how to find the hammock. But the savvy cheater-at-cleaning who wants to make the house presentable needs to know the best places to buy tools, the best ways to store them, and the best ways to put them into action. Here are some pointers.

BUYING

You will find the biggest selection of cleaning supplies, good prices, and brands you know at the big-box discount stores. So any time you can, buy your cleaning supplies there.

Janitorial supply stores are usually open to public, their prices are comparable to retail stores, and you can get larger containers of cleaners (often private labeled, but perfectly good). These stores are geared toward commercial cleaning people, however, and serving residential customers is not their priority.

At the supermarket, you might pay a little more and find less variety, but it's certainly convenient to buy an item or two during your regular grocery run.

STORING

Keep all of your cleaning tools in one spot in the house—a closet or in a corner of the laundry room, for instance—so you don't have to scramble all over the house looking

MICROFIBER: THE MIRACLE MATERIAL

Why are cleaning professionals ga-ga over microfiber cloths? Under the microscope, a conventional cotton fiber looks round—like a spaghetti noodle, says Tom Gustin, product manager for the Merry Maids℠ cleaning service. It just pushes dirt along as you wipe. Microfibers are much finer and split into tiny wedge shapes that actually scoop up dirt and pull it into the fabric.

Here's a simple experiment that will demonstrate the remarkable difference in cleaning ability. Make two dots of peanut butter on your kitchen counter, a teaspoon each. Wipe up one dot with a cotton diaper—wipe, fold the diaper, and wipe again until the peanut butter is gone. You'll have to wipe three or four times. Wipe up the second dot with a microfiber cloth. You'll probably get it all on the first try.

Now rinse the diaper in warm water under the faucet and squeeze. That brown smear will remain until you launder the diaper. Rinse the microfiber cloth and squeeze. The microfiber cloth will come clean, ready for use again.

for gear when it's time to clean. This will save you time and increase the likelihood of actually getting some cleaning done. Within this storage area, cluster your products by their use—mop, bucket, and other floor-care stuff together; cloths, vacuum, and other dusting implements in another spot. If you have more than one kind of mop, hang them on a wall upside down so you can tell at

DISPOSABLES SWEEP THE MARKET

Among newly introduced products, Swiffer® is one of the biggest homeruns of the last decade. It's a quick-and-easy way to give a room that "somebody cares" feeling in a minimal amount of time.

There are lots of spin-off products—and competitors—but the core Swiffer apparatus is this: a permanent 46-inch mop handle with a 10-inch-wide mop head, plus disposable mopping pads (either wet or dry) that are easy to slap on and pull off. This cleaning approach lops a huge hassle out of the floor-cleaning process—namely, filling a bucket, pouring in cleaner, hauling it around, dipping and squeezing out your mop, and pouring the water out at the end.

Disposable mop heads will snatch up dust and small particles, but they won't handle chunkier stuff like dead leaves from your houseplants, tracked in pine needles, or bits of dry pet food. You can, of course, use the mop to corral this stuff into one area and then get it up later with a brush and dustpan. At a certain point, the mop head will get overloaded with dirt (in my house, anyway) and lose its grabbing power. Stand over a trash can and pick off some of the debris with your fingers to get a little more mileage out of the pad. Also, you can flip the cloth over and use the other side.

Once in a while, when you've just put on a clean, dry cloth, use it to quickly wipe down the walls of the room. (Besides painting every several years, this is the only way that walls in my house get cleaned.) You can use the edge of the mop head to dust the tops of door frames, too.

a glance which is which, says Cynthia Braun, a professional organizer in Lake Grove, New York. Also, cluster all of your refill bottles in one spot and, at the end of each cleaning session, top off any bottles that you used.

If you have a second floor, keep a second cleaning station up there, fully stocked with everything you need to maintain the upstairs rooms.

USING

The best corner-cutting house-cleaners know that you need some kind of device for moving several cleaning items around the house with you as you work. This technique saves you from making multiple trips back to the cleaning closet. For most people, a tote tray is the way to go—a rectangular caddy with a raised handle and pocket-like bins all around it for holding squirt bottles, the whisk broom, cloths, and such. If you don't have a caddy, a plastic bucket will do in a pinch.

If you really want to show off your cheat-at-cleaning credentials, Braun recommends buying a tool belt at your home-improvement store. You can hang your most commonly used cleaning implements off the belt and you won't even have to bend over to reach for your caddy. When you're not wearing the belt, just hang it around the caddy handle.

I asked Tom Gustin, product manager for the Merry Maids cleaning service based in Memphis, Tennessee, to help compile a list of the most basic cleaning tools that any cheat-at-cleaning enthusiast would want to have in his or her closet. Aside from specialized tasks such as polishing silver, the following tools will handle virtually any household cleaning duty:

SCRUBBER SPONGE These are the household sponges that have an abrasive surface on one side for scouring tough grime. Scrubber sponges are color coded. Look for the kind with a white scrubber pad, meaning it's the least abrasive and least likely to scratch surfaces. "I would have two—one that you use for bathrooms and one that you use for kitchens and everywhere else," Gustin says.

TOILET BRUSH Yup, the wand that goes where others fear to tread. The all-plastic kind won't scratch the porcelain, whereas those with a wire center can. Make sure it comes with a little bowl-like stand that will catch drips when you're done. If you think *yuck* every time you see a toilet brush, switch to the super-convenient disposable variety.

VACUUM CLEANERS The hardcore cheater uses two vacuum cleaners, Gustin says—one conventional vacuum cleaner and one handheld vac. (Indoors, stick to the plug-in kind, since the recharging systems on some cordless models can be unreliable.) Use the big vacuum for broad floor cleaning and the handheld with its extension for cleaning corners, cobwebs, and tight spaces. With this one-two punch, you'll never need a broom. Gustin prefers the conventional upright vacuum cleaner to the canister or backpack styles. Look for a handheld that offers disposable paper dust bags as an option for easy, mess-free changes. If you can spare the expense, put a conventional vacuum cleaner on each floor so you won't have to haul it up and down the stairs. Use extension cords on your vacuum cleaners so you don't have to find a new electrical outlet every few minutes.

DUSTER Gustin likes lambs-wool dusters that come with an extension wand—they're great for dusting the tops of doors and the blades of ceiling fans. A good alternative: Fluffy, disposable dusting heads that fit onto an extension wand.

MOP Pass up the string mops, forge on past the sponge mops, and head straight for a flat mop. This device is good for wet or dry mopping and has a removable mopping pad that you can toss into the washing machine. They don't require wringing out and can reach under furniture more easily than conventional mops. Or jump whole-hog into one of the disposable mop systems—you just throw away the mopping pad when you're done.

BUCKET You'll need an all-purpose container for hauling liquids for cleaning windows, cars, floors, and more. Gustin uses a conventional round, 10-quart model.

BROOM Gustin actually never uses a broom, but you'll need one if you didn't run out and buy a handheld vacuum like he told you to.

CLEANING CLOTHS Microfiber cleaning cloths are superior at grabbing up dirt. Acceptable alternatives are cloth diapers or surgical "huck" towels.

Cleaners At the very least, you'll want each of these:

* ❋ Disinfecting cleaner for sanitizing
* ❋ All-purpose cleaner
* ❋ Glass cleaner
* ❋ Toilet bowl cleaner
* ❋ Floor cleaner

DISPOSABLE WIPES: TOSSING OUT A NEW STRATEGY

A few decades ago, disposable cleaning wipes had one lowly function: cleaning babies' bottoms. Baby wipes made perfect sense. Laundering anything that's covered in poop is pretty unappealing. Disposable diapers were a hit, after all, so why not wipes?

Then product researchers discovered that parents were cheating. They were using baby wipes for unauthorized purposes—say, wiping sticky fingers, doing touch-up cleaning in the bathroom, or blotting up stains on the couch. "Whoa," cried the ever-attentive product researchers, "maybe we ought to create a full range of disposable wipes for lots of different uses!"

So household-cleaning wipes emerged in the 1990s. Then dry, electrostatic wipes and cloths burst upon the scene in 1999, and the disposable wipe market has been expanding steadily ever since.

WARY OF WIPES?

Not all consumers have bought into the idea of disposable wipes. More than a third of all Americans have never tried any kind of disposable wipe, according to a survey done by the Soap and Detergent Association. That's too bad, because they offer enormous benefits:

- ☀ **Super convenience.** Everything you need is right there in one compact package—the cleaning cloth plus the cleaning chemical you need, all premeasured.

- ☀ **Portability.** Wipes usually come in convenient, resealable packaging that fits easily into a purse, glove box, desk drawer, gym bag, suitcase, or picnic basket. They're perfect for people on the go.

- ☀ **No mess.** There are no cleaning tools to wash or put away after the job is done. Just toss the wipe in the trash.

- ☀ **Tough on germs.** Whatever germs aren't killed outright by the wipes are just tossed into the trash can. They don't linger on your sponge or cleaning cloth, only to get spread around your home again.

- ☀ **Versatility.** While some wipes have narrow, specific purposes—everything from spiffing up your jewelry to cleaning blinds—many are good for a wide variety of cleaning tasks.

- ☀ **Reasonable cost.** Wipe users surveyed say the convenience definitely outweighs the expense.

So if you've been reluctant to plunge into the world of disposable wipes, you're in for an eye-popping surprise. Your cleaning chores are profoundly more tedious than they need to be. "I think you could probably clean your whole house using wipes," says Janet Nelson, a Ross, Iowa–based spokesperson for The Maids Home Services[SM].

Disposable wipes are easy to find—they're now a staple in supermarkets, discount stores, and home-improvement stores. They're incredibly easy to use as well, but there's one rule that too many people ignore, says Brian Sansoni, vice president of the Soap and Detergent Association: Read the package label first. You'll find any safety warnings on the label. Also, you'll find out what your wipes can and can't do. Not all kill germs, for instance, not all can be flushed down the toilet, and some (such as furniture polish wipes) shouldn't be used on floors because they'll make them slippery.

You may be concerned that disposable wipes aren't environmentally friendly. They don't actually amount to a lot of refuse, however—less than five hundredths of 1 percent of solid household waste, whereas newspapers and plastic make up 10 percent. Also, some brands have started making their packaging from recyclable materials.

Read on for specific advice on how to get the most out of disposable wipes around the home and when you're out and about.

WEDDING DAY JITTERS

Disposable baby wipes can mop up or erase any number of stains, marks, and splotches on your clothing or upholstery. Acting quickly is important. Janet Nelson, spokesperson for The Maids Home Services, has a quick-thinking friend who used a diaper wipe to solve a wedding day crisis. Someone had gotten a spot of blood on the bridal gown. Dabbing the spot with a wipe removed it entirely.

WIPE OUT HOURS OF LABOR

Use disinfecting wipes on food preparation surfaces and utensils to protect your family from bacteria that can cause serious illness. Check the packaging to make sure that the wipes you're using will kill germs. Carefully follow the label's instructions for disinfecting, too. You'll probably be told to wipe the surface down and let it air dry for 10 minutes. Then you may need to wipe again with a wet paper towel to remove chemical residue.

Remember that not all wipes are intended for all purposes. If your wipes promise to disinfect hard surfaces, they may be too harsh to use for hand washing or wiping baby bottoms, for instance.

TUNE UP THE BATHROOM In Chapter 5, we discuss how to clean your bathroom in 7 minutes (12 minutes for the deluxe job). If even that seems like too much slave duty in the throne room, you can double or triple the amount of time between cleanings with the use of disposable wipes. Just perform this easy, 1-minute routine twice a week:

Take an all-purpose or glass-cleaner wipe and clean the mirror and the window, then use it to pick up any accumulated dust or grime around the top of the tub, the top edge of the tile and, last, the base of the toilet. Toss the wipe out. Now take a disinfecting wipe and clean the faucet, the countertop, the toilet handle, and the toilet seat. Toss it. Take another disinfecting wipe and run it across the top rim of the tub, the sides, and across the drain to pick up any hair. Done!

STOP DIRT AT THE DOOR Stash a package of general-purpose wipes near any door where kids and pets come and go, suggests Joni Hilton, creator of Holy Cow™ cleaning products in Sacramento, California. Hilton says she keeps wipes near the back door, particularly in the summer. When kids come in from playing, grimy shoes and hands get a wipe down.

BREAK THE SPONGE HABIT Disposable dishwashing wipes could put a barrier between your family and disease. Unfortunately, the sponges that often are used for dishwashing can collect food particles down in their dark, moist recesses. "They're a germ factory," says Sansoni. Disposable dishwashing wipes will change that. They come already filled with dishwashing detergent and have a soft side and an abrasive side for scrubbing. You can use them a couple of times, Sansoni says, and just throw them out.

SECRET INGREDIENT: ALCOHOL Keep alcohol-based wipes in the kitchen. Not only does the alcohol kill germs but it cuts grease, too. These wipes will make quick work of the stovetop and those grubby stove knobs, for instance.

THINK BIG Many disposable wipes are tiny things—smaller than a standard washcloth, Nelson notes. Many cleaning jobs around the house—like wiping down an entire toilet—will require two or three wipes. To make your life even easier, keep an eye out for the larger, thicker wipes, which pick up more grime without

MESSY DOGS? FETCH A WIPE

A pet expert based in New York City, Charlotte Reed, shares her two-bedroom apartment with a parrot, 13 finches, two Persian cats and three dogs. She uses disinfecting wipes daily on counters where she prepares food, on the floor around the pet-food bowls, around the litter boxes, and under the 67-inch-high birdcage.

She keeps her pets away from newly wiped areas until they've aired out, so they aren't exposed to the disinfecting chemicals. She's also reluctant to use harsh cleaners around her birds, so for cleaning around her feathered friends she uses mild antibacterial hand wipes.

Since the dogs romp around outside frequently, they're particularly wipe intensive. When they come in, Reed uses little puppy gates to confine them to the kitchen until they've been cleaned up. General-purpose wipes work well on their paws. It's particularly important to wipe their feet in the winter, she says, because sidewalk salt will irritate their paws if it's not removed.

requiring frequent changes. You can often find these in the diaper section of your supermarket.

KEEP THEM UNDER WRAPS Most wipes come in a resealable container that will keep them from drying out. But if a package you've opened is going to be sitting around for several weeks, pop it into a zip-closing plastic bag for extra protection.

KEEP BUGS AT BAY Viruses that cause colds and flu can live on surfaces around your home for as long as 72 hours. So if someone in your home is sniffling and sneezing, regularly disinfect any commonly touched surfaces. This will reduce the chance of that infection getting passed along. Check the label on your wipes to make sure they'll kill cold and flu viruses. Wipe down appliances (don't forget the refrigerator handle and the microwave touch pad), counters, tables, cabinet handles, doorknobs, light switches, telephones, television controls, remotes, and video game controllers.

SEND WIPES TO SCHOOL One in five parents say their kids' schools lack the proper personal hygiene products needed to prevent illness. So why not take a proactive role with your child? Slip a hand wipe into her lunch box each day and instruct her to clean her hands before she eats. Put it in a plastic bag to prevent drying, or use the kind that comes individually packaged.

Germ-killing wipes, disposable mop heads, miracle fabrics—the space program may be attention grabbing, but science affects you much more directly in the cleaning closet. When you become a fan of innovative cleaning products, your chores become negligible and white space opens up on your calendar—free time for more important things. Less work. More fun. That's what cheating is all about.

CLUTTER CONTROL
MADE EASY

If eliminating the clutter in your home sounds like a lot of work, consider how much work co-existing with that clutter *causes*. Professional organizers say if your home weren't cluttered, 40 percent of your housework would evaporate. Also, if your office is orderly, you save yourself *weeks* of time each year—time that's typically spent looking for papers and other materials. Yup, de-cluttering your home is itself a way to cheat at cleaning: It requires less effort than not de-cluttering.

Now, stop groaning—nobody's going to tell you to get your home ready for a *House Beautiful*® photo shoot. That kind of "perfection" is no more real world than a Hollywood back lot. More reasonable goals leave room for the occasional messy dresser top, jumbled car trunk, or chaotic pantry shelf, goals such as:

* Being able to find possessions when they're needed.
* Having a home you're comfortable showing to friends and colleagues.
* Having a place in your home for every possession and a simple, ongoing process to get it there.

THE CLUTTER-BUSTER'S PLEDGE

1.

Every possession has to earn its keep.
It must have a function in my daily life.

2.

Every possession will have a home.
No more setting things down "just for now."

3.

I will not measure my personal value by my possessions.

4.

Sentimentality is a home wrecker.
I will use it sparingly when deciding what items to
keep and what items to dispose of.

5.

De-cluttering is an ongoing lifestyle,
not a finite project.

6.

Absolutely everything I own will, at some time,
become of no use to me.

7.

No one, not even my kids, will ever establish
a museum devoted to my worldly goods.

In this chapter, we'll look first at the "mental" side of clutter busting—simple ways of thinking about clutter that will help your home automatically fall into order. Then we'll tackle the physical aspects of clutter: working with containers, shelving, and other hardware and getting optimum use out of the storage spaces available to you. Naturally, this chapter is brimming with the world's best big-impact-for-minimal-work, corner-cutting advice.

THE INS AND OUTS OF CLUTTER

Imagine a child's toy box. Once a month, the child gets one new toy and puts it into the box. Every 6 months, the child stops playing with one of these toys— it's either broken or he finally admits that he's outgrown it, and he gets rid of it. What's going to happen over time, with more toys going into the box than are coming out? The toy box will overflow into an unsightly mess, and the child won't be able to find the toys he wants.

Your house is much like that. Most of us have many more possessions entering the house (new stuff) than we have exiting the house (worn-out stuff). It doesn't take a math genius to realize that this will eventually overburden all storage systems in even the largest homes. Possessions will be spilling out onto the floor, swamping the counters, and stacking to the ceiling in the garage. It's clutter.

Why does this happen? In broad terms, we are the beneficiaries of the Industrial Revolution. Never in the history of humans have so many goods been available for so little money. Just to make sure that we remain suitably wanton in grabbing up new possessions, a mammoth marketing machine eggs us on with hundreds of "buy" messages every day. This explosion of consumer goods is so recent, historically speaking, that society hasn't developed strong enough defenses against the onslaught. After all, there's very little money to be found by providing the more helpful kinds of messages, such as "Purge your possessions and live more simply" or "You don't really need a third television." So businesses don't do that. As a matter of self-preservation, you're going to have to reinforce the "buy-less" lifestyle all on your own.

Start with "The Clutter-Buster's Pledge" on p. 24. These seven simple commitments will help you curtail your hyper-buying ways, break your irrational emotional bond with possessions, and manage the stuff you do keep so that you have the kind of home environment you really want. Photocopy the pledge, tape it to the inside of your closet door, and review it before every shopping trip. If a mere "attitude adjustment" can slay the Clutter Monster once and for all—well, that's the very best kind of cleaning cheat.

STEP UP THE OUTFLOW

As you stem the flow of goods into your house, of course, your clutter problems will become easier to manage. However, there's a second part of the equation on which you also can have a major effect: the flow of goods out of your house. Here are some easy ways to improve your home's "outflow"—above and beyond taking the trash out each week.

QUESTION YOUR POSSESSIONS When you're de-cluttering and you're not sure whether you want to keep an item, ask yourself these five questions, says Kerul Kassel, a productivity consultant in Saint Cloud, Florida:

1. When did I last use this? If you haven't used it for 6 months to a year, get rid of it. (Seasonal items are an exception.)

2. Will I be able to find this again? This applies in particular to papers. If the item doesn't have a proper "home" where you'll be able to find it again, you might as well toss it.

3. What shape will this be in when I retrieve it? Aging computer equipment will be useless in a jiffy. The same goes for fashion items and food.

4. Is it costing me more to store this, on the off chance that I may need it some day, than it would for me to borrow or buy it in the future? Think in terms of space in the home and the mental burden of dealing with the item: Do you want to be caretaker of this thing for the next 5 years to 10 years?

5. Is owning this thing *truly* improving the overall quality of my life?

CLUSTER THOSE OUTBOUND ITEMS Create a little "way station" in your home for items that you've decided are headed out the door, says C. Lee Cawley, a professional organizer in

---

6 INDICATIONS THAT IT'S JUNK

Can't decide whether that 80-pound concrete gargoyle is junk or a treasure? Lindsay Peroff, of the clutter-removal company 1-800-GOT-JUNK?℠, says the following factors indicate that an item is junk:

1. You can't remember the last time you used it.
2. There's a layer of dust on it.
3. It's broken.
4. It's out of date.
5. You can't remember why you saved it.
6. You just don't want it in your home any more.

WHY WAIT UNTIL YOU DIE?

New York City architect Evan Galen has an interesting strategy for helping you sort through possessions that clutter your home. "Imagine that you've died and your family is coming around to look at your stuff and deal with it," he says. "Whatever they would keep that you don't especially need, give it to them *now*."

If you have an item that your family would not want—and you don't want it either—get rid of it now, he says.

Alexandria, Virginia. These could include items you're donating to a thrift store, a tool you borrowed from a neighbor, rental videos, library books, dry-cleaning, and clothing you need to return to a department store. If these things are lying all about the house, you won't remember to take them with you the next time you're running errands—they'll be that much more clutter. If they're all assembled near the door, you'll remember to snatch them up on your way out. Cawley likes to hang a shoe bag–like organizer on the back of her door. You also could hang an organizer on the back of your coat closet door or put the items in shopping bags on the floor of the coat closet.

GET ON A CHARITY'S PHONE LIST Many organizations regularly pick up donated items from residences. Phone around to find the groups that will call you the day before they plan to have a truck in your neighborhood. Make sure you have a clear idea of what kind of items the charity accepts. Some won't take furniture, for instance.

SELL YOUR CLUTTER TO OTHERS Make a yearly yard sale an institution in your home. Don't just scramble around the day before a yard sale, looking for disposable items in your house. All year long, sock items away in boxes in the corner of your basement—items of obvious value that nevertheless have no place in your life. Three months before the day of your yard sale, distribute a flier among your neighbors, asking them to schedule their yard sales on the same day. Have them share the cost of a classified ad in the newspaper on the day of the sale—bargain hunters from miles around will be attracted to a street with multiple yard sales. Call around to find a charity that will agree to pick up all of the leftover items from you and your neighbors on the day after the sale. And make this a personal rule: No yard sale item may come back into the house.

HIRE A PRO TO TAKE IT AWAY It's a sign of our times that businesses such as 1-800-GOT-JUNK?[SM] are thriving. "We find the main reason we're growing is that people are spending money storing junk they're never going to use," says Lindsay Peroff, a representative of the company based in Vancouver, British Columbia. Her company will send employees to your home to pick up any clutter you ask them to. This saves you from having to load the junk, truck it away, and arrange for dumping—the company takes care of it all. Their services are particularly advantageous if you're overwhelmed by a mountain of possessions you just want out

A DIRTY STORY XXX

ONE MAN'S JUNK . . .

You see some strange sights when it's your job to remove clutter from other people's homes and businesses. Lindsay Peroff, of the clutter-removal company 1-800-GOT-JUNK?, says the following items are among the more peculiar unwanted possessions they have hauled away for clients. (They make sure the owner is aware of the value of any item.)

- Prosthetic legs
- 18,000 cans of sardines
- 13 huge porcelain Buddha statues
- 19,000 pounds of frozen animal carcasses
- Antique rifles
- A defused bomb from World War I.
- An antique silver set.
- A 1954 Martin® guitar. (The owner said, "Do whatever you want to with it." It sold for more than $8,000 on eBay®.)
- Half a truckload of expired dog food.

A junk-removal crew also came across a totally unexpected item hidden amid one resident's clutter: an engagement ring that had been missing for 30 years. *That* was returned to the grateful owner.

of your life. Peroff says an average job costs $260 and fills half of a truck the size of a Federal Express[SM] delivery vehicle. The company has 200 locations in North America, covering most large cities and their suburbs. There's probably a branch—or a similar company—near you.

ORGANIZE BY STATIONS

Trying to de-clutter a typical home is enough to make anyone hyperventilate. However, Kassel has a deliciously easy trick for organizing any home—a technique that strikes at the heart of clutter: View your home as a collection of "stations" for performing the household's various functions.

Let's consider an obvious example: Food preparation is a core function of the home, and the station for that is invariably the kitchen. You probably do an adequate job of ensuring that all items you need for food preparation are quickly and easily found right there in the kitchen—not in the basement, not in the garage, and not under little Joey's bed. As you stand in your primary food-fixing spot, the items you need most—cutting board, knives, and frying pan, for instance—should be right at your fingertips. Infrequently used items should have homes farther away—your monster-size soup pot might go on a high shelf in the pantry, for example.

How does the idea of stations in the home control clutter? Well, in a home organized by function, items naturally gravitate toward where they need to be. The "home" for each item becomes more readily apparent, and an out-of-place or nonfunctional item will stand out like a streaker in the village square. If an object in your home is not serving any purpose, you have to ask yourself why it's there—and set it on a fast track out the door. (Okay, you might argue that art objects aren't part of a "station," but your display items do serve a purpose and need to be managed as a group.) Also, the stations concept performs the psychological trick of breaking your home down into smaller, easily managed compartments. You may not be able to de-clutter the entire house when you find a spare 10 minutes, but you can do wonders with your sewing area in that amount of time.

When you regard your home in terms of stations, an interesting strategy emerges that will save you a lot of time and bother: Every

THE ABCs OF CDs

Stop alphabetizing your CDs—right now. If you have all of your music neatly arranged from Abba to Zappa, you have to reorganize them every time you bring home a new CD. Instead, professional organizer C. Lee Cawley recommends that you organize your music by broad categories such as "Classic Rock," " '80s New Wave," "Jazz," and "Party Music." For each category, leave 20 percent of the space open to accommodate growth. That way, you don't have to move all of your CDs around each time you buy a new disk. Also, you don't have to return a disk to one precise slot on the shelf—anywhere on the shelf will do, as long as it's in the correct broad category.

"It's all about retrieval," Cawley says. That is, don't arrange your collection according to how you want to put CDs *away;* arrange it according to where you will look for the CDs when you want them. Besides, who do you think you are? A librarian?

If space is at a premium in your entertainment area, here's a supercompact way to store your CDs and DVDs: Throw out all of the plastic cases for your disks. Buy binders filled with the special sleeves made just for CDs, and slide each of your disks into these pockets. Tossing out the cases may feel radical at first, but it's liberating once you get used to it. The binders keep all of your disks together, make them easy to browse, keep them clean, and take up much less space on a shelf. If you're willing to put a tad more work into this system, pull any liner notes out of the CD cases and tuck them into a pocket of the binder. For DVDs, photocopy the case, hole punch the paper, and clip it into the rings of the binder.

station deserves to be completely outfitted with the tools and materials necessary to perform the assigned function. This will save you enormous amounts of time walking about the house looking for the myriad objects you need, say, to prepare a package for mailing. Your mail station will have tape, envelopes, boxes, stamps, scissors, labels, and anything else you need to get a package ready. No trekking to the kitchen or sewing room for scissors. The extra expense for duplicate supplies is nominal (those supplies *will* get used, after all) and the payoff is huge.

Here are quick notes about just a few other stations you might have in your home. Depending on your lifestyle, you'll likely want to invent some of your own:

WORK STATION. Everything you need for conducting business, managing finances, and corresponding. See Chapter 8 for more on home offices.

OVERRUN BY BOXES?

Every time you buy a small appliance, you read the following instructions in the manual: "Save all packaging material in case you need to return this appliance to the manufacturer." So now 500 cubic feet of empty cardboard boxes have overrun your basement.

To heck with that—throw those boxes away. In the unlikely event that you need to ship an appliance, just take it to one of those private mailing stores. They're experts at safely packing up any kind of delicate object you can imagine. Simply plop the bare appliance on the counter and give the clerk the shipping address and phone number.

CLEANING STATION. Stock a portable cleaning caddy with spray cleaners, dusting cloths, brushes, and wipes. Have a cleaning station on each floor of the house.

LAUNDRY STATION. This contains everything you need for clothing management—washer, dryer, detergent, stain remedies, and iron and ironing board (if you must). You need a bar for hanging garments and good light for inspecting clothes for stains.

FITNESS STATION. A welcoming place with plenty of room for your treadmill, stationary bike, and weights, plus easy access to any audio or video gear you need.

AUTOMOTIVE STATION. Typically in the garage, carport, or shed, it contains car-cleaning materials, auto tools, extra windshield fluid, oil, and coolant.

CRAFT OR HOBBY STATION. Put all of your craft or hobby tools, materials, and reference books in one place, organized in easy-access storage containers. Consider such needs as good lighting, a work surface, and ventilation.

TOOL STATION. An unused wall in the basement is ideal for a large pegboard or some other wall-mounted tool-organizing system. Have a worktable nearby, plus small grab-and-go toolkits already outfitted for your most common jobs. You need plenty of small containers for sorting hardware.

ENTERTAINMENT STATION. Cabinets for television, sound system, electronic game systems, plus generous storage for CDs, DVDs, game controllers, remote controls, and headphones.

DESIGN DIRT AWAY

AN OFF-THE-WALL STORAGE IDEA

To add an enormous amount of storage space—and therefore reduce clutter—in even a tiny home, why not build a hidden, shallow closet that runs the entire width of one wall? This works in any room—and even in a corridor, says New York City architect Evan Galen.

Galen likes to build these wall-size closets from floor to ceiling, on invisible hinges and then paints or wallpapers them to look like other walls in the room. They take only 8 inches of space out of a room, but they can hide plenty of shelves, hanging clothes, cleaning gear, and more.

Gift-wrapping station. This is the spot for all your wrapping paper, ribbon, tape, scissors, gift tags, plus a broad work surface. You might want to combine this with a mailing station.

Cawley recommends one more kind of station in the home: Each person in the house should have a personal staging area or launch pad. This is an assigned, dedicated spot where that person can park her purse, briefcase, cell phone, PDA, and keys. When she goes out into the world, all of the objects she needs to take along are right there. When she comes home at night, she drops everything in the same place. Kids need launch pads, too, Crawley says, for their book bags and shoes. The launch pad might be a drawer near the door, a bin, a basket, a shelf, or part of a counter.

SIMPLE STEPS FOR ATTACKING CLUTTER

No one is immune to clutter. As carefully as you might train yourself and your family to stop clutter before it starts, little infestations are inevitable now and then—a mound of magazines and books on the coffee table, Lego® pieces and action figures spilling across the family room floor, a car trunk brimming with tennis equipment and broken umbrellas. That's only natural. But you can make a clutter-busting lifestyle just as natural with these simple steps, which were partially inspired by Courtney Shaver, a representative of The Container Store®, based in Coppell, Texas.

1. **NARROW YOUR FOCUS.** Which are you more likely to accomplish over the next month: A 5-hour de-cluttering session, going top-to-bottom in your house? Or five separate 1-hour de-cluttering sessions, hitting one clutter hot spot at a time? The latter, of course. If you wait until you can tackle the entire house, you'll never get around to it. Make a habit of launching 1-hour clutter attacks once or twice a week. Having that one corner of your home gleaming with order will inspire you to start plotting your next attack on clutter.

2. **PULL AND PURGE.** Drag everything out of the area that you're de-cluttering. If your target is a pantry shelf, for instance, take all of the cans, boxes, kitchen gizmos, paper towel rolls, and jugs of juice off the shelf and spread them out on the floor. Be ruthless about disposing of anything you don't need, has expired, or otherwise has no function in your life.

3. **CLEAN.** You won't see your pantry this empty for months or years to come, so vacuum and dust it thoroughly. Some of the items you're saving could stand a wipe down, too.

4. **CATEGORIZE.** Cluster all the like things together. In the pantry example, you would put the pasta and canned spaghetti sauce together, the soups and stock together, the baking ingredients together, the snack foods together, and the paper goods together.

5. **SET PRIORITIES.** Decide what items you need easiest access to (they'll go on the mid-level shelves) and what items are used less often (high shelves, low shelves, and remote nooks).

6. **CONTAIN.** Decide how best to display and contain your items (use bins, baskets, hooks, and mini-shelves, for instance). Your arrangement should make the best use of

the space available. Items should be visible and accessible. Use a flexible storage system that can adapt to changing needs.

A 10-year-old I know very well had two bookshelves in his bedroom that were chock-full of books he wasn't using—most of them meant for younger kids. The rest of his room was a mess because he was out of storage space. Hoping to create more storage for him, I asked him to pull off the shelves all the books he was willing to sell in the next yard sale. He pulled out 25 slim volumes. Disappointed, I then asked him to remove all of the books he was willing to put into storage in the crawl space. He filled several boxes with 400 books!

The moral of the story: Storage space is an important psychological tool. One reason homes stay cluttered is a reluctance to part with possessions. Putting them into storage is a comfortable alternative. When these items have been out of sight for a year, it will be easier emotionally to give them away or sell them.

Storage is a sort of magic wand for creating an orderly house. This applies not only to items you want to stash away for the long term but also to items you want to keep orderly—but still accessible—for daily use. Let's take a look at how to best manage the storage spaces you have and how you can easily create new storage space when you need more.

WORKING WITH CONTAINERS

Give yourself permission to go crazy with containers. They're one of the most basic tools for home organization, and they're usually inexpensive. Here are some ideas for working with containers, from professional organizers and The Container Store.

USE TRANSPARENT CONTAINERS If you have items stored in opaque, unlabeled containers, you're going to forget what's in there. Those objects may be out of your way, but retrieving them will be a hassle. So make sure any storage containers you use are either see-through or labeled.

STACK THOSE BINS Vertical space in the typical home is woefully neglected. Stacking bins in your office, entertainment area, pantry, bedroom, or craft room will add tons of storage while only occupying a few square feet of floor space. For convenience, look for bins with slide-out drawers on the side.

TURN STACKS ON THEIR SIDE If you have a spot in your house where papers collect—say, on a dresser, counter, table, or credenza—professional organizer C. Lee Cawley says you can bring them to order with a snap of the fingers. All you have to do is turn the pile onto its side. Buy a vertical folder organizer from an office store and plop it in the same spot where those papers gather. Create a folder for each category of paper and sort the documents into the files. The papers take up no more space, yet they're instantly retrievable and look better to boot.

PUT SUPPLIES ON WHEELS Rolling carts are a powerful storage strategy, particularly for supplies that you need access to only for temporary work periods. Roll the cart out while you're working, then roll it back to a closet or a remote corner of the room when you're done. This works particularly well for cooking, office supplies, shop tools, and arts and crafts.

COVER THE CARDBOARD Alexandria Lighty, owner of the House Doctors Handyman Service[SM], likes storage boxes that blend in with the decor of the room where they're used. This is neither difficult nor expensive to achieve. Drop by an office-supply store and pick up a set of corrugated cardboard boxes, the handled kind meant for holding office files. Spritz the exterior of each box with spray glue and cover them in a fabric that works well with the rest of the room. For instance, you could cover the boxes in the same material you used for the room's curtains. Park these boxes on a shelf. When it's time to straighten up the room, pull the boxes out, dump the out-of-place objects into them, and slide them home again.

A LITTLE HELP FROM YOUR FURNITURE

Lighty likes to outfit her rooms with furniture that's designed to keep clutter off the floor and out of sight. Here are some of her favorites:

ARMOIRES. Lighty has stationed one of these closet-like cabinets in her living room, her dining room, and in each bedroom. In the main living areas, her armoires house the televisions, game systems, and related gear. They're smaller and less imposing than the typical entertainment center, and she can change the tone of the room just by closing the door to hide the TV. In the children's bedrooms, armoires provide a compact hanging space that's easy for kids to manage themselves.

FOYER CREDENZAS. Many homes have some kind of surface near the front door where people coming in drop their purses, hats, keys, and such. Why not use a long dresser, one with six to nine drawers, and assign a drawer to each member of the household? That way the miscellaneous personal items will be hidden—but also easy to find when each person dashes out the door for the day.

STORAGE BENCHES. Shop for the kind of bench that doubles as a storage box, and park it in the foyer or in the mudroom. Your children can toss their book bags in there when they get home from school. Little tykes will love stashing a jacket, hat, and gloves there, since they usually can't reach such items in a conventional closet. If you ask arriving guests to remove their shoes, a bench-box near the door hides the pile of footwear better than the commonly used basket.

DAY BEDS. Unlike sofas, day beds are built high enough that storage bins can be stashed underneath. With a few pillows across the back, you have a comfortable seating area, plus a backup bed for overnight guests. Use a bed skirt to hide the bins below.

MANAGING YOUR STORAGE ROOMS

When you have a bulky object you need to store away, where ya gonna turn? To the garage, attic, basement, crawl space, or shed, of course. These spaces are the utility infielders of the home front, the locations of choice for yard tools, shop tools, bicycles, out-of-season clothes, food bought in bulk, rarely used kitchen gear, backup refrigerators, sports equipment, and much more. Because they house such a hodgepodge of possessions, they stretch your organizational skills to the limit. With a few savvy techniques, however, you can vanquish those cluttered obstacle courses that build up in

GREAT · GEAR

CRAWL-SPACE HELPERS

A storage area that is impractical, inaccessible, or uncomfortable to reach will rarely be used. The traditional crawl space presents a number of challenges to the homeowner. Because of the low ceiling, you have to scrape and bruise your knees while you move storage items around. You can't stand straight up, of course, so moving heavy boxes more that a yard or two is a Herculean feat. And because crawl spaces are often damp, you risk starting up a mold farm on your stored goods. The following items, available at any home-improvement store, should be standard gear for any crawl space:

- **KNEE PADS AND WORK GLOVES.** These will protect your hands and knees as you crawl about on the concrete. Store them permanently on a hook or shelf right at the entrance to your crawl space.

- **DOLLY.** A flat, four-wheeled dolly makes it easy to whisk heavy objects from one side of the crawl space to another. Tie a rope to the dolly so you can sit still and pull objects toward you.

- **DEHUMIDIFIER.** Installing a dehumidifier in your crawl space will help to keep moisture and mold at bay. So you don't have to empty water from the dehumidifier manually, run a hose from its collection bin to a drain.

your storage rooms. Who knows—you might actually be able to park your car in your garage again.

Here's how to get optimum, organized use out of your storage rooms with the least amount of effort, according Lighty and her colleagues at House Doctors Handyman Service:

✳ Cover the perimeter of the room in wire shelving, pegboard, hooks, and similar storage. With this single measure, you will triple your home's storage capacity. Wire shelves and pegboard are sturdy, don't hold dust, and don't require painting, so upkeep on them is zero.

✳ Use heavy-duty hooks mounted on overhead beams to hang such bulky items as hoses, extension cords, and bicycles. If you have open beams, look for the easy-mount style that will slip right over the beam, or grasp the beam, and hang down. If the beams are covered by drywall, use screw-in hooks.

✳ Use tall laundry hampers and garbage bins (you'll clean them first, right?) to hold basketballs, hockey sticks, football pads, helmets, and other bulky athletic equipment.

✳ Suspend a shelf from the ceiling to hold long, flat items such as skis, snowboards, and canoe paddles.

✳ An old golf bag makes a great holder for long-handled tools such as hoes, rakes, and tree pruners.

✳ Allow each family member to hang no more than two coats in the main coat closet. Other coats can be stored in each person's private closet, and they can be rotated seasonally. This way, there's plenty of hanging space for guests in the main closet. Also, people will be more likely to hang their coats—instead of dropping them on the furniture—if it's easy to find a spot in the closet.

HUNT DOWN NEW STORAGE SPACE

Gather up a pen, a memo pad, and a measuring tape. Take a 20-minute tour of your house, from your attic to your basement, from the garage to the shed. Jot down notes about every space in your home that could conceivably be turned into storage. Note the location of each space and its measurements. Include in your list the following:

* Open walls where racks, shelving, or organizers could be installed.

* Odd gaps that remain from the building's design—for instance, the space under stairways or open area above cabinets.

* The backs of doors, where you could install hooks, racks, or organizers.

QUIT WAITING FOR PERMISSION

Tired of arguing with family members who get absurdly attached to items cluttering your house—your husband's 3-year-old hunting catalogs, for instance, or little Jeanie's 17 Popsicle®-stick creations on the kitchen counter?

Well, think about it: Nobody's really keeping track of each and every one of those items. Occasionally pick out one innocuous item and toss it out without asking permission. Bury it deep in the kitchen trash can, or toss it in there just as you're taking out the garbage. If, by some astounding chance, someone realizes it's missing 6 months later, you can just shrug your shoulders and say you haven't seen it lately. This falls into the "little white lie" category. That's okay. That's why we call it cheating.

✳ Current storage space that can't be fully used. This would include closets where there's more space than necessary above the top shelf.

You don't need to convert every spot on your list into storage immediately. Identify the locations on your list that fall within the most clutter-prone areas of your home, and start your conversions there. Home-improvement stores, organizer stores, hardware stores, office-supply stores, and discount stores offer multiple ways to create functional, convenient storage out of any of the odd spaces in your home. Keep the list for future reference.

"Utilize every bit of space," says New York City architect Evan Galen. In a home office, for instance, "A space between a column and a wall might be only 9 inches wide, but that could hold a year's worth of paper on adjustable shelves."

Now you are armed with the corner-cutting secrets for keeping an orderly and clutter-free home. Combine an organizer's outlook with some inexpensive storage equipment and a penchant for cheating, and your home will be ready for a photo shoot in no time. Maybe not for *House Beautiful*® but surely for *House Pretty Darned Good.*

SPOUSE, KIDS, FRIENDS, AND HIRED PROFESSIONALS

One of the most delicious ways to avoid household cleaning is to get somebody else to do it. The work gets done, and you don't have to lift a finger.

Now, I know I'm sauntering into tricky territory that's rife with gender-powered land mines. That's because, historically, women have done far more of the housecleaning than men. We all know why—back in the Ozzie-and-Harriet days women stayed home and vacuumed the living room twice a day in their pearls and high heels. Several decades later, two-career couples are the norm, but women are still typecast as the primary housekeepers.

The situation is improving, though. University of Maryland research shows that women's hours spent at housework were cut in half between 1965 and 1995, while men's housework hours doubled. Research released in 2005, however, indicates that women on average are still doing 61 percent of the household cleaning. And they're really, really steamed about that.

So in this chapter we'll examine how to get your significant other to do more cleaning—particularly if he's doing an *insignificant* amount of it. And I'm here to tell you that you can achieve this and still have your relationship intact at the end of the day. (In the unlikely event that you happen to be male and carry an unfair cleaning workload, this advice will work for you, too. Just switch the pronouns around.) We'll also examine how to get the kids to provide more cleaning help. And remember, hiring professionals to clean your home is actually a reasonable approach for many beleaguered couples.

ESCAPING THE GENDER TRAP

If you want help with cleaning the house, you're going to have to ask for it. There is a whole complex of reasons why you got stuck with an unfair share of the cleaning. To turn the situation around will require a little gumption and some communication skills—applied in the right place, at the right time.

First, consider this news flash: Men and women are different! Apparently, you and your spouse are on different planets, looking at the cleaning issue through two vastly different lenses. Do *not* expect your spouse to share your priorities for cleaning, to use the same methods you would use, or to clean to your specifications.

"Men don't see dirt the same way that women do," says Sandra Beckwith, the author of *Why Can't a Man Be More Like a Woman?* If children spill a little fruit juice in front of the refrigerator, a woman will leap for the paper towels. The spill will make enough of an impression on the husband so that he avoids stepping in it, but it won't register as something that needs to be cleaned up. "I think it's truly a genetic thing—their brains aren't wired to see it," Beckwith says.

Upbringing also is a factor. Many girls are brought up with housekeeping woven into their play, whereas boys emulate Dad sitting on the couch watching sports. Thus gender stereotypes get perpetuated.

Here are other ways that men and women differ when it comes to cleaning:

PRIORITIES. A clean and tidy home is not a priority for men. Women know that cleanliness in the home is better for health and that furnishings last longer when they're clean. Women in general are more attuned to health issues and are usually the health-care brokers in the home.

RESEARCH. Women will read instructions on the label of a disinfecting cleaner. Men will just use the product—or ask a woman how to.

TECHNIQUE. Men approach a cleaning task like a military assault. Beckwith pictures a guy entering the bathroom wearing goggles and a bulletproof vest, a sponge in one hand and a spray bottle in the other. He sprays everything in sight, wipes quickly, and backs out fast. Women will take several cleaning products and tools into the bathroom for different purposes, and will do the cleaning slowly and methodically.

ATTENTION. Men come equipped with special filters that prevent certain information from reaching the brain. Hard as it is to believe, your spouse may truly not know where the mop is.

ASKING YOUR SPOUSE FOR HELP

Once you appreciate the gender differences with respect to cleaning, you're ready to ask for more help. "You're going to be resentful, tired, and cranky if you're doing it all yourself," says Susan Newman, Ph.D., a social psychologist at Rutgers University

STUPID MEN TRICKS

Author and speaker Sandra Beckwith likes to regale audiences with her collection of "Stupid Men Tricks"—goofy things that guys do and women would never consider. Where does she get her material? Unfortunately, everywhere she turns.

On a radio call-in show, for instance, the male types were just lining up to outdo each other. One fellow recalled that when he was single he used to stuff his dirty socks into a drinking glass, run the glass through the dishwasher, and then put on the socks and drink out of the glass. Another caller said he was above that—this superior being liked to dry his T-shirts in the microwave, flipping them over every 10 seconds to dry them evenly. As they say, guys, don't try this at home.

"Now you see why I stress the importance of training," Beckwith says. "If that's how they do laundry, they need help."

and author of *The Book of No: 250 Ways to Say It—and Mean It.* "If he doesn't see that, you're going to have to tell him—that you're not his maid."

If you're newly married, it's important that you and your mate have a full and frank discussion about dividing up the household chores evenly, says Jen Singer, a parenting writer and a stay-at-home mom. Think of it this way—you're establishing patterns that will last for decades. It's a lot easier to agree on an equitable division of labor in the glow of an early relationship than it will be to change entrenched habits years from now. Furthermore, if you take on too much of the cleaning, you're going to be overwhelmed when you have children. So make a detailed list of all of the cleaning duties that need to be done in the home and divide them up—each of you getting some chores you enjoy, as well as some that are nasty. Chart out who's going to do each duty and how often it will be done.

If you've been married for years, and it's time to redistribute the workload, plot out in advance the discussion points you want to make, approach your spouse in an rational state of mind, and spell out the housework situation—what needs doing and who's currently doing what. Tell your spouse that the workload looks uneven, and tell him how that makes you feel, says Beckwith. (*Pop quiz:* Which phrase is less emotionally charged: "burdened" or "pissed off"?) Remark that it looks as if he had more leisure time than you do—you want extra time to spend with your husband and less time vacuuming. Ask which duties he would like to take on—and let him decide. Again, it will help if the two of you work together to make a list of the cleaning chores, assign your name or his name to each task, and note how frequently each will be done.

Following are other ways to make sure that cleaning chores shift from your to-do list to your spouse's.

MAKE YOUR WORK VISIBLE Does your spouse have a Magic Underwear Drawer? He puts used undies into a hamper and clean ones materialize in the dresser! No, no, no. You need to find subtle ways to remind your spouse of all of the work you do, says Singer. So if you're going to launder his clothes, deliver

---

FIVE VERY MANLY
THINGS ABOUT CLEANING

If you're the kind of guy who fears that housecleaning is a threat to your manliness, here are five points to keep in mind:

1. Being in charge of a cleaning job is a valid excuse to buy tools.

2. When you clean, you get to wear your rattiest jeans, T-shirts, and sneakers.

3. A guy who can clean is able eat all the junk food on the couch that he wants—and hide the evidence.

4. Any guy who can leap into action at a party and remove a fresh wine stain from the carpet will impress the heck out of everybody.

5. You get to hunt down and kill fierce wildlife. Okay, we're actually talking about germs, but they're still dangerous little beasts.

his laundry in a basket to the bedroom—but let him put everything away. Also, when the two of you are relaxing in the den in the evening, having the "How did your day go?" discussion, don't hesitate to list all of the cleaning chores you accomplished. You did the work, so take the credit.

PICK THE RIGHT TIME Discuss your need for more help at a time when your spouse won't be distracted or resentful—not while he's watching his favorite sports team on television and not the moment he gets home from work and needs to unwind. Otherwise, an angry undercurrent will scuttle your discussion.

PROVIDE TRAINING Women often know exactly how to perform cleaning functions, but men often don't, Beckwith says. Tell your spouse the key things he needs to know about loading the dishwasher, for instance. ("There are men who load the dishwasher with the glasses face up," she says.) Make sure he knows where the detergent is, how much to put into the dispenser, and how to operate the controls. Provide any training by *showing* how it's done—not telling.

LOWER YOUR STANDARDS This may sound condescending, but it's not. Some women's standards for cleaning are "ridiculously high," says Beckwith. If you criticize your spouse's cleaning efforts or redo his work, he'll quit helping. Be happy that some amount of cleaning was accomplished, even it it's not the way you would have done it.

STICK TO YOUR GUNS If your spouse is supposed to handle a particular cleaning task and he doesn't get around to it, don't do it for him, says Newman. That's a trap: The workload will drift back to the same old inequitable arrangement.

SCHEDULE THE WORK Your grandmother probably had a rigid schedule for housekeeping duties—there was a wash day and an ironing day each week, for instance. Modern homemakers tend to approach their tasks randomly as they find the time, says Singer—and that often means that work piles up undone. Small, self-imposed deadlines will help you and your spouse keep up with the work. For instance, Singer makes sure she has all of the breakfast dishes put away in the dishwasher before the kids leave for school in the morning, and she changes the bed sheets every Tuesday.

PRAISE AND REWARD No matter how lacking your spouse's clean-ing effort might have been, find something nice to say about the job—and throw in a reward: "Wow, shiny bathroom faucets! Why don't we drop the housework for now and go to a movie?"

GET SELECTIVE WITH YOUR CLEANING If you're having trouble making your point about needing help, ensure that any duties that specifically affect your husband get done last or not at all—washing his clothes, sorting his socks, and picking up his shirts from the dry-cleaner, for instance. "Sorry about that, Herb—I had to vacuum *the entire house* today by myself."

TRY EXTORTION If your spouse is reluctant to do his share of the cleaning, says Beckwith, hire a housekeeper to alleviate the burden—once every 2 weeks might be all the relief you need. Also, take the family's dirty clothes to an outside laundry for cleaning and folding. Hire a cook for a day to prepare a week's worth of meals (do an Internet search for "personal chef services.") If your spouse objects to these expenses, remind him that you've been asking for help. This will motivate your spouse to do more.

A DIRTY STORY
XXX
WORLDS APART

When you stay at home with the children, you and your spouse are often living in different worlds. Parenting writer and stay-at-home mom Jen Singer borrowed her husband's car once and accidentally dribbled some sesame seeds from a bagel onto the clean floor. (It's clean because the kids are rarely in his car.)

In good-natured retaliation, her husband sneaked into Jen's car and poured a half bottle of sesame seeds onto the floor. He sat back and waited for a reaction—and waited, and waited. You see, Jen's car is the prime vehicle for transporting the kids; it's a rolling museum of soccer balls and juice boxes. When hubby finally mentioned the seeds, Jen reports, "I said, 'Are they next to the lollipop sticks or the sand from the beach?' I didn't notice."

SANTA, RELATIVES, AND FRIENDS

During the gift-giving holidays in many industrialized countries, consumer spending goes into absurd hyperdrive. How many more scarves, gloves, and ties can our closets handle? How many more swirling, chopping, and grilling gizmos can we cram into our pantries? Do you really need a cell phone, iPod™, or digital camera that's only one generation improved over the one you already have? Here's a thought that will help return some sanity to gift giving: Why don't we redirect some of that spending in a way that will lighten our cleaning workload and thereby relieve some stress—particularly around the holidays?

Imagine this scenario: A couple decides that rather than dumping money into unneeded jewelry and neckwear for Christmas, they will spend a couple hundred dollars on a cleaning service that will scour the household from top to bottom. They have itdone in mid-December and can entertain guests hassle-free during the coming weeks.

Or try this variation: You and your spouse decide to have a cleaning service visit your home once a month during the coming year. Start up a cleaning kitty, tossing in some of that cash you would have spent on unnecessary merchandise. Invite your in-laws to contribute as well (in lieu of the annual fruitcake gift).

Singer remembers fondly when she was a totally exhausted mom with a baby and a toddler in the house. Her mother took pity on her and hired a cleaning service to do a thorough, top-to-bottom cleaning of the house. That left only light maintenance cleaning for weeks to come.

The yellow pages and the Internet will put you in touch with professional house cleaners in your vicinity. However, the most reliable way to find a good house cleaner is word of mouth, says Judi Sturgeon, a professional house cleaner and home health aid based in Ambler, Pennsylvania. Ask your friends, neighbors, and co-workers for the names of people who do excellent work.

There's one big warning in this gift-giving business, notes Beckwith, and it returns to the issue of gender differences: Under no circumstances should a man give a woman a cleaning device or a kitchen appliance—unless she specifically asks for it. Men sometimes forget this crucial detail because they like practical gifts.

LITTLE PEOPLE, BIG HELPERS

Do your kids drift dreamily through family life like wealthy guests at a sun-drenched beach resort? Do they toss dirty shirts into the corner of the room only to have them reappear fresh and clean on a closet hanger the next day? Do they have a clue how to open the dishwasher? Do they turn green and yell "Mom!" at the first glimpse of cat vomit?

As long as you're redistributing the cleaning duties in the home, include the kids in the process. From a mercenary point of view, children are a good source of low- or no-cost labor. But they need to learn how to clean for their own good as well, says Newman. You're training them to be competent adults.

FINDING THE RIGHT WORDS
Explain to your kids that cleaning the house is one of the things they have to do as a member of the family. Most children have no idea what life is like within other families, so you actually have a free hand in deciding how yours will operate. "If you set patterns and standards, this is what they grow up with and this is the way they think life is. As a parent, this is your prerogative," says Newman.

Explain to your children the problems involved in keeping the house clean, and involve them in finding solutions. They'll take more ownership of those solutions and participate more willingly. As with your spouse, make sure your children have the tools and the training they need to do each cleaning job well.

You will probably get occasional whining, back talk, and dragging of feet. But be firm on these points, says Newman: Tell them no is not an answer, and that later is not an option. Say, "We're your parents. We're not your friends. You can tell a friend

MAID TO ORDER

Choosing a housecleaning service depends on your personal preferences and circumstances. Your biggest decision involves whether to hire an independent individual to clean your house or a full-blown housecleaning business, says parenting writer Jen Singer. Keep these factors in mind:

* **A service that has several employees will always be able to show up on time. If they send in a team, the work will get done faster. The service may have specialists who will do a particularly good job cleaning such features as carpeting or upholstery. You won't know the workers, however, and the job will probably cost more.**

* **If you use a single, independent house cleaner, you'll know the worker and be more comfortable with that individual in your house. The job probably will cost less, and the worker will be more willing to handle odd tasks for you—such as taking phone messages or running errands. However, with one worker, the cleaning will take longer, and if that housekeeper gets sick or delayed the work won't get done.**

you're not going to play, but you can't tell your parents you're not going to pitch in."

Most children are very adaptable, and they have a strong desire to please their parents, Newman says. "If a parent just says, 'I need help,' that often will get a child to pitch in." When you praise their efforts, they'll be more willing to participate, too.

Put the kids' duties on a chart in a prominent place—on the wall in the kitchen, for instance. Include in the chart the chore to be done, the child who will do it, and the day it's to be done. (When possible, use classy names for the duties—"Chef's helper," for instance.) To prevent squabbling, rotate these responsibilities weekly or monthly.

A WRINKLE SOLUTION FOR YOUR LITTLE SQUIRTS

Children are not renowned wardrobe planners. How many times has your daughter pleaded with you, just before bedtime, to iron a wrinkly blouse—because she's just gotta, gotta, gotta wear it to school the next day?

Author and speaker Sandra Beckwith knows the scenario well. Forget that hassle of setting up the ironing board and heating up the iron, she says. Put the blouse on a hanger, spritz it with wrinkle-release spray, and smooth the fabric with your hands. By morning the blouse will be dry and wrinkle free.

Wrinkle-release spray also is a blessing for travelers who want to make their suitcase-squashed clothing presentable.

"It has totally transformed how we do laundry," Beckwith says.

When the kids do their jobs, keep your feedback positive. Don't fret if a T-shirt isn't folded just so or they missed a dust bunny in the corner of the living room. "Don't get too hung up on quality," says Beckwith. "You have to lower your standards once in a while or your head will explode."

Should you reward your children for cleaning? Theories about this vary widely from family to family. One reasonable approach: Establish a specific set of basic duties for your children that they will not be rewarded for—that work is just part of being a family member. If the kids get their basic chores done and do extra cleaning as well, that deserves a reward—money, extra privileges, treats, or a movie.

AGE-APPROPRIATE CHORES

Want your children to be happy little helpers around the house? Make sure they have a reasonable chance of performing their cleaning chores well—with training and supervision, of course. Here's a look at duties that children can start tackling at various ages, according to experts:

1. **PRESCHOOLERS:** Take plastic plates to the sink, help set the table, put toys away, put coats away, dust (within reach).

2. **AGES 5–8:** Make bed, put book bag in order, put clothes in hamper, set table, rinse dishes, load dishwasher, wash pots, some bathroom cleaning, rake leaves, shovel snow, sweep.

3. **AGES 9–11:** Sort laundry, vacuum, dust, take out garbage, clean windows, scoop out cat litter boxes.

4. **AGES 12 AND UP:** Just about any cleaning duty, including running dishwasher, cleaning bathroom, laundering clothes.

APPEAL TO THEIR PLAYFUL SPIRITS

Kids are naturally fun-loving creatures. They'll help you clean the house more readily if there are playful aspects built into the work. Try some the following approaches.

PLAY BEAT THE CLOCK Set a timer for 10 minutes and tell your kids, "If we can get this room clean before the timer goes off, we'll go out for ice cream." You might not even have to use a reward system, says Sturgeon—often kids just like racing against the clock.

MAKE IT A TEAM SPORT Children will enthusiastically help with the cleaning if they're competing against others, says Beckwith. Have your spouse take one child to clean the upstairs bathroom while you have another child cleaning the downstairs bathroom. Provide each team with a checklist of tasks to accomplish and the tools to do the job—then shout, "Go!"

STRIKE UP THE BAND Lively music will inspire your kids to keep moving as they clean. Crank up the stereo or let them wear their iPods.

GET SILLY To make the chores more fun, break out the Halloween costumes and let each person dress up in an absurd outfit while you all clean. Try this while you rake leaves in the front yard—the neighbors will giggle about it for years.

TURN TOOLS INTO TOYS Let children have fun with their cleaning tools. Some kids like to play with the bubbles while they wash dishes in the sink, for instance, and others enjoy writing their names in the bathtub with foamy cleaner.

Now you are fully equipped to call in reinforcements. Sure, some of your family members may be touchy about taking on more cleaning; but you have feelings, too, and you deserve relief. An extra pair of hands around the house is too great an asset to ignore.

SANITATION *AND* SANITY:
KITCHENS AND BATHROOMS

Usually, the veteran, card-carrying cheater at house cleaning is happy to ignore that which cannot be seen by himself or guests. There is a significant caveat to this philosophy, however. Sanitation, health, and safety have to be based on science—not on corner cutting and looking the other way. We stay sane by concentrating on our top priorities, and this has to be one of them.

The cheating in this chapter, then, lies in maintaining laser-sharp focus on what's important and casting aside what's not. Fortunately, the secrets of sanitation around the house are simple and easy. By instituting a few basic practices, you can protect yourself from many of the germs that are lurking in your home. There are a lot of myths about home sanitation, too, so this chapter also provides plenty of ways to save yourself effort and angst.

You'll find much of this chapter devoted to sanitation where household germs do the most damage—in kitchens and bathrooms. You can't see these germs, of course, so we do the next best thing—attack the specific spots in your home where scientists tell us they are most likely to be. And, once your empire is secure from microbial invasion, you'll find shortcuts for keeping your kitchen and bath presentable and orderly.

GIVE GERMS A ONE-TWO PUNCH

Bacteria can live for hours on surfaces and viruses can survive for days. People who touch those surfaces can easily transfer those germs to their mouths and become sick; keep them clean and you seriously reduce the risk of food poisoning, flu, colds, and other maladies. Your number one defense in this battle is a commercial product called disinfecting cleaner.

Notice that the term *disinfecting cleaner* has two words in it. They're both important—a chemical tag team. First, check the label of your product and make sure that it uses the term *disinfect*. Use of this word has to meet Environmental Protection Agency (EPA) standards, and it means that the product kills bacteria and viruses. The term cleaner is crucial, too, because you want chemicals that are designed to loosen dirt from the surfaces that soil clings to. This way, the disinfectant can to do its job better. A disinfectant without cleaner is designed for use on surfaces that have already been cleaned. A cleaner without disinfectant is designed only to remove dirt, and the label of such a product will not promise to kill germs.

You can buy disinfecting cleaners wherever cleaning products are sold, including supermarkets, home stores, and discount stores. You could mix your own, but the commercial products are more convenient and provide

PUT THE SQUEEZE ON SPONGES

If he were to be reincarnated as a salmonella bacterium, microbiologist Charles Gerba would want to make his home on a kitchen sponge. It's dark inside, it's moist, it's got tiny traces of food embedded in it, and you smear it all around the room, providing plenty of places to multiply. Germ heaven! Well-intended housekeepers everywhere are wiping down myriad surfaces with a sponge, thinking they're cleaning—when in reality, they're providing a job relocation service for salmonella, *E. coli,* and other microbial creeps.

"Some of the cleanest kitchens we found were actually those of bachelors," Gerba says. Among the reasons: They used their sponges less and therefore spread fewer germs.

The good news is that de-bugging your kitchen sponge is easy. You just have to remember to do it. Any one of these methods will work:

❋ If you're regularly using your kitchen sponge to wipe up after using a disinfectant cleaner you're golden. Your sponge is no longer a bacteria colony.

❋ Equally labor free: Buy antimicrobial sponges, available in supermarkets and discount stores.

❋ Put your kitchen sponge in the dishwasher just before you wash a load. Germs can't take that kind of heat. Make sure you secure the sponge so it doesn't get snagged in the inner workings of the dishwasher.

❋ Dampen your sponge and microwave it on high for 30 seconds. Take care when you pull it out—the water inside will be scalding.

precisely the right balance of ingredients, says microbiologist Charles Gerba, Ph.D., of the University of Arizona in Tucson, a scientist who spends much of his professional life analyzing household germs. "The homeowner doesn't have to be a chemist any more," he says.

Park a bottle of disinfecting cleaner under the kitchen sink and under each bathroom sink. Squirt this stuff every day on the commonly touched hard surfaces, including counters, sink, faucets, faucet handles, toilet handle, toilet seat, refrigerator handle, and cutting boards. This will take only you 8 seconds per room. Read the fine print of your product so you're clear on how it works. Typically, once you have spritzed the liquid on, you have to let it sit for a specific period to get the germ-slaying done, usually 30 seconds to several minutes. Then you wipe the fluid up, rinse your sponge, and wipe again with the wet sponge.

YOUR HOME HIT LIST

Here's a rundown of commonly contaminated spots and simple methods for de-bugging them.

While the principles of sanitation apply to the bathroom as well, most of these observations involve the kitchen because that's where most of the harmful bacteria are found. At least a third of the disease-causing germs in your home hitchhike there on raw food. Also, people tend to do a much better job of cleaning in the bathroom. "The cleanest object in the house is the toilet seat, because people are so paranoid about it," Gerba says. "If you're going to lick anything in the house, lick the toilet seat."

Since you can't see germs, the best you can do is disinfect where they're most likely to hang out, thus reducing your chances of encountering them. If you disinfect the following hot spots, you'll be far safer from disease than most families. Be sure to check out "Put the Squeeze on Sponges" on the facing page before using that sponge!

A SECOND SKIN

Buy a box of thin, latex (or plastic) medical gloves at your drugstore and park it in a kitchen cabinet or the pantry. These inexpensive, throwaway gloves will get you through innumerable messy jobs, in or out of the kitchen, and save you a skin-scouring cleanup afterward. Just a few of the uses:

- Handling potentially germy foods such as raw chicken.
- Keeping the indelible scent of garlic or fish off of your hands.
- Handling dead presents dropped at the back door by the cat.
- Messy crafts.
- Painting.
- Polishing shoes.
- Changing the oil in your lawn mower.
- Cleaning the toilet.
- Cleaning up vomit.

THE KITCHEN SINK Think of your kitchen sink as a basket of bacteria, contaminated by raw chicken, meat drippings, and food scraps, all warm and moist. If you're peeling a carrot and it falls into the sink, assume it's contaminated and wash it off with hot water. Include the sink in your daily spray-and-wipe with disinfectant cleaner.

THE DISH TOWEL You mop up messes with it. You wipe your hands while you're preparing meals, smearing it with bacteria from raw food. Yes, your dish towel quickly gets as contaminated as the kitchen sponge. As part of your cleanup after a meal, switch to a fresh dish towel. Wash your dish towels in hot water with bleach. As with sponges, if you use your dish towel to mop up after use of disinfectant, the bacteria in it will curl up and die.

THE CUTTING BOARD Chicken, beef, pork, and even some fruits and vegetables wreak a peculiar kind of revenge when you cut them up—they leave bacteria behind on the cutting board. Think about this the next time you slice some chicken for stir-fry and then cut up a bell pepper. Do you really want to serve salmonella salad? At the very least, use one cutting board for your meat and another for your veggies during meal preparation. Then use disinfecting cleaner on both boards.

An easy alternative: I like to keep three hard plastic cutting boards available in the kitchen. After using one, I slide it directly into the dishwasher, which does a splendid job of disinfecting.

Wooden cutting boards won't stand up to this abuse, so I don't use them.

THE REFRIGERATOR DOOR HANDLE How many times do you pop the refrigerator open during meal preparation? Do you wash your hands first every time? No, you don't. A contaminated refrigerator door handle will quickly spread germs to every member of the family. So spray the door handle on all sides with disinfectant cleaner, wait the prescribed amount of time, wipe, and rinse.

TELEPHONES You might be surprised to hear that home telephones are abuzz with harmful bacteria. But think about it: You're putting raw steaks into a marinade when the phone rings. You pick up the receiver, you slam the phone down when you realize it's a recorded message, and then you hurry back to making dinner. You have just left a reservoir of germs on the telephone receiver. Disinfecting the phone is simple: Spray disinfectant onto a cleaning cloth and wipe the whole thing down—receiver, base, and buttons. (Don't spray directly onto any electronic equipment—the seeping fluid could damage it.) A disposable disinfecting wipe will do the job, too.

THE TV REMOTE Here's another popular microbial crossroads in the home—handled by many grubby fingers but rarely cleaned. As with the telephone, spray a cleaning cloth with disinfecting cleaner and give your remote a rubdown. Or use a disinfecting disposable wipe.

MORE SANITIZING STRATEGIES

Here are some more pointers, shortcuts, and surprising facts you'll want to know about sanitation in the home.

GO DISPOSABLE There's an easy alternative to kitchen sponges and dishtowels, which are famous for developing colonies of harmful bacteria. Instead, use nothing but disposable paper towels in the kitchen. "People say, 'Oh that's not environmentally friendly!' Well, if you get diarrhea and you use a lot of toilet paper, that's not environmentally friendly either," Gerba says.

WASH AFTER COOKING Here's a great item for the quiz shows: At what time during the day do you think people are likely to have the most fecal bacteria on their hands? Gerba conducted a study of germs on people's hands, and here's his final answer: After preparing a meal. People remember to wash their hands before fixing dinner, but it's not commonly done afterward, when their fingers are dripping with bacteria picked up from raw food. So scrub up with soap and warm water before you ring the dinner bell.

NO SINK? GO WATERLESS If you don't like scrubbing your hands at the sink so much or if a sink just isn't available, waterless hand sanitizers do a good job of killing the germs on your hands, Gerba says. They're available at supermarkets, drugstores, and discount stores. Keep a small container in your purse, briefcase, and desk.

On the other hand (sorry), don't be misled by dishwashing liquid that claims to be "antibacterial." Such labeling is somewhat deceptive, Gerba says. When you read the fine print, you'll learn that antibacterial dishwashing liquid is designed to kill germs on the hands—not on dishes. Many people use dishwashing liquid as hand soap when they're washing up at the sink, the manufacturers reason. To kill germs on your dishes, standard air-drying on a dish rack does a perfectly good job, Gerba says.

KITCHEN DISPOSABLES FOR MINIMAL MESS

Just about any time the food you're preparing meets a surface that you're going to have to clean later, there's a way to get a disposable object—usually paper, plastic, or foil—to take the "hit" instead. If this sounds wasteful, just remind yourself that letting food mess up your pans and counters has a cost all its own—you lose time doing the extra

THE GROUND RULES

You know the 5-Second Rule: When you drop a cookie on the floor, the thinking goes, it's okay to eat if you pick it up within 5 seconds. It's a time-honored, wishful-thinking rule of thumb for kids and grown-ups alike—usually cited as a way of excusing loutish behavior to by-standers. Well, you might get away with following the rule, but it has everything to do with luck and nothing to do with timing.

A food sciences intern at the University of Illinois at Urbana-Champaign decided to test the rule and came up with a surprising discovery. The floors she tested in high-traffic areas all over campus were relatively bacteria free, probably because the floors were dry and bacteria need moisture to live. You could eat an Oreo® off those floors.

Then the young scientist went into the lab and infected floor tiles with *E. coli* bacteria. When she dropped food onto those tiles, the bacteria made the leap instantaneously.

So if you drop a cookie onto the kitchen floor, "It all depends where it lands. If it lands where the dog pooped, time is not a factor," says microbiologist Dr. Charles Gerba. "It is always a gamble with germs. Most of the time it is not a problem, but once in a while you lose. The way to play the game with germs is to always keep the odds in your favor."

In other words, the 5-Second Rule is a crapshoot.

cleaning; you need to use cleaning chemicals; you put wear on your pans, counters, and scrubbing tools; you use water to rinse it all away; and you use up energy heating that water.

Here are some delicious ways to cut corners while cooking, using inexpensive products that are readily available at your supermarket.

WAXING POETIC Just think of wax paper as a long stretch of disposable countertop. When you're cooking, tear off 8 inches and lay the sheet on the counter near the stove. After stirring the marinara sauce, lay your drippy spoon on the wax paper. The moisture won't bleed through to the counter. Use the same surface for grating cheese and peeling carrots.

Cover the kitchen table in wax paper when you and the kids are decorating cupcakes. When the icing starts flying, the table will stay clean. (The icing in your hair will still require a shower.) When you're microwaving an open bowl of food, lay a stretch of wax paper over the top to contain splatters and prevent a tough, cooked-on cleanup later on.

FOIL IT AGAIN Spare yourself the misery of trying to scrub baked-on food from your pans. Line them with foil every time you stick one in the oven. Pat Schweitzer, senior home economist for Reynolds® in Richmond, Virginia, says this is the quick-and-easy way to fit your pan with foil: Turn your pan upside down and tear off enough foil to cover it. Mold the foil over the pan. Pull the foil off the bottom, turn the pan right side up, plop the foil into the pan, and fold the edges over the rim.

A SAFETY NET FOR YOUR PIE Put a foil- or parchment-lined pan on a lower rack of your oven to catch drips any time you're baking a pie, says Jennifer Armentrout, test kitchen manager and recipe editor for *Fine Cooking*® magazine, based in Newtown, Connecticut. Throwing away a stretch of foil or baking parchment is a heck of a lot easier than cleaning the oven of sugary, baked-on drippings.

BAG THAT BIRD Oven cooking bags are tough sacks that contain the meat you're cooking and keep the juices where you want them—in the food, not decorating your oven, pans, and other cooking gear. The nylon kind works in the microwave or oven. The foil version works in the oven or on the grill. The large ones will handle an entire turkey, a leg of lamb, or a beef roast, and smaller bags will fit a chicken or pot roast. A quick search on the Internet will turn up hundreds of recipes that call for cooking bags and will revolutionize the way you use your kitchen.

GO SOLO "Hot bags®" are a close cousin to the oven bag. These are foil envelopes in which you can cook individual meals— say, a boneless chicken breast with vegetables. Not only are the hot bags disposable but they also allow you to vary the contents of the meal according to each family member's taste.

SLOW COOKING, QUICK CLEANING Nylon liners for slow cookers are yet another cheat-at-cleaning variation of the oven bag. Slow cookers (a.k.a. Crock-Pots®) are already a great way to cut corners in the kitchen—in the morning, just dump the ingredients in, cover, turn it on, and dinner is done when you get home from work. However, nobody enjoys cleaning that cooked-on crust of food from the ceramic interior bowl of the cooker. Nylon liners put an end to that chore. Set the liner inside the ceramic interior of the cooker and then load in ingredients as usual. When the cooking is done, serve the food, toss out the liner, and your slow cooker is clean and ready for storage.

SHAKE THE DRY STUFF The next time you need to mix several dry ingredients—for baking, for instance, or spices for stir-fry—pour them into a plastic bag instead of dirtying a bowl. To blend the ingredients, all you have to do is hold the bag closed and shake. Toss the bag out when you're done. If this is a recipe you make often, mix twice the ingredients you need. After blending, pour out what you need, then zip the bag closed, label it and stick it in a cabinet—all ready for the next time.

MARINATE IN A BAG Do you marinate meat in a large baking dish? You're setting yourself up for an unnecessary cleaning job. Next time, mix your marinade ingredients in a measuring cup, pour the mixture into a large zip-closing plastic bag, add the meat, and place it in the refrigerator. Set the measuring cup in the dishwasher and there's no more cleanup.

STEP UP TO THE PLATE

A funny thing happens after you've had your second child. Corner-cutting takes priority. Erik Sjogren calls them MacGyver[SM] Moms—after the ingenious, ready-for-anything adventurer of television fame. These are the harried souls who see the wisdom of using disposable plates, cups, and flatware on a regular basis, says Sjogren, senior brand manager for Dixie® Tabletop, based in Atlanta.

Consumers traditionally look at disposable plates as an item for special occasions—picnics, barbecues, and quick snacks. Disposable dishware can work so much harder for you than that, however. To fully embrace disposable dinnerware, you probably need to get over two psychological barriers:

1. The notion that you're a Bad Parent if you don't serve your kids on your finest china. To heck with that. It's quality time—not quality dishware—that counts. If being able to toss out the evening's dinnerware buys you an extra 20 minutes to read to your kids, that's worth it. And that's the exact figure—Sjogren says research shows that using disposable plates, cups, and flatware at a full meal for a family of four saves you an average of 20 minutes. No plate scraping, no washing. Just run your arm along the table and push it all into the trash.

2. The notion that you're ruining the planet by using disposables. Well, favoring your ceramic dishware over disposables might not be as environmentally beneficial as you think. Washing a load of dishes in the dishwasher uses up several gallons of water and the energy to heat that water, plus it requires the use of cleaning chemicals, which get flushed away with the water. If use of disposable plates and cups allowed you to run your dishwasher every other day instead of every day, you would save at least 1,600 gallons of hot water per year.

J. Winston Porter, Ph.D., president of the Waste Policy Center consulting organization in Leesburg, Virginia, and former assistant administrator of the EPA, has closely studied the issue, particularly for the food-service industry. "It's not a slam-dunk to say you should always reuse," he says. There are a lot of variables, so you won't find a definitive answer, but he says the environmental impact of the two approaches is fairly equal.

Besides, it's getting easier to find environmentally friendly disposable goods. The paper plates I picked up at the supermarket are labeled "biodegradable in home composting," for instance. Watch the labeling for "green" products and encourage such manufacturers by voting with your dollars. While you're at it, do your wallet a favor and buy your disposable dishes in bulk at a wholesale club.

THE CORNER-CUTTING COOK

Abe Lincoln had it right: "Give me six hours to chop down a tree and I will spend the first four sharpening the axe." Use your brain, and you need less brawn. In terms of cleaning, this is particularly important in the kitchen—that daily maelstrom of veggie chopping, sauce slopping, and egg dropping. Aside from use of the disposables mentioned previously, here are more corner-cutting kitchen techniques.

WHILE YOU'RE COOKING

You remember the TWO philosophy from Chapter 1, right? It stands for Thinking Wins Out. During every second that you work in the kitchen, there is some way to make the cleaning chores go more quickly and easily. Playing a good-natured mind game with yourself will keep you on your toes. For every cheating shortcut you use while preparing a meal, award yourself TWO points on your mental scoreboard. After you use a cheat three times, it will become ingrained habit. You'll find your own shortcuts, of course, but here are some to get you started:

SAVE TRIPS Pile up three or more things—say, the wrapper from a block of cheese, trimmings from a bell pepper, and a garlic husk—to cart over to the trash can all at once rather than taking individual trips. A dozen steps saved. TWO points.

CLEAN AS YOU GO In that 30-second break you have while the onions are sauteing, clean off the cutting board, rinse, and set it on the drying rack. That's 30 seconds off your after-meal cleanup duty. TWO points.

MAKE YOUR PANS DO DOUBLE-DUTY Serve your enchiladas directly from the baking dish, then slide the leftovers, dish and all, into the refrigerator. That's a serving dish and a storage container you don't have to wash. TWO points.

CONTAINER CONSCIOUSNESS When you're hand washing a few items in the sink, put any larger bowls or pans in the sink first and sponge them out last. The smaller items you wash—say, a can opener and a knife—will dribble their soapy water into the containers, giving them an advance soak and re-using the detergent. TWO points.

BEFORE AND AFTER YOU COOK

Minimizing mess is not only a concern when you're in the heat of cooking. Here are some more brilliant kitchen ideas from the Ounce of Prevention Department, for the times between cooking sessions.

SHOP FOR THE CHOPPED Whenever you can, buy produce that is already partially prepared for you. This not only saves you work time in the kitchen but leaves your utensils, counters, and other gear clean. If you buy preshredded cheese, for instance, the grater stays smudge free. Prechopped veggies and greens are all ready for the salad bowls—no knives or cutting boards necessary.

MAKE A DATE WITH YOUR FRIDGE Refrigerators get cluttered because they're crammed full of items that may or may not be good anymore—nobody knows for sure, so nothing gets thrown out. Here's the simple way to fix that problem: Park a permanent marker near the fridge. No prepared foods—condiments, sauces, spreads, and such—go into the refrigerator without a date marked on them. So if you run across a bottle of barbecue sauce that was dated 6 months ago, you can toss it out without another thought. Mark the date on leftovers you put into the refrigerator or freezer, too. If you're using a zip-sealing bag, write the date on the plastic. If you're using plastic containers, apply a 2-inch strip of freezer tape and mark the date on that.

Before you make a grocery run, open the refrigerator and quickly review the fresh stuff: Toss out any aging fruits or vegetables; leftovers more than a day old get the heave-ho, too.

PUT YOUR FRIDGE ON ROLLER SKATES

If you could get behind your refrigerator without hiring a moving crew, you might actually vacuum up the dust that accumulates back there. The solution is simple: Set your refrigerator or freezer on a set of appliance rollers. These elongated roller skates are placed under each side of the appliance. With an easy pull, you can wheel the refrigerator away from the wall for cleaning.

Be ruthless—do not get sentimental over a browning pear that's squishy soft. For a deluxe touch, spray a little disinfecting cleaner onto your kitchen sponge and give a quick wipe to the surfaces you've cleared off in your fridge. The shelves in there are rarely more open than just before your shopping run. This will keep the interior of your refrigerator presentable until you get inspired to clear the whole thing out for a thorough cleaning.

CATCH THOSE DRIPS The juices from raw meat sometimes contain harmful bacteria—not something you want to spread around your refrigerator. So anytime you store meat in the fridge, put it on the lowest shelf to reduce the chances of the meat dripping onto shelving, other food or containers, says Jennifer Armentrout. Also, put a pan or other rimmed tray under the meat to contain potential drips—there are fruit and veggie bins beneath that lowest shelf, after all. "You don't want your meat dripping onto your lettuce," she says.

READ AHEAD When you're ready to start cooking, read ahead in the recipe so you know which ingredients are going to be added in at the same time. Those ingredients—wet or dry—might as well be mixed in the same container at the outset, rather than dirtying a number of separate containers. "That saves you cleaning a lot of little prep dishes," says Armentrout.

GREASE THE SKIDS Give your baking dish or pan a quick spritz of cooking spray if you're going to cook something that's likely to leave a crusty residue. You'll save yourself a ton of soaking and scrubbing time. If you give the cheese grater a shot of cooking spray before you shred your cheese, the metal will come clean with the quick swipe of a sponge. Before you fill a plastic storage container with a staining sauce (marinara, for instance), give the interior a shoosh of spray. The coating will prevent staining and make cleanup a snap.

A TRICK FOR STICKY STUFF Measuring thick and sticky ingredients presents a double quandary: It's hard to get all that molasses, honey, or corn syrup to pour out of your measuring cup—making the amount of ingredient imprecise. Furthermore, it's a mess to clean. Cooking spray comes to the rescue again, says Armentrout: Squirt the inside of your measuring cup with cooking spray before you pour in the ingredient. When you pour it into your mixing bowl, the sticky stuff will slide right out, leaving behind an easy cleanup job.

CONTAIN THE SPRAY When you use cooking spray, it's easy to spritz a little extra oil onto the counter or stovetop, creating an extra cleaning chore. Armentrout's simple solution: Open the door of your dishwasher and place the object you're going to spray on the inside of the door. Any extra spray that you get on the door will just wash away the next time you run the appliance.

GIVE FLOUR THE COLD TREATMENT Anytime a measuring cup or utensil comes into contact with dry flour, rinse it off in cold water, says Armentrout. Hot water turns flour gummy—a messy cleaning task. If you use cold water, all you need to do is rinse the flour off and possibly wipe with a sponge.

PRESORT YOUR SILVERWARE As you toss silverware into the dishwasher, keep it organized just the way you do in the silverware drawer—knives in one basket compartment, forks in another, and spoons in yet another. Doing this will take you zero extra time and, after you run the dishwasher, you'll be able to grab up a handful of silverware and drop it into the proper place in the drawer without having to sort.

RUB OUT POLISHING DUTY The next time you put your silver away, wrap each silver piece tightly in plastic wrap. If air can't get to the silver, it won't tarnish. If you'd like to spend a modest amount of money for more convenience, pick up a storage bag made of flannel that's specially treated to prevent tarnish. These are available wherever silverware is sold.

SMART CHOICES FOR A CLEAN KITCHEN

Think of all the inanimate objects surrounding you in the kitchen as chef's assistants— not only the appliances but the furniture and the trash can, too. If chosen and used intelligently, they'll save you a ton of time and effort.

WIPE OUT UPHOLSTERY STAINS The next time you choose upholstery for your kitchen chairs, ask the fabric store to send the material out to be laminated. The extra couple hundred dollars will be well worth it, says Deborah Wiener, an interior designer based in Silver Spring, Maryland. Laminated fabric makes wiping up spills quick and easy. The fabric also will last much longer, saving you the hassle of reupholstering in the future. If the word *laminate* reminds you of the hard-and-shiny surface of your driver's license, relax. Laminated fabric has a natural-looking matte finish.

LID LESSONS LEARNED When purchasing a trash can, make sure the lid will stand open by itself. You want to be able to toss in a trimmed-off broccoli stem from 6 feet away, saving yourself steps (and scoring TWO points). You don't want to have to touch the trash can during food preparation (you remember, germs). Lids that open with a foot pedal are a help (count on the mechanism breaking after 9 months), but that still requires you walking up to the can—steps you'd rather not take, if possible. The type of cover that swings on a center hinge won't do—it requires that you stand right beside the can and push against the lid.

POSITION BINS STRATEGICALLY Make sure your recycling bins are as close as possible to where the recycling materials are generated, says Cynthia Braun, a professional organizer in Lake Grove, New York. This means placing a bin for cans and glass in or near the kitchen. This ensures that refuse does not accumulate in inappropriate places.

THE MOUNT COUNTS If you ever have a choice about sink styles, go for the undermounted kind (also called an apron or farmhouse sink) in your kitchen rather than the drop-in kind, says Wiener. Drop-in sinks have a rim that sits on top of the surface of the kitchen counter. When you wipe the counter and push little bits of grime toward the sink, some of it gets caught against the edge of the sink and builds up over the months into a brown goo. With an undermounted sink, there is no obstruction and no dirty buildup.

MIND OVER SPLATTER On the stovetop, always use a frying pan or pot that's substantially larger than you need. This will help contain the splatter when the juices go flying. Just in case,

KITCHEN APPLIANCES: HANG 'EM

Before you buy any appliance that you plan to park full-time on your kitchen counter, look around for a model that can be mounted under the cabinet. Not only does this free up more counter space but your kitchen will look less cluttered and you won't have to move those appliances around when you wipe the counter down. Also, undercabinet appliances gather less dust, since there's no top surface for dust to settle on.

Microwave ovens, toaster ovens, can openers, and coffee makers are available in undercabinet models. If the chefs in your home need to be entertained while they work, drop by an electronics discount store for a clock radio, CD player, or television in an undercabinet design.

make sure there's an easy-wipe splatter guard on the wall above your stove. Whenever you can, cook in the microwave, where splatters are at least confined to a small interior that you can easily sponge off.

ARE YOU A FAN OF FRYING? When you fry food on the stovetop, make sure to turn on the overhead ventilator fan, if you have one. Otherwise, superfine droplets of oil will take to the air from your frying pan and waft about your kitchen, settling on walls, light fixtures, carpets, and more. This greasy film will build up over time, collecting dust and turning into a cleaning nightmare.

OPEN THE DOOR TO SHORTCUTS If your kitchen layout allows it, cook with the door of your dishwasher open and the dish racks pulled out. During the preparation of any meal, you'll find at least a half-dozen items—dishes, utensils, pots, and the like—that you use just once. Rather than setting those items down on the counter (which will then need cleaning) or in the sink (a temporary way station), put them where they'll eventually end up anyway—in the dishwasher.

BREAKFAST DISHES NEVER REST When you walk into the kitchen first thing in the morning, do you start pulling cereal bowls, plates, and glasses out of the cabinets for breakfast? Here's a better plan: If you turned on the dishwasher the night before, just pluck what you need straight out of the dishwasher. If you play your cards right, you'll rarely have to put the breakfast dishes away in the cabinets. They'll either be in use or in the dishwasher.

MAKE THOSE APPLIANCES CLEAN THEMSELVES

In the ideal cheat-at-cleaning world, every machine we owned would clean itself. Our only duty would be to kick back on the sofa until the little darlings were all sparkling clean. The good news is that we can get pretty darned close to that utopian state

GOING PLATELESS

Eating over the kitchen sink has a lousy reputation—supposedly the realm of slobs and lonely singles. However, sink cuisine shows a lot of promise for a cheat-at-cleaning enthusiast with tons of self-esteem and a burning desire to pare cleaning duties to the bone. Just in case you're unfamiliar with the particulars of dining at the sink, here are the steps for its most efficient execution:

1. Open the dishwasher and the kitchen trash can.

2. Wash your hands.

3. Get the containers of chicken wings and green beans out of the fridge, open them, and set them by the sink. (Reheating them in the microwave is optional.)

4. Get a paper napkin.

5. Lean over the sink, pluck the wings and beans out of the containers with your fingers.

6. Eat.

7. Don't set the chicken bones down anywhere—toss them straight into the trash.

8. Rinse your fingers under the faucet.

9. While the water's running, cup your hands to take a drink.

10. Wash down the drain any flecks of food that fell into the sink, then turn the water off.

11. Put the empty containers in the dishwasher and close it.

12. Wipe your face on the napkin, throw it out, and close the trash can. Belching like a warthog is optional.

CAN YOU DISH IT OUT?

Company's arriving in 3 minutes and you have a Pike's Peak of dirty dishes, pots, and utensils teetering beside the sink. What's worse, you don't have a dishwasher. What do you do?

Put all the dishes in the sink, add two squirts of dishwashing liquid, and fill the sink with hot water. Visually, this becomes "cleaning in progress" rather than "stack of goopy plates and flatware." Perfectly acceptable. To drive the point home, pull on a pair of rubber gloves when it's time to greet your surprise guests.

If you're desperate, hide the dirty dishes in the oven, unless, of course, the evening's meal is already occupying that spot.

with some appliances. Here's a rundown of common kitchen appliances and how they can actually help clean themselves.

BLENDER OR FOOD PROCESSOR Rinse it to remove most traces of food, then fill it halfway with water and add a squirt of dishwashing liquid. Close the blender or processor and turn it on for half a minute. Rinse again, then let the blades spin for a few seconds to throw off any remaining water.

COFFEE GRINDER Grounds left in your grinder can quickly go stale and taint the next pot of coffee you brew. Here's the easy way to clean your grinder after each use: Run ½ cup uncooked white rice through the grinder and throw it away. If you make a lot of coffee, just give your grinder the rice treatment once or twice a week. Other times, wipe it out with a damp paper towel.

COFFEE MAKER Put a new filter in the basket to catch any loosened mineral deposits. Fill the coffee maker's tank halfway with white vinegar and the rest of the way with water. Turn on the machine and let it run through its cycle. Turn the machine off and let the water and vinegar sit in the carafe for 5 minutes (to help clean the glass). Pour it out, wipe out the carafe, refill the tank with straight water, and run through the cycle again. Follow this procedure once a month if you have hard water.

DISHWASHER Cleaning the interior of a dishwasher usually isn't much of an issue—unless you happen to have those white deposits building up, indicating a hard water problem. This mineral buildup is not only unsightly but can interfere with the efficiency of the dishwasher. Use a product such as Glisten® or Jet-Dry® dishwasher cleaner often enough to keep the white streaks at bay. Put the cleaner in the washer according to the package directions and run the washer through a cleaning cycle. I use Glisten on my glassware to remove milky mineral deposits from those as well.

GARBAGE DISPOSAL Empty an ice tray into your sink and push all of the cubes into the garbage disposal. Then push a few lemon rinds down there, too (any citrus rinds will do). Turn on the cold water, turn on the disposal, and grind away until the ice and rinds are gone. The disposal will be clean and lemony (or orangey) fresh.

MICROWAVE OVEN Pour 2 cups of water into a microwave-safe bowl. Set it in the middle of the microwave and cook on high for 5 minutes. The steam generated will soften any cooked-on food splatters inside. Remove the bowl using oven mitts. Wipe down the interior with a damp sponge.

OVEN Self-cleaning ovens have been a common feature in kitchens for years. You have to follow the instructions for your specific model, but basically you run the oven through a superhot cycle, which incinerates anything on the oven's interior surfaces. When the oven cools, all that's left is a film of ash you can mop up with a sponge. Continuous-clean ovens are different. Their interior walls are treated with a chemical that will destroy small splatters at high temperatures (350°F and up). You still need to sponge them out once in a while and run the oven through a high-heat cycle occasionally, according to the maker's instructions.

GIVE YOUR TOILET A DRINK

You've had a party, and guests have left several half-consumed cans of cola all around the house. Don't waste it! The acid in cola is a useful cleaner. Before you go to bed, pour a can's worth of leftover cola into the toilet and let it sit overnight. In the morning, brush and flush. Your toilet bowl will be bright and stain-free. Or pour two cans' worth of cola down a clogged drain and let it sit for at least an hour before flushing with water.

Don't use cleaning chemicals on continuous-clean or self-cleaning ovens. If your oven isn't trained to clean itself, it can still come pretty close: Pour ½ cup of ammonia into a glass bowl and leave it inside your closed oven overnight. Then pour out the ammonia and use a damp sponge to wipe up the grime loosened by the fumes.

LICKETY-SPLIT KITCHEN CLEANING

No matter how many preventive measures you've taken to contain spills, splatters, and spouse, once in a long while you're going to put your hands on your hips and say, "This kitchen needs cleaning." I put the question to Janet Nelson, a Ross, Iowa-based spokesperson for The Maids Home Services: If you had a lavish 7 minutes to clean the kitchen, what precisely would you do? Here's a game plan based on her priorities. Gather your materials first, and keep moving.

1. Take that stack of papers off the counter and throw them into a folder to sort later while you're watching television. Toss other utensils, food items and such into holding baskets, cabinets, and drawers. Wipe down the counters. Nothing says "clean kitchen" like vacant counters.

2. Pick any kid toys or pet toys off the floor and stow them away. Use a whiskbroom and dustpan to sweep up any loose pet food.

3. Toss any dirty dishes into the dishwasher.

4. If your sink is now empty, spray it with disinfectant cleaner and wipe it down. Wipe the handles and faucet, then dry them with a dish towel to prevent spots.

If by some chance Venus, Mars, and Saturn should fall into alignment and you're in the mood for the deluxe *How to Cheat at Cleaning* 12-minute kitchen routine, do all of the above, plus:

1. Take the kitchen throw rugs outside and shake them furiously for 10 seconds.

2. Vacuum the kitchen floor and put the rugs back.

3. Spray disinfectant cleaner onto your sponge and wipe down the appliances.

4. Spray glass cleaner onto the window above the sink and wipe with a cleaning cloth or paper towel.

A THRONE ROOM FIT FOR A KING

If the Ladies Auxiliary were to devise The One True Test of Housekeeper Worthiness, they would probably base it on an inspection of your bathroom. Even knowing that in certain circles your reputation hangs in the balance, there's no way you're going to devote an hour a week to cleaning slavery in the throne room. Relax. Read on, and then invite the ladies over for tea and crumpets.

LICKETY-SPLIT BATHROOM CLEANING

Here's a 7-minute routine that will keep your bathroom looking harp. (Once again, a grateful toilet-brush salute goes out to Janet Nelson for her input.) As with the kitchen, gather your cleaning materials first and move as if you were meeting a deadline.

1. Clear the counter of any extraneous objects. Put toothbrushes, hairbrushes, deodorant, medicines, toothpaste, and such into cabinets and drawers.

2. Squirt toilet bowl cleaner around the upper interior rim of the toilet. Spray the seat and exterior with disinfectant cleaner. Spray disinfectant cleaner on the sink, faucet and handles, counter, and tub.

3. With a toilet brush, scrub the interior bowl for 10 seconds. Flush.

4. Spray glass cleaner on the mirror and wipe with a cleaning cloth.

5. Using a damp sponge, wipe and then rinse (in order) the sink and its chrome, the counter, the tub, the toilet seat, and the exterior of the toilet.

6. With the same cloth you used on the mirror, wipe down the chrome once more for extra sparkle.

7. Tear off a 6-inch length of toilet paper to scoop up any loose hair and other debris from the floor and corners of the room.

As you've come to expect, for the truly finicky, I'm offering the deluxe *How to Cheat at Cleaning* 12-minute bathroom cleanup. Do all of the above, plus:

1. Put the tub mat, bath mat, and towels into the washing machine. Hang out fresh towels.

2. Vacuum the floor.

3. Empty the trash can.

4. Spray cleaner onto a cloth and wipe down the doorknob and the smudges on the door, the light switch, and the cabinets.

ZERO-EFFORT BATHROOM CLEANUPS

What, you're back for more? Okay, here are some more labor-saving tricks for the bathroom.

REFLECTED GLORY The mirror is a centerpiece for the bathroom. When it's sparkling clean, it's easier to forgive a hair or two

---

SWITCH YOUR FOCUS

Conventional wisdom would have you scrubbing the light switches and doorknobs in your home, on the theory that these are common way stations for germs in the home. Save yourself the bother, microbiologist Dr. Charles Gerba says. His tests show that light switches and doorknobs don't typically accumulate many germs.

He shatters a myth about public restrooms, too: Have you ever watched a finicky person, fearful of picking up germs, use a paper towel to open a restroom door? Relax. The door handle is actually the cleanest place in a public restroom. Another surprise: Among toilet stalls, the one nearest the door is typically the cleanest. People gravitate toward the center stalls, which are therefore the germiest.

left in the tub. Professional organizer Cynthia Braun likes to keep disposable glass wipes under the bathroom sink for a quick mirror-and-sink touch-up. C. Lee Cawley, a professional organizer in Arlington, Virginia, has a similar routine: Every night she uses a facial wipe on her face. Before tossing it, she gives the faucet and sink a speedy wipe-down as well.

TRY SHOWER POWER Here's another way to add instant sparkle to your bathroom: Pull down that old milky looking shower curtain liner and hang a fresh new one, says Braun. Yes, an old liner can be cleaned, but when they only cost a few dollars they're hardly worth the trouble. Buy a few at a time and count on replacing them every 6 months. If you're not in the habit of using shower curtain liners, now's the time to start—they'll keep the finer outer curtain clean and help it last longer.

SPRAY YOUR CARES AWAY Park a bottle of daily shower spray in your bathroom. When the walls are still wet after your shower, give them a spritzing. No need to rinse. The spray will prevent buildup of hard water deposits and mold. The shower walls will be one cleaning chore you can cross off your to-do list forever. Buy shower spray wherever cleaning products are sold.

SEE SPOTS RUN To keep hard water stains from building up on your shower doors, every few weeks dampen a cleaning rag with lemon oil or baby oil. Wipe down the interior of the doors. The shower water will sheet right off them, rather than clinging to the doors, drying, and leaving spots.

So there you have it: By adding disinfecting cleaner and a couple of disposable products to your shopping list—and then applying a little know-how—you get a germ-free, hassle-free kitchen and bathroom. Looks like the deal of the century to me!

WHERE YOU LIVE: KEEPING IT CLEAN IN THE LIVING ROOM, DINING ROOM, DEN, AND BEDROOM

In the ideal world, the living areas around your home would just clean themselves. Well, you might be surprised to find out just how close we're getting. If you make wise choices, a lot of the materials you use to furnish the living room, dining room, den, and bedroom will make housecleaning a snap. There are some time-honored traditions around the home you can dispense with, too, saving yourself a lot of housekeeping grief. And there are some amazing new cleaning gizmos that require no involvement from you whatsoever.

If you could remodel the main living areas of your home with only one goal in mind—to make cleaning chores as easy as possible—how would you do it? What flooring, furniture, paint, lighting, and window treatments would you use in the living room, dining room, and bedroom? I put the question to Deborah Wiener, a Silver Spring, Maryland, interior designer who is known for clever home solutions. Her answers deserve a prominent place in any homeowner's plans. Remember the Materials on a Program (MOP) philosophy: There's no need to accomplish all of these suggestions right away. Rather, factor them into your long-term cheat-at-cleaning blueprint.

FLOORING: THE HARD TRUTH

Let's start at the bottom—with floors. Stone flooring is the easiest to care for. Combine it with one of the new disposable mopping cloth systems, and you're on Easy Street. "You just take out your Swiffer® mop, and that floor's going to be spotless in five minutes," Wiener says. Use slate, terrazzo, or some other stone product throughout the house. If that's not practical, use slate for part of the home—say, the foyer, down the hall, and into the kitchen. Then use hardwood everywhere else. Hardwood flooring is similarly easy to clean, but it requires a little more protection (from grit and water). Stick to lighter woods, since dark wood shows dust and pet hair more readily.

Protect hardwood floors with strategically placed area rugs—for instance, by the kitchen sink to catch splashed dishwater. Highly colored and patterned area rugs will hide spills and wear-and-tear more effectively than solid colors.

BROWN DELIVERS For seating, chocolate brown leather furniture is "the ultimate in easy care," Wiener says. It won't show dirt or marks, and pet hair won't stick to it. When you're buying a leather sofa or chair, remember that not all leather is finished the same. Here's how to make sure the leather you buy is high quality: When the salesperson isn't looking, run your fingernail across the sample fabric. If it leaves a scratch, keep looking.

While we're on the subject of furniture: Buy chairs and sofas with exposed legs rather than the skirted style. The skirts attract stains and dirt from kids' shoes.

For shelving and other storage-type furniture, according to Wiener, "Anything closed is better than anything open." Look for an entertainment center with doors on the cabinets, for instance. Dust will not be able to settle on the objects inside, and closed cabinets are great for hiding clutter when guests come over.

WITH SHADES, YOU'RE ON A ROLL On the windows, forget curtains and blinds. For ease of cleaning, there's nothing like the old-fashioned roller-type shades. Modern roller shades are available in hundreds of attractive fabrics and styles. To clean, just pull the shade all the way down, wipe with a cleaning cloth, and roll it back into place. The newer cellular or honeycombed shades are very popular and energy efficient, Wiener says. However, they can trap dust—or even the little toys of mischievous children—inside the cells. To clear the shade out, you have to take it down, turn it on its side, and shake.

INTERIOR WALLS: DUST IF YOU MUST

If I am ever caught washing the walls of my home with a sponge and pail of soapy water, would someone please just shoot me? Many of us have mothers or grandmothers who scrubbed their walls once a week, but life is too short. Sure, a little dust may cling to your walls. It's invisible, however, and will behave itself if you leave it alone.

If you insist on cleaning your walls, do this: Slap a fresh disposable electrostatic cloth onto your Swiffer mop handle (or whatever brand you're using), and give the walls a quick dusting. Start at the top edge of the wall and drag the mop head down until you hit the baseboard, some piece of furniture, or the family dog. Working your way around the room in this manner, you can cover a typical living room in 23 seconds.

While you're waving a dust-grabbing stick around the living room, you might as well snag any cobwebs against the ceiling. For a deluxe job, also drag the mop head along the top of each window frame and door frame.

THE 15-MINUTE TOUCH-UP

The phone rings, and it's your old college roommate wanting to drop by for a surprise visit—in 15 minutes! You gaze in horror around your unkempt living quarters. How will you ever cheat your way out of this one?

Focus mostly on the clutter, and then just one or two high-profile cleaning touchups, says Shannon Ackley, a professional organizer in Shelton, Connecticut.

- Throw the newspapers into the recycling or trash.
- Stuff books and magazines onto shelves and racks.
- Toss any toys into toy boxes or the kids' bedrooms—and pull those bedroom doors closed.
- Whip out a disposable wipe or dampen a paper towel with cleaner. Wipe down the bathroom sink and toilet.

Skip the vacuuming or dusting. A guest who's there for only an hour won't notice.

SCRUBBABLE IS LOVABLE

For wall paint, use only water-soluble, scrubbable paint. You'll pay a little extra for this in a premium flat paint, but it's unquestionably worth it. You'll be able to sponge up smudges and marks without fear of erasing the wall color at the same time. Flat paint is more delicate than the nail-polish-tough glossy finishes. Wash it using a sponge and a bowl of warm water with a squirt of dish-washing liquid. Use a light touch with the sponge, moving it in small circles against the surface. Use the same technique on high-gloss paint, too, before attempting a more stringent approach like glass cleaner.

Remember that darker wall colors will hide scuff marks and dents more readily than light colors. For trim paint, however, Wiener uses Benjamin Moore® Decorator White—not because she's a decorator, but because that color happens to be a perfect match for the correction fluid called Wite-Out®. She keeps a dozen bottles of it on hand so she can quickly touch up marred and scuffed trim.

SMUDGE-PROOF YOUR DOORS Doors attract lots of finger-smudges, Wiener notes, so paint your doors with a glossy finish, which will stand up better to repeated washings. Besides, wood looks better with glossy paint rather than flat. For hardware on your doors and drawers, choose a matte finish rather than a shiny finish. A matte finish won't show fingerprints. Only your CSI guy will know for sure.

Why do we call them "dust bunnies"? Do you think of the dust cavorting under the sofa as warm-and-fuzzy fluff? On the contrary, the dust in your house is a not so cuddly mixture of dirt and pollutants dragged in from the outside, fibers from fabrics, dander from your pets, your own sloughed-off skin cells, and even poop from dust mites. Inspired enough to fire up the vacuum cleaner? No matter how many corners you cut and tricks you pull, now and then you're going to have to actually clean something, and rounding up household dust is one of those core tasks you cannot completely avoid.

Fortunately, dusting is simple and easy. You can make a big impact on a room—give it that "somebody cares" look—with minimal effort. It gets complicated only when you throw obstacles in your own way—namely, clutter. So let's look at how to streamline this most basic of cleaning chores.

DUST BUSTING MADE EASY

Approach the room you're going to dust with all of your armaments assembled: the vacuum cleaner, electrostatic cleaning cloths (special dust-grabbing cloths available at supermarkets and discount stores), a Swiffer-type dry mop, and either a step stool or an extendable dusting wand that will reach high shelves.

Now, this will go more smoothly if you follow the "De-clutter, then clean rule." This means the couch cushions are picked up off the floor, the magazines are in their rack, the CDs and books are shelved, and the surfaces around the room are relatively free of odds and ends.

Once you're ready, an orderly set of procedures will allow you to accomplish a basic dusting of a typical living room in

FOCUS YOUR COLLECTION

There's a big difference between a collector and a clutterer, says professional organizer C. Lee Cawley of Arlington, Virginia. It's all in the presentation.

A clutterer has three Hummels displayed in the bedroom, two in the kitchen, and five in the living room. That's spread all about and unfocused—clutter. If you're going to have a collection, "honor" your prized pieces by doing it right. Put all of your collection in one display space (thus freeing numerous assorted surfaces around the house). A focused display place becomes a center of interest in the home, instantly changing that room from "Blah" to "Oh, wow!"

If you collect small, delicate objects, anchor each piece to its shelf with museum putty, available where art goods, containers, and collector materials are sold. With each piece securely stuck in place, you can clean them with a feather duster in just seconds without fear of tipping one over.

Leave 20 percent open space on your display shelf to accommodate new acquisitions, Cawley says.

6 minutes. For a *How to Cheat at Cleaning* deluxe job, well, that will cost you 9 minutes. (If you run over these times, either your room is too cluttered or you're trying too hard.) This dusting routine will work for just about any living area in the house:

1. Always dust from the top down, so that no dust you've knocked loose will settle onto an area you have already cleaned. Yes, you're using electrostatic cloths, which should grab and hold the dirt. However, if it's been a while since you dusted, there could be some escapees. Walk around the room in a circle, using your dry mop to snag any cobwebs from the upper corners of the room and using your dusting wand (or a step stool and a hand cloth) to wipe any high light fixtures, shelves, and ceiling fan blades.

2. Now, with a few clean electrostatic cloths, walk around the room in a circle again, this time dusting everything between your knees and your head—any shelves you didn't get before, the top of the television, window sills, and furniture. When one cleaning cloth is totally grimy, switch to another. Pay particular attention to any dust that's visible from a standing

or sitting elevation. (If you can see it, clean. Conversely, if it's not visible, it's optional.)

3. Run your mop or dusting wand along the baseboards.

4. Use your mop on any hard flooring. Vacuum any rugs.

You may now declare the room livable—unless, of course, you're going for your master's degree in housecleaning, in which case you would want to add the following enhancements to your routine:

1. Begin the entire dusting routine just outlined by moving all of the light furniture—chairs, end tables, standing lamps, magazine racks, and such—into the center of the room. When you get to the vacuuming stage near the end, vacuum around the perimeter of the room.

2. Put all of the furniture back into place.

3. Vacuum the center of the room.

4. Vacuum the sofa and chairs with the upholstery attachment. If there's time, use the narrow tool to vacuum around the cushions.

DUSTING EVERYDAY OBJECTS

Here's how to make cleaning go easier as you tackle common dust-collecting objects around the house:

PUT THE GRAIN UNDER GLASS *Pop quiz:* Which kind of surface is easier to care for—wood or glass? Glass, of course—just squirt on some glass cleaner, wipe with a cleaning cloth, and you're done. No special polishes are required, no anxiety about marks or water rings. That's why Cynthia Braun, a professional organizer in Lake Grove, New York, had every wood surface in her house covered in glass—desks, end tables, night stands, and dressers.

ERASING HOUSEHOLD BOO-BOOS

Oh, to be a school kid again—make a mistake, and all you have to do is whip an eraser out of your book bag. Wouldn't it be nice to have an eraser to fix all of life's boo-boos around the house, too—the marks on the floors, the cooked-on stove-top spills, the crayon scribbles on the wall, the smudged switch plates?

There is such a product, the Mr. Clean Magic Eraser®; and professional organizer Cynthia Braun of Lake Grove, New York, swears by it. "I have one of those under every one of my sinks," she says. She's particularly impressed that it easily cleans her white utensil holders when they get marred, grape juice stains on the counter, the grease-spattered teapot on the stove, and makeup smears on the telephone. It can make a wall look freshly painted and renew an old pair of sneakers, too.

Here's how it works: The eraser is the size and shape of a kitchen sponge, only it's white and stiffer. Just wet it under the faucet, squeeze out the excess water, and it's ready to clean. The pliable material of the eraser fits into the minuscule grooves of the surface you're cleaning and scoops out the dirt. Here's the big secret they don't tell you on the package, Braun says: It works even better if you use hot water.

When the eraser gets dirty, just rinse it under the faucet and squeeze again. After several uses, it gets crumbly. Toss it and get a new one. You can get them one or two at a time at the supermarket, but Braun likes to buy them in eight-packs at a discount store. It's not recommended for all surfaces, so read the directions and test an inconspicuous area before you do any large-scale cleaning with it.

Go to the yellow pages and find a nearby glass company. It will send a worker out to measure your wood surfaces. The glass probably will be installed on clear disks that create a teensy gap between the glass and the wood so no moisture gets trapped in between. You'll be able to admire the beauty of the wood, but it will be perfectly protected and you'll never need to clean it again.

SHOWER YOUR SHADES Stop dusting all of those little crevices in your pleated lampshades. It's quicker and more thorough to give them a shower, says Braun. Once a year, remove the shades from all of your lamps. Place them two or three at a time in the bottom of your bathtub with the drain open, turn on the cold water, and hose them down with your hand-held showerhead. (If your tub isn't equipped with one, just turn on the shower and turn the shade under the spray. It might be less messy if you just strip and climb into the tub to do this—we'll never tell.) No scrubbing or detergent is necessary and you'll be happy to see all of the dust from your lampshades swirling down the drain. Let your shades air dry in the tub, then reattach them to their lamps. Even the standard pleated fabric shades come through this process just fine, Braun says, but don't try it on wood or silk shades.

SHOWER YOUR PLANTS, TOO Your houseplants will enjoy a shower now and then, too. They'll breathe easier once you've spritzed off that coating of dust that accumulates. Here's how: Set each plant's pot into a plastic grocery bag and tie the top of the bag loosely across the top of the pot, leaving a hole for the plant to emerge. Place the plants in the bottom of your tub with the drain open. Turn on a lukewarm shower for 1 minute. Let the plants drip dry in the tub, and then return them to their positions around the house.

PICTURE THIS: ONE FRAME ONLY Limit yourself to one framed photograph in your living room—or at least one photo frame per child. Why? One of the surest ways to cut down the dusting chore in your living spaces is to just put less stuff out. The fewer things you have on shelves growing that little coating of gray fur, the quicker your cleaning will be. Picture frames are a particular problem in many homes, says Braun. People feel like they have to display scores of framed photographs, and each frame has multiple edges and grooves where dust will gather—plus that dust-grabbing velvet backing.

Keep a photo album for each child in your family. When you get a new photo of one of your kids, slide it into the display frame. Put the old photo into the album. When the child reaches middle age, he'll love receiving the album full of his pictures. Because all of the photos were sorted to begin with, no one will have to tear up a family album to distribute them among the kids.

PUT YOUR MENAGERIE UNDER GLASS Keep your knickknacks inside a cabinet with a glass door. This way, your prized possessions are still on display, but you won't have to dust them nearly so often, says Shannon Ackley, a professional organizer in Shelton, Connecticut.

PLAY AIR PIANO Cleaning that piano in your living room is a tricky business, since liquid cleaners could damage the keys. The quick and easy approach, according to Braun: Blast any dust off the piano keys with a can of compressed air (available at photo shops and computer stores). When you're not playing the instrument or cleaning it, keep the keyboard cover closed to prevent dust from settling on it.

The compressed air trick also works nicely with computers and other electronics, cameras, and chandeliers.

SOCK IT TO 'EM Suppose you'd like to quickly dust a room but there aren't any cleaning cloths handy. No problem: Just pull a clean athletic sock over each hand and go around the room wiping surfaces. Start with the finer, less dusty items (knickknacks), then wipe the broader surfaces where you'll pick up more volume. When you're done, just peel the socks off and toss them into a laundry hamper (right side out, so the socks don't trap the dust inside).

POINTERS FOR PAINTERS

Painting—it's astounding how much of a mess you can make while beautifying your living room. Here are some corner-cutting cleaning tips that will make the job easier:

- Always paint with water-based acrylic paint, not oil-based paint. To mop up drips, all you need is a damp sponge.

- When you're done painting for the day, but you have to resume the next day, don't bother to wash out your brush or roller. Just wrap it securely in plastic wrap and put it in the refrigerator. This will keep it from drying out.

- If your plastic drop cloths have picked up paint splatters, as they usually do, don't be tempted to save them for the next painting project—throw them out. If you're painting with a used drop cloth, you won't be able to tell the dry paint from the wet. You'll drive yourself nuts trying not to step on the paint drops for fear of tracking them around the house.

- Always use plastic liners inside your metal paint trays. They're available wherever painting supplies are sold. When you're done painting, you can just throw the liner away and keep the clean paint tray. If you pour paint directly into the metal tray, you'll have a tough cleanup on your hands. You also run the risk that traces of the paint will taint the next color you pour into the tray.

- From head to toe, wear the rattiest clothing you have for painting —even for a 2-minute job. Paint has a way of leaping unseen onto your clothing. When you're done with the paint job, strip off all of these clothes at once and drop them directly into the washing machine. This reduces the chance of smudging paint onto furniture or other clothing.

- Unless you're obsessive about cleaning paintbrushes as soon as you're done with them, they're going to stiffen up after three or four uses. Life's too short to fret over paintbrushes. Expensive paintbrushes are an AILment (Anxiety-Inducing Luxury). Buy only cheap ones and throw the aging ones out.

There's more to cleaning your living areas than just dust. Here are some sneaky ways to outwit other kinds of grime.

SPURN THE BURN Quit using your fireplace. Boy, does it hurt to say that. I know as well as anybody the charm of a wood fire behind a screen in the living room. However, the science is irrefutable: Conventional home fireplaces are a terribly inefficient source of warmth. In some cases they actually *increase* your cost of home heating by sucking furnace-warmed air up the flue. At the same time, the typical home fireplace pumps fumes and particles into your home, polluting the air and making cleaning an even harder task. Also, dirt and bugs inevitably hitchhike into your house when you haul in wood.

The easiest solution is to have the flue of your fireplace sealed off and quit using it. Put a little candle arrangement in there, and light them when you get a hankering for flame. Alternatively, you could invest in one of the new, high-tech, airtight fireplaces that draw air from the outside for burning. Or you could explore converting to a gas fireplace—some designs are considered energy-efficient. If you're going to make such an investment, research thoroughly and don't believe everything you read in the sales literature. Also, modern airtight, advance-combustion wood-stoves can be a good alternative, providing low emissions and efficient heat transfer into the home.

GIVE DIRT THE SLIP When you outfit your couches and chairs with slipcovers, your furniture cleaning chores become a trifle. Slipcovers—essentially a second skin for your furniture—can be used in a number of strategic ways. Because they come in a wide range of colors and styles, you can easily redecorate your living room without buying new furniture. If the thought of the kids and Fido tramping on the new furniture ties your stomach into a knot, let slipcovers take the dam-age rather than the actual upholstery.

You can always remove a slipcover before guests come over, if you want them to see the splendor of the original upholstery. Or you can pull the slipcover off, give it a shake in the backyard, and put it back in place—no need to vacuum! If the upholstery on old furniture is worn and torn, the addition of slipcovers will add years to its life.

Most slipcovers can be easily removed and washed in your home washing machine. To prevent wrinkles, dry them until they're just slightly damp and then put them back on the furniture to finish drying. If needed, you can use a warm iron on the slipcover right there on the furniture.

Your slipcovers will have the best fit if you buy them from the manufacturer of your furniture. However, you also can buy slipcovers in retail stores and online.

USE GARBAGE CANS GALORE

When trash is extremely easy to throw into a proper trash can, it's less likely to wind up in alter-native places—on desks, counters, dressers, floors, and shelves, for instance. That's why Braun stations trash cans all over the house, particularly in the spots where trash is most often generated (desks, vanities where makeup is done, the scrap-booking and other craft areas, bathrooms, the deck, and the garage). If you station a trash can out on the deck or patio, make sure it has a cover to keep rain and inquisitive critters out.

SLEIGHT OF HAND

PRESORT YOUR JUNK MAIL

What if all of your junk mail arrived with a sticker on it reading "Don't Bother to Open—Throw Me Out!" That would make your daily mail sorting go a lot faster.

Well, I have just such an arrangement —and you can, too. After a change of jobs a few years ago, I subscribed to five new magazines all at once. Knowing that a huge percentage of my junk mail is created when publishers sell their subscription lists to marketers, I gave each magazine publisher a different first name—the more unusual the better. (For all they knew, I was buying the subscriptions for relatives.) Years later, I'm still getting mail for all of these fictitious people. And for each piece of junk mail, I know which publisher I have to thank.

I also know immediately that anyone who would write to "Aloysius Bredenberg" has nothing to say that would interest me. So that letter goes straight into recycling. I once saved all of my fake-name junk mail for 10 months and amassed more than 15 pounds of it!

LINER NOTES A trash can that's easy to empty will get emptied more often. You may already recycle your plastic grocery bags by using them as liners in your trash cans. Squeeze five of those bags into a tiny ball and put them into the bottom of your trash can. Then install another bag as the trash can's liner—over the other bags. The next time you need to empty the can, there will be another bag in the bottom of the can just waiting to become the new liner. No running to the pantry for a replacement liner. You can use this strategy in the kitchen, too, by putting extra kitchen bags in the bottom of the kitchen garbage can.

LET RUGS TAKE THE BEATING Your wall-to-wall carpet will develop a path of soiled and worn fibers in high-traffic areas. To preserve your rugs, or to cover stained or tattered spots, lay down runners in high traffic areas. Choose colors and patterns that will hide dirt well.

BEDROOM SECRETS

It's no wonder that people have strong feelings about how their beds are arranged. You spend a third of your life with sheets, pillows, and blankets all comfy around you in this one confined space. Make sure that your ingrained habits aren't working against you, however. You might be creating extra housework for yourself or, worse, you might be inviting some tiny, health-damaging creatures to snuggle up with you.

QUIT MAKING THE BED

Approximately 60 percent of people surveyed say they don't make the bed every day. Are they slobs? Not at all—they're visionaries.

Sure, some of my advisers insist that there's great emotional value in making your bed every day. A tidy bed is a comfort to the soul, the thinking goes, and makes a more inviting place to retire to at the end of the day. If that's all it takes to make your spirit soar, by all means give your covers a quick tug at each corner and be done with it.

Be aware, however, that scientists say *not* making your bed actually appears to be healthier. Why? Because the average bed can house as many as 1.5 million hideously ugly microscopic creatures called dust mites. These miniature monsters produce allergens that you breathe in while you sleep, and this is a major cause of asthma and other illnesses. A 2005 study unveiled at Kingston University in London showed that killing the dust mites in your bed is simple. The mites thrive on the moisture in your bed covers and mattress. When you make the bed, you're sealing the moisture in—tucking the little dust mites in just the way they like it. However, when you leave your bed unmade all day, the moisture escapes and the dust mites die. I'm sold!

FAST • FORMULAS

SHAVING CREAM, IN THE NICK OF TIME

If you need to fix a carpet stain and you're out of commercial spot cleaner, there's a good backup plan right in your bathroom cabinet. Get your can of shaving cream and three paper towels. Squirt onto your fingertips enough foam to cover the stain. Rub it into the stain with your fingers and let it sit 1 minute. Blot up as much of the foam as you can with one dry paper towel and toss it in the trash. Wet the second paper towel slightly with warm water and blot at the spot to remove any excess foam, then toss it. Leave the third paper towel dry. Fold it up until it's just large enough to cover the stain. Press it down onto the spot with your knuckles to soak up as much water as possible, and then throw it away. Let the carpet dry for a few hours, and then vacuum.

GET CLEVER WITH YOUR COVERS

Maybe leaving your bed unmade all day is too radical for you, even if it is scientifically sound. No problem—there are plenty of other bed management tricks that will protect your health and save you a lot of bother.

SKIP THE TOP SHEET At first this will sound nuts to many Americans: Quit using a top sheet. That's right. The conventional American way of making a bed requires a fitted sheet on the mattress, then a flat top sheet tucked in at the foot of the mattress, and

MAKING THE BED: LET IT SLIDE

If you insist on making your bed, at least amuse yourself by getting the job done before you're even on your feet in the morning. An item in *The Scotsman*, "Scotland's national newspaper," describes how to make the bed while you're still in it. The technique involves sliding out from under the covers at the foot of the bed, so it's assumed that you're not using a top sheet. Perform all of the motions described here slowly and carefully so that the duvet doesn't get dragged out of position. Here's how it's done:

- If there's anybody else in your bed, kick that person out—you have work to do. Lie on your back in the center of the bed, under the duvet.

- Spread your legs until you have a foot pointing toward each bottom corner of the bed. This flattens out the lower part of the duvet.

- Grab the top corners of the duvet in your left and right hands and give it a little pull.

- Slowly move one hand toward your chin, grab the center edge of the duvet, and pull it over your head—thus flattening the central part of the cover—and return your hand to its corner. The bed is now made—you just have to get out of it.

- Using a very slow rolling motion with your posterior, inch your way toward the bottom of your bed, taking great care not to disrupt the duvet. It might help to leave your hands higher than your head, smoothing out the duvet if it needs adjusting.

- When your feet hit the floor, slowly crab-walk forward. When your arms come, free, support yourself on all fours until you're clear of the bed.

It takes a little practice before you can pull this off without a hitch, but it will give the household rebel in you a definite feeling of accomplishment first thing in the morning. I stripped down to my skivvies to give it a try. We'll not repeat what my wife said when she walked in.

then a bedspread or comforter layered on top. Well, forget that top sheet—instead, just use a duvet. A duvet, for the uninitiated, is a cover for a comforter. They come in a variety of fabrics, colors, and patterns, giving you a lot of flexibil-ity with decorating. They also simplify cleaning: Your comforter never gets dirty—the duvet does. Removing the duvet and washing it is a thousand times easier than washing a comforter itself.

Having the duvet directly against your skin is every bit as comfortable as sleeping with a top sheet. If you dispense with the top sheet, you have one less thing to wash, and suddenly making your bed is markedly easier—just give the duvet a quick yank at each corner of the bed and you're done in seconds. Top sheets, on the other hand, often bunch up underneath the top cover, making the bed look like a topographical map of the Appalachian Mountains. Europeans will find nothing new in this advice, since they typically forego top sheets anyway.

FIGHT THE MITE If you think dust mites might be a source of your allergy problems, you'll want to take extra measures to keep them away from you while you're sleeping. Here are two good moves, according to Jay M. Portnoy, M.D., the chief of allergy, asthma, and immunology at Children's Mercy Hospital in Kansas City, Missouri:

DESIGN DIRT AWAY

TAKE COMFORT IN A DUVET

A duvet comforts your comforter—gives it protection, anyway. It also makes managing your bed a snap—it's easy to straighten and easy to clean. Here are a few things to consider about buying a duvet:

- A cotton-polyester blend is easiest to care for. A few times a year, remove it from your comforter and toss it in the washing machine, just like a sheet.

- If you're using a duvet, quit using a top sheet. Simpler is better.

- Make sure your duvet is a good fit for your comforter. Your best bet is to buy one from the same folks who made the comforter itself. If you're buying from another manufacturer, remember that standardized sizes (twin, queen, and such) are not reliable—take a tape measure to your comforter and buy your duvet according to actual measurements.

❋ Buy dust mite covers for your pillows and mattress. These covers place a barrier between you and the allergens.

❋ Wash your sheets frequently in water that's at least 130°F.

PILLOW TALK Pillows take on a musty odor after a while, and the surest solution is this: Buy new ones every 6 months to 8 months. If you'd just like to freshen up a stinky pillow, put it in the drier with a drier sheet. If you're willing to put more work into your pillows, most of them are machine-washable—check the tag. Even down pillows often can be washed in a gentle cleaner such as Woolite®. (If you bought dry-clean-only pillows, what were you thinking?) Just make sure that any pillow you wash gets really, really dry before you put it back into action. It can take hours of machine drying (gentle or medium setting) to get all of the moisture out of a feather pillow. To punch up the loft of down pillows, it helps to put a couple of tennis balls into the drier with them.

GO PLAIN AND FANCY If you have a hankering for elegant, designer-type bedding, limit these touches to the bed skirt, toss pillows, and duvet. For practical living, the work-a-day bedding underneath (the sheets and pillow cases) ought to be plain ol' white. Why? So you can easily bleach them if they get dingy or stained, says interior designer Deborah Wiener. You can buy high-quality white sheets at discount stores for a reasonable price.

COLLAPSE YOUR COMFORTER Storing a comforter requires a significant amount of closet space. To save room, fold your comforter and slide it into a large trash bag.

Then put the hose of your vacuum cleaner into the bag, hold the plastic securely around the hose, and turn the vacuum cleaner on. The comforter will be compressed to a fraction of its usual size. Seal the bag closed with a twisty-tie. Use the same technique for storing pillows. This extra closet space will translate into less clutter in your bedroom.

BEYOND THE BEDCOVERS

The bed is just 40-some square feet of the bedroom. Here's how to keep the rest of your inner sanctum neat and clean with minimal effort.

TELL THE TREADMILL TO TAKE A WALK If you're crowding an office, exercise equipment, and a television into your bedroom, chances are nothing is getting accomplished there. The desk is dysfunctional, the treadmill is covered in cobwebs, and you habitually nod off in the middle of that late-night TV show.

"Ideally, the bedroom should just be for sex and sleeping—and that's it," says C. Lee Cawley, an organizer in Arlington, Virginia. So give everything but your bed, clothes, and dresser the heave-ho.

BE A CLOSET GADGET JUNKIE Every chance you get, browse home-improvement stores, discount stores, and department stores for the myriad clever devices that save space in your closet and make items easy to find. For instance:

* A belt ring, which holds a score of belts while taking up a mere 2 inches of hanging rod space in your closet.

* A mesh bag. Fill it with small accessories such as earmuffs, bandannas, and headbands, and hang it on a hook in your closet.

* A compact step stool stashed in or near your closet (the folding kind can slide under your bed) will suddenly make the highest shelves of your closet easy to reach—and no longer a museum of forgotten items.

* A shoe bag mounted on the back of a closet or bedroom door will get that jumble of shoes off the floor. It's also handy for storing other small items, such as rolled up scarves, pantyhose, and gloves.

TWO RODS ARE BETTER THAN ONE

Double the hanging space in your bedroom closet by installing two hanging rods, one over the other. Hang one rod 40 inches off of the floor and the other at 80 inches.

GIVE YOUR HAMPER SOME AIR Don't store your dirty clothes hamper inside your closet. Not only will that rob you of a huge block of storage space but also those musty used clothes will share their odor with the fresh garments in your closet.

HOOK YOUR BATHROBE Mount a handsome hook on the wall near—but not inside—your closet, and park your bathrobe there. Bathrobes often get full of moisture during your shower routine, and an open-air hook will allow it to dry more thoroughly.

MORE CLOSET, LESS CLUTTER If you ever get the chance to remodel your child's bedroom, devote a large chunk of the room to a seriously expanded closet, Wiener says. Include in that closet generous hanging space, shelving, and other storage. This will limit the need for furniture out in the bedroom at large—thus cutting down on clutter, dust, and nicks and scuffs.

"To me, putting everything behind closed doors is preferable," she says.

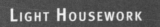

LIGHT HOUSEWORK

Here's where I advise you to throw out all of the lamps in your house. Bear with me for a moment—I'm not crazy. Remember: Cleaning would be extremely easy, just 90 seconds of dusting, if it weren't for all of the obstacles that you throw in your own way. You have to walk around lamps, coddle them like babies, and—worst of all—

they are exquisitely designed to gather dust and grime, whether they're hanging lamps, standing lamps, or table lamps. Look into the upturned shade of your floor lamp. Check your wall-mounted sconces, those hanging fixtures, and the pleated shades of those table lamps. Cobwebs, dead bugs, and dust, dust, dust. Lampshades get old and yellowed, too, and need replacing periodically.

What's the solution? Install recessed lighting throughout your house, says Wiener. This is the type of lighting that looks like a coffee can embedded in the ceiling. Light shines down into the room, but there is no bulky object intruding on the *space* of the room—nothing to tip over, nothing to trip over, and nothing to clean.

Most folks would want to hire an electrician to convert a room to recessed lighting. If you have easy access to the floor above (maybe there's just attic up there) this is a surprisingly easy job, Wiener says. If there's a finished room above, it's still not a terribly involved project—you'll just have to patch some drywall in a few spots. "I do it all the time," Wiener says.

Sure, installing recessed lighting requires a small investment, but it's a move that will pay off grandly over the long haul. Use the MOP philosophy: You might not convert the entire house at once. Just factor recessed lighting into your planning for the home and get it done when it's most strategic to do so—when there are workers at the house anyway installing ceiling fans or remodeling the kitchen, for instance. You'll save on labor costs if the workers don't have to make a separate house call.

Use extra-long-life halogen bulbs in your recessed lighting, Wiener says—they'll last 2 years or 3 years without a change, saving you a lot of bother. Also, put all of your lights on dimmer switches. One set of lights could illuminate the room over all, and other lights could be focused—say, on work areas or over the bed for reading.

Light has an enormous influence on the perception of cleanliness in your home. Think of yourself as the lighting technician

AD-HOC CLEANING

A half hour television show will typically have 8 minutes of commercials—and sometimes as much as 12 minutes. Why not use those minutes to catch up on some cleaning chores rather than allowing yourself to be hypnotized by Madison Avenue? Making good use of this "found time" means you won't have to devote part of some future weekend to these tasks.

Think ahead and gather any cleaning implements you'll need before your favorite show begins. To get you started, here are some cleaning tasks you can accomplish during a 2-minute commercial break:

* Sort that messy pile of papers into stacks such as "To be filed," "Take action on this," and "Throw away."

* Take the "To be filed" papers to your filing cabinet and put each in its proper folder. Toss the "Throw away" pile into recycling.

* Take a clean, dry dusting cloth and wipe down the entire entertainment center, working from top to bottom.

* Spray a cleaning cloth with disinfectant and wipe down all of the telephone receivers in the house.

* Pull the couch 4 feet away from the living room wall, scoop up all of those dust bunnies with a dusting mop, and put the couch back.

for your own theatrical production. You can toy with numerous variations and combinations of lighting sources, but there are two basic modes that you need to put the most thought to.

BRIGHT-AND-FUNCTIONAL MODE

Sure, brighter light will illuminate the dust and dirt in your home. But that's okay, because you're going to use the bright-and-functional mode only for you and your family. If the lighting helps you see dust on a living room shelf, you'll put that little dusting job on a mental to-do list.

For your day-to-day living, be generous with light. Walk around your house and examine every work area. Make sure good, bright light is provided for the task at hand. This includes reading areas, the office, the kitchen, the laundry room, craft and sewing areas, and the workbench.

If work around the house is not getting done often enough or well enough, poor lighting could be a contributing factor. For instance, Cawley often finds that a client's kitchen table is cluttered with work papers—so there's no place to eat comfortably. The resident doesn't realize that she is instinctively using the kitchen table as a desk because the light is better there. The home office—where those papers belong—is typically in a dark basement, a closet or some other odd corner of the house. Fix the lighting at your desk, and suddenly the kitchen table will be free for dining.

Yes, use of generous lighting means more power consumption and therefore higher cost. To compensate, install compact fluorescent bulbs (they fit into conventional bulb sockets) wherever you can in your home. While these bulbs are initially more expensive to buy than conventional incandescent light bulbs, they're cheaper in the long run—they consume much less electricity and last for several years. Use of fluorescents or other long-life bulbs also means, obviously, that you don't have to replace blown-out bulbs as often.

Also, open the blinds and curtains to let plenty of natural light into the house. It's free, after all. Scientists say that exposure to natural light can help alleviate depression in some cases. I'm not saying that sunlight will give you enough of an emotional bounce to clean the entire house, but at the very least you'll feel better about not having done it.

DIM-AND-SELECTIVE MODE

The dim-and selective lighting mode is what you use when guests come over. Any clutter, dirt, or dust you didn't get around to will be undetectable in the dark. For entertaining, turn off the lights in all areas where you don't want guests to go—the basement, the bedrooms, and your office, for instance. In the areas where your guests will roam freely—say, the living room, dining room, and kitchen—use dim lights in general, with a few narrowly focused lights emphasizing some nice feature of your home. In the living room, this might mean turning on just one corner lamp, plus a small spotlight on a painting (you've dusted the frame, of course). In the kitchen, the light focused over the kitchen table is on (you have a nice appetizer spread there), but the brighter over-head light is off.

Such devices as dimmer switches and three-way bulbs will help a lot with dim-and-selective mode. As needed, you also can remove 100-watt bulbs from some of your fixtures and replace them with 60-watt bulbs just before guests arrive.

MORE BRIGHT IDEAS

Maybe you're not ready to convert every single room to recessed lighting. All right, I'll still help you find some low-maintenance lighting fixtures. Here are some ideas from Jeff Dross, product manager and trend analyst for Kichler Lighting in Cleveland, Ohio:

FOREGO THE GLASS You don't exactly have easy access to a light fixture that dangles 10 feet above your head in a two-story foyer. So it pays to remember this law of lighting: Any enclosed glass fixture will become a highly visible burial ground for bugs that fry themselves against the light bulb. You'll need a ladder or scaffolding to get up there and empty their dead little carcasses out periodically. Instead, pick the kind of fixture that has a metal frame but no glass enclosure. Then your only cleaning task is removing dust and cobwebs. You can buy

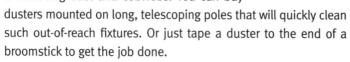

dusters mounted on long, telescoping poles that will quickly clean such out-of-reach fixtures. Or just tape a duster to the end of a broomstick to get the job done.

WARM IT UP Select lampshades in warm colors, such as yellows and oranges, as the light they throw will reveal less dirt, Dross says. Cooler tones—grays and blues—produce a starker, less forgiving light.

DON'T DANGLE Don't buy light fixtures with dangling elements—crystal chandeliers, for instance. Dusting them is a hopeless chore.

A NEW TWIST ON CANDLE POWER Light bulbs that are shaped like candle flame, the kind typically used in chandeliers, gather dust easily—but they're a breeze to clean, Dross says. Just turn the chandelier off, spray some glass cleaner on a paper towel, and quickly twist the towel around the bulb. "You'd be surprised at how clean this makes the whole room look," he says.

LOOK FOR LACQUER Make sure any brass or copper in the light fixtures you buy is lacquered—meaning it has a clear protective finish that you can clean with the simple swipe of a cloth. Stay away from unfinished brass and copper, unless you're willing to just let them corrode. Such fixtures are intended for people with servants who spend their days polishing.

ROUGH SURFACE, ROUGH GOING Avoid light fixtures that have glass with textured exterior surfaces. This kind of trendy glass collects dirt and is a pain to clean.

CLEARING THE AIR

Have you ever met a woman who uses way too much perfume? You almost smother under the tidal wave of sweet fragrance. Her good intentions are actually working against her—and she's oblivious to the problem, because her nose has acclimated to a high level of that particular scent.

Your efforts to "freshen" the air in your home can backfire in the same way. If you have odor "issues" in your home, layering on yet another scent—even a pleasant one—can create more of a problem than you had in the first place. Ironically, you are the worst person on the planet to judge whether your home smells okay, according to Pamela Dalton, Ph.D., an odor scientist at the renowned Monell Chemical Senses Center in Philadelphia. While your nose might be accustomed to a high level of artificial fragrance in your house, guests could be bowled over by the odor.

So here we're going to talk about easy ways to manage odors in your home without smothering innocent visitors. First, it helps to know just a little bit more about your nose and what it knows.

Smell is an old, primal sense, Dalton says. We are not programmed to detect the scents that linger around us all of the time. Rather, we are programmed to pick up changes in the scents that are around us. That's because in prehistoric times the primary function of our sense of smell was to detect danger ("Uh-oh, predator nearby") or food ("Mmm, ripe berries"). Messages about odor are processed in the brain in the same area where we store emotional memories. You could say that odors are hard-wired to our emotions.

That is why real estate agents' odor tricks really work. You know: When prospective buyers are headed to your house, you bake a loaf of bread, put on a pot of aromatic coffee, boil a cinnamon stick in water on the stovetop, or place a drop of vanilla on a light bulb and turn it on. Any of these homey odors will immediately put buyers in a positive frame of mind, imagining your home as a place of family, food, and comfort.

However, don't go overboard with home scents. If you have a fragrance-producing gizmo jammed into an outlet in every room, it's probably time to unplug and rethink what you're doing. "I'm not a big advocate of using a lot of fragrance products," says Dalton. When you overuse a home fragrance, you might unwittingly create the impression that you have something to cover up. So easy does it.

If your own nose is not a reliable judge of the air in your home, how are you supposed to know whether you have odor problems? Ask a friend to drop by, sniff around, and give you an honest as sessment, says Dalton. When you do, get right down to business—the human nose starts to get acclimated to its environment after only 15 minutes. Your friend can tell you whether there's a general mustiness about your home, an overwhelming floral scent, or if there are odor problems in specific places around the house—the refrigerator, the cat box, or a kid's closet, for instance. Make a "hit list" for remedial action.

Here's another easy way to get a read on your home's odor problems: When you return home after a week's vacation, what

A DIRTY STORY
XXX
EAU DE HOTEL

During a vacation, Cynthia Braun's husband stepped into their hotel room and wrinkled his nose. "This hotel room doesn't smell so good," he said.

Braun, a professional organizer, sniffed out the problem right away. During 16 years of marriage, her husband has gotten accustomed to the potpourri she spreads all over the house—plain ol' hotel smell wasn't good enough. So Braun whipped out her aerosol can of potpourri spray, spritzed the room, and the smile returned to her husband's face.

does the interior smell like? An overused gym locker? You may tell yourself that the house has been closed up and you just need to open some doors and windows to air it out. More likely, Dalton says, that's what your home really smells like to visitors.

SHEDDING LIGHT ON ODORS

Forget about air fresheners, forget about sprays, forget about potpourri. If you want the easiest, laziest, cheating-est way to freshen the air in your home, here's what you should do: Start changing your light bulbs. Yup. At this writing, special odor-killing light bulbs are just entering consumer markets. You might already be familiar with compact fluorescent bulbs, the power-saving, money-saving bulbs that last for years. The odor-killing bulbs are the same thing, except that they have a coating of titanium dioxide. When the chemical interacts with the bulb's light, it destroys the organic material in the surrounding air. This technology was developed by scientists looking for solutions to "sick building syndrome," caused by poor ventilation.

At first, you'll want to install a bulb near the cat box, in a musty basement, where smokers hang out, and any other place where odors are a particular problem. When you turn the bulb on, it takes about 10 minutes to start its odor destruction. The longer you leave

it on, the stronger the effect is. As your conventional bulbs burn out, you'll want to install titanium dioxide bulbs in every possible fixture for a whole-house odor shield. The bulbs don't perform miracles, but you will be able to scoop out cat boxes and change the litter half as often.

There are some caveats. The bulbs can do their de-stinking only when the open air can circulate past them, so they won't work in glass or plastic-enclosed light fixtures. The bulbs are a bit pricey, too. The less-costly brand, Fresh2®, is for $20 for a two-pack.

On the bright side: The odor-killing chemicals last for 3 years, and the bulbs themselves can last 7 years to 9 years. The 23-watt fluorescent bulbs also put out the same amount of light as a 100-watt incandescent bulb, meaning they provide a huge energy savings. At this writing, the bulbs are sold in some home stores, and discount stores are soon to follow. They're easy to find on the Internet.

BREAK THE MOLD

You may have seen scary reports about a creepy form of toxic mold chasing hapless residents out of their homes. Some people want to blame every disease known to humankind on mold. Others claim it's a lot of hype created by people who want to sue building contractors.

"The only reasonable place to be is in the middle somewhere," says Portnoy. The truth is, most houses have mold in them and little of it is toxic. While scientists don't know enough about how mold affects humans, there is evidence that it can trigger allergy symptoms and aggravate asthma. If nothing else, mold is worth controlling in the home because it looks and smells bad. When it gets out of hand, it can even weaken the structure of a house by digesting wood.

Mold needs two things to survive in your home. The first is food—which is the stuff your house is made of. If you remove this food, you won't have a house left. So let's move on to the second item, which is far easier to control: water. When the humidity—or moisture in the air—is above 50 percent, you're encouraging the growth of microorganisms, Portnoy says. A home's moisture problem is made worse by everyday living, including cooking, showering, other washing, and even people breathing in and out.

Many of the best ways to control humidity in your home fall into the category of one-time fixes, which means they take a little effort up front but continue to pay off far into the future:

* ❄ Central heating and air-conditioning systems typically include humidity controls, so make sure you know how to work them. Check your manual or ask a service technician.

* ❄ During warm months when you're not using an air-conditioner or if the air-conditioning doesn't dry the basement air enough, keep a dehumidifier running to pull the moisture out of the air.

* ❄ Make sure there are no leaky pipes in your house or a leaky shower stall dripping water into the basement.

* ❄ Check whether water is seeping through your basement walls. If you have a seepage problem, use a special moisture-blocking paint (available at home stores) on the interior of the concrete block. Outside, make sure all of your downspouts carry water well away from the house. If problems persist, you may need to have your yard regraded so that rainwater flows away quickly.

* ❄ Make sure your home is well ventilated. Exhaust fans that suck moist air out of bathrooms, kitchens, and laundry rooms and vent it to the outside will help control mold. If you have an older home that wasn't built with exhaust fans, installing them is a surprisingly easy job for a contractor. The next time you have remodeling, siding, roofing, or other building-type work done around the house, see if you can include exhaust fans as part of the deal.

SHOOT TO KILL Now and then, despite your best efforts at controlling moisture in your home, you're going to come face-to-face with the enemy. The minor mold incursions—a few telltale black spots on the grout in the shower or along the rim of the toilet—are easy to dispatch. Just pick up a bleach-based disinfecting cleaner (Clorox® is one brand), squirt it on, wait the prescribed amount of time, wipe, and rinse. The same cleaner will kill even moderate infestations of mold, Portnoy says, on wallboard, ceiling tile, and wood. Not only is the fungus killed, he says, but the bleach will lighten the mold stain and make it look better.

If you discover a large mold problem—say, in wallboard that has grown soft to the touch—the only solution is to remove the contaminated building material and replace it. Don't attempt this on your own, Portnoy says. The concentration of mold could be severe enough to be harmful. Ask professional home remodelers whether they handle cases like yours. Even if they don't, they'll have names of people who do. Just making the repair is not enough—make sure you figure out why the contamination happened and fix the source of the problem.

GREAT · GEAR

WATER, WATER EVERYWHERE

To discourage mold and dust mites, we need to keep the humidity in our homes under 50 percent. The ideal level for health and comfort is 45 percent, and 30 percent is too dry.

How the heck are we supposed to know, with any kind of precision, what the indoor humidity is? Easy: A hygrometer will tell you.

Most home hygrometers fall into one of two categories:

- **MECHANICAL.** These plastic or wood devices have a dial display and can be found for $20 or less.
- **ELECTRONIC.** These units have digital readouts, require batteries, and cost $40 or more.

These compact gizmos are easy to move around the house, but remember that they can take a couple of hours to acclimate to a new location. Don't position your hygrometer near a heat source. Hygrometers often can be purchased where indoor thermometers are sold—department stores, home stores, and hardware stores, for instance. Some hygrometers come combined with a thermometer in one unit.

If you find out that your house is too humid, adjust the humidity controls on your central air or central heating, or use a standalone dehumidifier.

OF MITES AND MEN (AND WOMEN)

The air in your home can be an invisible soup of impurities that can aggravate anybody's lungs and are a particular nuisance to people with asthma and allergies. These particles include not only mold but also dust mites, pet dander, smoke, and other airborne detritus. If you do have asthma or allergies, explore with your doctor what specific irritants you react to. Your doctor can supply more detail that's specific to your case than I can provide here. However, here are some broad strokes that any homeowner can make to yank impurities right out of the air with minimal effort.

FIGHT THE MITES Dust mites are microscopic insectlike critters that thrive on, among other things, the skin cells you leave behind in your bedding. The poop they produce is a notorious allergen. The humidity-reducing measures described earlier will help control dust mites. Wash your bedding weekly in hot water, and zip your mattress and pillows up in anti-mite covers, available in department stores and discount stores.

GET A HEAP OF HEPA FILTERS Buy high-efficiency particulate air (HEPA) filters for your furnace and vacuum cleaner. Also buy stand-alone air filtering machines to use in your living areas. HEPA filters remove from the air the kind of microscopic particles that are good at burrowing into your lungs. If you buy a HEPA filter for your furnace, consult your service folks—they may need to adjust the furnace's fan speed to accommodate the new airflow, Portnoy says. Special HEPA vacuum cleaners are available, or you can buy HEPA bags for conventional vacuum cleaners. HEPA filters need changing with a certain frequency, so pay special attention to the directions.

If you buy a stand-alone air-filtering machine, make sure you understand the unit's coverage area. Many can service no more than one typical room—and certainly not the entire house—so you may need more than one. Avoid the type of room air filters that emit ozone, which is itself a lung irritant, Portnoy says. Not all room units perform equally well, and price is not always an indicator of quality. So check consumer publications before you buy.

CHOKE OFF THE SOURCES OF POLLUTION We sometimes cling dearly to lifestyle factors that are ruining the air around us. Make the tough decisions and ban smoking from the house, quit using the fireplace, and stop lighting candles and incense. Quit using air fresheners, and don't store solvents, pesticides, and other chemicals in your home.

ALLEVIATE YOUR PET PEEVES If you're allergic to furry pets, foregoing them altogether is best. However, if you have dogs in the house, wash them weekly with a mild pet shampoo—not human shampoo and not common soap. Wash your cats, too, if you can get away with it—just wiping with a damp cloth will help. (And just in case you were thinking about it, don't spray your cat with disinfectant—believe it or not, Portnoy knows of people who have done just that.) Pet allergens and dust mites will cling to carpeting. Instead, use hard flooring and throw rugs that you can wash in hot water.

GET ALL YOUR DUCTS IN A ROW Sometimes mold will grow on old construction material left behind in ductwork, Portnoy says. Removing it is a good job for a duct-cleaning service. However, despite some of the advertising you'll see, regular duct cleaning isn't necessary.

MORE STINK STRATEGIES

Here are more ways to clear the air around your home:

USE ODOR ABSORBERS Baking soda and cat litter are two common household substances that are famous for absorbing odors in confined spaces—closets, lockers, drawers, pantries, and refrigerators, for instance. Just pour several ounces into a lidless plastic container and place the container in a hidden spot where it won't get tipped over. The baking soda or cat litter does all the work—you don't have to do anything but change it every 3 months.

KNOW YOUR SPRAYS It sounds Pollyannish to say "Read the label on your product," but it really does help to check the spray can of any odor-fighting product. If you know how the product works, you increase your chances of success in de-stinking the house. Some sprays work by killing odor-causing bacteria on surfaces, some kill bacteria suspended in the air, some trap odor molecules, and others just add a pleasing fragrance to the air (covering up— or adding to—the stink). So fit the product to the situation. In a shower stall, use a product that will kill mildew on the tile, for instance.

THIS ROBOT WILL SWEEP YOU OFF YOUR FEET

As I write this, there's a robot vacuuming my dining room. We truly have entered the age of *The Jetsons*. Only my robot isn't named Rosie and it isn't human shaped. My metal-and-plastic assistant is a cute little disc that's only 13 inches across and 4 inches high. Yes, it looks like a Foreman® grill on wheels. It's a revolutionary tool that is now available to any consumer for the price of a conventional vacuum cleaner. The Roomba® and its competitors will do for floor cleaning what the washing machine did for laundry and the dishwasher did for husbands: It takes care of a regular, necessary cleaning chore all by itself. While your robot is doing the vacuuming, you get to read a good book or go out to lunch—unless, like a number of enthusiasts, you can't resist following the little machine around the house.

The Roomba was devised by iRobot®, the same company that makes who-cares-if-they-get-killed robots for the military. While its cousins are exploring dangerous caves in Afghanistan, the homebody Roomba routs out dust and dirt in all of your living spaces. While the robot may sound intimidatingly high-tech, it's actually easy to use. It weighs no more than your purse or briefcase and has a convenient handle on top. Just turn it on, and the robot goes wheeling around the room, humming at the volume of a hair dryer set on low. The robot estimates the size of a room by seeing how far it can go in various directions without running into a wall, and then it uses math to design a cleaning pattern that will cover the entire floor.

It automatically adjusts itself to the floor surfaces it encounters—wood, tile, and carpet. (It does fine on low and medium pile, but it won't work on deep-pile carpet, shag, and such.) It can sense which parts of the floor are dirtiest and will concentrate on those areas. It also has side brushes and wall-following technology that help it clean corners and edges of a room. Because the Roomba stands just a few inches off the ground, it can vacuum where conventional vacuum cleaners can't reach—under couches, beds and chairs, for instance. Different settings instruct the robot to adjust to room sizes or even focus on one particular

CHECK YOUR ROBOT'S BREATHING

If the performance of your Roomba robotic vacuum cleaner takes a nosedive, check the filter—it may be time to replace it. You'll find an easy-access release tab for the filter on the bottom of the dirt bin, which slides out of the back of your robot part of the floor. A remote is available on some models, allowing you to turn it on from afar, direct it to specific dirty spots in a room, or pause the machine's cleaning cycle.

For recharging, the machine is connected to an electrical outlet. It can clean three average-size rooms on one charge. The newer units include a "home base" where the Roomba parks itself for recharging.

The first time I used my Roomba, I let it loose in the family room, living room, and dining room, which had been vacuumed with a conventional human-driven machine just two days before. The Roomba picked up an ounce of dust and other grime (yes, I weighed it on a postal scale)—a glob the size of my fist. This machine won't do a deep-down cleaning in your carpet—you'll still need to use a conventional vacuum cleaner for that—but it's perfect for a light cleaning every few days. Some Roomba fans say they now don't touch their conventional vacuum cleaners for months at a time.

JOIN A ROOMBA COMMUNITY

A search on the Internet will quickly lead you to an online Roomba discussion group, believe it or not. You can browse through the discussions, picking up advice about specific Roomba models, or you can get questions answered by people who have more experience than you. You'll find that a lot of owners get deeply attached to their robots—giving them names (R2D2 has been taken . . . many times over), racing them, debating what gender they are, and otherwise treating them like part of the family.

HELPING YOUR LITTLE HELPER

As independent as they are, robotic vacuums do need a little help. The human tasks are easy and fall into two categories.

READYING THE ROOM Before your Roomba goes to work, you have to prepare the room. If you're a parent, this will feel oddly like the child-proofing routine you do for babies and toddlers. The difference is, preparing for your Roomba is much easier and the stakes are much lower. It's not very likely, for example, that your vacuuming robot will sit on your cactus or stick a coat hanger into an electrical socket. Just scan the room for objects that might get pulled up into the robot's whirling brushes—plants that hang to the floor, blind cords, and lamp wires, for instance. If you have fringe on a carpet, you can tuck it under the rug temporarily. Secure the corners of small area rugs with double-sided tape. Make sure there are no objects, such as a rickety plant stand, that could be bumped over. The Roomba comes with "virtual wall" devices—little infrared flashlights—that mark off areas where you don't want the robot to go—say, through a doorless passageway.

Your Roomba may also need a little help if you have furniture that stands just a few inches off of the floor—say, the lower edge of a couch or cross-supports for an end table. Such furniture can trap your vacuuming robot. Some furniture can be raised on blocks or casters. If that's not feasible, create a physical barrier or use one of your virtual wall devices to shoo the robot away from trouble.

A DIRTY STORY
XXX

GETTING LUBRICATED

The Roomba robotic vacuum cleaner will spiff up your social life as well as your carpet. Roy Hinrichs, an Internet technology manager for a computer services company in Fort Worth, Texas, has a model with a remote control. During a social gathering in his home, Hinrichs sent his Roomba into the kitchen. His wife placed four beers on the robot's flat top. The little robot then returned to the living room and served the guests.

MAINTAINING THE MACHINE Roomba enthusiasts say some simple maintenance routines, performed after every three or four cleanings, will prevent breakdowns. In particular, you don't want long hair or other debris to get wrapped in the inner bearings or gears. To remove the robot's brushes for cleaning, all you need to do is turn the robot over, pop the wire guards off, and loosen a small Phillips-head screw. (The manual provides details.) Remove all of the hair and dirt you can find and reassemble the machine. You also can use the brush and crevice attachments on your conventional vacuum cleaner to suck dirt out of the workings of your robot. (An alternative: Blast the dirt out with compressed air.)

Assemble a small kit of the Roomba-related items you'll need frequently. These will include the following:

* ☀ A small Phillips-head screwdriver for removing the robot's brushes and cleaning inside.
* ☀ An old comb and an unbent paperclip to help extract hair and dirt from the brushes.
* ☀ Used drier sheets for dusting your robot and leaving behind an anti-static film.
* ☀ Extra filters.

These items will fit easily in a self-closing plastic bag. Store this kit in a cupboard near your Roomba.

You can buy a Roomba at discount stores, bath and kitchen stores, department stores, or on the Internet. Check how many "virtual wall" devices come with your unit—you may want to buy one or two extras. Get some extra replacement filters at the same time. You also can buy a battery

that recharges in only 2 hours, as opposed to the 12 hours it takes the standard battery. Just in case something goes wrong with your unit, buy from a retailer with a liberal return policy.

More robots could be joining your household in the near future. At this writing, the people who created Roomba were just unveiling a new floor-washing robot called Scooba®. Also on the drawing boards: machines for such tasks as washing windows and cleaning out gutters.

So there you have it—quite a collection of strategies that will make the main living areas of your home profoundly cleaner and more presentable for very little effort. Don't forget that when I suggest that you quit making the bed, install different lighting, or use a new kind of wall paint, you get to say, "No, I prefer my own approach." I'm not the God of Guilt ordering you around. If you weren't in charge, after all, it wouldn't feel like cheating.

LAUNDRY GOT YOU
OUT OF SORTS?

Jot down a quick list of the garments that you wear regularly, including clothing for work, casual situations, and outerwear. Sort your entries into two columns, one titled "Easy Care" and the other "Special Handling." Easy-Care items are those that can go into the general wash (award yourself a bonus point for each garment that's stain resistant or wrinkle free). The Special-Handling items require hand washing, delicate washing, delicate drying, or dry-cleaning. This exercise gives you a snapshot of how hard you're currently working for your wardrobe. If more than 5 percent of the clothing you regularly wear falls into the Special-Handling category, it's time to rethink the way you dress.

Unless you're a hermit, you have a valid need for the occasional piece of fine clothing, even if caring for it requires special effort. The trick is to keep such items to a minimum—nice showpieces that you mix in with a wardrobe that's predominately simple to care for.

Easy care is not the only issue. For most people, enjoyment of life is inversely proportional to the cost of the clothing you're wearing. If you spend the day in more than $500 worth of clothing, you're wearing a mental body cast—perpetually concerned about messing up those clothes and hoping your finery is creating the right illusion. That's self-induced stress. Sure, we all may enjoy the occasional silk shirt or cashmere sweater. But the stress-busting solution is to keep an eye on the balance and prevent your wardrobe from sapping too much of your physical and emotional energy.

So this is a chapter about adding "clothing sanity" to your personal agenda. In recent years, much of the working world has embraced Casual Friday—a good step. How about Casual Sunday through Saturday? Let's reserve suits for dinner at the White House. Let's dispense with men's ties altogether—an absurd garment if there ever was one. You have better things to do with money than fritter it away on fabric finery—pay for your kids' college education, pay down the mortgage, catch up on credit-card bills, or donate to charity, for instance. So let's look at some specific ways you can restore some clothing sanity to your life right now.

DESIGN DIRT AWAY

FABRICS FROM HELL

Some fabrics come with a guarantee: to make your life miserable. To simplify clothing care, follow the Materials on a Program (MOP) philosophy and quit adding these garments to your wardrobe. Here is Steve "The Clothing Doctor®" Boorstein's rundown of fabrics that are high-maintenance—and particularly vexing to travelers who try to haul these duds around in a suitcase. Just say no to:

- **ACETATE.** Difficult to iron—it shines up more quickly than chrome.
- **RAYON KNIT AND SILK KNIT.** Phew. Impossible to remove body odors.
- **SILK.** There are many grades of silk, and the cheaper variety doesn't clean well.
- **SILK-LINEN BLENDS.** These stain badly. Soft drink stains are particularly hard to get out.
- **VELVET.** Very water sensitive. "If you're a spiller, you want to stay away from most velvet," Boorstein says. Can't be ironed.

To reduce the chore of cleaning your clothes, start by making wise clothing purchases. If you consistently buy only easy-care clothing, over the months to come your laundry hassles—stains, wrinkles, delicate care, and dry cleaner trips—will be reduced by two thirds.

Once again, technology has come to our rescue. "Wrinkle-resistant clothes started out looking like people were wearing Teflon®," says Steve Boorstein, a.k.a. The Clothing Doctor, author of *The Ultimate Guide to Shopping and Caring for Clothing*. However, wrinkle- and stain-resistant fabrics have improved so much over the last decade that you can actually build an entire wardrobe out of such clothing without looking like a dork. When you stray from the wrinkle- and stain-resistant clothing, make sure you're selecting a fabric that's known for easy care. When you assemble your wardrobe with this strategy, you'll happily whistle your way through laundry day.

LABELS: THE CRUCIAL CHECKPOINT

To make sure you're getting an ideal garment for your cheat-at-cleaning wardrobe, pay careful attention to the labels on the clothing you're considering. "It's amazing how many people don't," Boorstein says—especially when they buy coats, jackets, and other outerwear. Both the hangtag dangling from the sleeve and the sewn-in fabric-care label offer valuable information about caring for a garment. Give first priority to wrinkle-resistant, stain-resistant clothing. Also, the ideal label indicates that a garment can be both machine washed and dry-cleaned. This indicates that the manufacturer has tested both approaches in the laboratory. (On the care label, the international symbol that looks like a tub full of wavy water means "wash," and a simple circle means "dry clean.")

"I believe that the care of clothing begins the moment you begin to shop," Boorstein says. "If you are a stain magnet, you really need to make sure that your clothes can be dry-cleaned *and* washed."

Oddly enough, if a label only says "machine wash" you probably can dry-clean it as well. Such labels indicate that the manufacturer tested the fabric just one way in the lab.

FAST•FORMULAS

OLD JEWELRY: RISE AND SHINE

Revive the shimmer and shine of your old costume jewelry by giving it a quick bath in white vinegar. Pour 2 inches of vinegar into a ceramic bowl and slip your jewelry into the liquid. After 2 minutes, lift the jewelry out and give any nooks and crevices a light brushing with an old toothbrush. Rinse the piece under the faucet and press it gently from both sides with a towel to dry. If you have fine jewelry that you want to clean, be careful: Many of the softer stones—such as opals, lapis lazuli, turquoise, and pearls—could be harmed by the acid in vinegar.

More testing costs the manufacturer more money, and the U.S. Federal Trade Commission requires only one laundry instruction for each garment. So if you have a "machine wash" ski jacket that picks up a greasy stain from your car door, you need to take it to the dry-cleaner's. Trying to wash out an oil-based spot at home could set the stain. (More about stains in a moment.)

If a garment's label tells you that special care is required—say, dry-cleaning only or delicate washing—a little alarm should go off in your cheat-at-cleaning head. Is this piece of clothing really worth the bother or extra expense?

Another gift from modern technology is microfiber, Boorstein says. This is a broad term for manmade cloth designed at the microscopic level to take on certain characteristics. Microfiber clothing, often a rayon and polyester blend, has an excellent drape and does not wrinkle easily.

WANT YOUR WALLET WASHED?

Empty the pockets of your clothing the moment you take them off, says Steve "The Clothing Doctor" Boorstein, who spent years as the hands-on operator of a dry-cleaning business. Otherwise, you risk having important items ruined in your washer or at the dry cleaner's. (A dry cleaner should check pockets, but sometimes he or she will miss items.)

Here are just a few items that Boorstein has found in customers' clothing in his days on the cleaning front lines: expensive jewelry, credit cards, government IDs—even a $25,000 check!

Easy-care knits, particularly cotton-polyester-Spandex® blends, also will add clothing sanity to your life, says Pamela Brown, Ph.D., a professor at the Texas Cooperative Extension at Texas A&M University. Such knits are very forgiving in the laundry room, she says—just wash, dry, remove from the dryer immediately, and hang them up to let any last wrinkles fall out.

Buy clothing in dark colors and prints, which hide stains better than light-colored clothing. Even if there's a little residual stain left after you try to remove a spot, those traces are not likely to show on dark or patterned fabric. Also, neutral colors stand up to washing over the long haul, whereas intense colors fade more quickly. If you feel drab wearing subdued colors, perk up your wardrobe through the use of accessories such as belts, scarves, and jewelry.

PLAY INSPECTOR

Once you've found the perfect garment, it's time to run off to the cash register, right? No, keep your credit card in your pocket for just 60 seconds longer. You want to be sure that the garment is really as "perfect" as it seems at first glance. Lay the clothing out on a counter or hang it up and conduct Boorstein's six-point check to make sure it's in good condition: hooks, zippers, hems, seams, snags, and buttons. Test all of the moving parts, making sure the hooks work and zippers don't catch the fabric. Make sure that the hems and seams weren't damaged by some other customer trying the clothing on. Check that all of the buttons are in place. Are there extra buttons in case you lose one?

If you're buying a finer garment—maybe a nice blouse or a sport coat—also buy a sturdy, shaped, well-fitted hanger to go with it. A high-quality, contoured hanger will keep the garment looking its best. If you use an ill-fitting hanger, you could find a bizarre dimple in the middle of the shoulder, for instance, as you dress for your big presentation. Also, avoid the clip-style hangers that have a ridge where the clip bites the fabric. These will leave impressions in the cloth. Use only the type with a smooth clasping surface.

MANAGING YOUR CLOTHES

You get your new easy-care duds home, you snip off the tags, and you set these garments free in that stream of clothing that circulates throughout your house. This is a stream that meanders from your dresser and closet, to the hamper, to the laundry room, and back again. How smoothly and easily that stream flows depends largely on you. Here are some corner-cutting clothing management techniques to help it along.

LET YOUR CLOTHES HANG OUT

When you get home from work, you want to take a little break, right? Well, your work clothes need a rest, too. So take off your shirt and pants, empty all pockets, put the clothes on hangers, and change into your jeans and T-shirt. Then hang those work clothes out in the open—on the back porch, on a doorknob, or in the bathroom, for instance.

Why? For a few good reasons. First of all, unless you got those clothes really soiled you can wear them to work two, three, or even four times before laundering. Don't blush, Boorstein says. People who study clothing use had a focus group of white-

IT'S A TIE, NOT A BIB

If you must wear ties, spray them lightly with a stain-resistant spray such as Scotchgard®. You'll be able to mop up ketchup or wine drips without having a heart attack over the prospect of staining.

collar types—doctors, lawyers, stock-brokers, and the like—and you know what they found? These high-rolling professionals wear their dress shirts multiple times before washing them, particularly if they were wearing undershirts. So you can, too. Be-sides, over-cleaning your clothes is a kind of wear-and-tear in itself, so clean them only if necessary.

Here's why you hang those work clothes out in the open for at least 1 hour: Your clothes have spent the day sucking up mois-ture, odors, chemicals from work, and smoke from that bar where you ate lunch. Would you rather have these clothes air out—or share all of those fumes with the other clothes in your closet?

Inspect the clothes under a bright light, front and back, top and bottom. If you find grime or stains—say, around the collar, cuffs, or elbows—then they need to be laundered. Perspiration stains in particular must be washed within 24 hours. If you were to put them back into the closet for a week or two, the soil would oxidize into a permanent yellow stain. Also, give your clothes the sniff test—yes, under the arms in particular. If there's any odor, wash them. Otherwise, back into the closet they go, thus saving you some labor on washday.

STAINS MADE SIMPLE

You can find entire encyclopedias devoted to the subject of stain removal. However, if you stick to this incredibly simple rule you can't go wrong, Boorstein says: Water-based clothing stains go into your washing machine; oil-based stains go to the dry cleaner. In either case, wash (after pretreating) or dry-clean with-in 24 hours.

If the stain is on your own clothing, you probably have a reasonable idea of whether that stain is beer (water based) or a movie popcorn simulated-butter-like substance (oil based). However, on children's clothing it's harder to be sure what kind of stain you have, particularly if your kids' vocabulary never gets any more specific than "I don't know," "Nothing," and "Stuff." So here's how to tell water- and oil-based stains apart and how to deal with them.

WATER-BASED STAINS These almost always have a border around the perimeter that looks like a map. Examples: coffee, wine, and soft drinks. Apply a laundry pretreatment before washing (see "Stain Stopper" on p. 130, or use a commercial product). In most cases, the stain will come out fine in the wash at home.

When washing, don't forget which garments have stains—either run them through a separate wash, separate them from the other clothing in a mesh bag, or mark them with a safety pin. Remember that stains appear darker when they're wet and often are invisible, so you might not be able to tell by looking at the wet garment whether the stain has come out. Because machine drying will set the stain, let these clothes air dry

E M E R G E N C Y ✚

TOO EAGER TO GET IT OFF YOUR CHEST?

How many times have you seen someone in a restaurant rubbing furiously at a spot just dripped onto a blouse? Big mistake, says Steve Boorstein, author of *The Ultimate Guide to Shopping and Caring for Clothing*. It's okay to carefully blot at a stain with a fresh napkin to absorb some of the liquid. (*Blotting* means pressing down with the napkin, changing to a new part of the napkin, and pressing again.) However, never rub a stain—that could damage the fabric and ruin the color in the fibers. Just live with the splotch for the evening, and launder the blouse or take it to the dry cleaner's (depending on the type of stain) first thing in the morning.

If you're sure you have a water-based stain, blotting with a damp napkin might help, too. Club soda also is a famous emergency cure for stains (dampen a napkin with club soda and blot), but that also should not be used on oily stains or dry-clean-only clothing. It works fairly well on stains from wine, coffee, soft drinks, and some foods.

STAIN STOPPER

The earlier you get to work on a stain, the better your chances of getting it out. So when you do your evening inspection of the clothing you wore that day, here's a stain-busting formula that you can apply to spots right away. This pretreatment will hold you until laundry day. It is for water-based stains only. If you wiped french-fry grease onto your shirt, take it straight to a dry cleaner.

In a small plastic bottle, mix 1 ounce of clear (not blue or yellow tinted) dishwashing liquid with 6 ounces of water. Drip onto the stain enough of the solution to cover. Use a small brush to gently work it into the fabric. Clip a clothespin onto the stained spot so you'll remember to watch for it, and toss the garment into the hamper.

So you can grab them quickly when you need them, store the bottle, small brush, and some clothespins in a dresser drawer, in your closet, or even in the bottom of your laundry hamper.

instead—laid out flat or draped over hangers—then inspect them. If the stain is still visible on the air-dried clothing, wash again (pretreat, presoak, wash in an all-fabric bleach).

If you have a persistent stain that pretreating and laundering will not remove, take the wet (or air-dried) clothing to the dry cleaner, point out the stain, and tell them precisely what you did in an effort to remove it. Armed with this information, your dry cleaner has a better chance of getting the spot out. "It's time to be totally up front," says Boorstein, a former dry cleaner. "Full disclosure really helps."

OIL-BASED STAINS These almost always have no outline, and the stain typically has been absorbed into the fabric. Examples: egg roll grease, gravy, and hamburger drippings. Oil-based stains rarely come out in the wash, and if you do try to launder them, they will leave a blotchy remnant that will affect the color of the clothing. In most cases, it's worth the investment to dry-clean. If you insist on treating an oil-based stain at home, catch the stain fresh.

A myth-busting note: 70 percent of spot stain remover products say they remove all stains, which is impossible, Boorstein says. Tide to Go® is one of the best stain removers on the market. Its label faces up to its limitations—specifying that it is not for use on oily stains.

SOCK MATCHES MADE IN HEAVEN

The next time you're ready to buy some socks for yourself, go to your dresser, put every sock you have into a shopping bag, and donate them all to a preschool so they can make sock puppets. Yes, get rid of the seven pairs in various shades of tan, the three versions of navy blue, the green spectrum (khaki to deep forest), and the five brands of white athletic socks in various states of decay. Anything with a leprechaun, jack o' lantern, or Santa Claus on it—out it goes. Now you're ready to go to your clothing store and buy the socks that you will need to get you through only one week, says C. Lee Cawley, a professional organizer in Arlington, Virginia. For a man, depending on his lifestyle, that may be something like this: four pairs of white athletic socks for sneaker casual and five pairs of black socks for dress. If you insist, add three pairs of navy. Most important: All socks of the same color must be of the same brand and style. For women, Cawley's system isn't much different: several pairs of black trouser socks for dress and several pairs of white athletic socks for sports and sneaker casual, plus a few pairs in navy blue, gray, or brown (depending on the color of your dress trousers). Cawley also recommends limiting your pantyhose to black, nude, and—if you insist on getting complicated—gray or navy. Find a flattering, comfortable style, and buy them in bulk (usually 12 pairs at a time).

Why are we socking it to the sock drawer? Because owning 43 pairs of socks all in different styles and shades is a needlessly complicating element in your life. With Cawley's simplified sock plan, that hideous matching-up chore on laundry day will vanish. Your clothing choice when you dress in the morning will be a no-brainer. And you'll gain 2 cubic feet of space in your dresser drawer.

Photocopy, fill out, and post prominently.

A NOTE FROM
YOUR LAUNDRY FAIRY

This family's Laundry Fairy works only under specific conditions and guidelines:

1. **The Laundry Fairy does not pick up or deliver. Laundry days are _____. Laundry delivered in your laundry basket by _____ will be washed and returned to the basket. You may pick it up by the end of the day. Please return cleaned clothes to your dresser or closet promptly.**

2. **At times other than those stated in No. 1, you may use the laundry equipment to wash and dry your own clothes.**

3. **If you have special washing instructions or clothing requiring delicate care, please write the specifics down and refer to them carefully as you do the washing yourself. See No. 2.**

4. **The Laundry Fairy does not iron. Ironing lessons are available by appointment.**

5. **The Laundry Fairy assumes you intend for her/him to wash any items left in pockets, including wallets, candy, homework, frogs, video games, and love notes. You are responsible for the results.**

6. **Socks delivered inside out or balled up ("stink grenades") will not be laundered.**

7. **To reduce wrinkles, the Laundry Fairy will smooth and fold shirts, pants, and skirts. You may fold your own underwear and match up your own socks.**

Your humble servant,

The Laundry Fairy

THE PANTYHOSE SECRET: DOUBLE-BAGGING Pantyhose are a cleaning nightmare for many women. Here's Cawley's streamlined system: Buy two mesh lingerie laundry bags, one to hang on a hook in your closet and one to hold all clean pantyhose in your dresser. When you need a fresh pair, pull one out of the bag in the dresser—the color you need should be easy to grab. At the end of the day, drop them into the bag hanging in the closet. On laundry day, put the entire bag holding dirty pantyhose into the washer and then the dryer. Then slide it into your dresser and transfer the other lingerie bag to your closet.

GET A HANDLE ON SANDALS Every chance you get, wear sandals—without socks. Every day that you do represents a pair of socks you didn't have to sort, launder, dry, match up again, and deliver back to a drawer—an extra little toehold on sanity, if you will.

WASHING: LESS IS MORE

Here's welcome advice for anyone who does laundry: Do it less frequently. What most people think of as doing a normal wash actually is overwashing. Overwashing is not only a waste of time but has other undesirable effects as well: It puts more wear on your clothing, it uses up more detergent, and it increases the chances that detergent will be left in your clothes.

"Unless you have a child who has been on the playground making mud pies, most laundry just needs to be freshened," says Ingrid Johnson, a professor at the Fashion Institute of Technology in New York City. If the clothing you're going to wash has had everyday light wear—a day at the office, a shopping trip, or a day at school, for instance—use half the amount of laundry detergent that the package recommends and use the shortest, most

UP FRONT ABOUT WASHERS

The next time you buy a washing machine, go for a front-loading model, says Steve Boorstein, a.k.a. The Clothing Doctor. Here are the advantages of front loaders:

- They use only 5 gallons of water per load, compared to 20 gallons in a typical top loader.
- They whirl more of the water out of your clothes, so your drier has to use less energy to get them dry.
- They cause less abrasion on your clothes, meaning they'll look good longer.
- They have a larger capacity. They can easily handle big items, such as sleeping bags, that you would take to a commercial laundry otherwise.
- They generally come with more choices and flexibility in wash cycle settings.
- They're less likely to tangle up your clothing during the wash cycle.

delicate wash cycle available on your machine. "More than 90 percent of average soil comes out of most clothing within the first 2 minutes," adds Boorstein.

On the other hand, if your kids have been playing football or your spouse was knee-deep in muck in the garden, fine—give those ground-in-grubby duds the full laundry treatment: pretreating, presoaking, a full measure of detergent, and a nice long ride in the washing machine. There's just no need to give all clothing this treatment on every washday.

TIPS FOR THE LAUNDRY FAIRY

Here's advice for getting the clothes washing done with minimal effort.

TEACH YOUR KIDS RESTRAINT Children typically follow a wear-it-once philosophy and toss their clothes into the hamper whether or not they're dirty, says Brown, the Cooperative Extension prof. Train them in the quick clothing inspection techniques described earlier. Impress on them that they're lessening the household workload and protecting the environment (less use of energy and cleaning chemicals) when they wear clothing more than once.

GET THE DIRTY DUDS DELIVERED Make sure each member of the family has his or her own laundry basket for hauling clothes around. Let them know the specific day and time when laundry will be done. Anybody who wants the Laundry Fairy (that's you) to magically wash their clothes will deliver a basketful to the laundry room by that deadline. If they forget, don't wash their clothes. They won't forget again. And you won't have to forage around the house looking for clothes to wash. Photocopy "A Note from Your Laundry Fairy" (p. 132) and post it where everyone in the family will see it.

GET THE HANG OF DRYING When you're getting ready to haul your dirty clothes out of the bedroom on laundry day, open up your closet door, grab several unused hangers, and toss them into the laundry basket, too, says Cawley. Those hangers will be ready to spring into action the moment you pull a shirt or a pair of slacks out of the dryer—and hanging up dried clothing immediately means you'll keep wrinkles to a minimum. Install a hanging bar or rolling clothing rack in the laundry room just for this purpose. (Don't hang clothes on plumbing pipes running across the ceiling—you'll weaken the pipes' joints.)

DO YOUR PART Wrinkle-resistant garments can't do their wrinkle resisting all on their own—you have to help. Check the care label in the clothing. Typically, you'll be told to wash the garment in warm water, dry at a low temperature, and take it out of the dryer right away. Smooth the fabric with your hands, and hang it up. Don't expect razor-sharp creases. "It's a relaxed look," says Brown, "but it will be wrinkle free."

PUT YOUR CLOTHES INTO REVERSE Turning certain garments inside out will help protect them in the washing machine. Turn dark clothing (black jeans, for instance) inside out to reduce fading and the pick-up of lint. Also turn clothes inside out if they have anything fragile on the outside, such as hooks or zipper pulls.

FILL IT FIRST When you're starting up a load of laundry in a top-loading machine, first let the tub fill with water, then mix in

---

SLEIGHT OF HAND

A SHAKE PREVENTS WRINKLES

Do your clothes come out of the dryer with more wrinkles than a box of raisins? Here's an easy way to minimize wrinkles during the drying process: When you're transferring clothing from the washer to the dryer, give each garment a shake to untangle it. If you put clothes into the dryer all twisted up, they'll dry with those wrinkles immortalized in the fabric.

the additives (detergent, softeners, bleach, and such). Make sure all of the chemicals are dissolved before you put in your clothes. Giving your clothing a direct blast of cleaner is courting disaster, Boorstein says. "If you want to ruin a garment fast, put undiluted bleach directly on it."

A CURE FOR CARDBOARD CLOTHING If your garments come out of the wash feeling stiff, the detergent probably didn't wash out of the fabric well enough. To prevent this, Boorstein uses Country Save® laundry detergent. He also uses OxiClean's® Toss-n-Go™ ball, which has a very low residue and is rated least likely to remain in your clothes. In the United States, Country Save is most often found in natural-food stores and is easy to find on the Internet. OxiClean is sold in most grocery stores and on the Internet.

WASHER, WASH THYSELF Does your washing machine have bad breath? When you wash a load of clothing, billions of skin cells and other particles are left behind in the washer. To cure your machine of the resulting musty odor, run a quick wash cycle with no clothing at the end of the washday: Use the washer's briefest setting and pour in ¼ cup of bleach. An alternative: On washday, just launder your white undies as the last load, with bleach. When the cycle is done, leave the lid of the washer open until you use it again so the machine will dry out thoroughly.

For a super-deluxe cleaning of the washing machine, use a damp sponge on the under-side of the lid and the upper rim of the tub inside, particularly where water flows into the washer. Also, the holders for detergent and fabric softener can collect contaminants from clothing. Remove them and sponge them off in the sink.

WELCOME YOUR FAMILY INTO THE FOLD When you're done drying a load of laundry, slide the laundry basket up to the door of the drier, pop the door open, and drag the dry clothes into the container. If there are any shirts, skirts, or pants in the load, hang them up quickly, or smooth them out, fold them, and return them to the basket. Either way, you'll keep wrinkling to a minimum—beats the heck out of ironing them later. Just leave the socks, underwear, and such loose in the basket. Their owner can do his or her own folding and sock matching later. Leave each basket of clean clothing on the floor of the laundry room. Your family members will remember to pick them up when they run out of undies.

THE THREAT FROM "DOWN UNDER"

Speaking of undies, you might have to change your underwear. Oh, sure, you wear a fresh pair every day. What I mean is, some kinds of undies don't lend themselves to good sanitation. If you have the wrong kind, toss them out.

Here's why. Charles Gerba, Ph.D., a microbiologist at the University of Arizona in Tucson, got curious about sanitation issues involving the laundering of used underwear. His tests showed that the typical pair of used underwear contains a tenth of a gram of fecal matter, also known by the scientific term *poop*. That's equivalent in weight to one quarter of a peanut, he says. And that's a heck of a lot of nasty bacteria.

What happens when you wash dirty underwear with other clothing? Yes, some of the bacteria get washed down the drain. However, a significant amount of bacteria are evenly distributed among all of the clothing in that wash load—enough bacteria to sicken the person handling these clothes. The typical warm wash and the typical drying time do not kill them all.

The solution? Wash all of your underwear separately from other clothing in hot water with detergent and bleach, and then dry them for 45 minutes, Gerba says. That will kill the bacteria and make handling your laundry safe. Unfortunately, some of the more fashionable and decorative kinds of underwear call for washing in cold water with no bleach. Throw them away or convert them to cleaning rags, and then buy some undies that will stand up to the rigors of sanitation. You might have to give up on the idea of looking like a fashion plate in your skivvies.

HANDY HAND WASHING

Hand washing bras, lingerie, and other fragile items is a breeze as long as you follow the number 1 rule: Don't put much effort into it. "There's no reason to overwash clothing that doesn't require it," Boorstein says. Many sweaters can be hand washed too, but make sure you take cashmere to a dry cleaner. Here's his easy, no-fuss approach to hand washing:

* Run cold water in the sink until it's 4 inches deep.
* Add delicate detergent according to the package directions.
* Let the garment soak for 2 minutes.
* Swish the garment around with your hands.

* Drain the water, then refill with fresh water to rinse.
* Hang the garment up to dry.

Here's an alternative to hand washing sweaters that will save you some time and effort:

* Wash the sweater in your washing machine using cold water and the shortest, gentlest cycle.
* Spin the sweater for 10 minutes in the dryer, set on the lowest setting.
* Lay the sweater flat on a towel to finish drying.

TABLECLOTHS: TABLE THAT IDEA

The plates and glasses are tucked away into the dishwasher, the leftovers are packed into the fridge, the serving dishes are drying in the sink-side rack. Ahhh, you've just about recovered from your holiday feast—except for that battle-scarred white tablecloth. Ready to wrestle it into the laundry room?

Don't even bother, says Boorstein. The simplest—and really the only—cure for a feast-stained tablecloth in the United States is to drop it off at the dry cleaner's immediately. The reason is a sad tale of lagging technology. American washing machines are no match for the typical tablecloth stains—wine, gravy, butter, and wax, for instance. The water in typical American machines reaches only 110° to 120°F, but removing these stains requires water near the boiling point, at least 190°F. European washers have long had heating elements that boost the water temperature to the proper level. Front-loading washers with heating elements are a new item in the American market.

If you do try to launder that tablecloth at home without the temperature boost, here's what will happen: You'll wash the cloth. In the bad light in your laundry room, you'll fail to notice the faint, blotchy remnant of the stains. You'll fold the tablecloth and stick it into a drawer, where those remnant stains will oxidize. When the next big feast day comes, you'll pull the tablecloth out again, and then you'll stomp around the room ranting about the stains that magically appeared. "Every household in America has a table-cloth with yellow or brown stains," Boorstein says.

So skip right over all of that angst, and make a quick trip to the dry cleaner part of your postfeast cleanup routine.

<table>
<tr><td>

**NOW THAT
THEY'RE CLEAN . . .**

</td><td>

Sorting, folding, ironing, and storage. You work so hard for those darned clothes that they ought to cut you a paycheck every week. No matter. There

</td></tr>
</table>

are plenty of ways to cheat at the postwashing stage.

TAKING TURNS IS LOADS EASIER

Washing your family's clothing isn't labor intensive. The tough part comes before and after washing—sorting all of the stinky clothing into color-coded piles and then, after washing, "unsorting" them back into each family member's laundry basket. A weekly wash for a family of four could easily involve two loads of dark clothing, two loads of colors, two loads of lights, a load of towels, and a load of whites. How could you possibly cheat on laundering an inhibiting mountain of clothes like that?

Easy: The strategy is to peel the sorting out of the process. Just don't wash everyone's clothing on the same day. Pick a few different days of the week to wash clothes, and wash only one family member's clothing on each of those days. On Monday, launder your teenager Julie's clothes. On Tuesday, it's your spouse's turn, and so on. This makes the laundry sorting incredibly simple—each washday, all clothing comes out of and goes back into only one basket. You'll be able to get it all done in just a couple of loads. If the Laundry Fairy in your house is so astoundingly generous as to provide delivery service, each day's clothing needs to go to only one person's bedroom rather than several locations around the house.

YOU GOTTA KNOW HOW TO FOLD 'EM

If you've played air guitar, then you're going to have no problem playing "air laundress." After washing and drying, do you fold each garment by laying it flat on a surface and then meticulously folding each sleeve or plant leg into place? Switch to this in-the-air quick-fold technique, and you'll shave 20 minutes off of your laundry duty. Here's how it's done:

- ☀ Pick up a newly dried shirt with its front facing you. Hold it with a hand in the middle of each shoulder.

- ☀ With the shirt still dangling there in the air, turn your hands so that you fold each sleeve behind the shirt (along with a few inches of shoulder).

- ☀ Lower the shirt into the laundry basket so that the bottom half of the shirt hits the surface face down.

- ☀ Drop the top half of the shirt onto the bottom half, thus folding the shirt horizontally across the middle.

Practice this technique, and soon you'll be able to fold a shirt, T-shirt, or sweater in 1 second flat. Adapt the process to pants, skirts, and any other clothing—basically, you want to set a garment down only once, in its final resting place. No, this approach isn't as precise as folding on a flat surface. Any family member who complains, however, gets to do his or her own folding.

CURES FOR SHRINKING AND STRETCHING

It's a magic trick: Your teenager's sweater goes into the washer a perfect fit but it comes out the right size for her 10-year-old sister. Here are Boorstein's easy methods for handling clothing shrinkage and the reverse malady—stretching.

If there's a chance the sweater you're washing will shrink, whip out a tape measure and mark down its dimensions (height, width, sleeve length, and such). When the sweater comes out of the wash, lay it out still damp over a dry white towel on top of the washing machine or on a laundry table. Check the dimensions you recorded. If the sweater shrank, gently "reblock" the sweater by pulling easily with your fingers until it's back to its original size. Let it dry lying right there.

If you have a problem with your jeans shrinking, fold them the long way while they're still moist—so the legs are flat against each other. Pull at the top and bottom ends to stretch the jeans into shape. If the waist comes out of the washer too snug, wrap the waist (still damp) around the edge of the laundry table and pull. You can do the same for the tight collar of a dress shirt.

There's also an easy cure for stretched-out sweaters. Sweaters typically stretch in the neck, cuffs, or waist when you wear them, and stretching also can happen when a long garment gets wrapped around the agitator in the clothes washer. Just wash the sweater as usual. After washing, lay it out still damp on a dry, white towel. Then pinch, push, and squish the fabric together. The sweater will dry in that "tightened" condition and stay that way (until you stretch it out again).

To prevent stretching, pilling, and other damage, always wash your sweaters or long, stretchable garments in a mesh laundry bag, available in fabric stores. An alternative: Wash the garment in a pillowcase held closed with a thick rubber band.

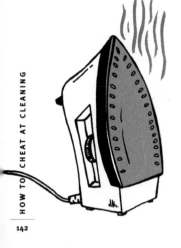

PITFALLS OF PRESSING

You can measure your cheat-at-cleaning success by how often you have to fire up the iron. Every other day? You are a slave to your wardrobe. Once a month? Not bad. Forgot where your iron is? Now, *that's* living!

If you insist on using an iron now and then—maybe you just can't live without a 100 percent cotton dress shirt—then you'll want to know how to keep the chore to a minimum. Here are the most common ironing mistakes, Boorstein says:

LEAKING ALL OVER YOUR CLOTHES It's usually the older irons that leak, so get one that won't. Read the manual and make sure you know how to operate that steam button. You might be flooding the steam chamber by pressing it too much.

SPITTING IMPURITIES ONTO YOUR CLOTHES Use distilled water in your iron unless your model is specifically designed for tap water. Otherwise, the steam function may spray staining minerals all over that blouse.

PRESSING TOO HOT When you're ironing, more is not better—you'll ruin the fabric. Use the heat setting that matches the fabric you're ironing.

SOME IRONCLAD RULES

Here are other ways to satisfy your pressing needs with a minimum amount of effort.

WASH YOUR FACE The face of the iron, that is. Using a clean iron will reduce the odds of staining and yellowing. Put some baking soda into a bowl and add enough water to make a paste. Wipe the paste onto your iron's face (while it's cool) with a damp cloth. Turn the cloth over, and wipe the paste off. You also can buy iron-cleaning products in supermarkets and discount stores.

A MINI BOARD FOR EASY IRONING

The wide-open parts of a blouse are a breeze to iron. It's the sleeves and nooks and crannies of the garment that take up most of your time. The job will go more smoothly if you use a sleeve board—basically a mini ironing board—to press those hard-to-reach spots. When you iron sleeves on a sleeve board, you no longer have to press the sleeves flat, creating those long creases. Sleeve boards are typically about 20 inches long and a few inches wide. Look for them wherever you buy ironing products or do a search on the Internet.

STEAM POWERED

How would you like to eliminate just about all of your ironing chores? Steve "The Clothing Doctor" Boorstein swears by his wrinkle-busting garment steamer. Let's say you have a crowded closet and a skirt came out wrinkled, or a knit shirt sat unused for months and now there are fold lines down the front. Just hang the garment on a knob, turn on the steamer, shoosh the offending spot, and the wrinkle will be gone in seconds. You get to skip the entire process of setting up your ironing board and pressing.

Boorstein swears by the Jiffy® Steamer brand, which offers a home model and a smaller travel version. "I now actually pack in a very different way—I never worry about wrinkles," he says.

MAKE SURE YOU'RE COVERED Impurities and laundry products such as starch can build up on your ironing board and transfer to the clothes you think you're cleaning. Boorstein's simple solution: Use two ironing board covers. When one gets soiled, wash it and use the spare in the meantime.

GO EASY ON THE TRIGGER When you spray clothes for ironing, use a minimum of water. If you soak the garment you're ironing, you're more likely to sop up impurities from the ironing board cover.

BUY A BEEFY BOARD A high-quality ironing board can make all the difference in the quality of your ironing. The problem is that a cheap ironing board will sometimes bend in the middle, causing the iron to dig into the fabric you're ironing and cause a mark. Buy an ironing board that's so sturdy it feels as if you could sit on it.

USE AN INTERMEDIARY Certain fabrics are sensitive to high heat and can turn shiny if you set the iron too hot. This applies in particular to acetate, gabardine, certain twills, and polished cotton. Use a muslin pressing cloth between the iron and the garment to protect such fragile fabrics. Or just turn the garment inside out and press the reverse side. Never iron velvet—period.

DO IT DAMP Pull your blouse out of the dryer while it's still slightly damp and iron it right away. This way, your blouse won't have to recover from dryer-induced wrinkles. "That will cut down on 50 percent of your ironing time," Boorstein says.

REMOTE STORAGE

It's the rare person who feels as if he or she had enough closet space. As ruthless as you might be about weeding out unused or unnecessary garments in your wardrobe, it seems like there's never enough rail space for everything you want to hang. You already know the basic solution: Use other locations as temporary storage. You might rotate seasonal items in and out of your bedroom closet, you might fold up clothes and store them in containers, or you might permanently park infrequently used garments (an evening gown or tuxedo) in some remote part of the house. But there's more to storing clothing than just shifting them from one spot to another. There are precautions to take and a few myths to be busted, says Boorstein.

CLEAN IT FIRST Before you store any clothing, first make sure every item has been washed or dry cleaned. Always empty the pockets.

BAG THE BAG Always remove the dry cleaning bag—the clothes need to breathe. Leave those little paper shoulder covers on—they'll keep some dust off.

TUCK THEM IN When you're storing clothes in a remote closet, line the garments up on a hanging rail and throw a clean, unbleached sheet over them all. This will keep dust at bay and protect them from fading. (Yes, even low light will have some effect over time.)

FORGET THE MOTHBALLS Avoid mothballs. They leak, you can't remove their odor from clothing, and they're toxic.

SURRENDER THE CEDAR You know that time-honored notion that cedar products protect your stored clothes? "It's a fallacy," says Boorstein. To protect your clothes, the cedar must have a strong, pungent odor, but 99 percent of cedar chests and drawers in use do not do any good because they've lost that scent. Restoring that odor requires reconditioning of the wood, which no one is going to bother with.

HIRE IT OUT If you use a dry cleaner's storage service, they will clean and store clothing in a climate-controlled facility. Before you do this, however, make a computerized list of all of your items (year after year, you'll be able to edit the list on your computer). Check your home insurance to make sure that it covers off-premises storage.

The bottom line is that laundry, like dishwashing, is a cleaning duty that just never quits. It accounts for a large percentage of the time you spend cleaning every week, and as with many large tasks there is no single way to cut corners. The cheating lies in multiple techniques that whittle away at this monster that has taken over your life. You might not even realize how onerous the laundry has become until you feel the relief that comes with wise buying, clever management, and savvy dirt busting. It's time for a little laundry revolution in your home. So get going—you have nothing to lose but your chains . . . and your stains.

YOUR DESK AND
WORK AREAS: WINNING
THE PAPER CHASE

Keeping an orderly home office is not just about aesthetics. Your personal and professional reputation is on the line. If your home office is dysfunctional, you miss appointments, pay bills late, spend hours looking for lost documents, and offend clients and colleagues.

On the other hand, nobody wants to be a slave to a filing cabinet and an anal-retentive office system. My computer doesn't have enough disk space to hold all of the school-marmish rules for how to run a home office. Chances are you've read an article or two about how your home office "ought" to be set up and run—complex systems, baffling software, and, just to make us all laugh, a spotless desk at the end of each day. Your eyes cross, you tell yourself you'd rather stick your hand in a meat grinder, and you continue with your comfortably slobbish office habits.

Well, you're going to feel better after you meet Jeff Zbar of Coral Springs, Florida. On the workday we talked, he had a house full of kids. If that weren't distraction enough, there were no fewer than 20 personal, nonbusiness items vying for his attention in his home office (child art, a poster, quotes, his drum kit, and more). He gets a clear view of his desktop only every few weeks. He's a great believer in stacks of barely organized paper. He stacks magazines on the floor. And the most delicious thing: He's a successful consultant on the subject of home offices.

"I'm organized in my disorganization," says Zbar, who does business as The Chief Home Officer. "I fear people who have no paper on their desks."

In this chapter, then, we'll find out more about how Zbar organizes his own office. I'll share some easy, low-maintenance, no-slave-work techniques from other sources as well. If you have an office job outside of the home, you're going to find plenty of useful advice that applies there, too. Home offices are a highly individual thing, Zbar emphasizes, and it's crucial that you find a system that clicks for you.

"Tip number one is make your own rules," he says. If they work, fine. If not, have the wisdom to change them. Now, that's the *How to Cheat at Cleaning* spirit!

CLUTTER: HOW'S YOUR DESK STACK UP?

Zbar has a few core strategies that keep his home office ticking efficiently. Stacks, for instance. While stacks of paper are a no-no to organizational purists, Zbar manages swimmingly with a few stacks of paper on his desktop, all of them pertaining to current or near-future concerns. While an outsider might find no rhyme or reason to the content of each one, Zbar is confident he can find any paper he wants within seconds—and that's all that counts.

One stack plays a pivotal role in getting excess paper "out of my face," he says—the stack of papers that are ready to be filed. When a document has served its immediate purpose but must be kept for the future, onto the stack it goes. Every few weeks, Zbar spends 45 minutes on a Saturday morning putting these papers into their proper files. Similarly, every few weeks he totally clears off his desk—typically when he has finished a large project for a client. Cleaning his desk more often would interfere with his work, so to heck with conventional wisdom.

EASY-DOES-IT FILING

This brings us to filing systems. Zbar is a fan of the simple, no-frills approach—just a filing cabinet and oodles of file folders. ("There's a reason file folders come in boxes of 100," he says.) There's no need for computer-printed file labels or other fancy trappings. Start your filing system with broad categories. As needed, subdivide large topics into subtopics. For instance, "Insurance" might have subfolders of "Insurance—Car," "Insurance—Home," and "Insurance—Medical."

Don't make your filing system any more complicated than it needs to be. Consider how often you need to retrieve each kind of document. For instance, if you almost never need to retrieve old utility bills, you probably can use one folder for the power, water, phone, and cable bills. Making separate folders for each utility just makes the system more laborious to maintain.

Make maximum use of the vertical space around you. To keep surfaces in your office clear, mount everything possible on the wall—telephone, paper organizer, and lamps, for instance. Put tools, reference books, and computer peripherals on shelves above and around your desk. Use stacking trays or vertical files near your desk for sorting papers that are related to current projects.

Another area where simplicity is best: technology. "I'm not a believer in using technology that goes beyond what you need," Zbar says. Cutting-edge computerized gizmos, complex software, and other extravagances will sap not only your money but also your time and mental energy as you learn how to make them work. Heed the saying "The leading edge will make you bleed." Ask yourself, "Does this widget really make me more efficient and therefore more productive?"

There's a flip side to the issue of office technology: Make sure that the machines you do keep in the office are up to date and in good repair. Equipment that is obsolete, broken, or works only marginally will become more and more of a drag on efficiency as time passes.

CUT OFF CLUTTER AT THE SOURCE

Here are more ways to make sure clutter never gets a chance to smother your home office.

STAMP OUT MAIL MESS When you pull mail out of the mailbox, sort it right away so you don't have to handle it twice. Zbar has an outside trash receptacle near his garage where he drops all junk mail (after tearing it in half) so it doesn't even get into the house. He drops all bills into the top right-hand drawer of his desk, where he stores his checkbook and other family finance materials. Mail for his wife goes onto her desk. Magazines go onto a special "read-soon" stack in his office. Whatever you do, don't plop the mail down unsorted onto a desk or counter—it will just get absorbed into a monster clutter pile, never to be seen again.

GREAT · GEAR

HOME OFFICE WISH LIST

Your office is already stocked with paperclips, scissors, tape, and envelopes. Here's a list of less common office gizmos that professional organizers say will help you reduce clutter, save time, and save effort.

- **USB HUB.** USB connections are the standard for PC gear these days, but many PC towers offer only two or three ports—sometimes in a hard-to-reach place. A USB hub places several ports right on your desktop, meaning you'll never run out of room for USB headphones, flash drive storage devices, and such.

- **WIRE CHASE.** For easier office cleaning and an orderly look, bundle that tangle of cables behind your desk into a wire chase, a channel or tube that will hold them together. Also, use plastic zip ties (available at home improvement stores) to bind up excess lengths of wire behind your computer.

- **SMALL TOOL KIT.** Instead of running to the toolbox every time you need to make a little repair, keep a small tool kit in a desk drawer. Include a tiny screwdriver,

a tiny Phillips screwdriver, needle-nose pliers, and other tools you think you'll need.

- **COMBINED SCANNER-PRINTER-COPIER-FAX.** Consolidate your computer equipment as much as possible. Why have a separate scanner, printer, copier, and fax machine, when there are single units that will handle all of those tasks? This will save you several square feet of counter or shelf space.

- **LABELER.** If you need to worry about appearances for professional reasons, or if you just like sharp-looking labels, there are machines that produce durable, laminated labels for shelves, bins, binders, and envelopes.

- **SHREDDER.** How many cubic feet of bank statements, receipts, cancelled checks, ancient tax forms, medical papers, and other documents are you holding onto just because you're afraid, for security reasons, to throw them away? You need a paper shredder at your desk. Some models will also shred credit cards and CDs.

OPTICAL MOUSE: CASE CLOSED

With a simple equipment change, you can eliminate a cleaning issue and computer hassle from your life forever. The conventional mechanical computer mouse, the kind with a roller ball on the underside, has an annoying flaw. It likes to pick up dust and collect it inside the mechanism. Slowly, your mouse loses agility until you find yourself struggling just to move that little computer arrow from one side of the screen to the other. You have to disassemble the mouse, pluck out the gray fuzz with tweezers, and put it back together again. A better approach: The newer optical mouse. Instead of a roller, it uses light sensors to detect movement. It's a more accurate system, and no dust gets inside the case of your mouse, so it stays squeaky clean.

CORRAL THOSE ITTY-BITTY DOCUMENTS Receipts and credit card slips from everyday purchases present a quandary. They're official documents that prove you made particular purchases from particular stores. But how often do you really need to retrieve an old receipt? Two or three times a year? Here's a simple, no-effort way to keep your receipts organized in case you need them. Each time you make a purchase, put the receipt in your pocket. When you get home, put any receipt that you might need for taxes into a file in your office. Put receipts for high-priced items such as jewelry and major appliances into your home insurance file or a fireproof box. Throw away any receipts for minor incidental purchases— a candy bar, dental floss, or cellophane tape. All other receipts go into an easy-access shoebox or small drawer. Place the receipts in their container in chronological order (just plop the most recent receipts at the front). If you need to locate one of these receipts in a month or so, you'll have a rough idea of where to find it. When your storage container gets full, pull a handful of receipts from the back of the drawer. These will be a few years old and entirely useless by now. Run them through a shredder or drop them into a box labeled "Destroy" and toss them into a campfire.

DON'T FILE IT, GOOGLE™ IT Yes, stuffing papers into file folders will get them off your desk and keep your work area clean and neat. It's better, however, to throw away every piece of paper you possibly can, says Zbar. Before you put printouts of research into a folder, ask yourself: "Can I easily find similar material on the Internet any time I want?" If the answer is yes, then recycle those papers instead of filing them.

MAXIMUM STORAGE, ZERO SPACE Speaking of computers, conduct as much of your daily business on your computer as possible, and store your documents there electronically. Resist the temptation to print out documents that you can easily retrieve from orderly computer files. This keeps paper clutter to a minimum in your office. Word processing and e-mail programs typically allow you to make unlimited storage folders on your computer. As a memory aid, use an electronic folder system that follows the same logic as the hard-copy folders you keep.

QUIT WRITING CHECKS Sign up with your bank for electronic bill paying—it's simpler and faster than using checks, and it doesn't require stamps, envelopes, or a trip to the mailbox.

GET DRASTIC WITH PLASTIC Open your wallet and cut up all but three or four of the most useful and versatile credit cards you have. The fewer services you use, the less "mindshare" you have to devote to running your daily life, Zbar explains. Zbar limits himself to four cards: a debit card and credit card for the family, and a debit card and credit card for business. What's in your wallet?

TAKE CARE OF BUSINESS No matter how casual you might be about the order of your home office, there will be certain materials that need quick and careful filing. For instance, if you work out of your home office—as a telecommuter or a home-based business—slide all project-related papers into a labeled folder the very moment you're done with them. You want those papers at your fingertips if your client or boss calls to talk shop. If you want a sane approach to home cleaning, you have to focus on priorities—and your livelihood is a big one. Here are some other papers that you should put in their proper "homes" the moment they arrive—don't set them down in a pile: checks to be cashed, bills, tax documents, and car registration papers.

COMPUTERS: KEEPING A CLEAN MACHINE

In just about anybody's home office these days there is, front and center, a viewing screen attached by cable to a large whirring box. You need to keep your home computer "clean" in two senses: Keeping it dust free will help ensure that it runs properly, but it's even more important that you keep your computer clean digitally—that is, free from viruses, adware, spyware, unused programs, and other threats.

If you at all depend on the proper functioning of your home computer, here's my number 1, cheating-est, angst- and labor-saving recommendation: Develop a relationship with a professional computer technician—someone who makes house calls routinely to fix and maintain computers. Such a technician offers a level of service that cannot be found over the "help line" at a mail-order computer company or at the repair counter of a computer retail store. Find a technician who has several years of professional experience in troubleshooting and repairing home computers (the teenager down the block won't do). A talented technician will save you wheelbarrow loads of heartache. But don't wait for disaster—make an appointment with your new tech now to review your system even if it's humming along smoothly. Then he or she will know you and your computer whenever your hard drive melts down. Don't bother with a repair company that asks you to take your computer in and leave it for a few days.

Once you have a professional computer tech programmed into your speed-dial, you may be ready for level 2 of computer "cleaning," which also is pretty darned easy. The following concise lists will help you protect, maintain, and physically clean your home machine. If you hit all of these points, you'll be light-years ahead of the typical computer user. A tip of the hat goes out to advisers Joe Grant, owner, and Alexander Barco, technician, of Computer Medic in Dublin, Pennsylvania.

DEFENSE AGAINST INVASION

Think of the Internet as one big digital mud pit. The more you cruise through it, particularly with high-speed connections, the greater your chance of getting your system dirty—that is, infected with harmful, secretly delivered programs. Here's how to prevent that.

INSTALL A WALL Firewall protection will make your computer resistant to a wide variety of viruses (destructive programs), adware (hidden advertising programs), and spyware (hidden programs that provide data about you to outsiders). A firewall can come in one of two forms—hardware (a box that stands between your computer and your Internet connection) or software.

INOCULATE YOUR COMPUTER Buy special software for your computer that will detect and destroy viruses, adware, and

TAKE SPAM OFF THE MENU

Wish you could close down the pipeline that funnels unsolicited phone calls, junk mail, and e-mail spam into your life every day? There's no total solution, but in the United States adding your name to lists at two Internet sites will help:

- **THE FEDERAL TRADE COMMISSION.** Visit www.donotcall.gov and put your telephone number on the do-not-call list. Most telemarketers (some are exempt) will have a month to quit calling you.

- **THE DIRECT MARKETING ASSOCIATION.** Visit www.dmaconsumers.org, and click your way to the consumer assistance information. Add your name to the lists of people who don't want unsolicited telephone, mail, and e-mail marketing pitches. Some companies (not all) use these lists to purge their rosters. Over the following months, you should notice a marked drop-off in junk solicitations. Depending on how you register, you may encounter small processing fees or have to print out a form, fill it out, and mail it in. But if this reduces the marketing noise that assaults you every day, it will be worth it.

spyware. You'll probably need more than one program. This technology changes rapidly, so ask an experienced computer technician to recommend the best brands. (Don't just talk to the salesperson at the computer store.) Many programs allow you to schedule an automatic, full-system sweep. Do this at least weekly. To make sure your computer will recognize the most current threats, see that your software is updated frequently.

AVOID INTERNET "HOT" SPOTS X-rated Web sites often are brimming with hidden adware and spyware ready to leap onto your computer uninvited. Avoid such sites altogether. I'm not being judgmental —just presenting the bare facts.

BEWARE "FREE" DOWNLOADS Don't download third-party software, programming that is unbranded or branded with a name that's unfamiliar to you. Such programs are not as well tested as the famous-name software and may not be compatible with other software you rely on. Programming that you download from top software makers probably won't harm your computer, but read every word of the fine print first.

HANDLE ATTACHMENTS WITH CARE Whenever someone sends you a file attached to e-mail, do not open the file straight off the e-mail. Save the file to your disk so your protective scanning programs can check it over first. Delete all junk e-mail immediately.

NO-BRAINER MAINTENANCE

Some simple habits will keep your computer whirring happily and protect all of the good work you have stored on the hard drive. Because systems and software vary and change, I can't provide step-by-step details. However, the HELP function on your computer will provide easy instructions or your computer tech can walk you through it. Enter reminders for these procedures into your electronic calendar. Many of the following details apply specifically to the Windows® operating system and Microsoft℠ software because they're overwhelmingly the most commonly used. If you're a Mac® user, talk to your tech about the REBUILD YOUR DESKTOP, REPAIR PERMISSIONS, and DISK FIRST AID functions, as well as other routine maintenance.

BACK UP YOUR FILES This involves the mass copying of all the personal files you have on your hard drive to a large-capacity storage device that's outside of your computer—for instance, a CD, a zip disk, or an external hard drive. If your computer's hard drive crashes, your files might not be retrievable. With backup files, you can resume business immediately on another computer until you get your main rig repaired. Back up your files at least weekly—daily if you generate lots of data.

BABY YOUR HARD DRIVE Run the CHECK DISK function on your computer every 6 months. This will examine your hard drive and patch up any physical problems. Also, run the DISK DEFRAGMENTER program, which will rearrange the data on your hard drive so that it functions most smoothly.

UPDATE THE OPERATING SYSTEM When you hook up to the Internet, Windows should alert you when updates are available for the operating system. You also can get updates manually through the TOOLS menu on your Web browser. These updates are important for the smooth running and security of your computer.

PURGE INTERNET FILES Once a month, go to the TOOLS menu on your browser and click on INTERNET OPTIONS. Delete the temporary Internet files (also called the "cache") and cookies, which can bog down your computer and present security problems.

PURGE YOUR PROGRAMS Every 6 months, review your computer for programs you no longer use, and delete them. (Go to the CONTROL PANEL, which has a program deletion function.) Heaping unused programs onto your computer will slow the system down.

A PHYSICAL CLEANING, TOO

They have yet to invent software that will clean the physical dirt from your computer. Fortunately, it's almost as easy as hitting a DELETE button—although there are a couple of important cautions.

WIPE OUT DUST To remove dust from the exterior of your computer casing and a conventional screen, all you need to do is wipe it down with a lightly dampened sponge (water only) or paper towel. Never spray any fluid directly onto your computer—drips could damage the electronics. Use a disposable duster if you prefer. The newer LCD screens are plastic, not glass, so remember that they are particularly delicate. Use only a damp, soft, lint-free cleaning cloth on such screens. Wipe them with a gentle side-to-side motion, not in circles.

GO UNDER COVER I know, going inside your computer box is scary. But dust can build up inside, causing it to overheat. This will lead to expensive repairs. So once a year, unplug the machine and open up the case of your computer. Computer covers are held on in various ways, often by two screws you have to loosen on the back. On a typical computer tower, you usually want to remove the cover on the left side of the box (as you face its front). Put the brush attachment on your vacuum cleaner and suck the dust out, being careful not to bonk any of the electronics or loosen any connections. Then snap the cover back into place. Never blow inside your computer, either with your mouth or with compressed air. That could force dust into the workings of your CD drive or other devices, where it will do damage. While you have the vacuum all set up with the dust attachment, turn your keyboard upside down and give it a gentle shake. Vacuum up all of the potato chip crumbs that fall out, then give the keyboard itself a once-over with the brush.

MIND GAMES

Let's set aside hardware and filing cabinets for a moment. Clutter control in your home office depends a lot on the mental side of managing your workspace, too. Here's a look at how office layout, decision-making, and planning will lend some sanity to your desktop. A little brainpower expended up front will pay off handsomely in time and energy saved.

FIND THE RIGHT FREQUENCY Are the tools and papers you need for your day-in and day-out work easy to grab, use, and return to their homes? If they are, then the objects around you will naturally settle into order rather than accumulate in a chaotic

A CLUTTER-FREE DESK IN 5 MINUTES

You say the clutter on your desk is beyond repair? You would happily adopt clutter-free work habits—but that rolling heap of paper in your work area is so inhibiting that you never summon the courage to start? Or perhaps the problem is even more urgent—say, a client is dropping by within minutes, and your reputation will be ruined when she sees that desk?

Don't worry, we're going to have that desk cleaned off in 5 minutes. Just follow these steps:

1. Get two large cardboard boxes. Label the first box "To Be Filed," the second "My Desktop" and add the date.

2. Set a timer or just glance at your watch while you work. Spend 10 seconds grabbing up any papers from current projects and throwing them into a folder. Now take 3 minutes to move all the papers on your desk into one of the two boxes. Don't stop to think—you have time only to move papers by the handful. If you come across intact file folders or other materials that obviously belong in your filing cabinet, put them into the first box. That's probably 5 percent of the heap. All the other papers get shoveled into the second box.

3. Park the "To Be Filed" box near the filing cabinet. Put the "My Desktop" box into a short-term storage spot—the corner of the office, a closet, or the basement.

4. Quickly pick through any remaining junk on your desk. Throw the usable supplies into your supply drawer. Throw away the broken buttons, candy wrappers, ancient sticky notes, and dead bugs.

5. Wipe down the desk with a damp sponge or disposable wipe.

Now you can make a fresh start at your desk. If you ever think you need one of those old papers, you know right where they are. They're no more or less organized than they ever were—they're just not in your way any more. If a year passes and you haven't opened the "My Desktop" box, throw it out. Even if you never reform your work habits, you now have a crude system for de-cluttering the desk once a year.

heap. Here's an easy way to plan your workspace for maximum efficiency: Sit in your desk chair and look at all the items in your work area. Rearrange your possessions so they radiate away from you in terms of how urgent they are. The things you use several times a day should be within quick-and-easy grasp. Items you need two or three times a day should be within reach. Items you need two or three times a week should be no more than a step or two away from your chair. Items you need two or three times a month should be on the periphery.

To make frequently used items accessible, put extra effort into creating close-at-hand storage and making the best use of space:

- Some sleek-and-modern desks have no desk drawers at all, notes Elizabeth Hagen, a professional organizer in Sioux Falls, South Dakota. In that instance, substitute a stand-alone rolling file unit.
- Go vertical: Use shelves and stacking trays, and mount everything possible onto the nearest wall.
- The next time you buy a computer monitor, get a flat-screen model rather than one of the conventional, bulky, dust-magnet CRTs.
- Buy electronics that combine multiple functions into one unit rather than buying separate devices. This way, only one machine has to be within reach rather than several.

PUSH-BUTTON-EASY CLUTTER CONTROL

In a typical computer game, you have a mission to accomplish (say, make the world safe for humankind) and a barrage of unexpected matters to cope with along the way (that bug-eyed alien crawling out of a manhole). You have an array of tools and strategies available for wending your way through the game.

Working in your home office can be much like that. You have a main mission (often, keeping your financial empire intact) and myriad incidental problems to cope with along the way (responding to an e-mail from your bug-eyed accountant). As with the computer game, if you ignore the barrage of matters competing for your attention, they'll mount up and eventually eat you alive. Indecision about the papers on your desk will not only bury your work space in an unsightly heap but will reduce your efficiency as a worker, tarnish your reputation when you don't deal with matters promptly, and cost you business from people you've offended through neglect.

There's a simple secret for vanquishing desktop clutter forever. It's as easy as pushing a button every time a problem, large or small, presents itself. Think about it, says Hagen: All of the input that crosses your desk will come in one of five forms: paper, voice mail, e-mail, verbal requests (Mommy, I need a Halloween costume—tomorrow!), and things you think of on your own. For any of these matters, make a split-second decision—all you have to do is choose from one of five easy responses. In videogame terms, think of the following as the five buttons you can push every time input enters your life. Write these five terms down and post them in a prominent place at your desk:

Toss it Just throw the item away—shred it, recycle it, or delete it. Ask yourself about the worst-case scenario: What's the worst that could happen if I throw this out and I discover that I need it later? If you can live with those consequences, toss it. Learn to love this response. Remember: Willingness to throw stuff out is one of the prime *How to Cheat at Cleaning* virtues.

DELEGATE IT That is, pass the matter off to someone else. Pick the right person, clarify what you want done, verify that the other person understands (get him or her to repeat the instructions), get the other person's agreement to participate, and then specify a completion date.

ACT ON IT If acting on this matter will take 2 minutes or less, just do it immediately.

FILE IT FOR FOLLOW-UP If acting on this matter will take more than 2 minutes, put it in your to-be-done-later file, or on your calendar, under the appropriate date. (More on simple to-be-done-later files in a moment.) The beauty of filing for follow-up is that you don't have to perform the task immediately—just commit to when you will do it.

FILE IT FOR FUTURE REFERENCE When must-keep papers fall into your lap (tax materials, insurance papers, and medical records), store them in your standard office files. However, go easy on this approach, says Hagen: 80 percent of what we file we never look at again.

Notice that when you use one of these five responses, no papers are allowed to settle onto your desk. If you train yourself to immediately push one of these five buttons for every bit of input that crosses your desk, your work area will never be cluttered, colleagues will be impressed by your organization, and you won't ever have to apologize for having misplaced important materials. You will rule the world.

A DIRTY STORY
XXX

A LITTLE LIGHT READING

While it's an easy factor to ignore, light will make a big difference in the function of your office. Not only does light tend to lift your spirits, but the lack of light will render parts of your office unusable. You won't realize it, but you will confine yourself to the parts of the room where there's good illumination. Or you'll abandon your poorly lit office altogether and work elsewhere in the house—spreading chaos and clutter.

To make sure your entire office functions smoothly, install lighting that's strong and evenly distributed about the room, says New York City architect Evan Galen.

HOW SHARP IS YOUR SECOND BRAIN?

Every adult needs some kind of system—some kind of "second brain"—for reminding herself or himself what to do when, and for locating the relevant materials associated with it. At the simplest level, such a system might entail a calendar you can jot notes onto (or the computerized equivalent), a to-do list you keep on your desk, and a set of vertical files kept within easy reach for current active projects. If you have a homegrown system such as this and it works for you, stick to it. However, if you're exhibiting symptoms of disorganization—heaps of paper clutter, commitments forgotten, or paperwork lost—it's time to adopt one that is more orderly.

Hagen recommends an incredibly easy to-be-done-later reminder system that she calls "core files." When you're making rapid-fire, instantaneous decisions about all of the niggley problems that confront you daily, now and then you say, "I'll deal with this later." Maybe your mother called asking you to mail a photograph from last summer's vacation or perhaps a client sent an e-mail asking you to revise a report and return it within 2 weeks. If you jot a note to yourself and just plop it onto your desk, you'll lose the reminder and forget to follow through. However, Hagen's core files make sure that you get reminded to perform each task you have committed to and that you have all of the relevant papers on hand.

Drop by an office-supply store and pick up a couple boxes of hanging file folders. You will need an easy-access place to park these files—preferably a desk drawer. If you don't have one, buy a plastic file box that has the ridges to support hanging files and put it near your desk. Label one set of folders for each day of the month, 1 through 31. Label 12 more folders January through December. Finally, label a separate folder for each person that you interact with regularly—your spouse, each child, an assistant, or a colleague, for instance.

If you have to fly to Dubuque, Iowa, on the 18th of the current month, drop all of the relevant paperwork—ticket information, itinerary, and contact information—into the folder labeled "18." If the trip isn't until next April, file the material in the "April" folder. If your assistant is making the trip instead of you, put the papers into the folder with his or her name on it.

Now for retrieving the information you have socked away. At the beginning of each day, open up the folder that corresponds to the day of the month and check the tasks that you have committed yourself to. Everything you need should be right there. At the end of each month, open up the next month's folder and sort any materials and reminders that you find into the appropriately numbered folders. Whenever you encounter the people you have made the special name-labeled folders for, hand them the contents of their folders.

"This system will never crash on you," Hagen says. "Make it a part of your life, and you will have a clutter-free desk!"

9

THE GREAT OUTDOORS:
DECKS, SIDEWALKS, DRIVEWAYS, GUTTERS, SIDING, WINDOWS, AND ENTRYWAYS

It's a tough, damaging, grimy environment beyond the walls of your home. A lot of the outdoors is just plain *made* of dirt, so it's surprising that anything you leave unsheltered ever gets clean at all. Complicating matters are harsh sunlight, temperature extremes, air pollution, vegetation, wind, rain, snow, ice—and, of course, bird poop. Because many of the things we leave exposed to these elements need special protection—decks and sidewalks, for instance—cleaning projects often expand into waterproofing projects, too.

Cleaning the exterior of your house, the walking surfaces, and your outdoor possessions is a big, big job, one that can take over your life if you let it. Unless you cheat. Which means buying easy-care or no-care products to begin with; using cutting-edge, labor-saving tools; and following your priorities and forgetting about the rest. Or just saying to heck with it and moving into an apartment. This last option may of course seem rather drastic, so let's focus just on the cheating.

Inside the house, the hardest-working, most indispensable cleaning tool is undoubtedly the vacuum cleaner. For outside of the house, there's an equally powerful, multitalented appliance, although it's not yet as ubiquitous as the Hoover® in your closet: It's the pressure washer. This device will take an hour's work done "the hard way"—say, cleaning the garage floor with a mop—and reduce the task to a few minutes. You'll wonder why you went so long without one.

For the uninitiated, pressure washers squirt a super-fast stream of water out of a metal wand, knocking grime off surfaces that normally would require diligent scrubbing. Most pressure washers have devices that allow you to add detergent to the spray when desired. Light duties for a pressure washer include cleaning garden tools, lawn mowers, patio furniture, automobiles, and grills. Heavy duties include spiffing up siding, decks, driveways, and sidewalks. Because they do their cleaning through high pressure and not by the sheer volume of water, they actually use 80 percent less water than your garden hose.

BUY THE RIGHT PRESSURE WASHER

Before you open your wallet to buy one, first consider what you want to clean with a pressure washer. (Your rake and trowels after a gardening session? The 800 square feet of patio?) Then consider how those needs match up with the two basic types:

ELECTRIC. Electric pressure washers tend to have less power—1,300 to 1,700 pounds per square inch (psi). They're great for cleaning items with smaller surface areas. Although they tend to cost a little less, remember that you're going to find yourself tethered to an outlet.

GAS-POWERED. Gas-powered washers can have twice the pressure of electric models and can make short work of large surface areas. But although they clean faster, they're also louder.

Wielding all of this power also means you have to take precautions. You don't want to dig a groove into your deck or chip paint off your car—which can happen if you're not careful. So when you start to clean, hold the tip of the wand at least 2 feet from the object you're cleaning and slowly move closer if you need the extra punch. Protect your body, too. At a minimum, always wear goggles and shoes when you use a pressure washer, says Jon Hoch, who sells the devices online through his company Pressure Washers Direct, based in Romeoville, Illinois—preferably boots with rubber soles. As odd as it sounds, it's easy to cut your foot with a pressure washer if you're not wearing shoes. Sandals and flip-flops are a no-no.

If you want to save money on a pressure washer, Hoch says, two strategies will cut the cost in half: Either buy a reconditioned model, or split the cost with a neighbor and take turns using it.

Here are some more tips for using your pressure washer, whether you're cleaning the deck, siding, patio furniture, grill, garage floor, or driveway:

GET THE RIGHT CLEANER Pressure washers can do a lot of cleaning with pure water alone, but mixing in detergent makes them even more effective. Make sure the label on your detergent says it's okay for pressure washers.

LET THE SUDS SIT When using your pressure washer to apply detergent, turn off the washer and let the cleaner sit for 10 minutes before you rinse. This gives the detergent time to do its dirt-loosening job before it gets washed away in the rinse water.

TAKE CAREFUL AIM Don't go overboard with that blast of water. You don't want to force water into a light fixture or vent, or behind the siding on your house.

DECKING DECISIONS

If you're building a new deck, the kind of material you choose will have a big effect on the time you spend cleaning and maintaining it. Here are some things you'll want to know:

- **PLASTIC DECKING.** If low maintenance is your priority, this is the way to go. It's easy to clean and doesn't tend to fade. *Drawback:* As much as the manufacturer may try to create a wood look, you're gonna know it's plastic. Visit a showroom or home show that has a deck built of the material you're considering buying, and decide whether it's for you.

- **COMPOSITE DECKING.** These materials are usually made of 50 percent wood flour (ground-up wood, finer than sawdust) and 50 percent plastic. You get what you pay for. The higher-quality versions do a decent job of simulating natural wood. Those with a higher plastic content will last longer. Composite decking is easy to clean and doesn't require waterproofing, although you might want to use deck stain to help maintain the color. Note,

however, that this decking can bow in high heat, and mildew can degrade the wood flour component, weakening the boards.

- **PRESSURE-TREATED LUMBER.** The most common pressure-treated lumber for decking is either yellow pine or Douglas fir, depending on where you live. Of the natural woods, these are the easiest to care for. They come treated to resist rot and termites, but they still need protection from water damage. (Some decking now comes with pretreated waterproofing, but make sure it's labeled that way if you're going to skip the sealing process.)

- **EXOTIC WOODS.** Cedar, redwood, and tropical hardwoods require more care because you need to take extra steps to restore their color during your periodic cleaning and resealing. Consider these an AILment (Anxiety-Inducing Luxury).

BUY A BRUSH Pick up a siding brush that slips onto the end of your spraying wand. The light scrubbing action will help loosen dirt when you clean your siding.

HIDE YOUR MISTAKES First apply your pressure washer to an inconspicuous part of the object you're cleaning to make sure it won't be damaged.

THE WIND AT YOUR FINGERTIPS

Leaf blowers are another versatile outdoor power tool that make quick work of cleaning tasks, in particular blasting leaves, twigs, and dirt off your deck, patio, porch, sidewalk, and driveway. If you spend a miserable amount of time behind a push broom outside—or if you ought to, but you don't have time for it—take the leap into power blowing. Unless you have an enormous yard or you have to work far from a power outlet, the electric models are the way to go—they're less expensive, lighter, and less hassle to operate. Many models have a vacuum option, allowing you to suck leaves and debris into a bag. Some even mulch leaves and dump them into a trash can. The smaller, handheld blowers are fine for most homeowners, but if you need an enormous amount of power, check out the backpack or wheel-around models.

Be aware that these machines are noisy—loud enough that ear protection is a good idea. Be considerate of your neighbors, who might not want to be blasted out of bed at 7 A.M. on a Saturday. Many communities are so up in arms about the noise created by incessant leaf blowers that they're passing laws against their use.

In fact, Lance Walheim, a garden expert for Bayer® Advanced lawn care and pest control products, dislikes the noise of his own leaf blower so much that he uses a different power tool for getting his leaves off the lawn quickly: He puts the grass-clipping bag onto his lawn mower and mows the leaves up wherever they lie—no blowing, no raking. Mulching mowers do a particularly good job of grinding up leaves. The shredded leaves are compact, so they're easier to handle and fit into fewer lawn bags. You also can pour the shredded leaves onto your garden as mulch or onto your compost pile to rot.

THE SURFACES UNDERFOOT

What separates us from nature? Well, roofs and walls to be sure. But also the hard surfaces we create outside to keep our feet and vehicles from sinking into the muck. Our decks, patios, sidewalks, and driveways are extremely durable, built to withstand years of abuse from rain, snow, pollution, boots, tires, and children. Happily, the wind and rain often do a stellar job of keeping these surfaces free of dust and grass trimmings. Once a month or so, you might be inspired to take a 2-minute tour around the house with a leaf blower to give them a gale-force cleaning. (Use a push broom if you have tons of excess time and need the aerobic exercise.)

Over the years, however, these manmade surfaces grow dingy from embedded dirt that no power blower or broom bristle can budge. The solution is a special kind of cleaning involving tools and chemicals that do deep-down dirt removal. Once that's done, there's generally another step: adding a sealant that will help the surface shrug off damaging water and dirt in the future. Yes, it's a tad involved, but the alternative is to let these outside surfaces crumble into disrepair—taking you to a whole new level of expensive hassles.

Fortunately, cutting-edge tools and materials are steadily making the cleaning and protection of these outside surfaces easier. Here's how.

SIZING UP YOUR DECK

We associate decks with leisure living, so it would be a shame if such an amenity actually made your life miserable. Let's look at how we can clean and maintain our decks while keeping the work to a minimum.

Day-in and day-out cleaning of a deck is a simple matter—a quick sweep with a push broom or a squirt from the garden hose will usually do. But in the case of a wooden deck, every few years, and in some cases every year (depending on materials), you need to do a thorough, deep-down cleaning or it will quickly deteriorate and fall apart. The job can be broken down into three phases, but none of them is difficult if you have the right equipment and know-how:

1. **ASSESSMENT.** Figure out whether your deck needs resealing, consider what material it's made of, and

---

THREE STEPS FOR PROTECTING THOSE PLANTS

When you spray cleaner or waterproofing onto your deck, it's hard to keep some of that spray from splashing onto the nearby landscaping. Here's the easy way to protect your lawn and other plantings:

1. Before you treat your deck, take the spray nozzle on your garden hose and thoroughly water down all nearby plants.

2. Cover your plants with plastic. Plastic painters' drop cloths work well for this.

3. After cleaning or waterproofing your deck, remove the plastic and thoroughly spray the area again to dilute any cleaner that made it onto the ground.

THE LOW-MAINTENANCE LANDSCAPE

Many a cheat-at-cleaning enthusiast has stared out at the lawn and had a thought like this: "I should just landscape the entire yard and eliminate mowing forever." That's an admirable idea—but be careful. The cleanup and care of some landscaping features are actually more trouble than a few extra square feet of conventional grass, says Alissa Shanley, a landscape and garden designer in Denver, Colorado.

We asked Shanley how she would design a yard if low cleaning and maintenance were the top priorities.

- **PICK PATIOS.** A patio made of concrete, or a combination of flagstone and concrete, needs much less maintenance than a wooden deck.

- **COVER UP.** A permanent awning or roof over your patio will drastically reduce cleaning-oriented tasks. Dirt and debris will be deflected onto the lawn. Your outdoor furniture will be protected, so you'll be able to quit hauling it in and out of the weather. And once your patio is permanently "made in the shade," you'll have no further need for that annoying patio umbrella that keeps blowing over.

- **BRANCH INTO EVERGREENS.** Evergreen trees are low maintenance, because they don't drop any leaves you'll have to clean up. Many people cover their yards with conventional leaf-bearing trees, forgetting what a massive job the raking will be in the fall.

- **FOREGO THE FLOWERS.** Converting lawn into beds for shrubs and flowers is a mistake. Those plantings will require trimming and weeding. Flowers need deadheading so they'll continue to bloom, plus cutting down at the end of the season. If you're trying to reduce maintenance, this trade-off is not worth it. "I say let's do grass and hire your neighbor kid to cut it—that's the least maintenance if you want something growing," Shanley says.

- **FORGET THE FOUNTAIN.** People often tell themselves, "I'll just install a fishpond or fountain in my yard—and I'll never have to touch it!" Wrong, says Shanley. Fountains and ponds require constant cleaning. If you fall behind on cleaning them, leaves and debris will blow in, clog the system, and burn out the pump.

decide what you want your deck to look like once you've treated it.

2. **Cleaning.** A good cleaning will remove embedded dirt, mildew, and that gray tinge that wood develops when it's left out in the weather.

3. **Sealing.** Apply waterproofing to wooden decks periodically to protect them from water damage. If you want to stain your deck, use a waterproof seal that stains at the same time so you're not adding extra steps to the process.

If you're reading this book, you certainly don't want to deep clean and reseal your deck unless it's absolutely necessary. Victoria Scarborough, Ph.D., director of research and development for Thompson's Water Seal®, says this is the simplest way to decide if your deck's old waterproofing is still intact: On a dry day, pour a glass of water onto your deck's surface and watch what happens. If the water is absorbed into the wood and creates a darkened splotch, it's time to reseal the wood. If the water runs off or beads up, go find something else to worry about—your deck is fine.

TIME FOR PRESSURE CLEANING

If your deck needs resealing, there are a couple of issues to consider before you run off to your home-improvement store. What kind of sealer and stain are currently on your deck? This could affect what cleaner you use. Also, what do you want your deck to look like? Its natural wood color? Slightly stained to a new tone? An opaque color that still shows the wood grain? Your answer will affect what kind of sealer you buy.

Cleaning your deck will remove dirt, mildew, algae, weathered-gray wood cells, and remnants of old waterproofing—all of which can interfere with your new sealant. The certified *How to Cheat at Cleaning* method for removing this stuff from your deck is to

apply deck cleaner using your high-
pressure sprayer. (Remember, you
ran out and bought one after reading about them earlier in this
chapter.) A high-pressure sprayer is
powerful enough to gouge a groove into your deck's wood,
so take it easy. Scarborough recommends a setting of no more than
1,200 psi. Follow these steps:

- ☀ First use the pressure washer to rinse any surface grime
  off the deck.

- ☀ Add cleaner to your pressure washer, spray it onto the
  wood, and let it sit for several minutes, according to the
  package directions.

- ☀ Switch to plain water again and put on a narrow spraying
  tip (but not the narrowest). Sweep the spray back and
  forth across the wood to loosen the embedded dirt and
  rinse off the detergent.

If you don't have a high-pressure sprayer, your backup plan is
to apply the cleaner with a pump-style sprayer, which also is available at your home-improvement store. In this case, you'll need to
scrub the cleaner in with a synthetic broom before rinsing.

Not just any old cleaner will do for this job. Make sure your
cleaner is specifically made for decks. Deck cleaners come in
several intensities, too, so find one that's a match for your
situation. They will fall into these categories:

GENERAL CLEANER. For removing dirt, mildew, and old
oil-based sealant.

HEAVY-DUTY CLEANER. Removes not only dirt and mildew
but also old water-based sealant and tints.

CLEANER AND BRIGHTENER. Helps preserve the color of redwood and cedar.

STAIN REMOVER. Strips away the paint-like solid stain.

NOW SEAL THE DEAL

Once your deck is clean, it needs a fresh coat of waterproofing. Most sealants tell you to let your deck dry for 2 days or 3 days after cleaning. If you shop around, however, you can find newer sealants that can be applied as little as 2 hours after cleaning—meaning you can now clean and waterproof your deck all in the same day. Check what weather conditions are required—you'll probably need clear skies for the next day or two and temperatures between 50° and 90°F.

Keep in mind that the clear sealants generally have to be reapplied after 1 or 2 years, whereas the more opaque stains last 2 or 3 years. Whichever waterproofing you decide on, heed this advice: Wave good-bye forever to oil-based sealants and their messy clean-up requirements. Modern water-based sealants are as good or better than their stinky oil-based counterparts and can be cleaned up with simple soap and water.

There are a number of easy ways to apply waterproofing. A pump-up sprayer will do the job most quickly. (If you're using a tint, make sure the spraying mechanism can handle heavier pigments.) Rollers and paint pads will do the job fast, too—use an extension pole so you don't have to bend over and ruin your back. Use a conventional paintbrush to apply the sealant to the odd spaces around railings where pads and rollers can't reach. If the weather is ideal for drying, you'll probably be able to walk on your deck after 24 hours—check the directions.

SIDEWALKS AND DRIVEWAYS

Plenty of people go a lifetime without doing anything more to care for concrete than sweeping it or squirting it with the garden hose. There are good reasons to go a step further once every several years, however. Concrete has lots of pores, says Scarborough, which are "great traps for just about every icky, dirty thing that there is outside." This includes oil, grease, sap, and mildew.

A thorough cleaning of the sidewalk can add a "like new" touch to the appearance of your house. And adding sealer to the concrete has several benefits: Your sidewalk will slough off dirt and stains, so it will look clean with little further maintenance; it will repel water, preventing the damage that freezing and thawing causes; and it will make shoveling in the winter easier, because snow and ice will not be able to reach into the pores of the concrete and grip the surface.

Cleaning concrete is much like cleaning your deck. Buy a cleaner specifically made for concrete. Apply it according to the directions and let it sit for 15 minutes or so. If you have a high-pressure sprayer, use it to rinse and loosen any stubborn dirt. Otherwise, scrub with a stiff-bristled brush and rinse with the garden hose.

When the concrete is clean, apply the waterproofing with a pump-up sprayer or a roller. Look for a high-quality sealant that will last for several years.

If you have a single oil spot on a sidewalk or driveway—say, from a leaky automobile—you can find a number of driveway-cleaning products at your home-improvement store. But this tried-and-true home remedy might be all you need: Sprinkle cheap cat litter onto the spot, stand on the litter, and grind it in with your shoe, then let it sit. Cat litter is highly absorbent and will suck up the oil. After 3 hours, just sweep up the litter.

What if you have an asphalt driveway? Manufacturers say spreading driveway sealant on asphalt every few years will

FAST • FORMULAS

GETTING UP GUM

Nothing loves bubble gum more than an 8-year-old. The exception being concrete, which clings to the sticky stuff for dear life. Here's an easy way to remove those dirty-pink dollops from your sidewalk, says Dr. Victoria Scarborough, director of research and development for Thompson's Water Seal.

Pour on enough mineral spirits (or similar solvent) to cover the gum. The gum will immediately soften. Scrape it up with a putty knife. If there's gum residue left on the concrete, apply a little more solvent, scrub with a stiff-bristled brush, then hose the debris away.

prolong its life, protecting it from weather and UV rays. Skeptics say that driveway sealer adds little protection. But all agree on two things: It's particularly important to patch any cracks in your driveway with a crack-filler product so water doesn't undermine your driveway, and follow up with a sealant to provide a nice cosmetic touch, at the very least.

THE HOUSE ITSELF

Here's where we talk about housecleaning in the literal sense—actually cleaning the outside of the house. Your house has a number of systems designed to keep the outside on the outside, including the roof, gutters, downspouts, siding, and windows. In the course of performing this service, they get grimy with airborne particles, speckled with sap, festooned with leaves and twigs, and spotted by birds with uncanny aim. These systems work best and look their best when they're cleaned periodically. So let's see how they can be spiffed up with the minimum amount of effort. And just to make sure none of this outside grunge gets *inside* your house, we'll discuss how you can easily set up a mudroom as a last line of defense.

PUT YOUR MIND IN THE GUTTER

A lot of home maintenance involves making sure water goes where you want it to and nowhere else. Outside, this means keeping your rain gutters and downspouts clean. If your gutters are clogged, rainwater will back up and rot the fascia board of your house (the board under your roof line that gutters are attached to). Water from overflowing gutters can pool around the base of your house, too, causing the foundation to shift and the basement to flood. Dripping gutters also will dig a mini-trench in your yard and ruin landscaping.

If you want to make gutter cleaning a minimal task, there's a preventive secret I'll bet you never thought of: Give the roof a quick sweeping. Sweeping the refuse away while it's on the roof is a lot easier than digging it out of a clogged gutter later on. Walheim's approach is the easiest of all—get up there with a leaf blower and blast all the debris off your roof in just a few seconds. If you don't have a leaf blower, it's still a quick job with a push broom. Chase away all the bark, twigs, leaves, and dirt once or twice a year, particularly in the fall after the leaves have dropped from the surrounding trees, says Alisa LeSueur, executive director of the American Association of Rain Carrying System Installation Specialists, based in San Antonio, Texas. (If you decorate your house with Christmas lights, get that task done at the same time.) If you have trees that also shed debris in the spring, sweep the roof then, as well. If you're sweeping, use a dustpan to collect the debris, or shove it off the edge of the roof with enough force that it doesn't fall into the gutter. Two cautions: Make sure you're not sweeping debris onto someone's head down below and do

WHEN YOUR GUTTER RUNNETH OVER

How do you know you have clogged rain gutters? Easy: The next time it rains, grab an umbrella, go outside, and take a look at the bottom end of your downspout. If there's little water coming out, you know the rain is going somewhere else—and that can't be good news for your house, says Alisa LeSueur, executive director of the American Association of Rain Carrying System Installation Specialists. Also look up: Is water dripping off the sides of your gutter? That's another sign that your gutter is dammed up inside.

THE INS AND OUTS OF
GUTTER COVERS

A number of systems will help keep debris out of your home's rain gutters. These covers will save you some gutter-cleaning work, but none of them is totally trouble free, says Alisa LeSueur, executive director of the American Association of Rain Carrying System Installation Specialists.

With solid hood-style gutter covers, water flows over the solid hood, through a slot on the outside of the cover, and into the gutter. One style requires that you slide the inside edge under your roof shingles. Another requires that you lower the gutter. In one particularly expensive model, the gutter and hood are all one piece.

Screen-style covers are another option, but these are more likely to trap debris between the roof's edge and the gutter cover, requiring some rooftop sweeping.

Either style of cover can be overwhelmed by heavy rain, causing water to sheet off the side of the gutter.

Questions to ask your salesperson:

❁ Will I have to reposition my current gutter to accommodate this cover?

❁ Are special brackets required for installation?

❁ Will this cover work with my style and size of gutter?

❁ Will this work with my style of roof shingle?

roof work only when there's a buddy around to call for help if you fall.

Once the roof is swept, attack the gutters. Walheim says a leaf blower set on the vacuum setting will make quick work of a leafy gutter. Or slip on a glove and work your way down the gutter, pulling out any leaves and twigs and tossing them to the ground.

What if you've ignored the issue of rainwater for years, and now your gutter and downspout are choked with a few inches of slimy, composting leaves? Your neglect has made the job harder, but a few tricks will get you through. As mentioned earlier, sweep the roof, if possible, so there's no more debris rolling toward your gutters. Then take the following steps, in order.

REMOVE AN ELBOW If your downspout is clogged, you might be able to loosen up the leaves and twigs inside with your garden hose. Get on a ladder, stick the hose into the top hole of the downspout, and turn the hose on full blast. If that doesn't work, loosen the screws on the middle elbow joint, the most likely culprit. (There usually are three elbow joints on a down-spout—one at the top, a second one high up, and one at the bottom.) Turn your head to the side so you don't get a face full of water, remove the joint, and shake the leaves out. If the bottom elbow of the downspout is clogged, too, put on a work glove and reach in to pull the debris out. Or bend a wire coat hanger so that you can poke the hook into the elbow and yank the junk out.

Sometimes the top elbow joint is glued into place, so don't try to force that one off. Leave the downspout disassembled until the gutter above it is clean—there's no sense in clogging up the downspout again with debris from above. When you do reassemble the downspout, make sure that the "male" end of each piece is pointing down so that water is always directed inside the downspout, LeSueur says.

START SHOVELING Decide whether you want to tackle the job from the rooftop or from a ladder. Cleaning from the rooftop

eliminates the hassle of moving your ladder around, but you have to be comfortable working on your hands and knees at the edge of the roof. Also, decide where you want to put the muck that's pulled from your gutter. Throwing it onto the ground might be fine, or you may prefer dropping it into a bucket or onto a tarp.

If there are a few inches of rotting leaves and sticks in your gutter, you need some kind of mini-shovel to get it clean. Gutter-scooping tools are available at your home-improvement store. Buy the kind with an extension handle so you don't have to move your ladder as often. Or you can improvise—dig the debris out with a putty knife, a wooden paint stirrer, or a plastic motor oil bottle cut in half.

MAKE SOME RAIN Put your downspout back together and give it a dry run (or should we say "wet run"?). Rinse the gutter and downspout inside and out. Make sure that water squirted into the gutter is now running unimpeded out the bottom of the downspout. If a seam on your gutter is leaking, buy a caulking-style tube of gutter sealant at your home-improvement store and follow the package directions for filling the crack on the inside of the gutter.

There—that's as bad as the job will ever get. Now raise your right hand and take an oath to check your gutters at least every year and more often if there are trees near your house.

PUT YOUR
WINDOWS TO WORK

If your house has a lot of windows, you've probably found yourself outside on a ladder with a bucket and squeegee, thinking, "Some day, windows will clean their own darned selves." That day is here, actually. As improbable as it sounds to many people, homeowners really can buy windows that will clean themselves (on the outside, anyway). The key is a thin coating of titanium dioxide on the glass, which is activated by sunlight and speeds the breakdown of the organic material that can collect on windows—sap, resin, bird poop, and such. These windows also sheet off water quickly, so inorganic stuff like road dust washes away readily each time it rains—or with a quick squirt of the garden hose.

"I never clean them in my home—I never touch them," says Chris Barry, an engineer for Pilkington®, a Toledo, Ohio, company that makes self-cleaning windows.

As you might expect, replacement windows with self-cleaning glass cost more than conventional ones. But wouldn't you pay more if it meant you never had to wash windows on the outside of your house again? Now, I'm not suggesting that you tear out your current windows just to save a few hours' labor. However, if you're building an addition onto your home or if you're replacing old windows anyway, self-cleaning glass would be worth the investment. To get these windows for your home, do an Internet search on the term "self cleaning glass" and check out the manufacturers' Web sites, which will list window dealers they work with in your area.

Okay, I know what you're thinking: It could be years before you install self-cleaning windows, and you want to know how to cheat at window cleaning right now. No problem. Stop in at your home-improvement store or hardware store and pick up a bottle of outdoor window cleaner, the kind that attaches to your hose. Hook the bottle up according to the directions. You'll be told to rinse the windows, spray the cleaner on, let it sit for several seconds, and rinse again. That's it—no squeegee, no drying rag, no bucket, no ladder. The cleaner is formulated to run off, streak-free. You can even spray the cleaner through screens onto windows, and it will easily reach windows on the second floor.

Do you prefer the hands-on, up close and personal approach to cleaning windows? There are plenty of cheat-at-cleaning shortcuts even for squeegee-and-bucket fans. Tom Gustin, product manager for Merry Maids cleaning service in Memphis, Tennessee, recommends that you start with a squeegee that has a long sponge on the flip side and a socket where you can twist in an extension pole when needed. You also need a bucket that's wide enough to accommodate the squeegee, plus a dry micro-fiber cleaning cloth (this high-tech material draws up dirt rather than smearing it around like conventional cotton). Mix up the dirt-cutting window cleaner you'll find in "Yes, It Does Windows" on p. 183.

Now take the squeegee in your dominant hand and the cloth in the other and follow this quick procedure for each window:

1. Dip the squeegee into the cleaning solution and rub its sponge side over the entire surface of the window.

2. Draw the blade of the squeegee across the top of the window in one horizontal strip. Wipe the blade with the cloth.

3. Working from one side of the window to the other, wipe the remaining cleaning solution off the window in overlapping vertical strips. For each swipe you take, start

the squeegee at the top in the dry part of the window and draw down. Wipe the blade after each swipe.

4. Wipe the cloth over the edges of the glass to dry.

CONDUCT A SPOT CHECK

Now and then you'll run across spots, stains, or grime on your windows that are too tough for conventional cleaning. Here are handy tools that will help you dispatch those stubborn blemishes with a mere flick of the hand.

MILD ABRASIVE CLEANER A gentle household abrasive cleaner does wonders for those milky mineral deposits that can form when your lawn sprinkler splashes the glass.

ACID CLEANER Mild acid also will make quick work of splotchy glass. Look for a household cleaner that contains citric acid or use plain ol' white vinegar.

SCRUBBER SPONGE Carry a white scrubber sponge with you (the white ones are the least abrasive) to rub out stubborn spots on the outside of your windows.

RAZOR SCRAPER Also carry in your pocket a razor scraper, the kind with a retractable blade. This tool will eliminate the toughest stains, such as paint drops and hardened bird droppings. First wet the stain for lubrication, then slide the razor into the spot from the side. Move the razor in one direction only (sawing it back and forth could scratch the glass).

Two cautions: If you have self-cleaning windows described earlier, make sure you read the manufacturer's directions for care. You could damage the self-cleaning coating with aggressive spot cleaning. Also, while you might be tempted to use a pressure washer for cleaning your windows outside, Hoch doesn't recommend that. The pressure could loosen the putty that holds the glass in place.

MUDROOMS: NO DIRT MAY PASS

A mudroom is a dirt-catching zone that stands between your home and the great outdoors. If you stop the dirt there, you won't have to chase it all over the house with a mop or vacuum cleaner. Even if the designer of your house didn't bless you with an officially designated mudroom, equip your most commonly used entrance with the gear and systems that will keep bucket loads of grime out of your house. Depending on the traffic pattern in your home, your mudroom might be an enclosed porch, the entrance from the garage, or even the front entryway.

"A great deal of the dirt that comes into the house comes in on shoes," says Sarah Smock, a spokesperson for the Merry Maids cleaning service company. So the way you outfit your mudroom will depend a lot on what the residents of your house have wrapped around their feet as they come and go. Are you a single professional who wears nothing but leather soles? Everyday mats might be all you need. Got a family of six with kids ranging from 5 years to 17 years old? You need major dirt insurance.

MATS ARE A MUST Large, strong mats for wiping feet are your home's first and best defense against dirt. Put one just outside the mudroom door and just inside. Depending on your setup, natural fiber mats might work just fine, but remember that if your mats are directly exposed to the weather, synthetic materials will hold up better.

BE READY TO BRUSH Leave a stiff-bristled scrub brush outside your mudroom door to use on shoes and boots that are so messy that mats won't suffice. You'll find it's handy for muddy sporting equipment and yard tools as well.

USE HARDY FLOORING Mudrooms work best when you have an easy-cleaning floor that shrugs off water and grime. Tile works best. Some laminates are good for mudrooms, Smock says, but make sure you have the kind that stands up to moisture well.

CONTAIN THOSE SHOES Park by the door some kind of

device for containing drippy shoes and boots the moment they enter the house. A shallow plastic "boot tray," available at hardware stores, can accommodate several pairs of shoes, Smock says. Or stack a set of plastic buckets by the door—one for each child in the family. When a child enters with slush-covered boots, drop the boots into a bucket to dry off.

BE READY TO WIPE Keep a container of disposable wipes by the door to mop up messy hands, shoes and doggy paws. If your family tracks in a lot of slushy grime, a couple of old towels will be a godsend. A stack of old news-papers will come in handy, too. If your shoes are soaked through, ball up sheets of newsprint and shove them inside the shoes. Change them every 20 minutes until they've sucked up all of the moisture.

GET ORGANIZED Mudrooms inevitably turn into "a little bit of a dumping ground" as people come a go, Smock says. So add some features that will keep personal items tidy and organized. Plenty of coat hooks are a must, and a locker, closet, or cubby storage is helpful, too. Supply a bench for sitting on while people take off shoes (the lidded kind of bench can double as storage for out-of-season items). Establish a spot for posting messages for family members. Set up a family "in box" (for mail, fliers, and such) and an "out box" (for that package that's headed for the post office and the library books that need to be returned). Key hooks will help everyone keep track of keys for the cars, bicycle locks, and shed.

SLEIGHT OF HAND

ONE MORE CLEANING DUTY TABLED

Dorothy Burling, a retiree in Mishawaka, Indiana, didn't like the way the outer rim of her circular patio table collected dirt. So she bought a stretch of cloth-backed Naugahyde® to use as a handsome cover to keep the dirt at bay. She cut the material 5 inches wider than the table itself, and she also cut a 4-inch hole in the center to accommodate the umbrella pole, which keeps the improvised cover in place when the wind blows. When the cover gets dirty, she tosses it into the washing machine.

Any possessions that spend a lot of time outdoors have to be rugged in the extreme. Grime, water, temperature extremes, and ultraviolet light all damage their surfaces. Fortunately, this rugged nature makes them a breeze to clean and care for. Take the following easy steps to make your garden tools, grill, and patio furniture look better and last longer.

GET A HANDLE ON YOUR TOOLS

Caring for your garden tools is less about appearances and more about making them last. Start by investing a little more money for sturdier tools every time you need a new one. If you do, they'll be less likely to corrode and you won't have to spend time and money replacing them in the near future. Then, keeping your tools clean is simple, says garden expert Lance Walheim. Here's the bare minimum cleaning routine: At the end of your work session, lay your garden tools out on the ground. Use a putty knife to scrape off any caked-on dirt. Hose the tools off, wipe them dry, and store them out of the weather (in a shed, for instance). A quick hose-and-wipe will keep your outdoor power tools looking sharp as well, since most of them are now made watertight, says Dr. Trey Rogers, professor of turf grass management at Michigan State University in East Lansing, Michigan.

Are you willing to go a step further to clean and protect your garden tools? A thin coating of oil on your shovels, hoes, and trowels will prevent rust and make dirt less likely to cling to them. Try this old gardener's trick for giving your tools a super-quick oiling, says Walheim: Keep a bucket of oily sand in your shed. (You can just dump your used lawn mower oil in there, for instance, or add machine oil.) Whenever you have used one of your gardening tools, stab it into the sand for an instant coating, then hang it up. An alternative: Pour a little machine oil onto a rag and keep it handy for wiping off your tools. Wipe linseed oil onto the wooden handles of your tools to keep them from drying out, shrinking, and getting loose.

Sheds, of course, are all about protecting and storing tools in an orderly way. So don't hold back, says Walheim—cover every square inch of wall in your shed with pegboard and shelving. "That sure simplifies things," he says.

FOR THE GRILL OF YOUR DREAMS

The first priority for cleaning a barbecue grill is to get the grate grime-free because that's the part that comes into direct contact with your food. Either of these two approaches will save you a lot of scrubbing:

1. Remove the grate from the grill and drop it into a large plastic bag. Squirt it down with oven cleaner, close the bag with a twist-tie, and leave it for at least 2 hours. Then put on rubber gloves, remove the grate, wipe it down with a scrubber sponge, and hose it off.

2. If you have a self-cleaning oven, slide the grill grate(s) into the oven and run the appliance through its cleaning cycle.

To prevent food particles from clinging to the grates while you're cooking, spritz them with nonstick cooking spray before they get hot. When you're done cooking, scrape the grates with your metal spatula or a wire brush, then close the grill cover and let the grates cook in there for an extra 15 minutes. This will burn off excess food.

If you have a charcoal-burning grill, the only other crucial cleaning duty is getting rid of the ashes once the fire is totally out. Spread out a few sheets of newsprint on the lawn and dump the ashes onto it. Roll the paper up, folding the sides in to contain the ash, then drop the bundle into a plastic grocery bag and tie it off. Discard into an outdoor trash can.

REFURBISHING THE FURNITURE

Patio chairs, recliners, and tables seem like magnets for atmospheric grime. Suddenly their smooth and shiny surfaces are gray tinged and gritty. The solution: Give them a quick once-over with a high-pressure sprayer, says Tom Gustin of Merry Maids. To protect the finish of your patio furniture, use low pressure—1,200 to 1,350 psi. A general-purpose cleaner should be fine—unless it contains chlorine bleach, which will make the color of your furniture fade (particularly darker colors, such as brown and red).

To clean your patio umbrella, you may be able to get away with nothing more than a squirt from the garden hose. If stubborn grime is clinging to it, pour 1 gallon of warm water into a bucket and add a squirt of dishwashing liquid. Dip a brush (synthetic bristles) into the solution and scrub the umbrella. Then rinse with the hose.

If you have wooden furniture in your yard—or wooden fencing, for that matter—follow the same procedures for cleaning and sealing wooden decks.

Now that you have savored every word of this chapter, you are a certified Master of the Wild. Nothing that nature has to deliver can get past your pressure washer, squeegee, and mudroom. Okay, no one's going to fit you with a coonskin cap yet, and you won't be wrestling grizzlies anytime soon—but if one leaves a mess on your deck, you've got the situation under control!

10

CARS:
BACKSEAT ARCHAEOLOGY

I have donated my body to science. Not my flesh-and-blood body, mind you—my car's body. Far too much time, energy, money, and anxiety go into cleaning automobiles. The high-tech materials used to build our cars—both exteriors and interiors—are getting more durable every year. Shouldn't the effort expended in cleaning our cars diminish proportionately?

Here's how selflessly devoted I am to scientific inquiry: My car is 8 years old at this writing, and I haven't waxed it in 5. I don't wash it more than a few times a year either, not counting the occasional rinse if the buildup of road slush gets out of hand in the winter. I'm in good company. More than half of all Americans wash their cars less than once a month, and about 15 percent of American car owners never wash their cars at all.

My car looks . . . well, if not pristine it definitely looks okay. I'm betting the finish will still be in reasonable shape by the time the car is ready for the scrap heap. If my ride were some

ROADMAP FOR CLEANLINESS

You're not going to make your car-buying decision based solely on how easy it is to clean the vehicle. Nevertheless, here are some points to keep in mind. After all, the more often you make easy-care choices, the saner your life will get.

- Black cars show dirt most readily. White cars look terrible in the winter when they've been splattered with slush. Of all car colors, silver stands up best to dirt and slush, and the color has a good resale record as well.

- SUVs take twice as long to clean as compacts, and it's really hard to reach certain parts of an SUV with a wash mitt—the center of the roof, for instance.

- Fabric upholstery is much easier to clean than leather.

- If the car dealer offers to treat your upholstery with fabric protectant to ward off spills and stains, save yourself the $80. The new upholstery materials are so advanced that it's probably not necessary. If you want extra protection anyway, buy a can of Scotchgard and spray it yourself.

kind of show car—say, a Lamborghini® or a Rolls-Royce®—boy, I would be out in the driveway every weekend washing and waxing with the best of them. Driving myself nuts. But no, my rig is a modest, lozenge-shaped compact like a zillion others you'll see on the road. It's a tool. It gets me from point A to point Z with reasonable fuel economy.

We see this advice printed with astounding frequency: "Protect your investment by washing and waxing your car regularly." Huh? How did we come to view cars as an investment? No matter how well you care for it, a car loses roughly 50 percent of its value every 4 years. So that $20,000 beauty you bought will be worth $10,000 after 4 years, $5,000 after 8 years and $2,500 after 12 years. If your 401-K performed like that you'd cover your investment adviser in honey and stake him or her to an anthill.

Here's a much more sane way to think about your car: To get the most value out of your car, drive it until the wheels fall off. Then sell it to a teenager for $215, use it as a trade-in on your next car, or donate it to charity and take the tax write-off. Remember, neither that teenager, the dealership, nor the charity will give a beep if the car isn't glimmering with a showroom finish.

The "you-gotta-wax-your-car-or-it-will-rust" sentiment is antiquated thinking—just begging us to cheat. In truth, carmakers in recent years have made enormous leaps in preventing corrosion, particularly in the use of galvanized sheet metal and high-tech clear coat finishes. Two decades ago, it was fairly common to spot the occasional rusted-out rattletrap creaking down the street. The way today's cars are built, that's a rare sight indeed.

The typical car finish is 100 microns thick, about the width of two human hairs, says Robert R. Matheson, Ph.D., an auto finish expert for DuPont®. There are four layers in this coating:

* Electrocoat, which prevents corrosion.
* Primer, which smooths out the surface and protects the electrocoat from UV rays.
* Base coat, which provides your car's color.
* And clear coat, the tough transparent shell that protects the finish from everyday wear.

The most exciting advancements are being made in clear-coat technology. Around the year 2001, says Matheson, clear coats got tough enough that you could finally run your vehicle through a commercial car wash without worry that the process would do more harm than good. The problem was that the automated brushes would rub surface grit into the car's finish, causing minuscule scratches. Those days are gone, which is good news for people who love to "outsource" their cleaning chores. And even better news: Waxing is unnecessary, too. On top of modern clear coats, wax offers such a slim extra whiff of protection that it's not worth the effort.

So, just who is proclaiming that you need to wash your car weekly and wax it once a month or so? Not surprisingly, it's car-wash operators and the people selling car-wash products.

Am I advocating that you stop washing your car, period? Not at all. There are some very good reasons to wash your car now and then:

※ If your car is covered in slushy road salt or acidic, splattered bugs, which really can eat away at your car.

※ If you live in a region affected by acid rain. This includes industrialized areas such as the northeastern United States, but it's even more of a problem in the South, where acid rain is aggravated by heat and humidity. In fact, the problem is so extreme in Jacksonville, Florida, that, according to Matheson, car-finish scientists test their products there.

※ To slough off the gritty buildup on your car. Abrasion from road grit can work on your car's finish like sandpaper.

※ If you just plain feel better when your car sparkles like a Las Vegas casino sign. That's perfectly valid. Do what makes you feel good.

Since there are valid reasons to wash your car, the crucial question becomes: How often? The party line is every 2 weeks or so—what car industry folks call "reasonable care." At that rate of washing, even the finish on the cheapest cars will look good for 6 or 7 years, and the more expensive rides will still be sharp after 10 or 12 years. Those life expectancies are right in line with the rust-through warranties that car-makers are now offering—6 years is common, and some models offer a

12-year guarantee. New-car buyers hold onto their cars an average of 7 years, which means that many folks are trading in their cars before the body is even out of warranty.

What's the worst that could happen if you never washed your car? Let's say you buy one of the most inexpensive new cars—which generally means you'll get a weaker finish—and you expose it to the

worst conditions the environment has to offer. It *could* have a corrosion problem in as little as 4 years, says Matheson. That's not really a goal to aspire to. With just a little regular effort—say, washing every month or two, depending on conditions, and cleaning off those bugs and salt immediately—you'll add several years of life to that finish. Fortunately, there are plenty of easy, time-saving ways to get the job done. So before you strip down to your Speedo® and haul out the buckets and wash mitts, read on.

PAYING FOR CONVENIENCE

The pain-free way to wash your car, of course, is to pay someone else to do it—assuming you find someone who will do it right. Automatic car washes of old had huge twirling brushes that were capable of scratching circular swirls into the finish of your car. In a modern "conveyor" car wash—the type that moves your car along a track automatically—you're likely to find that a jungle of hanging, jiggling cloths does the cleaning. Or just a series of spray jets.

Look for a car wash that advertises soft cloths or "no touch." Commercial car washes also have superior equipment and a staff that's more practiced at car washing than you are. So for the investment of a sawbuck and 10 minutes of your time, you'll probably come away happy. You'll get a clean exterior, clean windows, and a quick cleanup inside. (Detailing your car—a meticulous cleaning inside and out—can easily run you $100 or so.)

HANDING YOUR BABY OVER

Here's how to get the most out of an automatic car wash.

BUY IN QUANTITY Try out all the local car washes. When you find one you like—and if you've decided that outsourcing this job is the way to go—ask the cashier if they sell books of tickets at a discount. Some companies will even add the tip into the cost of the ticket. That way, you won't even have to open your wallet. You also can just hand a car-washing ticket to some other family member so he or she can get the job done for you.

GIVE THEM A RUNDOWN If there's anything peculiar about the way your car operates, be sure to tell the car wash attendant when you hand over your keys. Maybe your car is prone to locking itself automatically or it starts up in an unusual way. A few simple words in this case can save you a ton of grief.

WATCH THE WIPE DOWN At the end of the car wash process, you'll usually find a team of folks toweling off your vehicle. Stand nearby and pay attention to their work—this will inspire them to do a better job, particularly if you're holding a few dollar bills in your hand that may or may not become a tip. This is your time to speak up if you think anything's amiss with the cleaning job.

DON'T BE A STREAKER Once you've had your car washed, wait a couple of hours before you roll the windows down. There will be moisture trapped in the door, and rolling the window down will streak them with water—which will dry and leave spots. So give the water in the doors time to evaporate.

<table>
<tr><td>

TAKE THE CASH OPTION

</td><td>

Want a little more control over how your car-washing is done? In a self-service car wash, you pull your car into a carport-like bay, feed money into the

</td></tr>
</table>

machine, and use a sprayer or brush to do the cleaning yourself. You can get in and out in 10 minutes or 15 minutes—quick enough that it still feels like cheating when compared to the elaborate production some folks mount on their driveways each weekend. In exchange for putting a little work into the operation, you're saving a few bucks compared to the cost of a full-service car wash. And you don't need to own any of the car-washing gear, other than towels to dry the car when you are done.

Here's how to get the best results from a self-service unit.

THINK AHEAD Before you head to the car wash, grab a couple of things around the house—including at least $5 in bills and quarters (you may not spend that much, but running out of cash when your car is still soapy really stinks). Also take along your drying towels. A couple of old, soft, 100 percent cotton towels will do. Alternatives are a natural chamois cloth or several of those smaller towels you can buy in auto-supply stores.

OVERPAY Most cash-operated car wash machines have a minimum fee just to get the water flowing, commonly $2. If you run out of time and your wash job isn't done, you'll have to pay

$2 more to get the washer going again. So overpay at the outset—two or three extra quarters ought to do it—to give yourself ample cleaning time.

GET IT WET Select the soap setting on the controls, and cover the car in soapy water from the high-pressure sprayer, working your way from top to bottom. Don't forget the wheels and wheel wells. Then set the sprayer on rinse, again working from top to bottom to get rid of all the soap. (If there's an applicator brush, make sure the car is wet before you touch the brush to the finish. Otherwise, you'll scratch the paint.)

NOW MOP UP Use the towels to dry your car. Drying is described more thoroughly in the car-washing instructions a little later, but basically it's best to dry in order of importance from a visual standpoint—windows first, then hood and trunk, followed by roof, sides, and wheels.

GO AND THEN STOP No matter how good a job you did toweling off your car, there still will be water hiding in the crevices. This water will dribble out once the car gets moving and will leave spots if left to dry on its own. So you're going to outwit the wet: Drive half a block and pull over. Mop up any drips that have appeared, and get on your way again.

PAY THE BALD GUY TO DO IT

Washing your car actually is an easy task. It's *drying* your car that takes most of the time and effort. So it's nice to hear of a product that allows you to eliminate the drying step altogether. At this writing, the Mr. Clean AutoDry Carwash® system is a unique product, but competitors are sure to follow. The initial kit will cost you around $20, which you might find worth it if you want to wash your chariot in the driveway regularly but like to keep the effort and time involved to a minimum.

The system comes with a spray handle, a replaceable water filter that slides into the handle, and a container of refill soap.

GETTING THE MOST FROM
A COIN-OP CAR WASH

Whenever you're about to depart for a self-service, coin-operated car wash, a little alarm should go off in your head. Maybe there are other objects around the house that would benefit from a quick, high-pressure soap-and-rinse session as long as you're going to be camped out in the car wash bay anyway.

Make sure any possessions you clean this way can stand up to the high-pressure spray without falling to pieces. Good candidates include the charcoal grill, outdoor furniture, wagons, tricycles, wheelbarrows, garbage cans, shovels, and rakes. Pull them out onto the floor of the washing bay and hose them down quickly at the same time you're cleaning the car. (Make sure you paid for enough time to handle everything.) Bring an extra towel or two to wipe these items down before you load them back into the car.

Of course, to haul bulkier items you'll need a station wagon or van. Even better: Put everything in the bed of a pickup truck and wash them right there, hosing out the truck bed as a final step. No need to unload them from the truck at all.

Be considerate of the folks who own the car wash. Chunky debris could clog the drains, according an industry source. So dump all of the ashes out of your grill and remove the moldy newsprint from the bottom of that garbage can before you leave the house.

You connect the handle to your garden hose and wet your car down with regular water. Then you change the handle to the soap setting, squirt soap all over the car, wash with a car-washing mitt or sponge, and rinse again. Final step: Set the handle on the auto-dry setting and squirt the entire car again with the "deionized" water. This water has been treated so that it sheets off the car quickly and dries without leaving mineral spots.

Not a bad deal for fans of corner-cutting gizmos.

LAST RESORT: THE HANDS-ON APPROACH

If you've made it this far into the chapter, you must be yearning for an honest-to-goodness, hands-on car-washing session in your driveway. That's okay, I'll help you anyway—and there are still plenty of ways to cut corners.

You probably know people who turn driveway car-washing into a bigger production than *The Lion King*—a 4-hour extravaganza starring several helpers, enough water to fill five hot tubs, and a dozen bottles of exotic cleaning substances. Let's simplify that: With the following approach—much of it suggested by Philip Reed, senior consumer advice editor at the car information company Edmunds.com[SM]—you can clean the exterior of your car in 15 minutes flat all by yourself.

FIRST, GATHER THE GEAR

Drop by an auto-supply store and pick up a few items. These will help you do the job so quickly that you'll never dread it again—absolutely worth the investment:

* **A car-washing wand.** This device usually consists of a telescoping handle with a brush or pad on the end.

Some models hook up to your garden hose, and with others you pull on a plunger to suck soapy water from a bucket into the handle. As an alternative you could buy a wash mitt—a fuzzy glove that looks like part of a *Star Wars* Wookie costume—but you'll find that reaching some parts of the car will be harder with this approach.

* **A car squeegee.** This is an incredibly fast way to dry not only your car's windows but other flat surfaces as well—the hood and trunk, for instance. Make sure the blade is pliable.

* **A wheel brush.** These brushes are specially designed to remove grime from the complex crevices of automobile wheels. The bristles are 2 inches to 3 inches long, flexible and sturdy.

* **A container of tire black.** for an easy, glitzy final touch. Get the kind with a wipe-on applicator. If you use the spray-on kind, some of the tire black can get on the wheels and attract dirt.

The other items you'll need can probably be found around the house: two buckets, a garden hose, a bottle of car cleaner (make sure it's specifically made for cars—just about any other cleaner, such as dishwashing detergent, will be too harsh for a

car's finish), and a natural chamois cloth or an old beach towel (you can buy terry towels specifically made for car washing, but since these things are barely bigger than a washcloth you'll need several to do the job).

NOW GET IT WET

Now consider where you're going to do the wash job. Direct sunlight won't do. The water you use will dry on the car's surfaces too quickly, leaving spotty deposits. Also, cold water splashed onto a hot car can cause spidery little cracks in the finish called crazing. So find a shady spot, preferably not under a tree that will drip sap or one that's holding a bird convention. Also, find a place where the wash water will flow off and disperse into the soil. Letting wash chemicals pour into a storm drain isn't a good idea.

Gear gathered, location chosen and hose hooked up, you're ready for the world's quickest at-home, bumper-to-bumper wash job. Follow these easy steps—in order.

1. Hose the car down. Get every inch of the surface wet. You want as much of the grime to loosen and flow away as possible. Any time you're squirting water at your car, try to keep it flowing in the direction it would go if you were driving through a rainstorm. Otherwise, you might force a quart or two of water into a vent or crevice where you don't want it to go.

2. Pour a gallon of water (cold is generally fine—check the directions on your cleaner) into one of the buckets and add the car cleaner according to the package directions— probably just an ounce or so if you're using a concentrate. Fill the second bucket with clean water for rinsing your brush. With the hose turned off, telescope your car-washing wand out to full length and use it to apply the soapy water. Don't scrub—let a light swish of the soapy brush loosen the dirt. Leave the wheels alone for the moment.

Aside from that, cover all outer surfaces of the car, including the windows and wheel wells. Dunk the brush into the rinse bucket frequently—so you're not dragging any accumulated grit across the car's finish—and then dip it into the cleaning solution again to continue soaping the car. If your brush touches the ground at all, rinse it before you touch it to the car again.

3. Rinse the car. If you have the type of washing wand that hooks up to a hose, rinse the brush one more time, turn the water on, and rinse the car, working top to bottom. If your wand isn't connected to a hose, use the spray nozzle on your hose to rinse the car. Again, leave the wheels alone for the moment.

4. Now you're in a race to dry the car before it dries on its own, leaving spots. If you're using a chamois cloth, wet it with the hose (not in that grubby bucket of rinse water) and squeeze it out. The chamois is now ready for super-absorption. But do *not* dry the car top to bottom, as you might be tempted to do. Dry the parts of the car in order

SLUSH BUSTER

If it's winter and little stalactites of gray, salty grime are hanging from the underside of your car, you can wash it all off in just seconds and forestall future corrosion. Go to your shed and grab the lawn sprinkler (you remember—the twirly little summer item?). Hook it up to the hose, turn the water on and, using the hose as a guiding pole, slide it under your car. Reposition it every 15 seconds until the entire bottom has been spritzed.

of importance. The windows come first. Nothing screams "clean car" like sparkling glass. Also, the cleaner the windows, the better the driver's visibility. Squeegee the windows quickly, wiping up any excess water at the corners and edges with your drying cloth. Then use your squeegee and cloth to dry the next-most-visible parts of the car: the hood and trunk. Towel off the roof, then dry the sides of the car. Use a light touch with any drying rag—a blotting action is best, rather than wiping. Pressing down on the rag as you wipe could harm the finish.

FINAL TOUCHES

Wheels and tires are the crowning glory of a car-wash job—where the rubber meets the road, as they say. The wheel covers are a particular challenge, as they can get covered in brake dust and many covers have a stylish design with hard-to-clean nooks and crannies. (Can you say "fashion victim"?) Dip the wheel brush into the bucket of car-cleaning solution and give each wheel and tire a 15-second scrub. Rinse with fresh water and dry with the cloth. Then apply the tire black to the rubber (following the package directions) for a glossy, fresh-off-the-showroom-floor finish.

Occasionally your car will pick up a stubborn blotch that defies conventional washing—hardened bug bodies or sap, for instance. Don't scrub at these—you'll do more harm than good. Go to your auto-supply store and buy one of the myriad products designed just for your problem. They generally require you to clean the car first, so now's the time to deal with it.

Also, if you insist on waxing your car, do it now. Reed says he never waxes his own car, and he doesn't know anyone who does. If you're going to wax, at least cheat a little bit: Pick one of the liquid waxes and follow the package directions. They're easier to apply than the firmer paste that comes in a tub.

FAST • FORMULAS

CLEAR SAVINGS WITH EASY GLASS CLEANER

For pennies, you can make enough glass cleaner to drown a hippopotamus. With the following approach, you not only save gobs of money, you simplify your life, too. Just mix up the windshield washer fluid in a jug and pour it into the little tank under your car's hood as needed. When you need glass cleaner for your home's windows, just dilute this homemade washer fluid with water. You'll never have to buy any kind of glass cleaner again!

- **TO MAKE WINDSHIELD WASHER FLUID.** Rinse out a gallon milk jug. Pour in 3 cups of rubbing alcohol and 10 cups of water. Add a squirt of dishwashing liquid. You can add one drop of blue food coloring so your solution looks like the commercial stuff—this also will remind people that the contents are not just water. Seal the jug. With a permanent marker, label the jug "Windshield Washer Fluid / Glass Cleaner Concentrate." Rubbing alcohol is toxic, so keep your jug away from children and idiotic adults. Store it, for instance,

on a high shelf in the garage. The rubbing alcohol will prevent freezing.

- **TO MAKE GLASS CLEANER.** When your squirt bottle of commercial glass cleaner runs out, save it. Go to your garage, where you'll find—if you've been paying attention—a jug labeled "Windshield Washer Fluid / Glass Cleaner Concentrate." Fill your squirt bottle one third of the way with this fluid and fill it the rest of the way with water. You can do the same mixing job, of course, in one of those empty squirt bottles you can buy at the supermarket, discount stores, or home supply stores. Label the squirt bottle "Glass Cleaner" in permanent marker.

If you need a larger quantity of glass cleaner—say, for cleaning the outside of your home's windows with a sponge-and-squeegee wand—prepare the amount you need in a bucket using the same proportions: one part homemade concentrate to two parts water.

A BREATH OF FRESH AIR

You can let the candy wrappers and doughnut bags pile up as high as you please on the floor of your car—your wheels will still get you to the supermarket and back without a complaint. But if you're ignoring a basic cleaning issue right there under your hood—the air filter—you're slowly choking your car to death.

The conventional wisdom is that you have to change your air filter every 10,000 miles or so. The hands-down easiest way to deal with a dirty air filter is to have your mechanic swap it out the next time you take your wheels in for an oil change. But if you can tell a hammer from a screwdriver and like to do your own light maintenance on your car, changing the air filter is simple task. And if you've been changing your own air filter every 10,000 miles, you'll want to know about the innovative K&N® Filter. This baby is good for 50,000 miles. And if you follow the manufacturer's simple directions for brushing, spraying, and rinsing the filter, it will be good for another 50,000. That saves you a whole lotta hood-popping, hand-griming work.

While the conventional replacement air filter is made of paper, the K&N Filter draws air through oil-covered cotton to snag impurities and to allow top-notch airflow at the same time, according to the car info experts at Edmunds.com. You won't be surprised to learn that it costs several times more than a conventional air filter, but if you like to reduce work and hassle, this is clearly the way to go. You can pick one up at your local auto parts store. The warranty on the filter is good for 10 years or, for goodness sake, 1 million miles.

If this inspires you to pop the hood on your car for the first time in a long while, the air filter lies inside that large, black plastic casing that's typically hovering right over the engine (sometimes to the side). Let the engine cool first. In most models, you can just pop open the clasps on the side of the casing with a screwdriver (sometimes there are screws to remove). Lift the cover, and you'll find the filter inside. If it's showing a lot of dirt buildup, you know your filter is impeding airflow and reducing your engine's performance. Time for a change!

DEPARTMENT OF THE INTERIOR

It's amazing how a few small changes will make you feel so much better about the interior of your car. If you only have 90 seconds to invest, try this:

* First, do a little backseat archaeology. Open a car door, grab the first fast-food bag you can find, cram all of the other miscellaneous trash into it, and throw it away. You'll do this more frequently, by the way, if you have a trash can stationed near the driveway—in a handy corner of the garage, for instance.

* Pull out the floor mats, give them a shake, and put them back in.

* If you have crystal-clean windows, passengers will forgive the other foibles inside your car. So squirt glass cleaner onto a couple of paper towels and wipe down all the windows. Don't use glass cleaner on the plastic windows of a convertible, however. Hose them off with water and blot them dry with a towel. (Don't scrub or wipe in circles—that could scratch them.) Then apply a clear-plastic cleaner according to the package directions (spray-and-wipe products are available at auto stores).

HAND VAC: WINDS OF CHANGE

Maybe you're on a roll now, and you're ready to go for the full *How to Cheat at Cleaning* all-out supreme deluxe 5-minute interior detailing. If so—if you really want to commit to the next tier of car interior cleanliness—then invest in a battery-powered hand vacuum. Why? Because of the Accessibility Theorem: "A cleaning task will be accomplished on a frequency that is

TAMING THE TRUNK JUNK

Does the inside of your car trunk look like a junkyard on wheels? Here's a simple way to keep the contents of your car's trunk under control: Store some kind of container back there where you can stuff all the miscellaneous items—tools, flashlight, work gloves, jumper cables, medical kit, maps, and such.

The size of the container should leave plenty of room for the things you commonly haul temporarily (tennis racquets, book bags, and grocery sacks, for instance). The container also should have handles so you can lift it out to make room for the occasional enormous item you need to jam in there. You'll also be glad that everything's contained if you have to retrieve your spare tire from underneath the trunk floor. One quick lift and all your paraphernalia is out of the way.

My favorite trunk container: A plastic "milk crate" from a discount store. It's cheap, lightweight, has handles, and you can see through the sides to find what you're looking for. If you're hankering to throw more money at this matter, an auto supply store will happily sell you a car trunk organizer with multiple storage bins and pockets. However, an old gym bag would serve just as well as the one I inspected.

inversely proportional to the distance between the object to be cleaned and the materials necessary to clean it." That is, if it's a hassle to get to your cleaning gear, no cleaning gets done.

Now, in the case of an automobile interior, vacuuming is a core function. But dragging the home vacuum cleaner out to the driveway is a chore for anybody. Then you have to hunt around for a really long extension cord. For a lot of people the situation is worse: They have to clean their cars on the street or in an alleyway, well out of reach of the home Hoover. So a battery-powered hand vac, or one that connects to your cigarette lighter, is the solution: Just store it in the trunk, and you'll never again moan about cleaning the inside of your auto. (Don't store it in the backseat—some kid will decide to vacuum the back of your head while you're changing lanes on the freeway.) If you have the kind of hand vacuum with a wall-mounted recharging station, you might want to hang it in the garage, where it will be close by.

Whatever kind of vacuum you're using, here's how to clean the interior in 5 minutes or less:

1. As above, pull out all of the trash—anything too big for the vacuum—and throw it away.

2. Pull out the mats, shake them, vacuum them, and then vacuum the interior carpet. Move the front seats forward and back to get to some of the hidden—and often grungy—parts of the carpet. If your vacuum has a narrow nozzle, use it to get beside and between the seats and to vacuum any other nooks and crannies you can find.

3. Use an upholstery attachment to vacuum the seats. If you use seat covers or seat pads pull them out, give them a shake to remove the debris they've collected, and then pop them back into place. (Auto-supply stores sell car seat covers that will protect your original seats from damage—or hide the rips and stains you already have. There are two basic approaches: fabric that closely covers the entire seat, or L-shaped pads that cushion your back and your buns. These are particularly handy if kids, dogs, or fraternity brothers frequent your automobile.)

4. Assuming you just washed the outside of your car, take your still-wet chamois, sit in the driver's seat, and look around. Wipe up any dust and dirt that's within your sight. (After all, you're the one who spends the most time in this car, so your viewpoint rules.) Wipe the dashboard, the area around the instruments, the glass over the instruments, the steering wheel, the horn area and the steering column. Wipe the cup holders, the center console and cubby. Keep changing to a fresh part of the chamois as you go.

NOW STOW YOUR STUFF

You're done! Time to gather up all your implements and put them away. Keep the hand vacuum in the trunk or hanging in the garage so you can use it whenever the whim strikes. Try to keep all of the other gear—the washing wand, chamois, car cleaner and such—together in one place. You could stash everything in a bucket, for instance, and park the bucket near the garden hose for easy access next time you need to clean your car. Assuming you ever feel the need again.

BABIES, TODDLERS, AND PETS: THE THINGS WE DO FOR LOVE

We invite little creatures into our homes—both the human kind and the animal kind—and what do we get in return? A relentless source of pee and poop. Not to mention hand and paw prints everywhere, floors littered with toys, food flung about wantonly, and furniture and clothing festooned with animal fur.

Making it all worth it, however, are mountains of love, devotion, and companionship. Not for a moment will I suggest you forego parenthood or pet ownership. 'Tis better to have loved and lived in filth than to have never loved at all. But you can actually *have* it all—the kids, the pets, an orderly home, and even your sanity—as long as you keep a few core concepts in mind:

- ✳ Be willing to spend money in exchange for convenience (one of the primary rules from Chapter 1).
- ✳ A little training pays off big-time for both children and pets.
- ✳ The less exposure you have to excrement, the happier you'll be.

The first 6 months of parenthood is a hazy, sleep-deprived confusion punctuated by periods of unbridled joy and horrifying surprises. Complicating matters further, when you're new to parenting a torrent of possessions flood into your home that you have never had to manage before—diapers, baby blankets, bottles, ointments, baby clothes, mobiles, teensy food jars, a high chair, a baby swing, a stroller, and thousands of stuffed animals. If there ever was a time for convenience items, organizing tricks, corner cutting, and cleaning cheats, this is it.

Most of the baby-related items that clutter a new parent's home can be easily organized by "stations"—just like the adult stations described in Chapter 3 for food preparation, mailing, crafts, and more. So you want an assigned spot for each diaper-changing item within easy reach of the changing table, an assigned spot for each sleep-related item near the crib, and an assigned spot for each bath-related item near the tub. Plotting out where every little baby thing goes may sound terribly persnickety, but the failure to make these decisions is the road to ruin, says Dana Korey, a professional organizer based in Del Mar, California.

"I think people really need to decide what they need in each space—make the decision to decide," she says. "The better you contain your items and divide them up by category, the easier it will be to maintain your system."

The diaper-changing station is a prime example, she says. Think about it: When your baby is on the changing table, you want to be able to keep one hand on her so she doesn't roll off. This means that all paraphernalia related to changing should be within super-easy grabbing distance—preferably on a nearby shelf in lidless bins so that you don't have to struggle to open things with your one free hand. Having to open a cabinet or a closed container will get old by your 2,000th diaper change. Position everything in the order you typically use them for a diaper change—for instance, wipes first, then ointment, then powder, and then fresh diapers. Make sure there's a pedal-operated diaper pail at your feet.

DIAPERS: CHANGE IS GOOD

Speaking of diapers, few things will have as big an effect on a new parent's sanity as the kind of diapers you choose. When you have your first child, you may develop this vague notion that using cloth diapers, rather than disposable ones, is somehow more wholesome, more pure, more environmentally friendly, and more healthful for the baby. Because nothing is too good for your offspring—who will, after all, win a Nobel Prize some day—you're

going to smugly turn your nose up at disposable diapers and wrap your child's bottom in cushy cotton. After a couple months of leaky diapers, diaper changes every other minute, and shocking messes to launder, you'll realize your monumental mistake—a classic "What was I thinking?" situation.

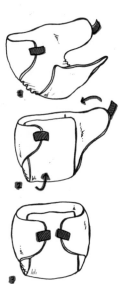

The experts who analyze such things scientifically say that the pure-and-natural reputation of cloth diapers is a huge misconception. The truth is that in terms of health, cost, and environmental impact, neither cloth diapers nor disposable diapers are superior—it's a wash, so to speak. But in terms of convenience, disposables are unquestionably the winner. So leap,

SLEIGHT OF HAND

A BOXFUL OF MEMORIES

Crayon scrawls, finger paintings, Popsicle® stick sculptures—the urge to save these treasures is irresistible. However, your child's creative work can quickly inundate the shelves and counters in your home. Also, works you hope to preserve will quickly become tattered when they're lying in random heaps. Professional organizer C. Lee Cawley, of Arlington, Virginia, has the solution: Set up memorabilia boxes for each child.

A wide, flat storage box will do the trick. Cawley likes 14½-inch by 11½-inch cardboard boxes. They're 3 inches deep and have metal corners, plus slots on the side for labels. To help preserve the contents without paying the high price of official archival boxes, line each box with two layers of acid-free archival tissue paper, which you can buy at storage or craft stores, or online.

Label each box with the child's name and grade range—for instance, "Christina, Preschool–1." When your child brings artwork home, pick out the best piece of the week and put it in her box. Don't mix papers you're saving for posterity with papers that are important here and now—the T-ball schedule, for instance. The memorabilia boxes will be powerful keepsakes to give to your children when they reach middle age.

wholeheartedly and guilt-free, into the convenience of disposables.

Managing disposable diapers is easy, but from a cleanliness standpoint there are some things to remember. The one drawback to disposables is that they contain the poop and pee so well that it can be hard to tell when it's time to change them. At least once an hour, stick a finger into the waistband of your baby's diaper and look in to see if anything inter-esting is going on. Wearing a loaded diaper for too long will give a baby diaper rash.

If you have solid poop in a diaper, shake it out into the toilet and flush before you throw the diaper out. Roll the used diaper up into a ball and use the waistband tapes to secure it before you toss it into a plastic-lined diaper pail (remember, you want a pedal-operated lid). This way, the diaper will take up less space and will contain its own filth and odor somewhat. Wash your hands immediately after each diaper change. Once a day, take the diapers out to the garbage can and replace the diaper pail liner. (You can do it less often if you pick up those special odor-reducing trash can liners at the supermarket.) Once a week, spritz the pail with disinfecting cleaner inside and outside, and wipe with a paper towel.

So there—with that one diapering decision you're going to save yourself a ton of grief and grime.But there are plenty of other sanity-preserving strategies that parents can implement. Let's take a look.

TIME FOR CLEANING TRIAGE

New parents know the word *overwhelmed* intimately. Jen Singer, a writer on parenting and a stay-at-home mom, says that when a baby arrives it's time to revise your standards for home cleaning. Stick to a few narrowly defined priorities, tasks that directly affect your life—"cleaning triage," she calls this. For instance:

- ✳ You have to have a steady supply of onesies for the baby to wear, so get the laundry done.
- ✳ Empty the diaper and garbage pails daily to keep stink and messes under control.
- ✳ Ignore the dishes until the end of the day, when the kids are in bed.
- ✳ Let the dusting go, unless your mother-in-law is coming over.
- ✳ Vacuum the floors once a week.
- ✳ Clean the main bathroom, but leave the others alone.
- ✳ Let everything else go.

Singer has two rarely used rooms in her house. To limit cleaning chores, she shuts the doors to those rooms and leaves them alone until they're needed—for holidays, for instance. "I can shut the doors to the living room and leave it for a month," she says.

THE INCREDIBLE VANISHING JUNK HEAP

Children are not renowned for keeping their bedrooms neat. You can start training your kids to keep an orderly environment at the toddler stage, however. (You can reasonably expect them to perfect these skills by the time they're, say, in their early 30s.) Here's the secret for instantly creating the appearance of order in a household with children, particularly if you have visitors: Close the doors to their bedrooms.

It's a tad trickier to keep the rest of the house neat and clean when the kids play outside of their bedrooms, but the following corner-cutting ideas will help you there as well. (Make sure you also check out Chapter 4 for advice on getting kids to help with household cleaning.)

PUT PLAYTHINGS IN THEIR PLACE

Toddler toys are a lot like liquids—that is, they spread out to cover any space that contains them. To preserve your sanity, Singer recommends a few simple toy-management measures:

* Institute no-toy zones in the house. No toys may enter the home office, for instance. If possible, confine all toys to one playroom—or even the child's bedroom.

* Supply a generous number of toy boxes. At specific times of the day, have the kids participate in putting toys away. In this situation, brainwashing your kids is perfectly acceptable, so sing the Barney® cleanup song.

* Limit the influx of toys. If Grandpa hauls a new toy into the house every time he visits, establish some ground rules. Tell him, "You know, you've become Santa Claus to these kids—every time you arrive, they expect a toy. I'd rather they appreciate you for you."

* Encourage the outflow of toys. Before any birthday or gift-giving holiday, go through all the toys with your kids and decide which ones can be thrown out or donated to charity. Take your children on the ride with you to the Salvation Army℠, so they learn a lesson about giving to people in need. "I call this 'making room for Santa,'" Singer says. "Santa won't come unless you get rid of some of this stuff."

GET A VIDEO BOX FOR THE TOTS
If you have a small child in the house, store all of his videos in one lidless box that he can easily reach on a low shelf, says professional organizer C. Lee Cawley, of Arlington, Virginia. The typical humongous living room entertainment center—the kind with myriad doors and drawers—is too complex for a little kid to work with. The result: The child never learns to find his own video, watch it, and return it to its storage area. The parents get to do all of the work. An open box stuffed with Thomas the Tank Engine® videos may not be the trendiest decorating scheme, but at least your child can clean up after himself and keep clutter under control.

GET THE HANG OF COAT RACKS Coat racks are a kid-friendly accessory, says Alexandria Lighty, owner of the House Doctors Handy Man Service℠ in New York City. If you have one in the foyer, your children will readily use the coat rack rather than tossing their jackets onto the floor when they enter the house. Stationed in a child's bedroom, a coat rack is a handy place to hang pajamas or any other clothing that has trouble finding its way to the closet. These clothes may be more visible than if they were in the closet, but at least they're up off the floor.

BUY AN AMPLE NIGHT STAND Many parents make the mistake of purchasing a cute little night stand to go beside a toddler's bed—one that's barely big enough to hold a little lamp, says Korey. Get one that's large enough to accommodate all the things a youngster might need while in bed, including the lamp, a book, a water glass, tissues, and a flashlight.

An organizer that hangs off the side of a child's bed also makes a handy spot to stash items that a youngster might want in the middle of the night, Korey says. Such organizers typically have a "tongue" that slides between the mattress and the box spring, allowing several shoe-bag-style storage pockets to dangle down the side of the bed. What's more, it creates a solution to clutter without eating up shelf or dresser-top space.

THE FEEDING FRENZY

We've already discussed how to manage what comes *out* of your baby—the end product, so to speak. But putting food *into* your baby makes almost as much of a mess. Here's how to cope.

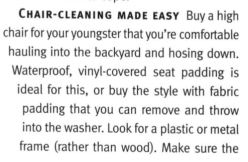

CHAIR-CLEANING MADE EASY Buy a high chair for your youngster that you're comfortable hauling into the backyard and hosing down. Waterproof, vinyl-covered seat padding is ideal for this, or buy the style with fabric padding that you can remove and throw into the washer. Look for a plastic or metal frame (rather than wood). Make sure the high chair has a removable plastic tray that you can wash in the sink or just plop into the dishwasher. The tray on the highchair should have a high rim, which will keep some percentage of the baby's food off of the floor.

WHEN THE FOOD FLIES . . . Don't even consider feeding your baby unless you have a couple of basic accessories on hand, says Judi Sturgeon, a professional house cleaner and home health aid based in Ambler, Pennsylvania:

* A baby bib with a pocket at the bottom for catching food (this will keep the pureed peas off the furniture and floor). When the bib isn't in use or being laundered, give it a permanent spot hanging off the back of the high chair.

* A clean, damp cloth for easy wiping of face, hands, and surfaces, so the mashed carrots don't get smeared all over the house.

OUT OF THE HIGH CHAIR, INTO THE TUB Arrange your household schedule so that bath time comes right after dinnertime. This way, you don't have to do a perfect job of cleaning the baby's face and hands. The bath will take care of that.

HANDY HABITS Training your toddler to adopt these habits will save you tons of cleaning, says Sturgeon:

* Eating over the plate—a good lifelong habit that will keeps crumbs and dribbles contained.
* Washing her hands *after* eating, so she doesn't smudge the walls, floors, doors, and furniture.
* Washing hands as soon as she comes inside the house, so she doesn't bring dirt and germs home from day care or the backyard.

THE FURRY CLEANUP CREW Having a dog in the home at the same time that you have a baby is not a bad idea at all. I have a cousin who eliminated 90 percent her baby-spill cleanups by allowing her eager dog to lap food up off of the floor.

YOUR FURRY FRIENDS	Two factors are crucial to mess-free pet ownership, says Melissa Laiserin, a PetSmart[SM] dog behavior expert based in Phoenix, Arizona:

* Training your pet to do what's appropriate.
* Supervising your pet to correct behavior and forestall disasters.

Naturally, the primary behaviors you're concerned about are peeing and pooping. The key to potty training is watching your pet closely for signs that he has to relieve himself. So, when you first bring your pet into the home, make sure you can spend plenty of time close to him. If your dog is walking in circles and sniffing, or running back and forth, he's gotta go—move him quickly to his official potty spot. This is usually either a spot in the yard outside, a puppy training pad inside, or a container of litter, which is available now for small dogs. If you find your dog squatting inside, you're too late.

Reward your dog when he gets it right. Depending on the dog, the reward might be a small treat, verbal praise, or a scratch behind the ear. (Although I'm using dogs as an example, Laiserin says that the same training rules apply to cats as well—it's a myth that they can't be trained.)

Learn your pet's "bathroom" schedule. A dog will typically need to relieve himself within 20 minutes of eating and drinking, within a half hour of vigorous exercise, and first thing in the morning. As a precaution, let him relieve himself just before you go to bed, too. Puppies can delay relieving themselves for 1 hour per month of age, Laiserin says. This means your 4-month-old woojums will need to go out at least every 4 hours.

Good training also will help prevent destructive behavior, Laiserin says. First, eliminate the temptations. Make sure there's a lid on your kitchen garbage can, for instance; and, if possible, position it behind closed doors. Dogs particularly love smelly socks, so put them in a hamper, not on the floor. Make sure the kids keep their toys picked up. And consider the messages you're sending the animal during playtime. If you play tug-of-war using a worn-out sneaker, can you blame your dog for chewing up a perfectly good one the next day?

Sprays are available in pet stores that will help train your animals to avoid certain places (your home office, for instance) and to quit chewing on certain objects (the couch cushions). Also, the folks who make invisible fences for the yard (the dog gets an annoying shock from his collar when he strays out of bounds) are now offering similar systems for interior use. This allows you to make rooms or entire floors of your house off-limits to animals.

Now let's take a look at easy ways for pet owners to cope when preventive measures fail.

PET ACCIDENTS: "IT" HAPPENS

As with so many other cleaning tasks, disposables are the very best cheat-at-cleaning approach when you're fixing pet messes. Particularly with feces or urine, you want products that eliminate the yuck factor—allowing you to have minimal exposure in terms of sight, touch, and odor. Disposable cat boxes that come prefilled with litter certainly fill the bill. You can find any number of ingenious poop-scooping devices that allow you to quickly slide pet feces straight into a plastic sack that you can drop right into a waste bin.

Now and then, however, you come face-to-face with the pet-owner's nightmare—pee or poop right on the dining room carpet. This is a serious situation. Not because it will tie your stomach in a knot, but because you can't afford to let the odors linger even subtly in your carpet. If your pet detects waste odors in the future,

PET BOWLS: HIDE THE EVIDENCE

A lot of people feed their pets on the kitchen floor, but you can use a more out-of-the-way place for feeding if you don't like the sight of the pet's bowls—and the food that gets flung about—in your kitchen. Find a place with a hard (preferably tile) floor for easy cleaning. You also want quick access to water for bowl refills and a nearby place to store the pet food. A utility room, laundry room, or mudroom would probably do nicely.

To keep messes under control, place your pet's food and water bowls on a tray or a plastic mat with a raised rim. Wash the mat and bowls weekly in hot water and dishwashing liquid, then rinse and dry.

she may think this spot has become her new official bathroom, and history will repeat itself.

Solid poop is the easiest to cope with. Fold three paper towels on top of each other and tent them over the poop. Lift the excrement straight up into the towels, then either drop it into a plastic bag and tie it off to throw away, or drop the poop (not the towels) into the toilet and flush. If there are traces left on the floor or carpet, mix a cup of warm water with a squirt of dishwashing liquid and blot at the spot until it's gone, then rinse with fresh water. Finally, fold up two paper towels until they're the size of the wet spot and press down firmly with your fist for a minute to draw up the water.

For anything messier—say, runny poop, pee, or vomit—you need a special weapon: an enzyme-based clean-

FAST·FORMULAS

THE CURE FOR FURRY FURNITURE

What makes pet hair cling so vehemently to your furniture and drapes? A static charge. Here's a little trick that will kill that electrical grip and make hair cleanup easy, says Lisa Peterson, the Newton, Connecticut–based spokesperson for the American Kennel Club[SM].

Fill a spray bottle one quarter of the way with liquid fabric softener and the rest of the way with water, seal the bottle, and shake. Stand near your hair-covered furniture or drapes and mist the air with the solution (don't squirt it directly onto the fabric). The hair will lose its static charge and fall to the floor. Now all you have to do is vacuum. You'll find that the nonclinging hair gets vacuumed up without the least bit of resistance.

An alternative: Warm up a drier sheet in the drier and wipe it across your furniture and drapes to kill the charge.

er. No pet owner should be without this stuff—it's the one sure way to eliminate the lingering odors from pet accidents. Follow the directions on the package of your cleaner. The procedure will go something like this: First, dispose of any solids as described above. Then, use the blotting method with fresh paper towels to sop up most of the liquid. Apply the enzyme-based cleaner and leave it for the prescribed amount of time (it can take hours or even days for the enzymes to thoroughly break down the organic material that

HAIR ON THE SIDE OF CAUTION

Are you reluctant to buy a dog, fearing that a pooch might leave a blanket of fur on the furniture and carpet? Do you get itchy eyes and a runny nose run when you're around dogs? Here's a list of dog breeds that are known for minimal shedding of hair and minimal shedding of the dander that annoys allergy sufferers, according to the American Kennel Club.

- Bedlington terrier
- Bichon frise
- Chinese crested (they're hairless!)
- Irish water spaniel
- Kerry blue terrier
- Maltese
- Poodles
- Portuguese water dog
- Schnauzer
- Soft-coated wheaten terrier
- Xoloitzcuintli (hairless)

would otherwise cause lingering odors). Then rinse again with water, blot with paper towels, and let it dry. Now, that wasn't so bad, was it?

THEY PUT THE "FUR" IN FURNITURE

Next to pee, poop, and vomit, pet hair on your clothing and furniture seems like a refreshing little diversion. But your own tolerance for furry clothing and furniture is bound to wear thin. You're going to want some easy ways to keep it off your furnishings and to clean it up if your prevention efforts fail.

People often associate allergies with pet hair, but actually it's pet dander that will inflame your eyes and make your nose run. Fortunately, the procedures for preventing or cleaning up pet hair in the home often reduce the amount of dander present as well. See Chapter 6 for more about cleaning and allergies.

VACUUM YOUR PET To people who have pets that go berserk at the merest glimpse of the vacuum cleaner, this is going to sound insane. But you really can vacuum dogs—and even cats—to prevent their hair from decorating your house. You can buy pet vacu-ums that have special grooming attachments, or use a conventional vacuum with the upholstery attachment, says Lisa Peterson, a spokesperson for the American Kennel Club. (Whatever you do, don't use the beater brush.)

Vacuuming your pet will be easiest on everybody's nerves if you start the practice while the animal is young so she grows up accustomed to the noise and the suction. Otherwise, you will need to introduce the vacuuming process very gradually. For instance, start by brushing your animal with the attachment—with no hose hooked to it and no vacuum cleaner in sight. The next time you brush your pet, have the vacuum cleaner turned on—but in another room. Keep moving the machine closer each time you brush until you can hook the hose to the attachment and apply light suction (on many vacuums, you can vent the hose to reduce the air flow). People swear that indoctrinated cats will come running, begging to be groomed, when they hear the vacuum cleaner turned on.

During shedding season, vacuum your pet daily. If the weather is nice, do the job outside so that escaped hair doesn't end up in your house. Otherwise, do the job on hard flooring, which is easier to clean up, says Peterson.

If you're afraid the vacuum cleaner will give Fido a heart attack, use one of the conventional animal brushes that are available at pet stores. When you drop that glob of fur you've collected into the trash bin, say a little prayer of thanks that this stuff isn't spread all over your furniture.

GOOD FOOD, FINE FUR Premium, nutritious pet food will give your pet the healthiest possible coat, says Rashelle Cooper, product buyer for PetSmart. A healthy coat will mean less shedding and less allergy-aggravating dander. So ask your vet what the optimum diet is for your animal.

Washing your dog frequently also will help control shedding and dander. Ask your vet what the ideal frequency is for your pet. If you do it regularly from an early age, your dog will grow up used to the process and will put up less of a fuss. Use a shampoo that's formulated for pets—not a human shampoo. For between washings, you can buy disposable wipes that promise to control shedding and dander as well.

THE SELF-CLEANING LITTER BOX

Chicago entrepreneur Alan Cook had always adroitly avoided cleaning his girlfriend's cat box. But after they were both laid up with food poisoning for a week, he could no longer ignore the stench from the neglected receptacle. He was horrified by the "absolutely disgusting" cleaning chore.

"I asked myself: We can put people on the moon—why can't we make a litter box that cleans itself?" he says.

Thus began a year's worth of research. There were some mechanized cat boxes on the market, and he began to analyze their failings. He spoke with customers in the pet aisle of the supermarket. He huddled with buddies from MIT and NASA. The result of his investigation: The ScoopFree™

self-cleaning litter box. The unit comes in two parts: the main casing, which plugs into an outlet, and a cartridge that lies under the casing and contains super-absorbent litter crystals. An infra-red sensor alerts the box when there's a cat "customer" using the litter. A timer starts, and 20 minutes later—assuming the cat doesn't return—a motorized rake drags through the litter and pulls any solids into a closed compartment, where the poop will dry out and shrink without releasing odors.

There's nothing to clean and nothing to dismantle. You just pull out the old cartridge, throw it in the trash, and replace it with a new one periodically (every 20 days to 30 days if you have one cat, and every 10 days to 15 days if you have two). An automated cat box would be particularly beneficial for elderly people or children if you have doubts about their ability to handle a conventional cat box. "It's the Swiffer principle for the litter box," Cook says.

Most cats do a good job of cleaning themselves, although there are plenty of cat shampoos and other cat-cleaning products to be found in your local pet store, too.

ERECT SOME BARRIERS Peterson uses several coverup strategies to put a barrier between her pets and her furnishings. Because her dogs like to sleep on her bed, she covers the bed with an old, tight-weave sheet to protect it from loose hair and dirt. Throw rugs and runners protect her nice carpet from hair, dirt, and doggie accidents—particularly in high-traffic areas. (She can roll the throw rugs up and stow them in a closet when guests come.) In the car, Peterson prefers leather upholstery, which pet hair will not stick to. Manufacturers offer seat covers that will protect your upholstery, too, but Peterson says it's not safe to let your pet roam freely in the car. She uses heavy plastic airline crates for her animals. You also can buy grates that will confine your pet to the cargo area of an SUV, plus protective covers for the floor of the cargo area.

TOOLS TO THE RESCUE To remove pet hair from upholstered furniture, pull on a pair of latex gloves, dampen them, and sweep your hands over the upholstery. The hair will bunch up and then is easy to remove with your fingers. Brush any excess hair off your gloves into the trash can, or rinse it off in the sink. Specialized tools are available at your pet store for the removal of pet hair, too, including squeegee-like wands and velvety mitts.

To pluck pet hair off your clothing, tear off 8 inches of packing tape, wrap it around your fingers sticky side out, and pat at the offending hair.

PUT WIPES EVERYWHERE If your dog or cat is your best friend, then disposable wipes are a close second. Station a cylinder of wipes in your bathroom, your kitchen, at each door, and in the glove box of your car. They'll be handy not only for quick hair cleanups but also to clean off paws as your pets come in the door. If you have large dogs, keep old towels near the door for wiping wet or muddy feet.

Speaking of paws, Peterson says they'll pick up less dirt in the first place if you trim the fur between and around your dog's toes with a small pair of scissors. Shorter toenails on your pet also pick up less dirt, so keep them clipped.

DOES FIDO PASS THE SNIFF TEST?

One of the great mysteries of the universe is why dogs like to roll around in certain disgusting substances they find outside. If your dog is suddenly sporting a new manure-like fragrance, a bath might be all that he needs. If the foul odor persists, however, consult a veterinarian. A number of medical maladies produce foul odors, including skin, ear, dental, and anal problems.

Inside the house, dog beds and other favorite hangouts (your nicest couch, probably) are known to develop a funky odor over time. A number of spray and powder fabric fresheners are available in pet stores and supermarkets—choose an odor-absorbing product rather than a perfumey one that will just add to the stink. Also available: sacks of odor-absorbing chemical that you can hang in pet areas to keep them smelling fresh.

Cats add their own brand of stench to a household. You might be tempted to mount a regular household air freshener near your cat's litter box, but that could have disastrous consequences. Cats are notoriously finicky about odors, and if they are driven away from the litter box, they're going to find alternative places to pee and poop—none of them fun for you. For the same reason, don't use strong-smelling cleaners on your cat box. Warm water and dishwashing liquid will clean it nicely.

To keep your cats happy and odors down, scoop the waste out of the litter box into a plastic bag every day, tie it off, and throw it into your outdoor garbage can. (The plastic has not been made that can totally contain this brand of stench, so get it out of the house.) You also have to totally replace the litter with a certain frequency. If you're using as many litter boxes as you have cats (recommended), then clay litter will need changing at least twice a week, and the modern clumping litters can stretch for 2 weeks or 3 weeks. So in the name of cheating, see if your kitty will go for the newfangled stuff.

To make the changing process simple and to keep the inside of the box clean, use a plastic litter box liner with a drawstring top. You just lift the whole mess out of the pan, throw it away, and install a new liner. (Perform this air-fouling operation outside if possible.) Before you put fresh litter into the box, pour a thin layer of baking soda into the bottom. This will help absorb odors without repelling Muffy. Or cruise the aisles of your local pet store, where you'll find any number of other nonoffensive products for absorbing cat box odors, including sprays and granules that you sprinkle over the litter.

Now you're ready. With a little training, some modest expenditures, and a few crafty measures to throw a barrier between you and the nasty stuff, you can embrace your beloved youngsters and pets without fear. Ain't love grand!

Index

FIVE
MINUTES
IN
HEAVEN

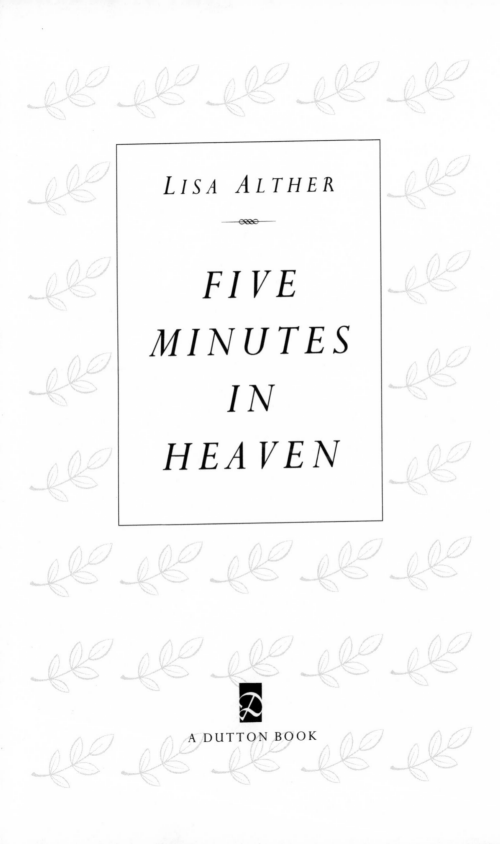

LISA ALTHER

FIVE

MINUTES

IN

HEAVEN

A DUTTON BOOK

DUTTON

Published by the Penguin Group
Penguin Books USA Inc., 375 Hudson Street, New York, New York 10014, U.S.A.
Penguin Books Ltd, 27 Wrights Lane, London W8 5TZ, England
Penguin Books Australia Ltd, Ringwood, Victoria, Australia
Penguin Books Canada Ltd, 10 Alcorn Avenue, Toronto, Ontario, Canada M4V 3B2
Penguin Books (N.Z.) Ltd, 182–190 Wairau Road, Auckland 10, New Zealand

Penguin Books Ltd, Registered Offices: Harmondsworth, Middlesex, England

First published by Dutton, an imprint of Dutton Signet,
a division of Penguin Books USA Inc.
Distributed in Canada by McClelland & Stewart Inc.

First Printing, May, 1995
1 3 5 7 9 10 8 6 4 2

Grateful acknowledgment is made to the following for permission to reprint from previously published material:

Frank Music Corporation: Excerpt from "Unchained Melody," lyrics by Hy Zaret, music by Alex North. © 1955 (renewed) Frank Music Corp. All rights reserved.

Gold Hill Music, Inc.: Excerpt from "Love the One You're With" by Stephen Stills. © 1970 Gold Hill Music, Inc. (ASCAP). All rights administered by this music corporation for the world. All rights reserved internationally. © secured. Used by permission.

Irving Music, Inc.: Excerpt from "Somebody to Love" by Darby Slick. © 1969 Irving Music, Inc. (BMI). All rights reserved internationally. © secured. Used by permission.

Satsuma Music and Becky Hobbs Music: Excerpt from "You Wanna Be Loved" by Lewis Anderson and Becky Hobbs. © 1976 Satsuma Music and Becky Hobbs Music. All rights reserved.

Webster Music Co.: Excerpt from "Twelfth of Never" by Paul F. Webster. © Webster Music Co. All rights reserved.

REGISTERED TRADEMARK—MARCA REGISTRADA

LIBRARY OF CONGRESS CATALOGING-IN-PUBLICATION DATA:
Alther, Lisa.
Five minutes in heaven / Lisa Alther.
p.   cm.
ISBN 0-525-93893-1
I. Title.
PS3551.L78F58   1995
813'.54—dc20
94-39252
CIP

Printed in the United States of America
Set in Perpetua

Designed by Steven N. Stathakis

This book is printed on acid-free paper. ∞

For Jody,
Scout,
and Dill

The only victory in love is flight.
—NAPOLÉON

PROLOGUE

TWO MEN LIFTED A GOAT, hooves wrapped with rope, from the trunk of a blue sedan. As they carried him across the tiled courtyard below, his bearded mouth fell open and he began to pant, . eyes rolling wildly.

The French would eat anything that couldn't outrun them, Jude reflected, recalling the weekend market, on rue Mouffetard, near her apartment during her junior year abroad from Vanderbilt. It had featured rows of glistening kidneys, livers, hearts, and tongues in graduated sizes. An entire aviary of birds had hung by their wrung necks, feathered wings limp by their sides. Rabbits still bearing fur had been slit down their bellies and laid open for inspection. But as Simon once said of his fellow Englishmen, no nation that loves animals will ever have a great cuisine.

Jude lit a cigarette and sank into a cushioned wicker chair in the sunlight coming through the glass doors of her sixth-floor walk-up. Still, Paris had a lot going for it. For one thing, it wasn't New York. And having spent the past several months spooning crushed Popsicles into Anna's mouth in her hospital bed at the Roosevelt, she welcomed the change.

It had all begun that night on Simon's deck near Provincetown when the wind shifted to the north, swirling the sand and frothing the surf. Anna had just died. Jude had spent the afternoon pacing the beach, studying how the hue of the sea altered in response to the sky, just as Anna's eyes had altered according to her moods and her surroundings.

When Jude got tired of walking, she scrambled up a dune, scooped out a hollow in the sand, and lay facedown, fitting her frame into its yielding contours as though it were Anna's body. She lay like that for several hours, eyes shut, hands beneath her thighs, listening to the breakers crash, and the foam hiss on the damp sand, and the seagulls shriek, and the dune grasses clash like a knife fight. And remembering the time she and Anna sneaked away from a conference in Boston to race horses down the beach, pounding through the surf, then sliding off their backs to watch from atop a dune as gleaming black whales dove and spouted against the far horizon.

As the sky turned to gore, she wandered home to Simon's tactful chatter and fortifying supper of roast chicken and mashed potatoes. They spread the dishes across the outside table and sat facing the darkening sea. As the tepid night air stirred Simon's black curls, they reminisced about Sandy and his operas, Anna and her poems, the delights of love, and the longing that won't quit when it's taken away.

Then Jasmine arrived, wearing a turban and gold ear hoops, en route to Paris. She strode across the deck, trailed by three young assistants, two women and a man, each dressed in gleaming white trousers and Mondrian tops, as though about to board a yacht at

Cannes. Jasmine was wearing a batik lavalava that made her resemble one of the exquisitely petite stewardesses on Singapore Airlines during Jude's interminable flight to Australia a few months earlier to speak on a panel about feminist editing at the Adelaide Festival.

While Jude subdued her urge to grab a beach towel from the railing and cover up her dingy gray gym shorts and Whale Watch T-shirt, Simon and Jasmine pressed alternate cheeks several times and gazed into each other's eyes as though they had only ten minutes left to live. Jasmine's father had fought with the French Resistance, and Simon's father had been his liaison officer at British intelligence. After the war, their families had visited back and forth across the Channel, and now Simon and Jasmine sold each other translation rights to their respective firms' books. Jude had first met Jasmine with Simon at the Frankfurt Book Fair. Since then, she'd run into her at the American Booksellers Association in Atlanta and the Feminist Book Fair in London and had spoken on a panel with her in Adelaide. She admired Jasmine's accessories, to say nothing of her intelligence and her élan.

Everyone sat down around Simon's glass-topped table to drink the Veuve Clicquot Jasmine had brought and to nibble Godiva chocolates. Alternating between Jasmine's basic English and Jude's and Simon's basic French, they discussed the Frenchwoman's gift for accessorizing, whether it was innate or acquired. Jude described her own bafflement when faced with a scarf. How did Jasmine know what size to pick for which location? Did French mothers give their daughters knot-tying lessons? And what about shoes? Jude had never seen Jasmine wear the same pair twice. Either their color matched or complemented her clothing, or they had some arresting feature like silver heels or straps that crisscrossed her ankles. At that moment, she was wearing golden stack-heeled sandals with thongs between the toes.

"Look at me," demanded Jude, holding up her sandy bare feet with their unpainted toenails. "I'm even underdressed tonight."

"But my dear Jude," said Jasmine, watching her with dark liquid eyes like melted chocolate chips, "you are famous for that. It is your trademark."

Jude blinked. "It is?" Her goal had always been to dress so appropriately as to pass unnoticed.

"Yes, one admires so deeply your indifference to fashion." Jasmine's gaze appeared ingenuous, but her eyes wrinkled slightly at the corners with a certain ironic amusement.

Simon was struggling to hide a smile.

"Thank you," said Jude uncertainly.

The soft sea breeze had mounted to a moaning gale, and the beach towels on the railing were whipping and snapping like flags in a windstorm. They moved inside. As Simon built a fire in his fieldstone fireplace, Jude showed the others through the house, with its walls of glass looking out on the dunes and its giant hand-hewn beams from an old barn in Vermont. The guests seemed a bit embarrassed as they peered into Simon's bathroom with its giant whirlpool tub, reminding Jude that house tours were an American phenomenon.

As Jasmine and her entourage were about to depart in a fog of Eau de Quelquechose for their guest house in Provincetown, she rested her magenta fingertips on Jude's forearm and offered her a job in Paris picking foreign fiction for translation. Jude was too bewildered to reply.

"So what do you think about my going to Paris?" Jude asked Simon as they propped their feet up on the fireplace ledge to commence a postmortem. The orange flames were dancing in Simon's neon-green eyes, converting the irises into small flaring kaleidoscopes.

"Go, Jude," said Simon as he munched a mousse-filled chocolate seashell. "Simon says go. But leave your corpse collection at home. Life is for the living."

This seemed generous of him, since Jude had been living with him and working for him in Manhattan for over a decade. But maybe he was as sick of her grief over Anna as she was.

"What was that nasty crack concerning my wardrobe all about?" she asked.

Simon smiled. "It means she likes you."

Jude gave an astonished laugh.

"If people bore her, she ignores them. When they intrigue her, she provokes them. Like a cat toying with a mouse."

"Charming. And exactly why is it you think I should work for her?"

"A change of venue would do you good. Some new faces and new neuroses might take your mind off the old ones."

IN ANY CASE, here she was now, trapped in the middle of a Kodachrome postcard, the city spread out below her from the dark highrises of La Défense to the domed Panthéon, the Seine snaking through the center, side-winding past the feet of the Eiffel Tower. Despite her year here during college, she'd never before seen this astonishing view, having passed her days in dusty classrooms on the Left Bank listening to lectures on European history and continental philosophy, and her nights in movie theaters working on her fluency.

In his letters to her mother during the war, which Jude had perused as a child, her father had described seeing this panorama from the square before Sacré Coeur. He had also described being driven by his sergeant through the streets of Pigalle, at the base of the butte where Jude now sat. He had been in the grip of pneumonia, lost and feverish and searching for a hospital. Gaunt women and children clamored around the jeep when his driver stopped to ask for directions. A young woman bared her breast and held it out to them in the icy

wind. An urchin perched on the running board and began to scrub
their combat boots with a filthy rag. Jude's father handed them all his
francs and cigarettes before desperately speeding away.

The sun was hot. Sweat popping out at her hairline, Jude stubbed
out her cigarette and threw open the glass doors, shivering in the
breeze that was stirring the creamy chestnut blossoms below. She
plopped back down in her chair.

*On the horizon, the Smokies formed a rolling blue rim notched with
knobs like the knuckles on a fist. Down in the valley, the lazy ocher river
drifted toward the mountains, carrying a leafy poplar branch on which perched
five cawing crows. Wisps of cloud were floating across the summer sky, furling
like breaking waves. Gradually, they assembled themselves into Molly's features,
bits of cerulean becoming her irises. She said in her voice that had always
been too husky for such a small person,* "You may think I'm dead, Jude, but
I'm not."

Jude jerked alert. Molly's features were still there, projected
against the silver-blue haze above the Bois de Boulogne. Apparently,
Jude couldn't escape her, even by crossing the ocean two decades
later.

"Fine," snapped Jude. "But where the hell are you?"

As Molly's face evaporated, Jude groped for another cigarette.

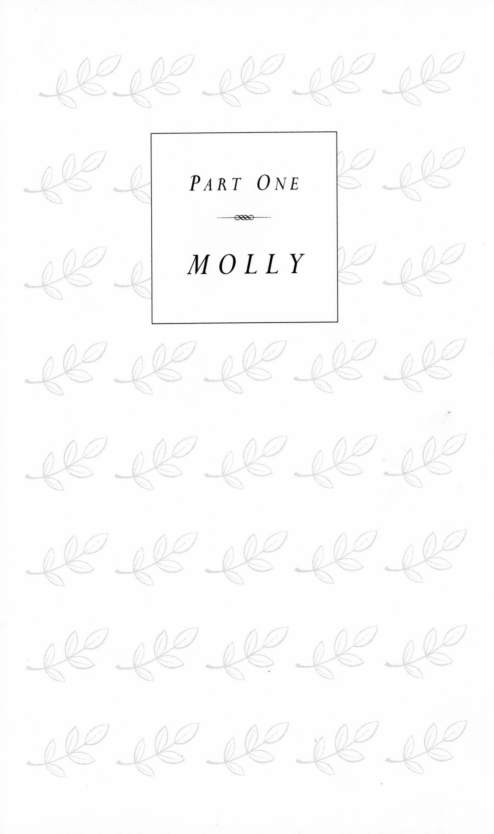

PART ONE

MOLLY

JUDE PEDALED NEXT DOOR on her purple tricycle to inspect the new cellar hole. Careening down the mound of orange clay, training wheels spinning, dark braids lashing like reins on a runaway horse, came a bare-chested girl in shorts. Her bicycle flipped halfway down, hurling her headfirst to the bottom. She jumped up, laughing, chest and cheek streaked with clay like Indian war paint. Righting her bicycle, she stroked its saddle, murmuring, "Easy, boy. It's okay."

"Are you all right?" asked Jude. She had never met another girl who didn't wear a shirt. Her chest was really tan, too, as though she never wore one. Whereas Jude had pale patches from the top her father made her wear at the golf club pool.

"This is my stallion," she replied. "I call him Stormy because he runs like the wind. What's yours called?"

Looking down at her tricycle, Jude said, "I don't know really."

She felt embarrassed that she'd never thought of her tricycle as a horse. She could hear Ace Kilgore barking commands to the Commie Killers in the field across the street. They all rode bicycles, too, making them rear up on their hind wheels to mount curbs. Ace could even balance like that and then twirl around in midair and race off in the opposite direction. Jude was the only kid in the neighborhood who still rode a tricycle. But her father had promised her a bicycle with training wheels for her upcoming birthday.

A blond woman in a sundress covered with flowers the color of tangerine peels appeared from behind the mound, long skirt swaying as she picked her way across the clay in high-heeled white sandals. "My gracious, Molly, what have you done to yourself now?" Taking a flimsy handkerchief with eyelet edges from her white handbag, she dabbed at the clay on Molly's cheek. "Goodness gracious, what am I going to do with my wild child?"

Molly shoved her hand away. "Momma, don't be such a worrywart."

Molly's mother smiled at Jude. "Well, hello there. You must be our new neighbor?"

"What's your name?" asked Molly, leaning over to pick at a scab on her kneecap.

"Jude." A screen door slammed down the block, and Jude could hear ice cubes clinking in glasses on someone's back porch.

"That's a nice name," said Molly's mother. "I'm Mrs. Elkins and this is Molly."

"How do you do, Mrs. Elkins," said Jude, as her father had just taught her.

Molly was watching a white mare's tail flick a far-off mountain-top. The rubber band had broken on one of her braids, which was slowly unplaiting like blacksnakes coming out of hibernation in the spring.

Mrs. Elkins smiled. "Well, my goodness, Jude, aren't you polite, now. I can see you're going to be a good influence on Molly."

Molly's blue eyes narrowed and shifted to gray.

Back home, Jude stood on a chair before the bathroom mirror, wiping at her cheek with a Kleenex and saying in a sugary voice, "Goodness gracious, what am I going to do with my wild child?" Then she pushed the hand away with her other hand, saying, "Oh, Momma, don't be such a worrywart."

"What you doing, Miss Judith?" called Clementine from the kitchen.

"Nothing. Playing." She wondered if Clementine could be persuaded to wipe her cheek with a Kleenex. Probably not. She skipped into the kitchen, where Clementine sat humming "Take Time to Be Holy" and snapping beans for supper. Jude tried to climb onto her aproned lap, but she straightened her legs so that Jude slid down them to the linoleum. She lay there tracing with a finger the grouting between the fake red bricks. "You love me best, don't you, Clementine?"

"I likes you, Miss Judith. But I got childrens all my own what needs me to love them best."

"But so do I."

Clementine had rolled her stockings to just below her knees. A ladder like a tiny cat's cradle ran down one calf and disappeared into her giant white oxford. She said her mother had called her Clementine because of her feet, huge even when she was a baby. Sometimes she sang Jude the song for which she'd been named: "Light she was, and like a fairy/And her shoes were number nine./Wearing boxes without topses,/Sandals were for Clementine."

"You got your daddy to love you best."

"But he doesn't. He loves Momma best. But she doesn't love him best, or else she wouldn't have gone away."

Clementine paused in midsnap to look at Jude stretched out on the linoleum. "Sugar, I done told you that the good Lord took your momma home two years ago."

"But where is she? Where's His house at?"

"In heaven with the angels."

"Well, I wish He'd take me there, too."

"Hush now, honey. That ain't for me and you to say. The good Lord takes us when He wants us and where He wants us."

"How come?" Jude stood up and draped her arm across Clementine's shoulders, one skinny leg straight and the other bent, a flamingo in a red linoleum marsh. Sniffing, she picked up Clementine's familiar scent of furniture polish, snuff, and the vanilla extract she dabbed behind her ears when her husband was about to pick her up.

Clementine glanced at her. "Sugar, go put you on a shirt, why don't you? Little girls wear shirts."

"I don't want to be a girl." With her fingertip, Jude touched a tiny silver curl, like a spring from a broken watch, which was peeking out from beneath the red bandanna Clementine tied around her head like a knitted winter cap.

"But that's what the good Lord made you. It ain't no choice. Just like it ain't no choice if your skin be brown or white."

ONCE JUDE PROVED THAT she could pee standing up, the Commie Killers were forced to accept her as a member, even though she was a girl and the youngest kid in the neighborhood. But fair was fair, and the Commie Killers' mission was to spread justice throughout the land. They consoled themselves with her promise to hide them one at a time in her father's office at her house as he examined patients. You had to lurk outside the door until he went into the bathroom between appointments. Then you slithered across the floor on your belly and slid beneath the huge maroon leather sofa. You could hear him discussing all kinds of interesting things with naked people you later saw walking around town fully clothed. From a certain angle, you could even catch a glimpse of the examining table.

On the day of her initiation, Jude concealed her tricycle in the pine grove by the path to Ace Kilgore's headquarters. Someone dug a cellar hole in the field across the street from Sandy Andrews's house before going bankrupt. Ace and his gang had constructed a network of trenches, bunkers, and tunnels in the abandoned hills of red clay, like an ant colony. Parents tried to prevent their sons from playing with Ace. He threw snowballs with rocks in them at little children. And he tied twine with tin cans on one end to dogs' tails. Once, he and his platoon pushed a junked refrigerator onto the train tracks in the valley, causing the engine to derail. Jude's father said he might get sent to reform school. Every kid in the neighborhood tried to avoid meeting his eyes, which were a dull shoe polish black. If he caught you looking at him, you became the target of an interrogation regarding your secret espionage activities for the Russians.

Nevertheless, every boy in Tidewater Estates sneaked away to Commie Killer meetings except Sandy Andrews, who was a sissy. They made their mothers rip the patches off their fathers' old army uniforms and sew them on their jacket sleeves, and they pinned their fathers' multicolored bars on their chest pockets. Ace had the most because his father had been a hero in the war. Jude made Clementine retrieve her father's olive uniform jacket from the attic. It stank of mothballs, but it sported the requisite bars and patches, which Clementine agreed to stitch onto her jacket if her father gave his permission. Instead, he forbade her to have anything to do with Ace Kilgore.

Jude used to play with the neighborhood girls at Noreen Worth's, but she was tired of diapering dolls with handkerchiefs and rolling around the playhouse floor speaking in tongues. Besides, Noreen, whose father was a Holiness preacher, claimed Jude was a bad

Baptist because at Jude's church people just sat in their pews and kept
quiet. She had also played a few times with Clementine's daughters
in Riverbend. But all they ever did was jump rope, turning two ropes
really fast and chanting things Jude couldn't understand. Whenever
Jude tried to jump in, she ended up on the ground, trussed like a calf
for branding. She found it hard to believe that these were the children
Clementine loved more than herself. So, despite her father's stern
injunction, Jude found herself irresistibly drawn to the Commie
Killers.

The hideout was dark inside, apart from the light from a white
candle stuck in the clay floor. The boys were wearing only Jockey
briefs, so Jude hurriedly stripped down to her white cotton panties.
Ace passed out several round Quaker Oats boxes and wooden spoons.
As some drummed, others danced. Watching from the corner of her
eye, Jude copied their writhing, hopping movements, like an Indian
war dance. Ace's father's colonel hat with the golden eagle above the
brim kept slipping down over his eyes. So excited was Jude finally to
be a full-fledged defender of the American Way that she had goose
bumps all over her flesh. She thought she could hear a cat yowling
from the corner of the cave.

The boys were kneeling in the dirt as Ace leapt from one to
another, thrusting his hips against their briefs with sharp jabs while
the drummers pounded a syncopated beat. His face was dripping sweat
in the candlelight and his licorice eyes gaped like the sockets in the
skull on her father's office counter.

Jude got down on her knees, but Ace pushed her over with his
foot. "Girls can't do this," he growled in a strange voice. "Men do
this."

Then they crouched in a circle around the candle and Ace placed
a cherry bomb in his palm. Gravely, he extended it to Jude. She took
it. His lieutenant Jerry Crawford, a tall, gawky boy who had smiled

shyly at Jude when no one else was looking, carried a cage over from the shadows. Inside was a matted barn cat Jude had seen lurking around the neighborhood. Her eyes were flashing chartreuse. One of her ears had been ripped off during a fight and the tip of her tail bent at a right angle. Several boys put on work gloves, dragged her from the cage, and pinned her against the dirt floor. Jude stroked her forehead with an index finger.

"Don't pet Hiroshima," said Ace. "She's been very bad."

"Why do you call her Hiroshima?" asked Jude.

Ace grinned, white teeth flashing like Chiclets in the shadow cast by the visor of his colonel hat.

"Why has she been bad?"

"She's been stealing my dog's food. But you ask too many questions, little girl. Just shut up and shove that thing up her hole."

Jude looked at the red cherry bomb with the green wick, then at the snarling, struggling cat.

"If you want to be a Commie Killer," said Ace as he struck a match, "you have to do it. And you have to do it now."

As eerie shadows danced on the walls of clay like the flames of Hades, Jude looked at him with horrified comprehension. "No," she whispered. "Don't, Ace. Let her go. Please." She looked to Jerry, who was staring hard at the floor.

"Hurry up! Do it!" ordered the boys as the cat hissed and howled.

Jude scrambled to her feet and ran toward the doorway, clutching the cherry bomb.

"Go bake cookies with that faggot Sandy Andrews!" someone yelled.

"If you tell," called Ace, "we'll hunt you down and do this to you."

Jude stumbled through the maze of trenches, sliding on the slick orange clay. She'd get Clementine. Clementine would make them stop.

She heard a bang. Slipping and falling, she lay for a moment in the sticky mud in her underpants, too stunned to get up.

Pedaling her tricycle fast toward home, she could hardly see the sidewalk through her angry tears. She had saved herself and left the cat to die. She was not a Commie Killer, she was a coward. And if she told, Ace would do that to her next. She couldn't jump rope, and she couldn't speak in tongues. The Commie Killers were not champions of democracy, they were murderers. She would always be alone forever and ever in this horrible place where bullies tortured the weak just for fun. If only she could be safe in heaven with her mother. She stopped pedaling to wipe her wet cheeks with a muddy forearm.

"Don't cry, Jude," said a husky voice beside her. "I'll be your friend."

Jude opened her eyes. Molly was standing there, barefoot, shirtless, smoky eyes troubled, hand on Jude's handlebars.

"You better not," said Jude. "I'm in big trouble. I may be killed."

"I don't care. I'll help you."

As Jude stood in the aisle leading to the altar, the adult choir in their white robes and red cowls were singing "Jesus Loves the Little Children." The dreaded Ace Kilgore was directly in front of her. His brown hair had been furrowed like a plowed field by the teeth of a comb, and he was wearing a red polka-dot necktie. It matched that of his father, who was the usher assigned that morning to lead the children to the Sunday school building.

Ace and his father also had matching black eyes that seemed just to absorb the rainbow light through the stained-glass windows rather than to reflect it as everyone else's eyes did. The other adults tried to avoid Mr. Kilgore's stare just as the kids avoided Ace's. He was always buttonholing Jude's father outside the church, trying to argue about Senator McCarthy. Mr. Kilgore's voice would grow louder and louder and his face more and more red as he described the agents of evil who were infesting the country like vermin.

Spotting Jude in line behind him, Ace leaned back to whisper, "We gonna get you, Goody Two-shoes."

Jude flinched, picturing the cat cowering in the dirt.

Molly, standing beside her, said, "Just shut up, goofball."

Ace looked at her, startled. "Who are *you?*"

"That's for me to know and you to find out."

"Well, we'll get you, too, ugly. And lynch you with those long black braids of yours."

The choir was singing: ". . . red and yellow, black and white, they are precious in His sight. . . ."

"You and what army, cat killer?" asked Molly, whose irises had shifted to a dangerous battle gray.

Ace narrowed his eyes and glared at Jude. "Don't you worry, little lady. The Commie Killers know how to take care of rats, and friends of rats." Grabbing his tie, he pulled it upward, nooselike, mouth lolling open and tongue hanging out.

"Why don't you go eat a vomit sandwich?" suggested Molly as their lines parted before the carpeted steps leading to the altar, on which stood a golden cross with Christ writhing in agony. Jude was impressed by her new friend's courage. No one ever talked like that to the Kilgores.

"MAYBE THERE'S SOME WAY to make a tunnel fall down with the Commie Killers inside it," mused Molly as they sat at a long table coloring pictures of Jesus tending baby lambs.

"I think we should ask Sandy Andrews to help us," said Jude.

"He's a child progeny." She selected a fat ocher crayon for Jesus' hair and beard.

"What's that?"

"He taught himself to read and write when he was four, so they let him skip first and second grade. My dad says he's so smart that they may have to send him away to school. I'm glad I'm not that smart."

"Do you think he'd help girls?"

"Maybe. He doesn't have any friends. He doesn't like to kill things."

"WHY ARE SOME PEOPLE so mean?" Jude asked Clementine, licking chocolate frosting off a beater while the morning sun through the kitchen window turned the red linoleum to orange. When she woke up that morning, her stomach had clenched with dread. The Commie Killers were going to get her. They were going to do to her what they'd done to that cat. Then she remembered her new friend, Molly, who had promised to help her, and she began to feel a faint flicker of hope.

"The good Lord made them that way so the righteous could be tested."

"Like a test at the hospital?"

"Like a test ever day of the year. You gots to be kind to them what treats you cruel." Clementine was spreading the frosting with swirling strokes of her spatula, making chocolate waves.

"How come?"

" 'Cause one fine day they gets ashamed of acting so ugly and they turns to Jesus. And then you wins yourself a golden crown."

Jude studied Clementine, picturing a golden crown atop her red bandanna head cloth. "But what if it's not you they're ugly to? What if they're ugly to something else?"

"What ugliness you seen, Miss Judith?" She paused to study Jude, who was winding her tongue around a beater blade to get at the frosting in back, which was still gritty with sugar.

"Nothing. I'm just wondering."

"A good person will put up with ugliness coming at themselves. But you gots to fight for them what's small and weak." She narrowed her eyes suspiciously at Jude.

To escape her X-ray vision, Jude dropped the beater in the sink and dashed out the kitchen door. Molly was riding Stormy down the sidewalk. She had attached playing cards to the spokes with clothespins to make a whirring sound, and she was wearing sunglasses and a winter cap with earflaps. She landed her airplane on the sidewalk in front of Sandy Andrews's house, elaborate whooshing and sputtering sounds emitting from her mouth.

Sandy was watering the foundation shrubs with a hose. Jude noticed that he was wearing socks and sandals instead of the black high-tops required by the Commie Killers. The shrubs had been clipped into triangles and cubes, like dark green building blocks.

"Hey, Sandy," called Jude from her tricycle, which she'd decided to name Lightning. "This is Molly. She's moved into that new house next door to mine." Molly was hanging her cap by its chin strap from her handlebars.

"Hi," said Sandy, not looking up.

"We're in trouble." Jude dismounted from Lightning. "Will you help us?"

He glanced at her irritably. "How can I say when I don't know what it is?"

"It'd be dangerous for you if we told you."

Sandy put his hand on his skinny hip and said nothing, studying the stream of water from the nozzle, the sun backlighting his blond head and casting a shadow over his face, which was freckled like a permanent case of the measles. He had a cowlick like the thumbprint of a giant to one side of his hair just above his forehead, which gave an interesting lilt to his crew cut.

"Ace might kill you," added Jude.

Sandy looked at her. "That fascist? Just let him try."

"What's a fascist?" asked Molly, tying Stormy to a yew branch by the fringe on his handgrips.

"Never mind. Come up in my tree house, where no one can hear us."

Sandy had never before let Jude visit his tree house. It had a retractable stairway that could be locked, and only Sandy knew the combination. It also turned out to have beige carpeting, a shelf of the *World Book Encyclopedia*, and a shortwave radio with as many dials and switches as Dr. Frankenstein's laboratory. Sandy said he'd built it from a kit. The walls were papered with postcards bearing the call numbers of ham radio operators he'd talked with all over the world. Half a dozen chessboards with games in progress were set up along one wall. A telephone sat on the rug.

"Come over here," said Sandy. He showed them a telescope on a tripod, pointed out the window. Through it, Jude could see right down into the Commie Killer trenches across the street, a grid of red clay gashes and hillocks stretching the length of the field. When Sandy moved the tripod to another window, she could see Mr. Starnes down in the valley, mowing the alfalfa by the river on his ancient wheezing tractor. He was wearing a battered felt hat low over his ears and was spitting tobacco juice from the corner of his mouth. Downriver, his wife was breaking off blossoms in the tobacco patch, the weathered wooden curing shed behind her. And beyond them stretched the mountains, range after range, separated by deep coves and valleys where creeks were flowing and farmers were mowing and a train mounded high with tree trunks and coal chunks was crawling along like a fat, lazy caterpillar.

"BUT I CAN'T DO IT myself," concluded Sandy after explaining his plan to the girls, who were sitting cross-legged on the carpet by the phone. "My mother won't let me out of the house after dark."

"Mine won't, either," said Molly, "but I can sneak out."

Jude's father rarely noticed where she was after dark because he was so busy changing dressings on patients in his office, or counseling them on the phone about their sunburns and ingrown toenails, or writing up their records at his desk, or rushing to the emergency room to stitch up their wounds from knife fights and motorcycle wrecks.

"Maybe you can spend the night at my house," said Molly as they climbed down the tree-house ladder, "so we can sneak out together."

As they stepped onto the lawn, Sandy raised the ladder behind them, like the drawbridge of a castle.

WHILE JUDE WATCHED FROM the kitchen doorway, Mr. Starnes, in faded overalls and clay-caked work boots, got out of a rusted red pickup truck and lifted a burlap-wrapped ham from the back. Jude grimaced. Clementine would take slices off it and soak them in water to get the salt out, and Jude and her father would have to eat it with grits and biscuits for the rest of their lives. Mrs. Starnes, wearing a floral housedress and leather oxfords with thin, white socks, carried a foil-wrapped cake. Since Clementine had already gone home to Riverbend for the night, Jude went out on the back porch to greet them.

"My dad's on the phone right now. He'll be out presently."

"My gracious, Jude, haven't you grown up, now!" said Mrs. Starnes. Her hairdo looked as though she'd removed her rollers and forgotten to comb out the hair.

"Yessum."

"I declare, if you don't look just like your daddy," said Mr. Starnes, propping one boot against the bottom porch step.

Jude frowned, preferring to look like her mother, since her father was nearly bald. Mr. Starnes's boot smelled of manure.

"Where's your shirt at tonight, honey?" asked Mrs. Starnes.

Jude shrugged, crossing her arms over her scrawny chest. "It's too hot."

"I'll bet you a dime you won't run around without no shirt in a few years here," chuckled Mr. Starnes. His eyes were as washed-out as his overalls, like clear cat's-eye marbles.

It had rained at the end of the afternoon, forked tongues of lightning striking the distant mountaintops as though the sky were a lake swarming with angry cottonmouths. Then, as the sun shone through a gap in the banks of black clouds, a rainbow had appeared, arcing across the river right down into Mr. Starnes's tobacco shed. At Sunday school, the preacher said a rainbow was God's proof that, even after trying to drown everybody for being so wicked, He forgave them. Sometimes God acted like a big baby.

But now the sky had cleared and the sun had set, turning the faraway mountains the color of grape jelly. Bullfrogs had started to croak in the reeds along the riverbank and fireflies were flickering like birthday candles among the leafy branches of the sweet gums in the valley below.

"That daddy of yours," said Mrs. Starnes, "we think he's pretty special."

"Yessum," said Jude. Now she'd have to hear about each stitch her father and grandfather had sewn in these people's mutilated bodies, each ancestor whose life they'd saved by operating by lantern light with a carving knife on a kitchen table in a remote mountain cabin during a thunderstorm, after a journey across a swollen creek on horseback in the middle of a midwinter night.

"Yessir," said Mr. Starnes, "I recollect the day my paw lost his arm in the combine. . . ."

Jude's father appeared in the doorway in his usual white dress shirt, open at the throat, sleeves rolled to the elbows. Sighing with relief, Jude picked up the foil cake from the porch floor. "Thank you, Mrs. Starnes. My daddy and me loves your cakes." Sniffing the foil, she detected caramel frosting, her favorite.

Her father looked at her with a raised eyebrow to indicate that she'd made a grammar mistake. As she carried the cake into the kitchen and cut herself a large slice, she tried to figure out what it was. Shrugging, she went into the back hall, where she'd been playing Ocean Liner, which Molly had taught her that afternoon. They'd pasted numbers on all the doors for cabins. Striding down the hallway munching her cake, she lurched from side to side on her peg leg. A storm was brewing in the nor'west and it was time to batten down the hatches, whatever they might be. She steadied herself with her free hand against the cases that held her father's arrowhead collection. On his days off, they drove the jeep down into the valley and dug up the moist black silt by the river. As they sifted the soil, he told her about the people who had lived in the valley long ago—the Mound Builders, the Hopewells, the Copena, the Cherokees, each tribe replacing the previous one, all the way back to the dawn of time, when the valley had formed the floor of an inland ocean full of bizarre sea creatures. When the ocean dried up, the Great Buzzard swooped down from heaven to scoop out the mountain coves with its wing tips.

The arrowheads and grinding stones had been made by the Nunnehi, the Cherokee Immortals, Jude's ancestors who lived underneath the mountains and at the bottom of the river and who came to help their descendants when they were in trouble. In autumn, when the whining winds from the north whirled the leaves off the trees, you could sometimes hear them murmuring to one another in the Wildwoods. And in the summer when you cast your line into the river for fish, if it got snagged, you knew the Nunnehi had grabbed it just to remind you that they were always there. And sometimes when the water was really calm and the breeze stirred tiny corduroy ripples across its surface, you could catch a glimpse of the roofs of their houses on the river floor.

As the Starnes's truck pulled away, Jude's father took her sticky hand to lead her into the den, unaware that the swells were running high and their ship was about to capsize. "My daddy and *I love* your cakes," he said. After turning on the radio, he sank into his brown leather armchair. John Cameron Swayze was talking about soldiers being brainwashed by the Communists in Korea. "Oh, Lord," her father said with a sigh. "Poor, suffering humanity."

"Why do they always bring us those awful hams?" asked Jude.

"That's how they're paying me for Mr. Starnes's appendectomy."

"Money would be nicer." She stroked the back of his chair. The leather was crazed with age cracks like the inside of an ice cube.

"No doubt. But they don't have any. Besides, some people consider country ham a delicacy."

"Not me."

"Yes, I know." He smiled.

"Daddy, why are some people so mean?" Jude straddled the arm of his chair, facing the back. It was her new horse, named Wild Child. The other arm was Molly's, which she'd named Blaze. That afternoon, they had been lassoing Molly's boxer, Sidney, in midgallop with pieces of Clementine's clothesline. Time after time, they played

"Git Along, Little Dogie" on the record player—until Clementine marched in and turned it off, announcing, "Miss Judith, if I hear 'yippy tie yay, tie yo' one more time, I gonna bust all your daddy's furniture into firewood and chase y'all round the backyard with a carving knife." Impressed, the girls had switched to Ocean Liner.

"Well, I guess they're mean because they're unhappy."

"But you're unhappy, and you're not mean."

He looked at her. "What makes you think I'm unhappy, baby?"

"Because you miss Momma."

He frowned and lowered his head. "That's true. But I used to be happy when she was here. Maybe that's the difference. People who've never been happy are mean. The rest of us are just sad."

She could smell his aftershave lotion, like cinnamon toast. Leaning over, she licked his cheek. The stiff hairs prickled her tongue and the cinnamon lotion tasted disappointingly bitter, canceling out the sweetness of the caramel frosting.

"Don't, Jude," he said, frowning and wiping his cheek with his hand. "That tickles."

Wrinkling her nose, Jude tried to scrub the terrible taste off her tongue with the back of her hand. Then Wild Child reared, hurling her off his back and into her father's lap. Leaning her head against his chest, she shoved a thumb into her mouth and felt his heart thudding against her cheek like a frog's throat.

"Baby, don't suck your thumb, please. It'll push your front teeth out. You'll look like Bugs Bunny."

Jude giggled.

"Don't you think you should wear a shirt?" he asked. "You're getting to be a big girl now." He patted her pale smooth belly.

"I don't want to be a girl."

"How come?"

"Girls are too boring."

"So you want to be a boy?"

"No. Boys are too scary."

"Well, what do you want to be, then?"

"I want to be in heaven with my momma."

He said nothing. When Jude looked up, his eyes were wet and red.

"I have a friend," offered Jude. "She lives in the new house next door. She's named Molly. She's going to be in the second grade. She doesn't like shirts, either."

"That's good, baby. I'm glad there's someone in the neighborhood now who's closer to your own age. I don't want you playing with Ace Kilgore and those other big boys. They're too rough. Promise me you'll stay away from them?"

Jude said nothing for a long moment. She didn't like to lie. But she wasn't really lying, since she now meant to stay as far away from them as she could. "I promise," she finally said. "Can I spend the night at Molly's house sometime?" She twisted around in the chair until she was reclining in the crook of his arm.

"Sure. If it's okay with her parents." He was gazing at a photo on the end table—of Jude's mother in a low-cut gown, standing inside a wine bottle.

"Why's she inside that bottle?"

"She wasn't really. It's trick photography. It was an ad for a winery."

"She was pretty, wasn't she?"

"She was the most beautiful woman I've ever seen." He was looking at the far corner of the ceiling, where Clementine's dust mop had missed a spiderweb. "I was an intern in New York. I first saw her surrounded by photographers on a corner near Central Park. She was wearing this big old picture hat the wind kept trying to blow off.

I just stood there staring at her until she got annoyed and asked them to make me leave.''

Mr. Starnes had said Jude looked like her father. Did that mean she wasn't beautiful like her mother? ''Why did she have to die?''

''Well, I came back home from the war in France, and we were very happy to be together again. So we decided to give you a baby brother. But your mother's brain started bleeding. She became unconscious and the baby died in her stomach. And then she died.''

''But I didn't even want a baby brother.''

MOLLY'S MOTHER INSISTED THAT Molly say her prayers, even though Jude was there, so the three of them knelt by Molly's bedside, beneath the pink dotted swiss canopy, as Molly recited her blessing list, which included her bicycle, Stormy, and her dog, Sidney. She concluded, ''And God bless my new pal, Jude, and keep her safe from harm. Amen.''

''Do you want to say your prayers now?'' Mrs. Elkins asked Jude.

''I don't have any.''

''But you need prayers, Jude. It's easy. Just try.''

So Jude mumbled, ''God bless my dad, and Clementine. And Grandma. And my momma in heaven. And Mrs. Elkins. And God bless my new pal, Molly, and keep her safe. But not Ace Kilgore. Amen.''

Mrs. Elkins looked at Jude questioningly as she smoothed her blond pageboy with one hand. But then she just stood up and folded back the bedspread. ''Good night, sleep tight, and don't let those old mosquitoes bite!'' she called as she closed the door.

Molly and Jude scrambled up on the bed. Each grabbed a pillow. Every time Sidney tried to crawl onto the mattress, they beat him back with the pillows. The bed was a raft, adrift on an ocean full of ravenous sharks with flashing white teeth. Sidney crouched down on his front paws, cropped tail wagging frantically. He began to bark.

"Oh, shut up, Sidney," muttered Molly, dropping her pillow. "Sharks don't bark." She collapsed with a bounce on the mangled sheets.

Sidney crept up the bed and slithered between Molly and Jude, where he lay panting dolefully in time to the pulsing locusts outside. Molly's father had started snoring down the hall, like a monster growling in a cave. He looked like a monster, too, with dark, curly hair all over his arms and eyebrows that stuck straight out like the bristles of a toothbrush. Molly said he drove around to farms buying cowhides that got cut up and turned into belts at the tannery Sandy Andrews's father owned.

Molly went downstairs to the kitchen, wearing only her shorty pajama bottoms. When she returned, carrying two bowls, she paused for a moment, framed by the doorway, bare chest tanned and smooth except for two pink nipples like cinnamon valentine hearts. Her black hair, which Jude had never seen unbraided before, was floating around her face the way Jude's mother's hair did in a photo on Jude's bedside table. In that photo, she held Jude's chubby cheek against her own on Jude's first birthday. She had a white rose in her hair, perfect white teeth, and pale dreamy eyes.

"Why are you staring at me like that?" asked Molly when she reached the bed and handed Jude a bowl of raspberry sherbet.

"I didn't realize you were beautiful," replied Jude.

"I am not," said Molly, eyes blazing in the faint glow coming through the window from the streetlight. "If you want to be my friend, take it back right now."

Crossing her fingers, Jude said, "Okay, I take it back."

Leaning against the quilted headboard, they licked the tart sherbet off their spoons in a strained silence.

"Do you like God?" Jude finally asked.

"Sure. He's okay." Molly offered her spoon to Sidney, who daintily poked at the sherbet with his large pink tongue.

"I don't."

"How come?"

"He took my mother to His house. She wants to come back home now, but He won't let her."

Molly set her bowl on the bed for Sidney to finish. "Well, I guess I don't like Him anymore, either, then."

Jude decided that Molly was her new best friend.

Once the lights were off in all the houses down the street, they pulled on their shorts and tiptoed down the carpeted stairs and out the front door. The locusts were so loud that they seemed to be gathered inside Jude's head. Swarms of fireflies were making the star-specked night sky sparkle like a black diamond. Jude and Molly trotted across the straw-strewn lawn, the dew chilly on their bare feet, Sidney at their heels.

At Sandy's house, they found the hose coiled behind the foundation shrubs as Sandy had promised. Dragging it across the street, they stuck the nozzle into a Commie Killer trench. Then they re-crossed the street and turned on the faucet that protruded from the foundation bricks.

Crouched behind the geometrical yews, ducking a circling mosquito, Jude asked, "Why do you think Ace is so mean?"

"Momma says people are mean because they get up on the wrong side of bed in the morning," said Molly, arm draped across the panting Sidney.

Jude broke a piece off the tall triangular bush beside her and sniffed it. It smelled like the golden liquid Clementine mopped the kitchen linoleum with. She held it out for Molly to sniff. A hoot owl started calling in the Wildwoods.

Every time sleep threatened, one poked the other with an elbow and they gazed blearily at the constellations scrolling past overhead. Jude pointed out the Pleiades and told about how the Cherokees used to make would-be braves count the number of stars in the cluster. They discussed the difficulties of needing glasses before glasses had been invented. Then Molly explained that stars were actually light shining through holes in the night sky. Behind the black, everything was white.

"Maybe that's where your mother is," said Molly. "Behind the sky."

"Is that really true?" Jude asked. "Or did you make it up?"

"I can't remember."

At the first hint of dove gray in the eastern sky, as a pale silver sliver of crescent moon arced above the headstones in the cemetery on the hilltop, they turned off the faucet and dragged the hose into Sandy's parents' toolshed.

"VERY FUNNY," SAID ACE as the two girls pedaled past the abandoned construction site the next morning, purple circles under their eyes like bruises.

"What?" asked Molly.

"That." Ace pointed to the sea of orange mud where the Commie Killer headquarters had been.

"What happened?" asked Molly, blinking her baby blue eyes.

Jude chewed the inside of her lower lip to keep from grinning.

"You tell me, pukeface."

"Did it rain again last night?" asked Jude.

"Tell your parents to start saving for your funerals," said Ace, gazing at them through his opaque black eyes like Sergeant Friday on "Dragnet."

———

JUDE PEDALED LIGHTNING TO HER grandmother's large white brick house on the next block to welcome her home from her trip to Savannah for a Daughters of the Confederacy convention. "I told your granddaddy," she once explained to Jude, "if he expected me to leave behind my beautiful colonial Virginia, he'd have to build me a new dwelling place. I wasn't gonna live out my life in his hillbilly shack." After constructing his bride's neo-Georgian mansion and leasing the farmland in the valley to Mr. Starnes, Jude's grandfather sold off the rest of his family farm for house lots and a golf course. Her grandmother named the resulting development Tidewater Estates. Jude and her father now lived in the "hillbilly shack," a rambling house of chinked logs built by Jude's great-grandfather, a half-Cherokee herb doctor.

Jude remembered removing the knitted mitt from her grandfather's three wood so that he could tee up in his backyard and drive his golf ball across the river to the first green of the golf course, whose fairways scaled the foothills like a grassy roller-coaster track. Then he descended the cliff to the river's edge, put his golf bag in a boat, and rowed across the water to continue his game. Having been a left-handed bush league baseball pitcher before his conversion to medicine, he had a golf swing that was the envy of the county.

Following her husband's death the previous year, Jude's grandmother circled the globe twice on the *Queen Elizabeth*, sending Jude postcards and dolls from each country. Jude steamed the stamps off the cards and saved them in an album. And she removed the elaborate national costumes from the dolls to amputate limbs and extract organs. Then she stitched the incisions with needles Clementine threaded for her, as she had watched her father do when she went with him on house calls to hill farms.

Jude mounted the brick steps, white columns on either hand. Standing on tiptoe, she lifted the knocker hanging from the teeth of a huge golden lion head. A row of shiny cars waited by the curb, so her grandmother was probably having a club meeting. She went to one almost every day she was off the high seas—bridge club, garden club, Junior League, Bible study group, DAR. What Jude liked best about her grandmother was how glad she always seemed to see Jude. If you interrupted most adults when they were with other adults, they looked at you as though you were a skunk wandering in from the woods.

An unfamiliar young woman in a starched white uniform and ruffled black apron answered the door. "I reckon you be Miss Judith?" Her front teeth were gapped like a derelict picket fence.

Jude nodded. Her grandmother always hired farm girls from the part of Virginia where she herself had grown up. Her father had been chief of staff at the Confederate Veterans' Home on the outskirts of Richmond. They had lived on her mother's family farm on the Rappahannock River near Fredericksburg, which had supposedly been a land grant to her forebears from King James I for their agreeing to leave England. Jude's grandfather, descending like the Troll King from the misty mountains to the west, had done his residency at the Veterans' Home, wooing and winning the boss's daughter in the process.

"Your grandmaw, she's having her a Virginia Club meeting this morning," the girl said. Accustomed to chopping tobacco and herding cows on hillside pastures, the maids usually found Jude's grandmother's recipe for gracious living as incomprehensible as Jude did. They rarely lasted longer than a few months.

Through the hall archway, Jude could see women in pastel summer suits and flowered hats seated around card tables covered with embroidered linen cloths, eating chicken à la king from flaky pastry shells with her grandmother's Francis I forks, which had silver fruit all over the handles. Her grandmother always insisted this silverware would be Jude's when she died, but Jude didn't even know how to cook. When she grew up, she planned to go for dinner every night to the Wiggly Piglet Barbecue Pit on the Knoxville Highway, where waitresses in short shorts, cowboy boots and hats, and lariat-string ties took your order at your car window.

Sandy Andrews's mother was saying, "But you know, I think I like Tennessee almost as much as I do Virginia."

Jude's grandmother answered, "Yes, but I believe you get a better class of people in Virginia, don't you, Mavis?"

Fortunately, Jude's grandmother had insisted that Jude's father drive her mother across the state line to a Virginia hospital when she went into labor with Jude—so Jude would be able to attend these meetings when she grew up.

Her grandmother spotted Jude in the doorway. "Why, hey there, darling!" She stood up and strode over on spike heels so high that she looked like a toe dancer. Her silk suit was the color of a robin's egg, and the skirt just barely covered her kneecaps. Her hair was also blue, and at her throat was the pearl necklace she wanted Jude to have when she died. In the center were big creamy-pink pearls separated by tiny knots, and the pearls got smaller and smaller toward the ends. The necklace was very pretty, but Jude wished her grandmother wouldn't always talk about dying. When she bought a silver Cadillac in the spring, she'd said to Jude, "This will be the last car I'll ever buy on God's green earth." (Apparently, she thought she might buy another in heaven.) And each time Jude saw her now, she said, "Honey, this may be the last time you ever see me alive, so take a good long look."

"Evelyn, go get my little Virginia granddaughter a Popsicle," said her grandmother. As Evelyn headed toward the kitchen, she whispered, "Honey, where's your shirt at today? Virginia girls always wear shirts."

Evelyn returned, thrusting a cardboard box of Popsicles at Jude.

Her grandmother said, "Now, Evelyn, I've taught you better than that. Remember, you're in high society now."

Evelyn stomped back to the kitchen and returned with a monogrammed silver tray holding several Popsicles.

Jude took a cherry one, saying, "Thank you, ma'am."

Her grandmother murmured, "Darling, you don't need to say 'ma'am' to the servants."

LICKING HER RED POPSICLE, Jude pedaled to the cemetery at the end of the block. She wished her grandmother would stay home more often. When she was gone, Jude tried to avoid going past her big, empty house because it made her feel sad and lonely. What if one day it really was the last time Jude saw her alive, as had already happened with her mother and her grandfather?

Walking across the field to the wrought-iron gate, Jude stooped to pick clover blossoms, until she had two bouquets. To one side were the graves of soldiers killed in the War Between the States and of pioneer mothers who had died having babies. Sometimes their babies were buried beside them with toy headstones. Some of the graves had sunk in the middle when the wooden coffins rotted, and several stones had broken off or fallen over.

Jude placed a bouquet by her grandfather's headstone, a shiny, red granite obelisque that read: "A savior in life, with his Savior in death." He had had kind hazel eyes behind thick lenses in wire-frame glasses that perched like a giant insect on his aquiline nose, funny earlobes that hung down like a bloodhound's jowls, and a cute little double chin that puffed out like a bullfrog's throat when he laughed. Her grandmother said he had spent hours holding Jude over his head playing Flying Baby while Jude's father operated on soldiers in the belly of a troop ship in the mid-Atlantic, with torpedos plowing past and alarms screaming overhead.

Jude remembered sitting on his lap on his screened back porch, watching the Holston drift toward the Smokies. He told stories in his soft mountain drawl about cutting off men's arms and legs in a big tent by a river in Belgium. About a pit like a buried silo, full of German prisoners. About climbing down into it on a ladder, with a big red cross on his chest so they wouldn't hurt him. About a muddy field honeycombed with foxholes, where dead trees poked up like broken toothpicks. About tangles of rusted barbed wire that looked like a blackberry patch in the autumn. About men in metal helmets hanging from the wire, screaming while huge birds swooped down to tear at their wounds with sharp beaks and claws.

Jude's grandmother had come out of the house to ask, "Charles, do you really think it's a good idea to tell this child your horrible war stories?"

He looked up at her through his thick lenses. "She needs to know what she's up against. I wish I had known. All the soldiers at your daddy's hospital told me what an honor it had been to lose their limbs for the South. So I thought I was going to march in a uniform and be a hero."

"Jude's a girl, dear, not a boy."

"She's a human being. We're all in this mess together. That's the only thing that makes it bearable."

For a moment, he looked as if he was going to cry. Jude's grandmother reached for his hand, as small and supple as a woman's, with which he had hurled an unhittable curveball, with which he could chip and putt like a professional golfer, with which he could operate by feel in otherwise-inaccessible sites. As she stroked and kissed it, he began to look less miserable. Then she returned to the kitchen to work on her file box of secret family recipes, which had gotten her elected president of the Virginia Club. She claimed the South Carolina

Club had nothing to equal her Brunswick stew, which she'd adapted to modern times by replacing the squirrel meat with beef.

"Did you ever shoot people?" Jude asked her grandfather, standing up in his lap and patting his cheeks with both hands to cheer him up.

"No. My job was to patch up the ones who got shot, so they could go back to their trenches and kill some more Germans."

"But why?" asked Jude. She studied one of his cheeks carefully. Tiny hairs were sticking out of it like dark blue splinters. She wondered if they hurt him.

Her grandfather shrugged. "Most people are scared as treed coons, and scared people turn nasty."

"Scared of what?"

"Scared of living. Scared of loving. Scared of losing. Scared of dying. Scared."

"Are you scared?"

"Sometimes."

"Not me. I'll never be scared," said Jude, not yet having met Ace Kilgore.

"Not if I can help it, honey," he murmured, kissing her frown lines.

SQUATTING BY HER MOTHER'S GRAVE, Jude placed the second bouquet on the edge of her stone, a simple rectangle of cream-colored marble with forked green veins that branched across it like lightning. Her inscription read: "At Rest at Last in the Arms of the Lord." One day her mother was in the kitchen at home, baking butterscotch brownies and wearing a bulging apron covered with pink roses. The next day she was asleep in a white hospital bed and wouldn't wake up, even when Jude sang "Rise, Shine, Give God His Glory" right in her ear. And the day after that, she was here in this mound, being kept warm by a blanket of beautiful white flowers that smelled like her favorite perfume. And Jude's grandmother from New York City was weeping silently by the grave with a dead fox draped around her neck. It had tiny claws and glittery orange eyes. Her husband, Jude's other grandfather, who wore a gangster hat low over his eyes, kept wiping the orange clay off his shiny black shoes with a white handkerchief.

In a low voice, Jude began to tell her mother about Ace and the cat. When she got to the cherry bomb, she heard rustling among the dried milkweeds left over from winter. Looking up, she saw the Commie Killers in army fatigues and face masks, crawling on knees and elbows like evil insects, rifles cradled in their arms.

Jumping up, she looked all around.

"So," said Ace, leaping to his feet and aiming his rifle at her, "I guess we better show you what happens to little girls who talk too much." His father's colonel hat slipped down over his eyes.

Jude ran toward the sidewalk. Someone tackled her. They dragged her, kicking and biting, to a sunken grave. Pushing her into it, some held her down while others piled fallen tombstones across the mouth of the hole.

"A perfect fit!" announced Ace. "See you around, kid, as the line said to the circle." And the Commie Killers vanished.

Jude could hear a lone cicada droning like a chain saw from a nearby walnut tree. Six weeks until the first frost, Mr. Starnes always said. She pushed at the stones above her head, but they wouldn't budge. She tried to figure out how much clay lay between herself and the skeleton below. What if it reached up and dragged her down into the earth in its bony arms? Maybe if she stayed perfectly still, it wouldn't realize she was there.

She was so scared that she could hardly breathe. What if the stones came crashing down and smashed her into a human pancake?

She wished her grandfather would help her, as he had promised, but he was lying on the other side of the graveyard, probably just as scared as she was.

She paused in her panic to wonder if the tiny blue hairs on his cheeks would have kept growing so that he now had a long beard, and dagger fingernails like Dracula, and toenails that would one day sprout from his grave like blanched asparagus spears.

What if a nest of black widow spiders had been disturbed when the Commie Killers picked up the broken headstones? What if the black widows were crawling all over the stones just above her head? What if they didn't realize that she wasn't the one who had wrecked their home? She sank as far down in the grave as she could. But then she remembered the skeleton below and tried to twist sideways out of its grasp.

She lay there in the dark, eyes closed, breathing as little as possible. At Sunday school, the preacher was always talking about how great nature was because it displayed God's handiwork. But what about black widow spiders? What about copperheads? What about leeches and mosquitoes and bats and ticks and wasps? What about Ace Kilgore?

Gradually, her body relaxed into the contours of the sunken grave. Ace was right: She fit like Cinderella's foot in the glass slipper. This was what it was like to be dead, and it wasn't so bad. If she stayed like this long enough, she *would* be dead and she could join her mother in heaven and never have to see Ace Kilgore again.

Billowy white clouds were drifting like spinnakered sailing ships across an indigo sea of summer sky. Beautiful smiling women in white bathrobes were reclining on them, waving as they passed. One woman with curly black hair and full red lips looked exactly like Jude's mother.

"Wait!" called Jude. "Take me with you!"

But they seemed not to hear.

A dog began snuffling and yelping up above. Jude kept her eyes tightly shut, struggling to return to her mother.

"Jude, are you okay?" called Molly through an opening between the broken headstones. Sidney was beside her, whimpering and flailing frantically at the stones with his paws.

"I guess so."

"Don't worry. We'll get you out," said Sandy, freckled face looming in the window of light. "It's just a question of leverage."

THEY SAT IN SANDY'S tree house drinking grape soda through straws that bent like gooseneck lamps. The Commie Killers, shirtless in the hot afternoon sun, were redigging trenches across the street beneath a Confederate battle flag that hung limply from a pole stuck in the mud. The phone rang.

Answering it, Sandy said, "Oh, hi, Nicolai." He reached for a notebook. "Let's see, what do I have for you today? Oh, yes, queen to king's bishop four. Okay. Talk to you soon."

"Moscow," he explained, running his hand over his cowlick in a futile attempt to smooth it down. "Right, so first of all, Jude, don't ever play alone again. If Molly hadn't seen your tricycle, you'd still be in that grave. I can't spend all day at my telescope watching out for you two. I'm in the middle of some very important chess matches. Why don't you play with Noreen next door?"

"She's a girl," said Molly.

"We're not really girls," said Jude. "We just look like it."

NOREEN AGREED TO LET Jude and Molly be her sons if Sandy would be her husband.

"Okay," said Sandy, standing outside the shed attached to Noreen's parents' garage, "but I'm the kind of father who spends all day at the office. And my office is my tree house. And only my sons are allowed to visit.''

''But pioneer fathers don't go to the office,'' said Noreen from the doorway. Her dark naturally curly hair was parted on one side, and a red plastic barrette shaped like a bow held it back from her face on the other side. The frames of her glasses matched her barrette.

''They go hunting, don't they?'' asked Sandy, walking toward his yard. ''Pretend I've been eaten by bears. Pretend you're a widow.''

''You're no fun,'' said Noreen.

''Sorry about that.''

''Well, all right, come in, Jude and Molly.'' Noreen stepped aside. ''Sit down. We're having supper.'' Supper consisted of dried clay patties served on wild grape leaves atop an orange crate.

Noreen's ''daughters'' were a puling bunch in flared shorts with matching halter tops. Red plastic barrettes shaped their hair into bizarre lumps and mounds, as though their skulls were deformed. Most dandled dolls, nursing and burping them as they ate, and discussing their infant antics in wearying detail.

''Sister Serena, would you please read our Bible lesson for today?'' asked Noreen.

Serena handed her bundled doll to the girl beside her, then picked up a Bible and opened it at its marker. ''In my Father's house are many mansions,'' she read haltingly in a high-pitched voice. ''If it were not so, I would have told you. I go to prepare a place for you. And if I go and prepare a place for you, I will come again, and receive you unto myself; that where I am, there ye may be also.''

''Halleluia! Praise the Lord!'' shrieked Noreen, keeling over into spasms on the floor.

Jude watched as the other girls set aside their dolls and writhed on the floor, babbling in something that sounded like double pig Latin.

So it was true? "Where I am, there ye may be also." Her mother was going to come get her and take her to God's house. Everyone said her grandmother lived in a mansion. If heaven had many mansions, would it be a development like Tidewater Estates?

Whoops erupted outside. Through the playhouse window, Jude could see the Commie Killers war dancing with feather bracelets at their wrists and ankles. Ace appeared in the doorway in a chicken-feather headdress, a dish towel belted around his bony hips. His face and chest were painted with lipstick lightning bolts. The girls stopped rolling on the floor and began to wail. Holding up his hands for silence, he pointed at Molly and Jude. "We wantum those two shirtless ones. You squaws havum nothing to fear."

"No! Don't take my sons!" Noreen leapt to her feet and shielded them behind her back.

Ace shoved her aside, and his warriors dragged Jude and Molly into the yard. Ropes knotted around their throats and wrists, they were led toward the Wildwoods.

"I'm telling!" screamed Noreen. "Momma!"

"Hush, darling," called her mother from the screened porch, where the Missionary Society was meeting. "Momma's praying."

"Sandy!" Noreen yelled toward the tree house. "Your sons have been captured by the savages!"

"YOU'D BETTER LET US GO," said Molly, wrists and ankles bound to saplings so her body formed an X. Her ribs looked like a xylophone. "My uncle's a state trooper."

"So what?" said Ace, who was flicking the blade of his jackknife with his thumb. "So's mine."

"What are you going to do to us?" asked Jude, bound nearby. She kept picturing that red-and-green cherry bomb. On top of it all, she felt guilty: Molly wouldn't be in this fix except for her. Silently, she summoned the Nunnehi, the Cherokee Immortals, who her father had said would emerge from beneath the mountains and under the river to help you if you were in trouble. But no one showed up.

"We haven't decided yet, ma'am. We may play crucifixion. Or we may leave y'all here as supper for the mosquitoes." After closing his knife and fastening it to his belt, he walked up to Molly and glared right into her eyes with his dead black ones. "Are you now or have you ever been an agent for any foreign power?" he demanded.

"Excuse me?" said Molly, screwing up her face with contempt.

"So you won't talk?"

"Talk about what?"

Slowly, he extracted a chicken feather from his warbonnet. Smiling, he stroked Molly's armpit with it.

"Please don't, Ace," pleaded Molly in a wimpy voice Jude had never before heard from her. "I'm ticklish." She began to struggle against her ropes.

Delighted, Ace continued. The other warriors plucked feathers from their bracelets and joined in on both girls' armpits.

Jude caught on quickly, and she and Molly writhed and grimaced, screaming for mercy as loudly as possible.

Jude was standing on the porch steps before her mother's mansion in heaven, white columns on either hand. Her mother was in the doorway in a low-cut emerald evening gown, smiling, arms outspread, wavy black hair stirring in the breeze.

"Momma, is it really you?" asked Jude.

A siren whined up the hill from town. The boys, feathers frozen, looked at one another.

"I told you my uncle would get you," gasped Molly.

"Holy crow!" whispered Ace, seeing two flat-brimmed hats skimming along above the bushes. The Commie Killers took off through the undergrowth, feathers of torture spiraling to the forest floor.

BY THE CURB IN FRONT of Sandy's house was a khaki-and-forest-green highway patrol car, red light flashing on its roof. Molly's uncle Clarence, holster on his hip, black boots to his knees, opened the back door for Sandy.

"Wait a minute, Uncle Clarence," called Molly. "What are y'all doing?"

"Arresting him, sweetheart." He closed the door. Sandy looked through the window at Molly and Jude and shrugged helplessly.

"But Sandy saved us. You should arrest Ace Kilgore instead."

"We come up here in the first place to pick up Sandy," said Uncle Clarence as he circled the car to the driver's door, "and he told us about y'all. But this son of a gun here tapped into the phone line. He's been calling free all over the world for pert near two year now. He owes the phone company two thousand dollars, plus fines. Your young friend here is in real big trouble, missy."

CHAPTER

3

O N JUDE'S FIRST DAY OF SCHOOL, Molly, a second grader, walked her along the busy highway past the sign with the winged red horse in front of the Texaco station. As they approached the redbrick school building, which resembled the state mental hospital across town, with wire mesh in the window glass and a chain-link fence around the playground, Molly assured her that Noreen's report of a spanking machine in the principal's office was untrue.

"They always say that to frighten the first graders."

In the tiled hallway outside her classroom door, Jude saw several children crying in the arms of distraught mothers, clutching their skirts, clinging to their legs, begging to be taken home, like the pictures at Sunday school of sinners in hell pleading with the Lord for salvation.

Struggling not to be a crybaby, Jude opened the door and

marched into the room. She sat down at the desk pointed out by the teacher, whose chin when she smiled almost touched her nose, like the witch in *Hansel and Gretel*. A piece of manila paper and a box of new crayons with sharp tips sat on her blond wooden desktop, so Jude began to draw a puffy white cloud floating in a blue sky, with a woman in a white bathrobe standing on it, smiling with bright red lips. She made the hair yellow so no one would know it was her mother. As she colored, she began to feel less miserable. She liked the oily smell of the new crayons, the rough texture of the paper against her fingertips, and the bright colors she could spread in any pattern she liked.

"That's very nice, Jude," said the witch, bending over her picture, smelling like flowers that had been left in a vase too long.

"Thank you."

"Is it an angel?" She rested a bony hand on Jude's shoulder.

"Sort of." Jude would never reveal that the angel was her mother. There was no telling what a witch might do with that information.

"So how do you like first grade?" asked Molly in the cafeteria at lunchtime. She had sneaked away from the second-grade table to eat the peanut-butter-and-banana sandwich from her Donald Duck lunch box with Jude.

"All right." Jude took the wax paper off a stack of Oreos Clementine had packed for her. "Except my teacher was making fun of how this boy was holding his pencil, so he threw it at her. And then she spanked him in the cloakroom." Jude separated an Oreo to lick off the sugary white filling. "School is really scary, isn't it?"

"Yeah. But girls hardly ever get in trouble," said Molly. "Just boys, 'cause they always say what they think. They don't understand that nobody cares."

After lunch, Jude and Molly stood beside the high fence around the playground, the only girls in blue jeans, holding hands and watching the Commie Killers play softball. After the Commie Killers' run-in with Uncle Clarence, Jude's father had hired a bulldozer to destroy their trenches. So when they passed Jude on the sidewalk now, they called her "Public Enemy Number One."

Noreen's gang was in a grassy corner, hurting one another's feelings, then making up via networks of earnest intermediaries. Spotting Jude and Molly, Noreen sauntered over in her plaid dress, which had a black patent-leather belt to match her Mary Janes. Her stomach bulged out beneath the belt like a beach ball.

"Why do you spend all your time with that baby first grader?" she asked Molly.

"Because she's my friend." She let go of Jude's hand.

"When you get sick of her, you can come play with us."

"I'm not going to get sick of her, Noreen."

Jude was grinding a pebble into the dirt with the toe of her oxford. She glanced at Molly, aware of her sacrifice in being best friends with a first grader. Even though Molly's voice was calm, her eyes were icy cold.

"You two look like boys in those blue jeans," said Noreen. "Wouldn't your mothers buy you new dresses for the first day of school?"

There was a horrified silence as Noreen remembered that Jude's mother was dead. She whirled around and stalked away, dust coating her glossy Mary Janes.

"Look. There's Sandy." Touching Jude's shoulder, Molly pointed across the playground. He was sitting with his back to the brick wall of the building, playing chess against himself on a tiny portable set. The teacher on duty, a hunched old woman in a navy blue Brooklyn Dodgers cap, was standing over him gesticulating wildly. Sandy folded up his chess set and slipped it into his shorts pocket. Teacher hobbling at his heels, he marched to the softball diamond.

When the Commie Killers saw him coming, they groaned as though they had stomachaches. One yelled, "Oh, no, here comes the convict!" Although Jude's father, who had gone to high school with the president of the phone company, had gotten Sandy excused from the wiretap charges, the Commie Killers wouldn't let him put his criminal past behind him.

The teacher handed him a glove and directed him to right field. He stood there with one hand on his hip, the other holding out the leather glove like a skillet waiting for a flapjack. When Ace hit a fly ball, Sandy's expression as he watched it arc and fall in his direction was one of pure terror. He missed it, and Ace converted his error into a grand-slam home run.

During the next inning, Sandy walked up to the plate, optimistically hefting a black Louisville Slugger. Ace motioned the outfield closer, yelling, "Easy out!" Which it unfortunately was.

After school, Jude and Molly stood toe-to-toe at the crack in the sidewalk marking the boundary between their yards. Each crossed her arms and placed her hands on the other's shoulders. For a long time, they looked into each other's eyes. Jude could see herself and the maple tree behind her reflected in Molly's irises. The bright blue disks were scored with lines, like miniature blueberry pies sliced into a hundred pieces. Around each pupil was a tiny translucent golden ring like a butter rum Life Saver after you'd sucked it for a long time. Gazing into the black pupils, Jude felt suddenly dizzy, as though she were spiraling down the funnel of a whirlpool.

They smiled gravely and patted each other's shoulders, chanting in unison, "Best friend. Buddy of mine. Pal of pals."

After changing from school jeans to play jeans, Jude sat at Molly's kitchen table, spinning a marble around the lazy Susan, pretending it was a Las Vegas roulette wheel. Molly had been mixing them cocktails from several liquids they both liked to smell—vanilla extract, Pine Sol, cherry cough syrup. But each had tasted worse than the last. Now Molly was telling a story her teacher had read that afternoon about an orphan boy who was raised by wolves and had never learned to speak. He was discovered by hunters and taken to live in a cottage on the edge of the forest.

Molly and Jude spent the rest of the afternoon prowling through Molly's house. Their vocabulary consisted of hand gestures and facial expressions. In the bathroom, Jude seized a comb and displayed it to a mystified Molly, who manipulated it in various ways, trying to discover its function.

"What are you two up to now?" asked Molly's aproned mother, lounging in the doorway in her neat blond pageboy, arms folded across her stomach. Startled, the girls stared at her with wide-open eyes.

"What's going on?" She gave a perplexed laugh. They dashed from the bathroom to seek shelter behind the sofa in the knotty pine den, which enclosed them much as the wolves' lair had.

Jude was so enchanted with this game that she continued it at supper that night, marveling over the unknown delicacies served her on a round disk by a black creature in a white uniform with a red scarf wound around her head. It was wonderful to be handed food after a lifetime of chasing moles in the forest.

"So how was your first day of school?" asked a large, pale, hairless one at the head of the gleaming wooden table.

Jude gazed at him as she ate with a bizarre silver twig, unable to comprehend the howls coming from his mouth.

"What's wrong, baby? Cat got your tongue?"

The dark one led Jude up some steps to a pool of water and removed her soiled fur. Jude dipped her toe into the pool. The water was hot! She had known only icy forest ponds and streams. She climbed in. How delicious to float in the warm liquid while the friendly black one rubbed a small slippery stone that smelled like dried rose petals across her coat.

"How you like school, Miss Judith?"

Jude looked quickly at the dark one, whose mouth was making strange sounds.

"You ain't telling, huh?"

"WHAT A NICE DOG," said Mrs. Murdoch as she strolled down the aisle and peered at the picture Jude had just drawn. "I think we need to hang this one on our bulletin board up front, Jude."

"It's not a dog," said Jude, not looking up. "It's a wolf." The wolf was sitting in its cave in the forest, sniffing the morning air.

"Speak up, young lady. I can't hear you."

"I said it's not a dog; it's a wolf."

"A wolf? What an idea! Why is it a wolf?"

" 'Cause I like wolves. I think they're nice." Jude finally looked up. Mrs. Murdoch's bright red lipstick covered an area much larger than her actual lips, and her eyebrows had been plucked out and redrawn as crooked black arches. She looked like a messy clown.

Mrs. Murdoch laughed, chin nearly touching her nose. "You may like wolves, young lady, but they are definitely *not* nice. They are vicious wild animals. Think about the wolf in *Little Red Riding Hood* for just a moment."

Jude said nothing. She was thinking about the boy who got spanked in the cloakroom.

"Well, Jude?"

"Yessum."

"So you agree that wolves are vicious wild animals?"

"Yessum."

"Now, we would not want a vicious wild animal on our bulletin board, would we? Because it would scare us all half to death and give us bad dreams at night. But your wolf could just as well be a dog, couldn't it? And then we could hang it up and look at it without fear."

"Yessum."

"So you can practice your letters by writing D-O-G here along the bottom."

"Yessum," said Jude miserably, printing D-O-G beneath her wolf. Maybe she wouldn't be an artist when she grew up after all.

Mrs. Murdoch sat down at her portable organ in the front of the room and began furiously pumping the foot pedals. "Rise, children!" she shrieked, gesturing upward with her palms. "And lift up your voices to the Lord!"

"BABY, I HAVE TO GO back to the hospital after supper," said Jude's father as he laid a slice of Mrs. Starnes's German chocolate cake on a dessert plate painted with grape clusters and cantaloupe slices. He passed it to Jude. "To work on some reports. Molly's mother said you could spend the night there. Would you mind?" He picked up his fork and studied it.

Jude inspected his lowered face, which was turning bright red beneath his five o'clock shadow as he flicked and stroked his fork prongs. Why was he so embarrassed? He often went back to the hospital after supper if Clementine could stay late. It was no big deal. "Sure. That's fine, Dad."

The next morning, Jude and Molly raced down the hall from Molly's bedroom and into the bathroom to brush their teeth before school. Molly's father was standing in front of the sink shaving. He

was entirely covered with curly black hair, except for his white buttocks and a pale little slug that nestled in a mat of fur between his
legs.

Finally, Molly asked, "Daddy, what's that?"

Nicking his chin with the razor, he looked down at Molly's pointing finger. Clutching the slug with his free hand while the shaving
cream on his chin turned pink, he said, "It's my penis, and I never
want to hear you say that word again!"

Molly and Jude crept from the bathroom, teeth unbrushed, and
gathered their books from Molly's room in silence, exchanging wolfspeak signs with their fingers that said, He's covered with fur. Can he
be a brother?

JUDE'S GRANDMOTHER WAS SERVING garlic grits from a silver
casserole dish on her Sheraton sideboard. She was using a pitted serving spoon that her own grandmother had buried in the backyard at
the family farm near Fredericksburg to prevent its being stolen by the
Yankees. Unable to remember where she'd buried her cache, Jude's
great-great-grandmother spent the rest of her life making her yardmen
excavate the property. The week after they finally found it, she died.

"A little girl belongs in dresses at school, Daniel," her grandmother was saying, "not blue jeans. It's the talk of the town."

"Don't you find it sad, Momma," said Jude's father, loosening
his striped silk Sunday tie, "that this town has nothing better to talk
about than my daughter's blue jeans?"

"Don't get smart with me, Daniel. You may be a big man down
at the hospital, but you're still my son." She handed him a plate piled
high with fried chicken, grits, shelly beans, and a salad of molded
cherry Jell-O and shredded carrots topped with a mayonnaise rosette.

He buttered and ate a Parker House roll while his mother continued her critique of Jude's wardrobe.

Jude, whose skirt was hiked halfway up her thighs as she sat with her feet hooked behind her front chair legs, fixed her gaze on the glass goddess in the middle of the table. Baby's breath and pastel snapdragons were sprouting from her head. She clutched a bow and wore a quiver of arrows on her back. A pack of dogs was leaping up around her legs, which were laced with thongs from her sandals.

"Thank you, Momma," said her father. "I'm sure you're right."

Jude glanced at him, scratching her neck, which was itching from her scalloped lace collar. Often he agreed with his mother to her face, then ignored her behind her back. Hopefully, this was one of those times.

Satisfied, her grandmother resumed her account of the siege of Fredericksburg, told to her as a girl by a legless soldier at the Confederate Veterans' Home: "As the Yankees crossed the Rappahannock, Lieutenant Stevens hid behind a stone wall to shoot at them. All of a sudden, he saw a baby girl toddling down the street chasing a rolling shell casing, with bullets whistling all around her. He ran out and grabbed her and carried her down a side street, where he came to a young woman in a dirty ripped dress who was sitting on a pile of rubble."

"Ma'am," he said, "is this here your little girl?"

She and the child reached out for each other. "Sir," she said, "my cow's been shot. It's lying in that shed over yonder. You can go butcher it and take the meat if you want to."

"Thank you, ma'am," he said, "but the Yankees is coming fast, and I surely would be honored if you'd come along with me right now."

"Why, thank you, sir," she said, taking his outstretched hand with a coy smile, as though he'd just asked her to dance. "I don't mind if I do."

As he led her up the street, a shell exploded beside them. He woke up to find a starving hog licking the stumps where his legs used to be. The mother and her baby were lying dead beside him. Down the hill, he could see Yankee soldiers dressed in gowns stolen from the town houses. They were drinking fine French wines from the bottle and waltzing with one another around a bonfire of Chippendale chairs.

"There was no way in the world," Jude's grandmother concluded, "for our fine colonial cavaliers to prevail over that race of barbarians."

It was her favorite story. Although it was a good one, Jude had heard it a hundred times.

"And another thing, Daniel," her grandmother said as she ladled milk gravy over her fried chicken.

He looked up, the green beans on his fork slowly dripping fatback. "Yes, Momma?"

"This poor child has no mother. And the way you're behaving, running around with that floozy from intensive care at all hours of the night, now she has no father, either. It's not going unnoticed around town that Jude is practically living at the Elkins's while you cavort in back alleys with your concubine."

"Yes, Momma," he said, chewing his beans. "I'm sure you're right."

"What's a floozy?" asked Jude, studying the wallpaper over the sideboard, which featured a white columned mansion surrounded by women in hoop skirts and sunbonnets. This was what her mother's mansion in heaven looked like. One day soon, she was going to come take Jude there. It wasn't true that she had no mother. Just because no one else saw her didn't mean she wasn't real. "What's cavort?"

"Momma, tell us about Provence, why don't you?" said her father.

"Provence? Oh, Provence was lovely. You know, I believe I like Provence almost as much as I do Virginia. Except for all that funny food. And that strange language nobody understands except the French."

Her father laughed, running his hand over his bald spot. "I declare, Momma, you're the only person I ever saw who travels the world searching for Virginia. Why don't you just go to Virginia in the first place?"

She sighed and patted her red lips with her linen napkin. "Well, you know, Virginia's not what it used to be. Once, before that dreadful war, it was a gracious land of rolling pastures, where sleek cattle grazed and blackbirds sang. . . ."

"May I please be excused?" asked Jude, laying her napkin on the damask tablecloth, desperate not to hear again about the joys of plantation living.

"WHAT'S A FLOOZY?" Jude asked Clementine on her way out the door to school the next morning.

Clementine paused as she mopped the redbrick kitchen linoleum with the golden liquid that smelled so good and tasted so terrible. "Where you heard that word, Miss Judith?"

"My grandma said my daddy's running around with a floozy."

Clementine grinned, leaning on her mop handle. "That a fact? Good for him."

"What's a floozy?"

"A floozy is . . . um, a woman who likes to have some fun." She tucked a coil of springy hair beneath the edge of her head cloth.

"But what about my momma in heaven?"

"Sugar, be glad if your daddy's found him a new woman friend. He be a good man, and he been so lonely for so long. It don't mean he love your momma less. Fact is, I'd say he got him a graveyard love for your momma.''

''What's that?''

''A graveyard love be a love that lasts till you both be dead and buried in the graveyard. Like what I expect you got with Miss Molly. A graveyard love don't never end, no matter what.''

JUDE WAS OPERATING atop the desk in her bedroom on a doll her grandmother had just brought her from India. She had removed and set aside the red-and-gold silk sari. Now she was carefully snipping open the cloth belly with scissors. Reaching into the aperture, she extracted the wad of stuffing that was the dead baby. Once the baby was out, she hoped the mother could be saved.

After sewing up the incision with red thread, Jude discovered that her patient had stopped breathing. Turning her over, she administered artificial respiration, repeatedly pressing her back and lifting her elbows. But she still refused to breathe.

Jude had never lost a patient before. Feeling her throat tighten so that she could hardly swallow, she stumbled down the carpeted hallway and into her father's bedroom, which was painted lime green and had a gold quilted bedspread and velvet drapes. She searched the floor of his closet for a shoe box, intending to dig a grave in the backyard and make a headstone from a brick. Finally, she found a coffin, but unfortunately it was full of letters.

Carrying the box into her room, Jude plopped down on her bed and examined the French stamps on some of the envelopes, which featured the head of a woman statue with wavy stone hair. The letters were between her mother and father while he was away at the war. She removed one from an envelope that had an American eagle stamp. The paper was light blue, and the handwriting was small and squiggly. Right in the middle of the page, Jude spotted her own name.

Being in the top reading group now that she was in second grade, Jude used her father's dictionary to decipher the paragraph containing her name: "Your mother and I rode the train to our nation's capital last week. One afternoon we visited the National Cathedral. While we were looking up at the beautiful stained-glass window, we discovered that Jude, whom I was carrying on my hip, was blowing out all the votive candles in the rack beside us. Darling, I have my hands full with this marvelous child of ours! How I despise this awful war, which has taken so many men away from the wives and children who need them. . . ."

The letter paper smelled like her mother's favorite perfume. Closing her eyes, Jude remembered sitting on the pale green carpet in her parents' bedroom watching her mother get dressed for parties. She'd let Jude fasten the lacy tops of her silk stockings to her garter belt. Jude had been fascinated by the way the little padded buttons slid into the wire hooks. Then her mother would ask her to arrange the crooked seams down the backs of her legs into straight lines. After pulling on her dress, her mother would take the cut-glass vial of Narcissus perfume off her dressing table and dab her wrists and throat and behind her ears with the stopper. Jude would hold out her own wrist for a dab. After her parents' departure, she would lie in bed with her wrist to her nose, breathing in the sweet floral fragrance of her beautiful vanished mother.

Jude held the letter to her nose and took a deep whiff, gazing at the photo on her nightstand of her mother smiling into the camera, holding Jude's cheek to her own, black hair waving around her face like seaweed around a drowning swimmer.

Jude remembered the poor dead doll she'd left lying on the operating table. She got up and cradled it for a moment in her arms. Then she hurled it into the back of her closet and slammed the door.

Hiding the shoe box under her bed, Jude worked on the letters whenever the coast was clear. One evening, Clementine asked as she carried corn bread in from the kitchen, "Miss Judith, what you be doing alone in your room all the time, honey? You ought to be outdoors playing with the other children."

"Nothing. Reading. Thinking."

"I guess we're raising an intellectual here, Clementine," said her father as he cut the meat loaf. He still wore pale green scrub clothes from the hospital and looked very handsome with the candlelight reflecting off the ever-larger bald patch on his head.

"What's an 'interlectual'?" asked Jude, swinging her legs in her chair, pretending she was pumping really high in a swing.

He laughed. "An intellectual is someone who knows what the word *intellectual* means."

"I don't want to be one anyway," said Jude with dignity. "I want to be a medical missionary. Either that or a person who makes little girls' shoes that aren't silly."

"Same difference," said her father. "One heals souls and the other heels soles." He practically fell into his plate laughing.

Jude liked seeing him so happy all of a sudden. But it bothered her that he never stared anymore at the photo of her mother in the wine bottle when they sat together in his brown leather chair listening to John Cameron Swayze. Her mother was talking in her letters about how much she missed him, but here he was cavorting in back alleys with a floozy. It just wasn't right.

"I don't get it." Jude looked to Clementine for clues to her father's hilarity.

Clementine shrugged and limped toward the kitchen in her huge white shoes. Apparently, her arthritis was acting up, which meant rain was coming soon.

Her father sighed. "I wish there *were* some intellectuals around this place," he said, passing her the corn-bread squares, "to appreciate my bons mots."

"Ain't nobody here but us chickens," drawled Clementine from the doorway. It was the punch line from a joke they all loved.

As Jude and Clementine giggled, her father shook his head.

JUDE AND MOLLY CLIMBED into Jude's father's army-surplus jeep. When Jude was younger, he used to wrap her in a blanket and let her sleep on the backseat while he paid house calls back in the hills. If she woke up, she'd sneak over to the lighted windows, through which she might see tall, thin mountain people with gaunt faces and hollow eyes. Sometimes she'd watch her father lance boils or stitch wounds by lantern light.

Her father drove them across the pasture behind her grandmother's house and down through the Wildwoods, the olive hood bobbing and the power lift clanking on the back. The mountains lay spread out below them, a lumpy crazy quilt of rust and mauve and mustard and dark green.

As they sifted the dark loam along the riverbank in the slanting golden rays of the setting sun, Jude's father told Molly the story about his grandfather's mother, Abigail Westlake, whose forebears had lived in bark lodges by the river for centuries, fishing the slow-drifting waters and hunting the steep slopes of the Wildwoods. Later they put up a log cabin, growing corn and grazing cattle on the rich bottomland. By Abigail's time, they had built a plank house, brought slaves from Charleston, converted to Christianity, learned English, and begun wearing white people's clothing. Abigail's brother married a missionary from Baltimore.

One day, white soldiers came with rifles to round them up and march them off to a reservation in Oklahoma. When her brother tried to escape, a soldier shot him in the head. Coming home from gathering herbs, Abigail watched this from the Wildwoods, then hid in a cave while an unfamiliar white family moved into her family's house.

After several days, a neighboring farmer found her, nearly dead from cold and hunger and fear, and carried her back to his cabin on the ridge. He himself had recently arrived in America, having been evicted from his croft in the Scottish Highlands. He confronted the new family in her house and ordered them to leave. After they obligingly moved out, they burned her house to the ground. Jude's father pointed out the cellar hole, which was now overgrown with a tangle of Virginia creeper. An early frost had turned the leaves the scarlet of spilt blood.

Abigail learned from relatives who had survived the forced westward trek that her parents and sisters had died of typhoid in the Ozarks. As she lay in bed week after week trying to recover her will to live, she told the farmer about the dances in this valley when she was a child, at which warriors carrying red-and-black clubs painted their faces vermilion and circled their eyes with scarlet and black. About her cousins, who came down on horses from the deep mountain coves wearing deerskin leggings and embroidered hunting shirts and red-and-blue turbans, to watch the violent all-day ball games on the playing field downriver. About the shamen, who raked the ballplayers in their loincloths with turkey-quill combs to grid their flesh with blood for good luck. About the prophets who had recently begun painting their faces black and proclaiming the end of the Cherokee people.

The farmer told her about having his hut in the Highlands burned down around him in the middle of a winter night because he refused to leave to make way for a herd of sheep. About his wife and baby, who died as he dragged them from the fire. About being forced onto a ship in Ullapool with his young son, bound for no one knew where. About being dumped at Cape Fear on the Carolina coast and wandering across the Smokies in search of an unoccupied spot where he could farm in peace. About the recent Cherokee raid on his cattle, during which his son had disappeared.

Having loss in common, if nothing else, the two fell in love and married. Their son, Jude's great-grandfather, grew up learning from his mother which parts of which plants to use for which ailments. When he became a man, people arrived at his new log house from all over the region for his remedies. During the War Between the States, he patched up soldiers brought to him by both sides, but he refused to join either, having also learned from his mother a certain skepticism about the projects of white men, whatever their proclaimed creed.

Jude looked up from her digging to study her father. He had a big crooked nose just like her grandfather—just like the Indian on a buffalo nickel. And his cheekbones were so broad that his mahogany eyes seemed to be peering out from inside a cave. People always said Jude's eyes were just like his. While he talked, the valley came alive, with painted warriors paddling canoes up the river and shooting deer with arrows in the Wildwoods. With teams of men in loincloths catching balls in the nets of woven squirrel skin at the ends of their long wooden spoons. With bayoneted soldiers herding little children like cattle. With blazing houses and screaming people.

But when her father stopped talking, it all vanished and every-

thing fell silent, except for the whirring of grasshoppers in the withered alfalfa and the cawing of a crow from the top of a sycamore.

Her father scraped soil from a pointed shard of rock and handed
it to Jude. She and Molly looked at it. It was shiny black with a vein
of white down the center and pointed wings at the top for tying it to
an arrow shaft.

"Hang on to that," her father said. "Some ancient cousin of
yours probably made it."

Jude kept inspecting the chipped edges of the arrowhead with
her fingertips. It seemed strange that all that was left were these bits
of rock, herself and her father, and her father's stories, told to him
by his grandfather, who was told them by his mother. At school, they
played a game called Gossip in which everyone sat in a circle and one
person whispered something in the ear of the next, who whispered it
to the next, and so on. By the time it had gone around the circle, it
was completely wrong or stupid.

They drove up to the Wiggly Piglet, which featured an outline
of Porky Pig in flashing neon, with a slogan beneath that read: "Our
pigs are dying for you to eat." A high-school girl in a cowboy hat and
boots arrived to take their order of pulled-pork sandwiches and
peanut-butter milk shakes. As the girl strutted away, Molly reported
that she had had goose bumps on her thighs below her short shorts.

After the waitress returned, carrying their order on an aluminum
tray that she attached to their car window, Jude asked her father,
"Why did the soldiers want to march Abigail Westlake's family to
Oklahoma?"

"The white settlers wanted their land," said her father, handing
out the wrapped sandwiches. "That soil along the river is very rich
from centuries of flooding."

"But that's not right, just to take it like that."

He smiled faintly as he unwrapped his barbecue and poured extra sauce from a tiny paper cup onto the coleslaw atop his pork. "No, it isn't. But the Cherokees were sitting ducks. They believed that land belonged to everyone. It never occurred to them that it could be taken away."

"But you said they owned slaves?"

"Yes."

"Negro people like Clementine, who had to do all the work for free?" A speaker attached to the restaurant roof was blaring Hank Williams singing "I Can't Help It If I'm Still in Love with You."

"Yes."

"But that's not right, either," said Jude. The barbecue sauce was so spicy that her nose was starting to run.

"No, it's wrong. Very wrong."

Jude sat beside Molly on the backseat, sucking her milk shake through a straw, trying to figure out how the same people could be right and wrong, both at the same time. She glanced at Molly.

"When your grandfather told you those stories, did it make you sad?" Jude asked, watching the cowgirl write down the orders of three boys in ducktails who were sitting in a convertible with an elevated rear end and an elaborate chrome tailpipe. PARTY DOLL was painted on the fender. She and Molly had already decided to be waitresses here when they grew up, so that they could wear the cowgirl outfits.

"Yes. It made me sad to know that people would treat each other that way. It still does."

"Why do they?" asked Jude, determined to get this settled once and for all.

"Ah, the question of the ages." He wadded up his wrapper and napkin and stuffed them into the paper bag.

"But what's the answer?"

"Jude," he said, "I'm afraid you may be one of those people who spend their lives searching for that answer."

"But what is it?" Jude was starting to feel frantic, as though this was a joke that everyone knew the punch line to but herself.

"Well, I don't know exactly, baby." He turned around to look at her in the light from the flashing neon pig. "The Cherokees used to say that beneath different appearances, all creatures are merely manifestations of the Great Spirit. So that those who harm others unnecessarily disturb the balance of the universe and therefore harm themselves. But many people nowadays seem to feel separate and superior, so it doesn't bother them so much to hurt others."

"Which do you believe?" Molly asked.

"You don't need to believe or not believe something once you experience it."

Jude and Molly looked at him blankly.

"That means I agree with the Cherokees," he said.

Jude and Molly looked at each other. Jude thought that if anyone hurt Molly, she, too, would feel the pain. But if someone hurt Ace Kilgore, she'd feel glad. So which category did she fit into?

Your daddy's so sweet, Molly gesticulated in wolfspeak as he carried their trash to the can and handed their tray to the goose-bumped cowgirl. Jude felt proud of him.

Since her parents were out of town, Molly spent that night at Jude's house, and she taught Jude a game she'd just invented called Pecan. Jude lay on top of Molly, stomach-to-stomach, chest-to-chest, nose-to-nose. They looked cross-eyed into each other's eyes. Then Molly began to giggle. Jude could feel Molly's chest and stomach trembling and heaving beneath her own, so she started giggling, too. Soon it was impossible to tell who was and wasn't giggling.

Molly grabbed Jude's wrists and forced her over onto her side. Then she scrambled to her knees and sat astride Jude's chest, pinning her arms above her head. Breathing heavily, she look down at Jude with triumph, eyes so fierce that they were almost purple. "I could pin you like this with one hand tied behind my back,'' she announced in her husky voice.

"Probably," said Jude. But she hadn't been fighting back very hard because she had been too interested to find out what Molly would do next.

Before they fell asleep, they agreed that Pecan was such a good game that they should play it a lot, taking turns lying on top.

THROUGH THE BARE BRANCHES across the cave mouth Jude watched the river wind through the valley, a slithering brown snake. Holsteins stood to their knees in the water, patches of black spread across their barreled backs like continents on a globe. A hawk, fringed wing tips fluttering, swooped and dipped and floated on a column of air that was spiraling up from the valley floor. The Smokies rippled like blue sand dunes to the edge of the earth. Wispy puffs of smoke rose up from the mountain coves, where farmers were curing their tobacco.

A dozen yards below, Ace Kilgore was yelling commands to the patrolling Commie Killers, unaware of Molly and Jude overhead. Jude's father had shown them this cave, high up on a cliff, concealed by a thick tangle of mountain laurel, where Abigail Westlake had hidden while soldiers down below marched her family off to their deaths in the Ozarks. Jude and Molly were sitting on a cushion of pine needles, quiet as hunted game, playing Trail of Tears. They had even persuaded Sidney to halt his amiable panting.

Although she tried her best to stay out of Ace's way, Jude often stole glances at him on the playground or in the lunchroom or around the neighborhood. If she and Molly were wolf boys trying to pass unnoticed on the fringes of the forest, Ace was a wolf boy who had refused to come in from the wild. He was completely untamed, frightening but also admirable.

The Commie Killers swept down the cliff face on their mission of national security. Jerry Crawford, Ace's best friend, brought up the rear. He was much taller than Ace, but he always hunched over in an attempt to be the same height. A couple of the others, twins with sleek dark hair whom Jude and Molly called the "Panther Twins," were stronger and faster than Ace. But they always trailed around after him like docile guard dogs, executing his nefarious orders without a flicker of hesitation.

As their shouts faded, Jude extracted Girl Scout cookies and strawberry sodas from her knapsack. She handed Molly a candy cigarette, lighting it for her with an imaginary match. Cigarette dangling from her lips, Molly dealt hands for Over the Moon. Setting aside their soda bottles, they began drawing, exchanging and discarding in an arcane pattern understood only by themselves, since they had invented this game in which low cards were worth more than high ones. Sucking their cigarettes, they cheered and giggled and cursed.

When the game ended, they used the cards to outline the floor plan of the cabin they were going to build on the ridge overhead when they grew up. It would be filled with books and records, and there would be a separate room for drawing and painting. Outside would be a stable for their dogs and horses, with a fenced-in paddock. Their jobs at the Wiggly Piglet would pay for it all.

Jude inspected the floor plan that stretched across the pine needles. "What's that room for?" she asked, pointing.

"I just added it," said Molly. "It's for our babies. We can each have one."

Jude looked at her. "Oh, no, you don't. Not me."

"But it would be fun."

"Babies kill you."

"Not always they don't."

"Molly, I don't want you to die. Promise me you won't have a baby."

"Okay. Relax, Jude. It was just an idea."

Stomach knotted, Jude looked out the cave mouth as a huge, puffy white cloud drifted past like a giant cotton ball. Her mother was reclining on it, dressed in a skirted bathing suit, a white rose in her black hair.

"Is something wrong?" asked Molly.

Jude had told no one about sometimes seeing her mother. Everyone said she was dead. But Molly was her best friend. They told each other everything. "It's my mother."

Molly glanced around the cave. "Where?"

"Out there. See that cloud?"

Molly looked out the cave mouth. "Yeah, it does look kind of like a woman."

"No, I mean my mother is there, riding on that cloud. Lying on that thing that looks like a throne. Wearing a bathing suit. Now she's waving at us."

Molly stared at the cloud for a long time. "I don't see her, Jude," she finally said.

"You don't?" Jude blinked her eyes several times and then looked back at the cloud. Her mother was still there, tossing her a kiss.

"No. But I believe you, Jude. I believe she's really there."

But Molly's frown lines didn't go away, even after they returned to Over the Moon.

Finally, Jude rested her handful of cards on the pine needles. "What's wrong?" she asked, worried that Molly might be wondering if she really wanted to be best friends with someone who saw ghosts.

"Nothing."

Jude shrugged. "It's okay if you don't want to tell."

After a long strained silence broken only by Sidney's panting, Molly said, "Noreen passed a note around class today saying that you're my boyfriend."

"*What?* That's the dumbest thing I ever heard of."

"And during recess this afternoon, she and all her creepy little friends started singing, 'Molly and Jude, sitting in a tree, K-I-S-S-I-N-G. . . .' "

"But I don't even know how to kiss," said Jude, outraged.

"You don't?"

"Why would I?"

"I'll teach you," offered Molly.

Jude looked at her quickly. "How do you know?"

"I watch my parents—in the living room at night, when they think I'm asleep. I sneak halfway down the stairs and look through the banister." Laying aside her cards, she put the back of her hand to her mouth and opened her lips as though about to take a bite out of it. Then she pressed her lips hard against her hand and closed her eyes, twisting her hand and head in opposite directions.

"Okay. Try it," she said to Jude.

Jude copied her, sucking the back of her own hand with feigned fervor.

"Good," said Molly. "Now try this." She clutched the hand she was kissing with her other hand and turned her mouth aside to murmur, "Oh, my darling, I love you so much."

"Oh, my darling, I love you so much," Jude murmured to her hand, trying to imagine Molly's mother, who was as fragile as a flower, doing such a disgusting thing with Molly's father, who was covered like a bear with coarse, black hair and spoke in a voice that was almost a growl.

"There. You've got it," Molly said with satisfaction.

"But why can't Noreen just leave us alone?" demanded Jude,

letting her adorable hand collapse into her lap. "We've never done anything to her."

"Momma says she wouldn't tease us if she didn't like us."

They considered this bit of adult wisdom for a long time. It sounded far-fetched.

"What do you think we should do?" Jude lay back on the slick, fragrant pine needles, hands behind her head.

"You may have to prove to her that you're a girl."

"How?"

"If you show her you haven't got one of those dumb penises, she'll know you aren't a boy. And if you aren't a boy, then you can't be my boyfriend."

Jude giggled. "Maybe it would be better just to spend less time together."

"We can't let anyone come between us," said Molly.

"Nobody could ever do that."

They glanced at each other doubtfully.

"No," said Molly.

"But if we ignore each other at school," insisted Jude, "they'll think we don't like each other anymore, and then they'll leave us alone."

"We could still meet here every day after school," said Molly, looking relieved.

"Yeah. We're safe here. Nobody could ever find us."

After finishing her homework that night, Jude put on her pajamas and pulled the shoe box out from under her bed. Extracting one of her mother's letters, she climbed under the covers and decoded another paragraph: "This afternoon on your parents' lawn, while I was watching your father drive his golf ball across the river, Jude got a cardboard box from the garage and hung a dish towel over an upright stick inside it. When I asked her what she was doing, she explained that she was making a boat so she could sail down the river and across the sea to visit her daddy in France. Our child is the light of my life in these dark days, darling. Thank you for her, and for our nights of love that brought her into being.''

Smiling, Jude reread this several times. She had been the light of her mother's life. Wrapped in this new knowledge as though in her mother's arms, she sniffed the perfume emanating from the letter and caressed the back of her hand with her lips and remembered her mother leaning down in her long sleek mink coat to press her bright red lips against Jude's cheek as she lay in bed. If she woke up before her parents got home and smelled the smoke from the baby-sitter's cigarettes in the living room, she would get up and look in the mirror and touch the red lips imprinted on her cheek and know that everything would soon be fine again.

The next day, Jude was playing Red Rover with the other second graders when she spotted Molly helping Noreen mat down the tall grass in the far corner of the playground to form a warren of interconnected rooms. Noreen appeared to be the mother bunny and Molly the father. The other girls were apparently baby bunnies, because they were hopping through the grassy chambers sucking their thumbs and wiggling their noses.

Jude caught Molly's eye and glared at her. Molly gestured in wolfspeak when Noreen wasn't looking: Don't worry. You'll always be my best friend. I will never play Pecan with Noreen.

Meanwhile, Oscar, who had been kept back two years and was twice as large as the other second graders, had identified Mary, the frail girl who was holding Jude's hand, as the weak link in his opponents' line. He charged the two of them with bulging eyes and flaring nostrils. As Jude fell to the ground and was trampled beneath his pounding feet, she simply switched off the playground, like changing stations on the radio.

And there was her mother, dressed in her long mink coat, standing in the doorway of her mansion in heaven, arms outspread for Jude.

"How have you been, light of my life?" she asked.

JUDE SET HER ALARM for the middle of the night. Tiptoeing into her father's room, she stood by his bedside listening to his soft steady snoring. She felt guilty waking him up when he worked so hard, but it had to be done.

"Daddy?" she whispered.

He sat straight up from a deep sleep, well trained from his years of people pounding on the back door in the middle of the night, bearing the bloody victims of family feuds up in the mountain coves.

"I've been throwing up," she announced in her most pitiful voice. It was only a small lie, because she'd felt like throwing up ever since she saw Molly playing Father Bunny with Noreen.

He reached over to feel her cheeks and forehead with a cool hand. Then he got up, took her back to her own room, tucked her in, and laid a towel along her bedside with instructions to call him if it happened again.

The next morning, he came into her room in his navy-blue corduroy robe and thrust a thermometer into her mouth before going to the bathroom to shave. While he was gone, she held the thermometer against the bulb in the lamp on her nightstand. Then she furiously scrubbed her wool blanket back and forth across her chest and arms until a rash appeared.

When her father returned, dressed in a white shirt and smelling like cinnamon toast, he read the thermometer in the lamplight, placed a damp hand on her forehead, poked her rash with his fingertips, and told her to spend the day in bed.

Jude ended up spending the entire week in bed, eating meals

Clementine brought her on a tray and listening to Arthur Godfrey on the radio while Clementine ironed by her bedside. Her father ransacked the hospital library trying to diagnose her mysterious rash and fever. Molly came over every afternoon after school, bearing candy or cookies she'd saved from her lunch box or bought with her allowance at the drugstore on the highway.

"So how's Noreen?" Jude asked each afternoon.

Each afternoon, Molly averted her eyes and answered, "She's all right."

After Molly left, Jude would take out her mother's letter in which she called Jude the light of her life and sniff its fragrance and remember stroking her mother's calves with her hands as she straightened the seams down the backs of her silky stockings.

On Friday afternoon, Molly's reply to Jude's stubborn question was, "Noreen and I had a fight. We aren't speaking anymore."

To her father's relief, Jude was out of bed and back on her feet for the weekend.

MOLLY AND JUDE, KNAPSACKS on their backs, were weaving through the tangled maze of rock ledges and mountain laurel in the Wildwoods the afternoon following Jude's abrupt recovery from her unidentified disease. They had agreed it might be a good idea to play Pecan when they reached their cave, to make up after their week of estrangement. But when they arrived beneath the limestone outcropping, they found hacked, withering laurel branches strewn around the leafy forest floor. And printed across the pale gray rock face in red paint was DEATH TO ALL BOY-GIRLS!

Inside the cave, their playing cards, torn and twisted, were scattered across the pine needles. And in the middle of the floor, cold and stiff, a necklace of blood around its throat, lay a baby rabbit. Molly and Jude glanced at each other.

"I think we need to talk to Sandy," whispered Jude, groping for Molly's hand.

Molly extracted her hand to say in wolfspeak, Let's get out of here. They may be hiding somewhere, watching us.

Sandy lowered the ladder to his tree house, and they clambered up it as though pursued by enraged yellow jackets. Some maniac was screaming opera from a record player in the corner. A large, black typewriter sat on a low table. Stacks of paper lay everywhere.

"I'm writing a novel," said Sandy, fair hair as scrambled as though he'd combed it with an eggbeater. "It's about alienation on the playground. It's a metaphor for life."

"What's alienation?" asked Molly as they sat down cross-legged on the carpet.

"What's a metaphor?" asked Jude.

"Oh, never mind," Sandy said with a sigh. "What's up?"

"We're in trouble," said Jude.

"As usual." Sandy smiled tightly. "Now what?"

"I'm sure you've heard the rumors at school," said Molly. "That Jude is my boyfriend?"

He nodded. "The solution is simple. I've been wanting to tell you, but you haven't asked."

"What?" they asked in unison.

"Wear dresses and Mary Janes."

They looked at each other.

"It's the only way." Sandy pointed to the socks and sandals on his feet. "I wear these at home, but I wear high-tops at school. I play softball even though I prefer chess. If you look the way they look and do the things they do, they'll leave you alone. You can be yourself in private. Play their game, but know it's a game. Pretend you're double agents. Like on 'I Led Three Lives.' That's the theme of my novel:

the gap between appearance and reality. It's called *The Naked and the Clothed.*"

"It might work," said Molly, studying Jude. She started giggling.

"What?" asked Jude.

"You in those stupid Mary Janes!" Molly began rolling around the carpet, laughing. Sandy and Jude joined her, the tree house rocking on its branches.

After they calmed down and were lying on the floor gasping for breath, Molly said, "Sandy, you're a genius."

"So they say."

That night in bed, Jude read another of her mother's paragraphs under her sheets with a flashlight. This secrecy was unnecessary, since her father let her stay up as late as she liked. But public school was taking effect: She was starting to enjoy the rush of terror at possible discovery by a punitive authority figure.

"Darling, Jude wakes up crying in the night, and nothing will console her but to bring her into bed with me. Sometimes as I doze, I almost imagine it's you there beside me. But when I open my eyes, I see it's only Jude. She's an amusing little creature, but it's you I need, my precious love, in the way only you can provide. You are everything to me. . . ."

Ripping this letter into tiny pieces, Jude carried them into the bathroom and flushed them down the toilet. Then she stuffed the shoe box into the back of her closet and placed her dead doll patient on top of it. It didn't really matter if her mother hadn't loved her best, because she and Molly would wear Mary Janes and spend the rest of their lives together in their cabin on the clifftop.

ACE BRAKED HIS BICYCLE in front of Jude and Molly one afternoon as they were walking home from the grade school up the
hill from the highway. He was wearing chinos, with a bicycle clip on
one leg, a pinstriped oxford cloth shirt, and spotless white bucks, and
he reeked of Old Spice. There was a faint shadow on his upper lip,
and his chestnut hair was pomaded into a rigid flattop. Smiling so his
braces glinted in the weak autumn sunlight, he said in a cracking voice,
"Hey, ladies. How you doing today?"

"Fine, thank you," said Jude, glancing at him suspiciously over
her books, which she was clutching to her chest with both arms. He
had the same dull, dark wounded eyes, but everything else about him
seemed different now that he was in junior high. She and Molly had
heard that the Commie Killers were taking ballroom dancing lessons
at the Youth Center in case the graduates of Miss Melrose's Charm

Class invited them to be their escorts for the Virginia Club Colonial Cotillion. The notion of a room full of those gorillas waltzing in tuxedos with matching plaid cummerbunds and bow ties had reduced them to hysterics more than once.

"Mighty pretty day," he suggested.

As they walked, Jude noticed that the hand with which he was pushing his bicycle had nails chewed down to the quicks.

"Not bad," said Molly, eying this pleasant young Rotarian with curiosity.

Ever since Jude and Molly had started wearing skirts to school three years earlier, they had eaten lunch in the cafeteria and hung out together on the playground every day without being harassed by Noreen and Ace and their mobs. And after school, they donned blue jeans and raced their new horses down through the Wildwoods and along the river. Jude didn't really mind that her father had married his nurse from intensive care and moved her into their house, because Jude now spent most nights at Molly's, curled up with her and Sidney beneath the dotted swiss canopy like puppies in a litter. The only thing that bothered her about this arrangement was that she sometimes woke up in the middle of the night, to hear Molly's parents arguing in their bedroom. Occasionally, there were thuds, as though someone was throwing something. And then Molly's mother would start crying. But Molly always seemed to sleep right through it.

"Say, ladies," said Ace, running his hand up the front of his new scrub-brush hairdo, "Mill Valley has challenged Tidewater Estates to a football game. But we've only got eight players. Any chance you two would play?"

Molly and Jude glanced at each other. It might be a trick. Although the ancient wounds had healed, the scars remained to remind them.

"We need a full team if we're going to stand a chance." He

smiled at them smoothly, and Jude realized that he could have a fruitful career ahead of him as a horse trader.

"That's still just ten," said Molly, leaning over to straighten one of the white bobby socks that was sagging below her crinolined poodle skirt.

"Can you think of anybody else?"

"How about Sandy?" asked Jude.

Ace smiled with polite incredulity. "Sandy? Sandy Andrews? Sandy Andrews on a football field?"

"I played catch with him last year," said Jude. "He was working on his aerodynamics project for the county science fair. And believe me, Sandy knows how to throw a football."

"If Sandy doesn't play, we don't either," announced Molly.

Ace sighed with a sweet, long-suffering smile, a new facial expression in his rather limited repertoire. "All right. But you all ask him. He's not too crazy about me."

"I wonder if this is a good idea," mused Jude as Ace rode off down the hill. "Clementine always says that leopards don't change their spots without a whole lot of scrubbing."

"But he seems pretty scrubbed," said Molly. "We may as well give him a chance. If he's too obnoxious, we'll just quit the team."

ON THE FIELD ONCE pocked with their trenches, the former Commie Killers watched with amazement as Sandy repeatedly sailed the football over the heads of the enclosing tacklers and into Jude's or Molly's outstretched arms. Impressed, Ace promoted him to quarterback and Jude and Molly to ends.

Then they divided into two opposing lines. Crouching for drills like three-legged pit bulls, they collided time after time at a signal from Ace. The tenth time, Ace locked shoulder pads with Molly. Grinning at her with clenched teeth, he butted her backward down the field while she grimaced fiercely and struggled to dig her cleats into the turf and break his advance.

During the tackling drill that followed, Ace kept hurling himself through the air at Molly, bringing her crashing to the ground beneath him. Once, he continued to lie immobile on her like a sack of concrete, smiling up at Jude as Molly writhed and twisted beneath him.

"Get off me, you big lug!" Molly yelled.

Jude felt her hands clench into fists as she stood there watching. Apparently, the new, improved Ace Kilgore still had a few of his old tricks up his sleeve.

Laughing indulgently, he allowed Molly to push him aside.

"Drop dead, creep," she snarled as she struggled to her feet, face flushed and helmet askew.

Jude leaned over and asked her in a low voice, "Are you okay?"

"Of course I'm okay," she snapped, glaring at Ace as she straightened her helmet.

CLOUDS WERE SCUDDING LIKE hockey pucks across the bright blue sky. Noreen's crew wore red-and-white corduroy skirts, saddle shoes, and junior-high letter sweaters. Most sported jaunty ponytails.

"Girls?" the Mill Valley Butchers exclaimed when they dismounted from their bicycles and spotted Molly's black braids hanging down from her shiny red helmet.

"I know that ole girl," said one, pointing at Jude in her red jersey and padded khaki knickers. "She ain't nothing but a fifth grader."

"The Commandos got fifth-grade girls on their team! Oh, man!" They slapped one another's helmets with hilarity.

"You won't be laughing by the time this is over," snarled Ace from behind his plastic face guard.

"Better face it, rich boy," sneered Joe Sneed, "your ass is grass."

Joe's older brother Clyde, a former football star at the high school, home on leave from the marines, had come along as referee. The boys on both teams kept glancing at him as he stood there straight as a linesman's stake in his severe blond brush cut. He'd survived boot camp at Paris Island and killed Commies in Korea.

The Butchers won the coin toss, and Joe effortlessly returned the Commandos' kickoff for a touchdown, striding like a Louisville pacer through the scarlet maple leaves that were swirling like flocks of migrating cardinals across the plateau from the Wildwoods.

"Sorry, guys," Joe muttered to the Butchers as they trotted back up the field, shoulder pads jouncing like saddles. "I shoulda knowed this would be a waste of time."

For a while, Sandy strolled around the backfield in his cleats, hands on his hips, studying the Butchers and holding up a wet finger to assess the breeze. Jude and Molly fled to the sidelines each time the ball was snapped, while the Butchers ground the Commando line into the clay and massacred the ballcarrier. The afternoon gave every evidence of being a long and bloody one, and Jude couldn't imagine why she and Molly had given up cantering their horses along the river in order to be ripped to pieces by a gang of surly hoodlums.

Finally, Sandy announced in the huddle, "Okay, I'm ready."

Jerry Crawford centered the ball to Sandy. The Commando line turned suddenly impregnable, giving Sandy the leisure to fake a lateral and two handoffs to Ace and the Panther Twins so convincingly that the Butchers chased them down the field before realizing that Sandy still held the ball. Jude and Molly, meanwhile, were darting around midfield, causing the pursuing Butchers to collide with one another like enemy tanks. Sandy sailed a perfect spiral pass to Jude, who grabbed it out of the air and dashed untouched across the goal line.

Noreen's cheering squad went wild, prancing and twirling and turning cartwheels. They shook their red-and-white pompoms and thrust out their arms and legs in intricately choreographed patterns. Then they shouted in unison, with the same fervor they used to devote to speaking in tongues: "Hidy, hey, hidy, hoe! Iddley, widdley, waddley, woe! Our Commandos are the best! Better, better than the rest!"

The Butchers slunk home to the mill village after their defeat, and Molly invited the Commandos and the cheerleaders to her basement to celebrate their first victory with Cokes and butterscotch brownies.

"I have an idea," said Noreen as she drained the last of her Coke and brandished the green bottle like a fairy godmother's wand. "Let's play Spin the Bottle!"

The boys in their football uniforms eyed one another, grinning nervously and blushing behind their newly sprouted acne. Then they eyed the cheerleaders, who were draped decoratively around the steel jack posts that held up the ceiling.

"Good idea," said Ace, grabbing the bottle from Noreen. "Me first. Y'all girls get in a circle here."

Molly and Jude sat down cross-legged on the black-speckled linoleum as though before a campfire. Noreen and the other cheerleaders sank to their knees, tucked their feet beneath their hips, and braced their palms against the floor behind them so that their chests puffed out like robins in the spring. Ace stepped into the center of the circle, squatted, and twirled the bottle on the linoleum. It spun more and more slowly before finally stopping on Molly. She and Jude exchanged glances.

"Nobody has to play who doesn't want to," announced Jude.

"Fair's fair," said Molly. She stood up and disappeared in her football uniform behind the furnace with Ace.

Jude watched Jerry spin the bottle, praying it wouldn't land on her, wondering what was going on in the shadows behind the furnace. Would Molly really kiss their ancient enemy? Would she moan and sigh the way she had in third grade when she kissed the back of her own hand?

Jude watched in silent misery as the bottle inched to a halt. It was pointing at Noreen. She jumped up with a squeal, kicking back her saddle shoes in a coy pep-squad hop. As she and Jerry headed for the furnace, Ace and Molly emerged. Molly was blushing. She didn't look at Jude. But Ace did, grinning, his braces glinting in the light from the overhead bulb, which Molly had encased in a red-and-gold Japanese lantern.

Sandy's spin landed on Jude.

"She's too young," said Molly quickly. "She's just a fifth grader."

"She's only a year younger than I am," said Sandy. "I just skipped two grades, is all. Come on, Jude." He held out his hand.

In the dark beneath the cobwebbed heating ducts, Sandy whispered, "Thank God I got you."

"I'll say," whispered Jude. "Do we really have to do this?"

"We might as well get it over with."

As they tried to embrace, their arms collided and tangled. Then they bumped noses and began to giggle. Finally, Sandy managed to plant a peck on her mouth before they both doubled over with silent agonized hilarity.

Afterward, Jude and Molly changed from their football uniforms and walked to the pasture behind Jude's grandmother's house, where they kept their horses. Jude's father had bought them from a friend of Mr. Starnes who trained Tennessee walking horses for shows. These two geldings hadn't made the grade, but they were wonderful for riding because they were so happy no longer to have their hooves weighted for the ring that they seemed to dance on air as they ran. Tennessee walkers originally being bred for plantation owners to ride while surveying their fields, these two could cover miles without tiring, in a running walk as comfortable as rocking in a rocking chair. Although they had elaborate names and pedigrees, Jude called hers Flame because of a flaring white mark down his forehead, and Molly called hers Pal because he was a palomino, with a ghostly pale mane and tail.

On weekends, Jude and Molly rode downriver through pastures of bluegrass and timothy and fescue, past fields planted with tobacco and corn. Through bottomland studded with cottonwood, maple, sycamore, and sweet gum, their branches draped with lianas of wild grape that stirred in the breezes down the valley like serpents writhing in a jungle. After a picnic in the sun by the river, they headed back home along ridges thickly forested with oak and hickory and ash. In the fall, juicy orange persimmons fell into their laps as they passed beneath the overladen branches. And in the spring, dogwoods and redbuds starred the dark brooding woods with bursts of pink and purple and white, like fireworks that didn't fade.

That afternoon after Spin the Bottle, they cantered through Mr. Starnes's alfalfa field, alongside the low-leaning willows by the river. As Sidney leapt and barked beside her, Molly veered Pal toward the shore. Jumping the lip of the bank, Pal plunged into the water, throwing up a spray that glistened orange in the setting sun like sparks shooting from a fire.

Once Molly was thoroughly soaked, she headed Pal back toward dry land. He arced time after time up the rutted clay rise like a salmon leaping upstream. Molly threw her head back and laughed, dark wavy hair fanning out around her face, thighs gripping Pal's straining shoulders, fist maneuvering the rope she'd run through his halter for reins. For a moment, Jude couldn't catch her breath. Molly looked like the goddess on her grandmother's glass vase, the one with the bow on her back and the dogs leaping at her knees.

When Molly reached level ground, she dug her heels into Pal's flanks and lay down along his neck. He broke into a gallop, flying hooves hurling up clods of earth. As his cream-colored mane floated up and mixed with her dark hair, Molly glanced tauntingly back over her shoulder at Jude. Jude leaned forward and Flame shot off across the field after Pal like a land missile. Jude could see each muscle of Molly's back tensing and straining beneath the wet clinging fabric of her pale-blue work shirt.

When Jude and Molly finally slid off Pal and Flame in the stand of giant oaks on the cliff above their cave, the horses were covered with patches of white lather and dark sweat. The girls collapsed on a bed of leathery mauve leaves, laughing and gasping as their horses snorted and stamped and wheezed. In the tops of the huge old trees swayed globes of mistletoe the size of medicine balls.

After catching their breath, Molly and Jude propped themselves up on their elbows so they could watch the indigo mountains below, wave after wave of crenellated ridges like ripples on the sea, all being swallowed up by a maw of vermilion sunset. Jude could smell Molly's sweat and the rotting oak mold beneath the two of them, where a million earthworms were munching away. Molly's breath was stirring Jude's hair and tickling her ear. Suddenly, she recalled Ace's smug smile when he came out from behind the furnace and Molly's averted eyes.

"Do you still want to build a cabin up here when we grow up?" she asked Molly.

Molly turned her head to look at Jude. "Sure. Don't you?"

"Yes. But we haven't discussed it in a long time."

"What else would we do?" Molly reached out her little finger and interlocked it with Jude's.

"That kissing stuff was pretty dumb, wasn't it?" said Jude, relieved.

Molly didn't reply.

Jude's skin prickled with anxiety. "Wasn't it?"

"Yeah," Molly finally agreed. "Count on Noreen to dream up an ordeal like that."

"Sandy and I couldn't figure out what to do with our arms."

"You couldn't? Here. I'll show you."

Jumping up, she grabbed Jude's hand, pulled her to her feet, and arranged Jude's arms around her body. Beneath her fingertips, Jude could feel the damp cotton of Molly's shirt and the firm muscles of her back. Then Molly placed her arms around Jude, one hand holding a shoulder and the other Jude's waist.

"See? Simple." Smiling with just her eyes, she moved closer and kissed Jude firmly on the mouth.

As Molly's chest pressed against her own, Jude experienced an alarming sensation. It was sweet and nauseating, both at once, like eating too much fudge. Her teeth were set on edge and a shudder shook her limbs.

"What's wrong?" asked Molly.

Opening her eyes, Jude found herself staring directly into Molly's, which at that moment matched the blue of her shirt. "I don't know," she said. Shifting her hand down Molly's back, she discovered a piece of elastic stretching between Molly's shoulder blades. "What's this?"

"It's my new bra," said Molly, dropping her arms and stepping back.

"Why are you wearing a bra?" Mothers wore bras. Teachers wore bras. Marilyn Monroe wore a bra. But not kids.

"To support my breasts."

"But you don't even have any."

"I do so." Molly smiled.

"Where? Let me see." Jude reached out and undid her top button.

"Jude." Blushing, Molly turned away to rebutton her shirt.

"Sorry," said Jude, watching Molly uneasily.

The next afternoon while Molly was at the dentist, Jude walked through the revolving doors into Fine's Department Store on the main street of town. Glancing all around to make sure no one was watching, she sneaked into the lingerie department. All around her loomed beige plastic female torsos, severed at the waists, some headless or armless, others contorted into grotesque postures with their severed stumps of arms extended as though for a bloody embrace. Each sported a different type of brassiere or slip.

Clenching her molars for courage, Jude walked into their midst as though into an enchanted forest in which interlopers were chopped up and turned into bra-bearing statues. Reaching out to the nearest rack, she grabbed the first box she came to. After counting out her savings on the glass countertop, she shoved it at the gum-chewing salesgirl and fled.

Back in her bedroom, Jude threw off her flannel shirt and poked at the pale flesh surrounding her small pink nipples. It seemed no different from usual. But Molly always knew the right thing to do before Jude did. Inspecting the cardboard box, Jude read that the bra was size 36C. Removing the white cotton contraption from the cardboard box, she tried to figure out which strap went where. It was as confusing as when she was first learning to bridle Flame. Finally, she got the thing fastened and went over to look in the mirror on her closet door. The stitched fabric cups billowed atop her chest like luffing sails. Smiling proudly, she put her shirt back on and buttoned it. Then she turned sideways to the mirror to observe her new womanly contour.

AFTER EVERY FOOTBALL GAME, there was a celebratory session of Spin the Bottle in Molly's basement. Eventually, Jude had kissed each reformed Commie Killer at least once. These former marauders were so courteous and pleasant, even Ace Kilgore himself, that she was forced to admit that people could change. But try as she did to position her hands and mouth correctly, she felt very little except impatience as the boys pressed their lips against hers and ran their hands over the elastic that hung loosely between her shoulder blades. So she pretended that she was an orphan raised by wolves, participating in the rites of these strange creatures on the edge of the forest only to be polite.

One afternoon in early winter, Noreen announced that Spin the Bottle had become boring. Everyone nodded in agreement except Sandy, Molly, and Jude, who were wary of what she might propose instead. Her new game was called Five Minutes in Heaven. Each girl's name would be written on a slip of paper. Each boy would draw a folded slip. Then he and the girl he'd picked would be locked in the closet together for five minutes to "let nature take its course." Since there were nine couples that day, Noreen calculated that a complete cycle would require forty-five minutes. But several participants had to be home for supper before that, so she suggested locking up three couples at a time, one in the closet, one behind the furnace, and one in the outside stairwell, thus trimming game time to fifteen minutes. Those who ate supper late could play a second round if they wanted.

Jude watched with mounting dread as Noreen wrote out the

girls' names, tore the paper into strips, and folded them. She noticed that Noreen marked her own slip with a tiny X when she thought no one was looking, catching Jerry Crawford's eye as she did so. Then she mixed up the slips in the basket that had held the chocolate chip cookies. The first three boys selected one. Jerry unfolded his and gave Jude a look full of meaning. Noreen, meanwhile, looked at him with dismay. Then she glared evilly at Jude through her pointy new white cat-eye glasses.

Walking over to Jude, Jerry seized her hand and led her to the closet to which he'd been assigned. Within was an athlete's paradise —a croquet set, a kickball, fishing gear, a couple of rifles, a bicycle pump, a saddle and bridle, golf clubs and cleats, some deflated plastic beach toys. A badminton net was hanging off the upper shelf. Jerry closed the door, and he and Jude stood there in the dark, Jude wondering what they could possibly find to do with each other for the five minutes that stretched before them like the sands of the Sahara.

As Jerry leaned over to kiss her, his head became tangled in the badminton net. Struggling to free himself, he pulled the net off the shelf, along with several rackets and birdies. Jude also became entangled, and they spent their first two minutes in heaven trying to extract themselves. Finally, Jerry got them out by ripping the net to pieces.

Free at last, he put his arms around her and fitted his lips to hers. She could feel a fine stubble on his upper lip as he rubbed it against her own. Then he pushed his slimy tongue between her lips and into her mouth. She tried to push it back out again with her own tongue. This seemed to encourage him. Breathing faster, he started moving his tongue in and out like a striking snake. Jude turned her head aside, worried that she might throw up. Jerry put his hands on her waist, pulled her hips against his own, buried his stubbly face in the angle between her throat and shoulder, and began sucking her neck like a crazed vampire. She could feel some strange bulge in his football pants. It pressed against her belly like a concealed handgun.

The door flew open. Noreen was standing there looking deeply annoyed. "Time's up!" she announced like a teacher monitoring an IQ test. "Next!"

"So what did you think of Five Minutes in Heaven?" asked Molly after everyone had left. She grabbed the broom and began to sweep up the cookie crumbs on the linoleum.

"Not much." Jude was fitting the Coke bottles into the cardboard six-pack carriers, inspecting the bottom of each for its town of origin. So far, St. Louis was the farthest away.

"You didn't like it?"

"Did you?"

"It was okay."

Jude reflected that Molly's partner had been Sandy. No wonder she hadn't minded. Sandy always performed the minimum that he could get away with in these dumb games. "Jerry kept sticking his tongue into my mouth. It was disgusting."

Molly stopped sweeping to look at her. "You don't like Frenching?"

"What?"

"French kissing, it's called."

"You mean there's a name for it? I thought he'd made it up."

"You just need some practice. Here, let me show you."

Dropping the broom, she walked across the linoleum toward Jude. Jude watched her approach in her red football jersey, feeling strange. Was Molly really going to do that to her? With Molly, it might not be quite so revolting.

Extending the fingers of one hand, Molly placed her thumb beneath her index finger to form an opening. Wetting her lips with her tongue, she held this opening to her mouth. As Jude watched, she licked and caressed the aperture with her lips and tongue.

"Try it," she said.

Jude obeyed, looking at Molly as she did so, fascinated by the unexpected talents of this friend she thought she knew so well.

"I bet you'll like it better next time," said Molly, squeezing her upper arm.

Jude studied Molly, who was bending over to pick up the broom. With a stab of alarm, she wondered where Molly had learned to French kiss.

WHEN MRS. ELKINS ARRIVED in Molly's bedroom to say good night one evening, she was clutching a pink book called *New Life Abounding: A Guide to Christian Marriage*. Perching on the bedside beneath the dotted swiss canopy, she gazed at Sidney, who was panting amiably, filling the room with his sour dog-food breath.

"Girls, there's something we need to talk about," she said anxiously.

Jude and Molly, who were lying under the covers in their pajamas, looked at her with alarm.

"I suppose y'all have been wondering about babies and all like that?"

The girls glanced at each other.

"All right, so here's what happens," she gasped. "The daddy puts his pee-pee in the mommy's wee-wee, and a baby grows in her stomach. Oh, here, read it for yourselves." She thrust the pink book at them. Hyperventilating, she raced from the room.

Astonished by the concept that Mr. Elkins's tiny, pale pee-pee could somehow enter Mrs. Elkins's never-seen wee-wee, Molly and Jude spent several hours giggling nervously over the diagrams of this unlikely procedure. Molly pointed out haltingly that French kissing was merely this unappetizing act performed with the tongue. They gazed at each other with horror as they realized that each had done

this with various boys. Did this mean that they weren't "virgins,"
which the book said it was very important still to be when you gave
yourself to your new husband on your wedding night?

    As she slipped into an exhausted sleep toward midnight, Jude
finally understood that her father had killed her mother with one of
those strange lumps that lurked like hand grenades in the pants of the
new, improved Commie Killers.

CHAPTER

6

JUDE'S GRANDMOTHER looked up from soaking her baking-powder biscuit in redeye gravy to say, "Daniel, you're raising this child like a boy. Football, and horses without saddles, and jeeps in the pasture. And all this arrowhead nonsense. You may have gone to school in New York City, but you're every bit as much of a savage as your father was. I declare, I'm shocked to my core!"

"Yes, Momma. I'm sure you're right."

Jude realized that her father couldn't have cared less. He was beaming at his wife, whose belly was swelling with new life. Aunt Audrey's carrot-colored bouffant framed a foxlike face with small, pointed features. She was upset that Jude couldn't call her Mother. But each time Jude had tried, her throat had closed up, leaving her gasping like an asthmatic. Calling her Aunt Audrey was their compromise. Jude was trying to like her, but they had nothing in common except Jude's father. So Jude was polite to Aunt Audrey for his sake, and Aunt Audrey was polite to her for the same reason. Her father maintained she'd gained a mother, but she felt she'd lost a father instead.

"At least I wear shirts now," mumbled Jude.

"I beg your pardon?" barked her blue-haired grandmother. "Speak up, young lady."

"Nothing, ma'am."

"At the rate you're going, my dear, you'll never qualify for the Virginia Club Colonial Cotillion. And I refuse to ask them to lower their standards for you simply because I'm president." She returned the ladle to the silver gravy boat with finality.

Jude managed not to say that the only thing she wanted right now was to get this gruesome meal over with so she could go riding with Molly. Now that Molly was in junior high and Jude still in grade school, they saw each other only after school and on weekends. The Wildwoods were suddenly abloom and the alfalfa in the valley was greening up. The air had turned soft and steamy, and the soil would squelch under the horses' hooves when Pal and Flame loped along the riverbank in shafts of sunlight through the chartreuse willows.

Aunt Audrey said, "Yes, Jude, and you've got to think about how you're going to catch yourself a man when you get older." She plucked complacently at her bulging smock of rose linen.

Jude looked at her. If she wanted a man, she could always steal someone's father. Aunt Audrey was always making little jokes no one else thought were funny. It was pathetic.

That evening as Jude lay on her bed reading her assignment for Bible study class on the meaning of the lions in the story of Daniel, her grandmother phoned to say that Jude and Molly were enrolled in Miss Melrose's Charm Class at Fine's Department Store.

Jude held the phone receiver away from her ear and stared at it.

"They'll teach y'all how to dress and walk and sit," her grandmother promised.

"But I can already do that, Grandma."

"Not properly. Not like a young Virginia belle."

THE PROPER WAY TO WALK required placing one foot directly in front of the other as though crossing a tightrope, hips swaying side to side as ballast. Math texts balanced on their heads, Molly, Jude, Noreen, and several other apprentice charmers swayed along behind Miss Melrose (whose shiny false eyelashes and switchblade fingernails were all about an inch long) through the shoe department, down the escalator, past the waxworks of writhing plastic amputees in the lingerie department, and into the makeup department, which reeked of competing colognes.

"Now, girls," said Miss Melrose from behind the glass counter as she picked up a cotton ball and a bottle of caramel-colored liquid that looked like a urine sample, "at this particular moment in time, y'all's lovely little ingenue faces aren't anything but nasty old cell cemeteries."

Using the moistened cotton, she demonstrated on Noreen's oily forehead how to defoliate and moisturize these cemeteries. Then she promised to unveil the mysteries of eyeliner at the next session. Their homework assignment was to memorize the first ten silverware patterns in their *Learning to Be a Lady* handbook. She warned that they would be tested on this.

"Now y'all don't forget to bring you some high-heeled shoes next time," she called as they exited through the revolving door to the street, "and we'll practice our walk some more."

"Oh, please," muttered Jude as she and Molly headed home in the soft spring twilight, up the main street past the display windows at the five-and-dime. Jude felt acutely conscious of the incorrectness of her everyday gait, an ambling shuffle, faintly pigeon-toed. But Ace maintained that the fastest sprinters were always pigeon-toed, and it was true that Jude could outrun everyone else on the football team.

Molly was silent, which was making Jude uneasy. She had seemed alarmingly attentive during the skin-toning demonstration. The next thing you knew, she'd be wearing false eyelashes and a piecrust of makeup, just like Miss Melrose.

"I have something to tell you," said Molly as they passed their redbrick church, its white spire topped by a copper cross tarnished to the blue-green of bread mold. "I hope it won't hurt your feelings."

"What, for God's sake?"

"I'm having a party in my basement Friday night."

"A slumber party?"

"A boy-girl party. A Dirty Shag party."

"But you don't know how to shag."

"Yes, I do, Jude. They have sock hops at junior high during lunch break. To raise money for different charities."

"Well, I guess you could teach me to shag by this weekend."

"Jude," she said in a low, guilty voice, "it's just for junior high kids." She was staring at the sidewalk.

"Okay," Jude finally said. "So I'll just see you Saturday morning. We'll watch 'Fury' together. And maybe go riding. Or look for arrowheads in the afternoon with my dad."

"Great," said Molly. "You know you're my best friend. Nothing can ever change that."

"Yes, I know that."

They had reached the crack in the sidewalk between their two yards. For old times' sake, laughing, they put their hands on each other's shoulders, glanced into each other's eyes, and chanted in unison, "Best friend. Buddy of mine. Pal of pals." Molly seemed relieved to have made her confession, and Jude vowed always to help her feel free to do what she wanted.

Following supper and homework, Jude and Molly stood side by side in their shorty pajamas before the mirror in Molly's bathroom, setting their hair on rollers as big as frozen orange-juice cans. Then they encased the rollers in stretchy silver lamé hair nets that made them look like spacemen. Climbing into Molly's bed, they tried to discover a comfortable sleeping position that wouldn't result in stiff necks in the morning.

Finally settled on her side with Molly's chest against her back, Jude tried to relax, despite the fact that her ear was touching her shoulder. Molly twitched her legs irritably several times. Sighing, she sat up.

"What's wrong?" asked Jude, rolling over to look up at her in the glow coming through the window from the streetlight.

Molly reached under the covers and stroked one of Jude's calves. "Your legs. They tickle when we sleep like that. Couldn't you shave them?"

"I guess I could," said Jude. "I never thought about it." She ran her hand along one of Molly's calves. It was silky-smooth.

Molly rested her pumpkin head against the quilted headboard. "Jude," she said, "you know, it's not that easy for someone in junior high school to be best friends with a sixth grader."

Jude sat up and looked over at her. "I know it must be hard," she said, recalling her rash vow that afternoon to help Molly do as she wanted. "Do you want to see less of me?"

Molly said nothing for a long time.

God, Molly, don't leave me, Jude screamed silently. But she gritted her teeth and revealed nothing, as though bluffing during Over the Moon.

"No," Molly finally said. "But do please think about shaving your legs." She scooted to the far side of the bed and pulled the covers up to her chin.

Jude lay in the dark listening to the soft, steady whoosh of Molly's breathing. She could smell the floral cologne Molly had started splashing on her limbs after baths. She wanted to reach across the expanse of sheet and stroke Molly's hair. Or roll on top of her and lie nose-to-nose with their limbs aligned, giggling in unison and gazing into each other's crossed eyes. But they weren't children anymore.

Sidney yelped and snuffled in his sleep on his cushion in the corner. Baby frogs were peeping down by the river, and a coonhound was baying from some distant moonstruck cove.

Finally drifting off to sleep, Jude dreamed fitfully of losing her pocketbook, and being late for school, and having a flat tire on her bicycle, and having her teeth fall out in her hand at a party. Abruptly, she woke up. Molly's father was growling down the hall, followed by the high-pitched wail of her mother. Why couldn't they just be nice to each other and keep quiet? They were supposed to be the parents. Grabbing a tissue from the nightstand, Jude tore it up, plugged each ear with a wad, and tried to ignore their incomprehensible misery.

Toward dawn, she descended into an exhausted stupor.

She and Molly were lying on a raft in the river under a hot spring sun, floating past drooping willows that were mustard with new shoots. The raft rocked slowly in the current. Cawing crows were wheeling overhead. Sunbeams were flickering like hummingbird wings, back and forth across their flesh.

While the raft bobbed, the water began to flow faster and faster. She and Molly rolled toward each other and fitted their bodies together, interlocking their thighs and enfolding each other in their arms. As they were swept along

*down the river, their mouths met. They began to caress each other's lips with
their tongues.*

*The current raced more and more swiftly, as though about to carry them
over a waterfall. The rutted red banks rushed past on either side. And then a
towering wall of water rolled down the river and raised the raft high up
toward the sky, swirling it into the air like an autumn leaf on a whirlwind.
And Jude felt a sweet, haunting pain pulsing through her body, as though she
were being stung to death by a swarm of bees injecting her veins with honey.*

*And then the whole world burst apart like fireworks. Bits of Molly's and
her flesh flew off into the churning river and roiling sky. And they were no
longer Molly or Jude. They were each other and everything. The mountains
and the trees and the birds singing in the swaying branches. The river and
the pastures and the cows grazing on the lush grasses. They all formed a
whole. They always had and they always would, but she had lacked until now
the eyes to see it.*

Waking up in the scarlet rays of the rising sun, Jude discovered
that she and Molly were completely wrapped up in each other's arms
and legs in the middle of the bed, breasts pressed together. Molly's
eyes fluttered open and she stared blankly into Jude's, only inches
away, as though unable to remember who she was or who Jude was.
Slowly, the blankness faded and was replaced by consternation. Hurriedly, she untangled her limbs and scooted to the far side of the bed.

Glancing around bemusedly, Jude discovered that their giant
curlers had been yanked out and hurled around the room and that
their hairdos for that day were in ruins.

At school, Jude sat through her classes in a daze, constantly
reviewing what had happened between Molly and herself. It comforted
her to know that Molly was sitting in study hall at the junior high
school just then, also trying to figure out what it meant.

She watched a gray squirrel on a branch of the oak tree outside
her classroom window. It sat on its haunches munching an apple core

retrieved from the trash basket. Its fluffy, twitching tail was draped along its spine like a Mohawk haircut. As she watched, Jude thought maybe she finally understood what her father had always tried to explain to her. Beneath their different appearances, she and that squirrel were animated by the same force. It was the force that had joined Molly and her together last night. The Cherokees called it the Great Spirit, and Clementine called it graveyard love.

JUDE CRAWLED ACROSS THE LAWN to Molly's house, trying to pretend that she was an orphan raised by wolves who had just emerged from the forest. She was actually nothing more than a common Peeping Tom. But Aunt Audrey and her father were at the hospital having their baby, so no one would miss her. She lay in the shrubbery, looking through a basement window. Molly was dancing with Ace to "The Twelfth of Never." Ace had her arm twisted behind his back in a reverse hammerlock. Molly's hair was teased into dark cascades around her face. Eyes closed, she rested her cheek against his thick neck. Jude realized that Molly actually had the hips they'd been encouraged to sway at Charm Class.

Then there was a power failure and the lights went out. But the song continued: "Hold me close. Never let me go. . . ." So apparently it wasn't a power failure.

Yet the lights stayed out until Jude heard Mrs. Elkins's voice on the steps: ". . . and I insist that these lights stay on, Molly. If I have to tell you one more time, there'll be no more parties in this basement, young lady."

When the lights came back on, Jude could see Molly standing apart from Ace, who was wiping his mouth with the back of his hand. Molly's lips looked swollen. But how could she be kissing Ace Kilgore tonight after what had gone on between them last night on the raft?

Sidney came sniffing up to Jude's prostrate body. Whimpering, he lay down beside her, resting his chin on her shoulder. Jude draped her arm across his back. They watched Molly knead Ace's muscled shoulder with one hand while they resumed dancing, and Jude tried to figure out how to switch the lights off so that Mrs. Elkins would ban future parties. Closing her eyes, she willed the whole scene to vanish by the time she opened them.

Her mother was riding a puffy white cloud, a large picture hat clamped to her head with one hand. Smiling, she waved with the fingers of her free hand. Jude watched, worried to see her again after so many years, because her mother usually appeared whenever Jude was in for a bad time.

WHEN JUDE ENTERED MOLLY'S back door the next morning, Molly was sitting at the kitchen table eating a bowl of Cheerios. She had purple circles under her eyes, and so did Jude. Jude had lain awake all night trying to decide what to do about Molly's betrayal.

Plopping down in the chair beside her, Jude asked, "So how was your party?"

"Fine, thank you," said Molly without looking up. She tilted her bowl to spoon out the remaining milk.

"Was it any fun?"

"Yes, thank you." Still Molly wouldn't look her at her. And she seemed annoyed. Could she have seen Jude spying on her? Jude had believed that Molly should be free to do as she wanted, but that was at a time when she thought that what Molly wanted was to be with her.

Pulling herself together, Jude asked, "So do you want to go riding this morning, or what?"

"I'm afraid I can't." Molly leaned back in her chair, balancing on the rear legs like a circus tumbler. "It's one of Those Days."

"Which days?"

"I have cramps."

"Did you eat too fast?"

"No, I mean I have The Curse." Molly tossed her wavy black hair off her forehead with the back of one hand.

"The what?"

"My period. You know, like we read about in that pink book my mother gave us last year."

"You're kidding?"

"No."

"Since when?"

"Since yesterday."

"So you can have babies now?"

"Yes, I guess so," said Molly. She sounded vaguely pleased.

"Molly, for God's sake, be careful." Jude grabbed her forearm. "Babies can kill you."

"Your Aunt Audrey just had one, and she's still alive."

"She was just lucky."

"Honestly, Jude," said Molly, irritably wrenching her arm out of Jude's grip. "Grow up."

Jude looked at her angrily. "Fine," she snapped. "Have a baby. Die in childbirth. Get buried in the cemetery with all the other dead mothers. That's where you'll end up anyway if you get involved with Ace Kilgore."

Molly glanced at her guiltily. "What does Ace have to do with this?"

Jude said nothing for a long time, trying to decide whether to confess to what she'd witnessed through the basement window. "Noreen told me you have a crush on him," she finally murmured.

"What business is it of yours?"

Jude was stunned by Molly's contemptuous tone of voice, stunned that she didn't deny the crush, and stunned that she could even ask such a question. "How could it *not* be my business?" she asked in a low voice.

"What do you mean?" asked Molly, averting her eyes.

"After the other night . . . You know . . ."

"I don't know what you're talking about." Molly returned her chair legs to the floor, stood up, and carried her bowl to the sink.

Jude watched her in disbelief, feeling desperately lonely. The most important experience of her life to date had been just a dream. And the indestructible bond it had established between Molly and herself existed only in her own imagination.

"SO IF YOU KEEP your knees together tight, girls, and smile up at your date while you swing your legs under the dashboard, you can get into any sports car, no matter how small, without displaying all your worldly treasures.'' Miss Melrose was demonstrating her technique in her desk chair as she talked. The Charm Class was assiduously copying her movements, even though none of the boys they knew could drive.

As Jude secured her worldly treasures beneath her imaginary dashboard, she noticed that Molly had painted her fingernails pink. Now that Jude was in junior high, she, too, shaved her armpits as well as her legs. And she put on lipstick, eyeliner, and mascara every morning. Thanks to Miss Melrose, she knew never to wear white shoes before Easter or after Labor Day and not to make chicken salad with dark meat. But Molly was always one step ahead.

Except in the classroom. Despite her efforts to score poorly on the placement exams, Jude had been assigned to a special seminar, along with the nerds who played slide-rule games in the lunchroom while all the cool kids did the Dirty Shag in the gymnasium to raise money for cerebral palsy. Jude had also been elected seventh-grade representative to the student council, which was dominated by classmates who were Episcopalian and Presbyterian and who lived in the big, fancy houses of the Yankee mill executives along Poplar Bluff.

But Molly never even congratulated her on her student council victory. And if Jude tried to explain some of the ideas she was learning about in the seminar, Molly would just shrug and say, "Afraid you've lost me again, brainchild."

Some afternoons after school now, instead of racing Flame through the Wildwoods, Jude sat with Sandy in his upstairs bedroom discussing the big bang theory and natural selection and relativity. Out the window, they watched Noreen coaching Molly in Noreen's backyard for the upcoming cheerleader tryouts. Sometimes their lyrics reached Jude and Sandy through the open windows:

"Well, down my leg and up my spine!
We've got a team that's mighty fine!"

She and Sandy would pause in their discussion of Hegel's dialectic to giggle. Then Jude would frown at herself, feeling disloyal.

As they strolled home from Charm Class through the twilight, allowing their kilted hips to sway with every step, Jude said, "My dad said he'd teach us to drive the jeep down that hill behind the cemetery on Saturday afternoon."

"Oh, Jude, I'm afraid I can't."

"But it would be really neat to be able to drive, wouldn't it?"

"I'm afraid I'm tied up on Saturday afternoon."

"Doing what?"

"Jude, I'm not your slave. You don't need to know my every move."

"Sorry."

They walked in silence past yards full of tulips. Ever since Jude had realized that her experience on the raft with Molly had been just a dream, she hadn't known how to behave with her. It seemed impossible to recapture the unselfconscious accord of their childhood, but no guidelines for their distressing new separateness had emerged. So they often experienced awkward silences or irritated outbursts, followed by frantic attempts to backpedal to the harmony they used to take so effortlessly for granted.

"I like the white tulips best, don't you?" Molly finally said.

"Me, too," said Jude, accepting the apology.

"Actually, I'm going to the lake with Ace Saturday afternoon. To ride in his father's motorboat." She was trying to sound casual.

Jude glanced at her. Molly and Ace often danced together at the noontime sock hops. And although Molly never admitted it, Jude suspected that they talked on the phone a lot at night. Occasionally, the three of them sat together on the bleachers at lunch to watch intramural basketball. Ace and Molly weren't going steady, and they never went out on dates, but Jude could tell that Molly was sometimes preoccupied with him.

"But why Ace?" she finally asked, genuinely curious. "I just don't get it. Have you forgotten how mean he was to us?"

"There's a really sweet side to him that you've never seen, Jude. He may act tough, but inside he's just a sad, scared little boy." She was smiling fondly, as though describing the antics of her dog.

"Please spare me the details."

"Besides, there are reasons why he was so mean."

"Such as?"

"His father isn't a nice man."

"His father is the best lawyer in town. My dad says he was a big hero in the war."

"I can't say any more."

Jude studied her from the corner of her eye. "We've never had secrets, Molly." They were passing more tulips. Jude decided she hated them, especially the white ones.

"I promised Ace."

"So Ace is more important to you now than I am?"

"No, of course not, Jude. But he needs me. I think I can help him."

Reaching the crack in the sidewalk marking the boundary between their yards, they turned to face each other. Molly's shirt collar was peeping out from beneath her sweater. On it, Jude spotted a tiny dagger made from a straight pin, a piece of red plastic cord, and some multicolored beads the size of BBs. Noreen had started this fad, which had swept the halls of the junior high school. She and the other cheerleaders made sets consisting of a miniature dagger and sword. The boys bought them, and the cheerleaders donated the money to muscular dystrophy. The boys wore them crossed on their collars until they wanted to go steady, at which point they gave their girlfriends their daggers.

"What's that?" asked Jude, pointing at Molly's dagger as though at a scorpion.

Molly started, then looked quickly away. "Ace asked me to wear it today."

Jude said nothing for a long time. She was losing this battle, but she was damned if she'd make it easy for either of them. "What about me?"

"But Jude, you're a girl," said Molly gently. "You're my best friend, but Ace is my boyfriend. Why don't you get a boyfriend, too?

Then we can double-date to the movies. What about Jerry Crawford? Ace says he really likes you.''

"What about our cabin?" Jude asked doggedly. She didn't want Jerry Crawford. She wanted Molly.

"What cabin?"

"The cabin we were going to build on the ridge above the cave. With the paddock for Flame and Pal."

"But we were just kids then, Jude. It was like playing house." She was gazing at Jude with loving concern.

Jude felt the bottom drop out of her stomach, like a trapdoor to hell. She had known she was losing, but she hadn't realized that she'd already lost.

"Please don't do this, Molly."

Molly laughed weakly. "But I'm not doing anything."

As Jude walked up her sidewalk, she reflected that if she had one of those weird things growing between her legs, like Molly's father or the boys behind the furnace, she'd be able to slow-dance with Molly and go steady with her and all the things she had started wanting since entering junior high. Jude had no choice but to build their cabin alone, without Molly, who would be living somewhere else with Ace Kilgore and their mutant babies.

Aunt Audrey was upstairs talking to her new baby, Daniel junior, who was cooing and gurgling. Jude went into the kitchen and cut herself a piece of Mrs. Starnes's latest cake—chocolate fudge with buttercream frosting. Carrying her plate into the living room, she sat down in the brown leather chair whose arms she and Molly used to ride, lassoing Sidney with Clementine's clothesline. Reaching over to the end table, she opened the drawer and extracted the framed photo of her mother in the wine bottle, setting it up on the table. Her father always put it in the drawer now, explaining that it upset Aunt Audrey. And Jude always removed it, not explaining that it upset *her* to have

Aunt Audrey sleeping in the very bed in which her father gave her mother the baby that had killed her.

Yet the birth of Aunt Audrey's two babies hadn't killed *her*, so Jude was having to reexamine her assumptions. And she had to confess that she adored her little half brothers, with their toothless grins and tiny twitching digits and intense navy-blue gazes. Munching her cake, she stared at the photo of her beautiful mother, trapped in a bottle like an exotic flower. She wondered whether her mother had felt the same fierce devotion for her that Aunt Audrey seemed to feel for her babies. She thought probably so, judging by the look on her face as she held Jude's cheek to her own in the photo by Jude's bedside.

IN A TENT LIKE the circus big top, pitched in the middle of the county fairground on the outskirts of town, a visiting evangelist with a vanilla pompadour and a smile that wouldn't quit was enjoining the Baptist Youth from throughout the area to swear forever to forgo dancing, drinking, card playing, swearing, and the "illicit pleasures of the flesh." Jude watched from her folding chair beside Jerry Crawford as Molly and Ace joined the throng moving down the center aisle toward the front platform to be born again. She was appalled by the ease with which Molly was making a vow she'd never keep, loving Over the Moon as she did. Ace was evidently turning her into a liar. She'd been behaving very oddly since becoming pinned to him. Her blue eyes had lost their luster, and she walked like a robot, as though hypnotized by an evil wizard.

The new recruits for salvation gathered behind the glad-handing preacher, facing the audience. Meeting Molly's eyes, Jude gestured in wolfspeak, What the hell are you doing?

Molly looked away, smiling proudly up at Ace. The perpetually grinning agent of the Lord extended his arms as though walking a tightrope and invoked the Lord's blessing on "these the future leaders of our great Chrush-chen nation," who had pledged henceforth to lead new lives "swept clean by the push broom of Christ!"

Afterward, the Baptist Youth from Jude's church piled into their hay-filled delivery truck. As it rumbled down the road toward town, someone began singing "Jacob's Ladder."

Jerry leaned down, searching for Jude's lips in the dark. His Dentyne-fresh breath was warm on her cheek. Jude turned her head aside and feigned a deep commitment to getting the alto harmony just right on "If you love Him, why not serve Him?" Jerry sighed and rummaged through the hay for her hand, which he pinned beneath his own like copulating starfish.

In the middle of "This Little Light of Mine," everyone began waving flashlights around the truck. In the sweeping beams, Jude spotted Ace and Molly buried in hay in the rear corner, bodies pressed together, mouths gasping like dying fish. Apparently, they had decided to ignore the strictures against the illicit pleasures of the flesh.

Molly glanced up for a moment and her glazed eyes met Jude's. They gazed at each other for a long moment, and Jude thought that her heart was going to shatter into a thousand jagged shards right there on the blanket of hay. Eyes still interlocked with Molly's, Jude turned her head toward Jerry's and finally opened her lips to his. Through angry eyes, she watched Molly watch her as she drew Jerry's tongue into her mouth and placed his rough crustacean hand on her newly swelling breast.

As THEY WALKED HOME from school beneath the flying red Texaco horse, Molly announced that she and Ace had registered together for a Baptist Youth retreat in the Virginia mountains the next weekend. Although she urged Jude to sign up with Jerry, Jude had by now accepted her waterloo. She had been trying to save Molly from Ace, but she had finally understood that Molly didn't want to be saved.

Since she no longer had anything to lose, Jude said, "I wouldn't even go to heaven if I knew Ace Kilgore would be there."

Molly's blue eyes flared liquid ice. "Ace may not be very nice sometimes," she snapped, "but at least he's not boring."

"Meaning I bore you?" Jude clenched her jaws to keep from crying.

"No, you don't bore me," said Molly, retreating hastily. "It's just that sometimes I feel a little bit suffocated with you, Jude. It's like you want us to build a cabin on the ridge and stay children forever."

"Well, you won't have to worry about Ace Kilgore's suffocating you," muttered Jude, "because he'll probably be in prison soon."

"You and I are the ones who are in danger of prison," she said, staring at the sidewalk.

"What's that supposed to mean?"

"Some of the things we've done—they're just not right."

"Like what?"

"Oh, you know." Molly gazed across the street. "Playing Pecan. All that stuff."

"What was wrong with it?" It hadn't felt wrong at the time. It had felt right—for both of them. Now Molly, in addition to destroying their future, was rewriting their past.

"Two girls aren't supposed to do that together."

"Who says?" asked Jude weakly.

"God does," replied Molly with serene conviction. "The Bible says that a virtuous woman should be a crown to her husband."

Jude stopped walking and turned to look at her. "Since when have you cared what the Bible says?"

"Since I accepted God as my Lord and Master at that revival." She looked at Jude with defiance, blue eyes gone stone gray.

As Jude looked back, she felt her jaw fall open. Taking on God as well as Ace Kilgore was clearly hopeless. "But, Molly, I love you," she said softly, accepting defeat.

For a moment, Molly looked confused, her present self warring with a more ancient one. "Maybe I love you, too, Jude," she finally replied in a choked voice. "But not like that."

"Like what?" asked Jude with sudden urgency. She watched Molly closely.

Molly said nothing for a long time, staring hard at a cluster of red ants dragging a dead wasp along the pavement. "Not like that night on the raft."

THE SATURDAY AFTERNOON of the Baptist Youth retreat, Jude's father came into the kitchen to ask, "Do you and Molly want to go drive the jeep with me?"

Jude was lying facedown on the fake-brick kitchen linoleum. "Molly's gone."

He stood over her and looked down. "Oh?"

"She's in Virginia on a retreat."

"Didn't you want to go, too?"

"No." Jude had spent the past several days swinging violently between elation and despair. The dream about Molly and herself on the raft hadn't been a dream after all. Or if it had been, Molly had dreamed it, too. Together, they had experienced something profound. After loving each other for nearly a decade, they had set aside the boundaries that normally separated two people. They had merged with each other and with all creation. No one and nothing could ever take that knowledge away from Jude. But Molly wanted to. First she pretended it hadn't happened. Now she insisted it wasn't important.

That afternoon, Jude had forced herself to face the fact that Molly loved Ace *because* he was so awful. She liked the idea of saving a sinner, taming a wild beast, reforming an outlaw. Since he was a bad boy, she could feel like a good girl. Unless Jude could have a personality transplant and become even more wicked than Ace, there was absolutely nothing she could do to compete.

That night in the living room, Aunt Audrey passed Danny to Jude to hold as they all chuckled over the antics of Sid Caesar on "Your Show of Shows." Danny was cuddly and sweet-smelling in his flannel Dr. Denton's. Holding him upright, Jude let him tread her lap, his chubby legs churning as he pretended to walk. Then he reached out with his tiny, perfect fingers to grab her lower lip. Clutching it, he stared into her eyes with his open, trusting, quizzical gaze. He was so uncomplicated and innocent and vulnerable, loving to seize and examine anything within reach, loving to have any area of his soft velvet skin stroked by anyone anytime. How did an enchanting creature like this turn into an Ace Kilgore? Jude wondered.

Her father was holding Sam, his older son, on his lap. Sam also wore flannel Dr. Denton's. He was squirming as Jude remembered squirming, climbing all around the puffy leather armchair, experimenting to find the most comfortable position in relation to his father's large frame. Then he played hide-and-seek with Jude, believing that if he covered his eyes so that he couldn't see her, she couldn't see him, either. Her father laughed at this until his face turned scarlet. Jude was glad to see him so happy.

Molly was happy, too, with someone besides Jude. But Jude wasn't a lonely motherless child anymore. She was first in her class and in line to be secretary of the student council. The president, a ninth grader from Pittsburgh who lived on Poplar Bluff, had invited her to a party at his house the following weekend. She had a life apart from Molly and her father, just as they did from her.

The phone rang. Her father answered. His cheerful face contorted. "I'll be right down," he said in a voice turned suddenly terrible.

He stood for a moment with his hand on the receiver before facing Jude. "Baby, Molly's been in a car wreck. I have to go to the emergency room."

Aunt Audrey put her hands to her face but said nothing.

Jude looked up from her armchair. "Can I come, too?"

"Maybe you'd better not."

"It's bad?"

"It's real bad."

"I'm coming."

Jude sat in the waiting room with Molly's parents as people in rust-stained white rushed in and out. Ace's parents were there, too. Jude kept looking at Mr. Kilgore in his khakis and sports shirt, trying to figure out why he wasn't a nice man. Apart from his dull black eyes, he looked like every other father in town. Other parents Jude didn't know were also there.

Seven Baptist Youth had been riding in a car driven by a high-school junior. Ace had taunted him to go faster on the winding mountain road, yelling encouragement as the speedometer needle climbed higher and higher. He cheered as it reached fifty, then sixty, then seventy. Molly, who was sitting on Ace's lap beside an open back window, began yelling at the driver to slow down. The other girls screamed and wept.

The car missed a curve, skidded off the shoulder, and rolled down a steep embankment. Molly was thrown partway out the window on the first roll. On the second roll, the car landed on top of her.

Molly's mother was holding Jude's hand and crying softly. Molly's father was pacing the room. *Jude was on an ice floe at the South Pole, floating silently on a frozen silver sea.*

Ace came out on crutches, explaining to his mother, "So I tried to hold on to her. I tried to pull her back in. I had her around the waist. But then we were upside down and I lost her. . . ." He looked at Jude and stopped talking. She looked back at him. He swung out the door between his parents.

Hours later, Molly was rolled out on a stretcher. Her dark, wavy hair had been shaved off, and careful catgut stitches snaked across her skull like lacing on a softball. Her face was black and purple. One arm was in a cast. Plastic tubing from her nose and hand attached to bags of liquid on a rack being pushed by a nurse.

Jude's father appeared in green scrub clothes stained with Molly's blood.

"Is she going to be okay?" asked Jude. Adults died, not kids.

"I've done everything I can." But his maroon eyes were squinty, as though seeking refuge in the caverns formed by his high cheekbones.

Jude, her father, and the Elkinses followed the stretcher to a small room and watched orderlies transfer the body to a narrow white bed. Jude's father routinely saved lives, or so people all over town told her. He'd save Molly.

"Go home and have a rest," said Molly's mother, stroking Molly's inert arm.

"Good idea," said Jude's father. "I'm beat. We'll be back soon."

While her father showered and changed, Jude put some things into a paper bag—*Mademoiselle* and *Seventeen* to read to Molly once she was awake; nail polish so she could paint Molly's nails, which had gotten chipped during the wreck; a piece of Mrs. Starnes's orange-blossom cake, Molly's favorite, wrapped in foil.

Leaving the house to wait for her father in the car, Jude discovered Sidney sitting by the back door. She squatted down and patted him. Looking up, she saw Molly standing under the mulberry tree by the garage.

"Oh, you're back already?" said Jude, standing up. Sidney stood up, too, staring at Molly and whimpering.

As Jude walked toward her, she realized it wasn't Molly after all. It was just a shadow cast by the moon through the mulberry branches. But Sidney was still staring at the shadow, trembling all over.

WHEN JUDE AND HER father got back to the hospital, Molly was dead.

JUDE REFUSED TO GO to the funeral. She didn't want to hear Noreen keening by the grave as though over a lost football game. And she didn't want to meet Ace Kilgore's gaze. She lay on her bed eating raspberry sherbet and wondering if she'd gone on that retreat whether Molly would be lying beside her right now. Molly had once saved her from the Commie Killers, but she had not saved Molly.

She heard Sidney howling outside. Inviting him in, she let him lie on her bed and listlessly lick sherbet from her spoon.

She was gazing across a vast, empty snowfield that glistened under a merciless sun. She looked into the electric blue overhead for a cloud to carry her mother, but the sky was empty.

Out the window, Sandy and her father, dressed in suits and ties, were returning from the cemetery alongside Aunt Audrey, who was carrying Danny zipped into a padded powder-blue snowsuit. Their breath was frosty. Her father came into the house and up to her room. He sat down on the bed and patted Sidney.

"I don't know what to say, Jude. Just that I know how awful you feel right now. The years roll by and life goes on and new people come along. But some people can never ever be replaced."

Jude kept eating her sherbet. If he had just died in the war in

France, her mother would still be alive. Besides, he was a quack. He hadn't saved Molly.

Sometime later, Sandy appeared in her doorway, still dressed in his suit and tie. "I'm really sorry, Jude."

"Thanks."

"You'll always have your memories of Molly. No one can ever take those away."

Jude looked at him. "That may be all I ever had."

"What do you mean?"

"Do you think dreams are real?"

He shrugged. "I've read they're wish fulfillment. Or just random firings of neurons at rest."

"I thought Molly and I loved each other, but maybe I made the whole thing up."

"No, Jude. Molly loved you."

"Then why did she stop?"

"She didn't stop. But I think she got scared."

"Scared of what?"

"Scared of being different. Scared of losing herself in you. Molly wasn't as strong as you are."

Jude frowned. It didn't make sense. Molly was older. She had usually been the leader. And Jude didn't feel strong. She felt like crawling under her bed and never coming out.

He patted her awkwardly on the shoulder, and when she thought to look up again, he was gone.

That night she went down to her father's office and found an Ace bandage. Removing her shirt and bra, she bound her new breasts so tightly that they ached. Then she let Sidney outside to pee and got some more raspberry sherbet.

When Clementine arrived the next morning, Jude and Sidney

were lying on her bed surrounded by sticky bowls of melted sherbet, even though it was a school day.

"Sugar, I'm just so sorry," said Clementine.

"If Molly and I have a graveyard love, I guess we're halfway home," said Jude.

"You'll feel better by and by, I promise you."

Clementine stroked her back. Feeling the Ace bandage, she unbuttoned Jude's shirt and looked down at her tightly wrapped chest and the angry chafed flesh around the edges. "What you done to yourself, Miss Judith?"

"I don't want to be a woman," she said. "You become a woman, you love a man, and it destroys you."

"O Sweet Jesus, my poor lost lamb," murmured Clementine, taking Jude into her arms, rocking her and humming a gospel tune about Christ gathering His flock into the fold at twilight.

JUDE RODE HER BIKE into town. With her allowance, she bought a red-clay pot of white tulips. Holding it in one arm, she pedaled past her grandmother's huge white house. She'd just received a card from the Great Wall saying: "The Chinese are so polite and gracious, very much like Virginians."

Entering the cemetery, Jude walked over to the hillock of fresh clay that now encased Molly's bruised and broken body. As she set the clay pot among the withering wreaths from the service, Jude realized that to do anything at all, even to buy these flimsy flowers that would shrivel in the evening chill, was unnecessary. She and Molly had been dead to each other for nearly a year now.

"Best friend. Buddy of mine. Pal of pals," she murmured to the red-clay mound before turning away to ride back home, down the tunnel of arcing elms whose leprous limbs were coated with hoarfrost.

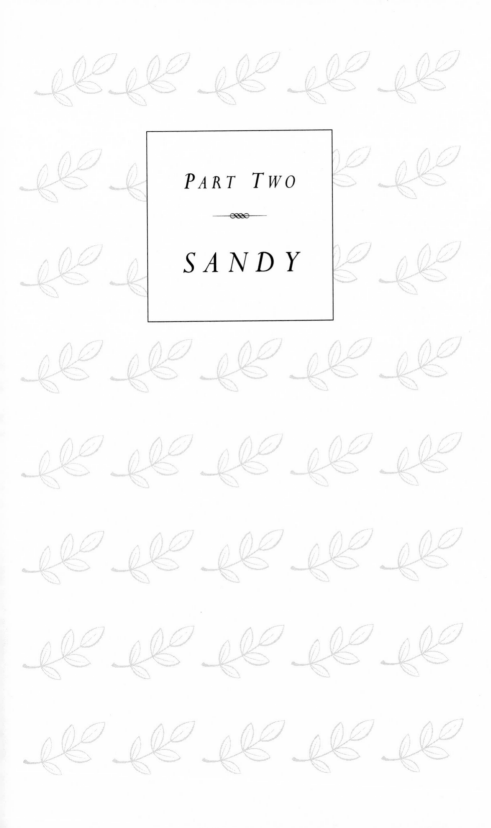

PART TWO

SANDY

"OH, MY," said Sandy as he opened the door of his Riverside Drive apartment and discovered Jude in her cream blazer, navy-blue A-line skirt, and tassled loafers. "A coed." He smiled whimsically. "Fancy that."

"And a hippie," said Jude, studying his octagonal granny glasses, bleached overalls, and the strawberry blond hair that curled like maple shavings around his shirt collar.

The focal point of the living room being an electric heater, they sat down before its orange glow in decrepit Danish-modern armchairs whose cushions were extruding foam. Not having seen each other for eight years, they had little to talk about except a past Sandy had repudiated, having refused to return home since leaving for college. They glanced at each other uneasily.

"Tea!" said Sandy. "Whenever the English are at a loss for words, they make tea. I'll make us some tea, shall I?"

"We're not British."

"No, but I worked at the National Opera in London when I was draft dodging, so I learned the drill."

As Sandy filled a kettle in the tiny kitchen and took tea bags from a canister on the counter, Jude studied his back. He'd filled out since high school, like a colt turning into a horse. He had a convex chest now and arms braided with muscles. The rumor around town was that, after dropping out of RPI, he'd been classified 4-F because of asthma. Most young men Jude had known at Vanderbilt were in ROTC, awaiting their chance to defend democracy in the Delta. When it came to fight or flight, Jude's ancestors had usually picked the latter, so her sympathies were with Sandy. If any one of her forebears had died a hero on some distant battlefield, disrupting the evolving chain of DNA, she wouldn't have been here.

Where would she have been instead? she wondered as she stood up and strolled across the battered parquet floor to peer out one window into an air shaft, then out another to the murky Hudson with the roller coaster of Palisades Amusement Park scalloping the far shore. A hallway with several doors off it led from the living room, the walls of which were papered with colorful posters announcing operas at the Met—FIDELIO and DER FLIEGENDE HOLLANDER and THE LOVE FOR THREE ORANGES.

The door to the outside hallway opened, and in walked a lanky young man with black curls and a drooping mustache. He wore a cracked, brown leather motorcycle jacket with a fur collar and a navy-blue Greek fisherman's cap. Studying Jude with the greenest eyes she'd ever seen outside of the cat kingdom, he said in a British accent, "Sandy's mate from childhood, I presume?"

"That's right. Jude."

"I'm Simon. One of Sandy's roommates."

"How many are there?"

"Four of us at the moment, I believe." He finally smiled, as though from duty. "Please. Make yourself comfortable, if that's possible in these collapsing chairs."

Both sat. Jude fiddled with a button on her blazer. Simon inspected the blue braid on the cap in his hands. Finally Jude asked, "How do you know Sandy?"

"We met at a bar in London."

"You're English?" The kettle in the kitchen began to whistle like Sandy's father's tannery back home at high noon.

"Yes."

"From London?"

"Yes."

"Have you been in the U.S. long?"

"A year."

"What's your job?"

"I'm a book editor."

Southern men were usually off and running with their autobiographies by now. Charm Class hadn't prepared Jude for the English. Fortunately, Sandy arrived with the tea. "Ah, Simon. I see you've met Jude."

"Yes. She's been interviewing me. The way you Americans always do."

Jude glanced at him. She was merely trying to be polite.

Sandy looked at him quizzically while setting the tea tray on a low table before the electric heater. "I'll be mother, shall I?" he said, attempting a British accent. He sat down, picked up a crockery pitcher, and splashed milk into each mug.

"So, Jude, why are you in New York?" Simon looked up from his cap with a sudden seizure of manners.

"I'm a Ph.D. candidate at Columbia. I just got my master's from Vanderbilt."

"What are you studying?"

"History."

"Where are you living?"

"On West Sixty-Seventh Street, near Central Park. With my grandparents—my mother's parents."

Sandy handed them each a mug, then held out a jar of honey while Jude spooned some into her tea.

"How do you like it?"

"Fine, so far. But I've just arrived."

Simon tossed down his tea and stood up. "I'll leave you two to reminisce over steamy nights in the slave quarters. I've got to change and go out. Lovely to meet you, Jude."

They watched him stride on long legs across the ratty maroon carpet, which smelled of mold.

"It's good to see you again, Sandy," said Jude as Simon vanished down the dark hallway. "Growing up appears to agree with you."

"And with you. Did you drive all the Sig Eps at Vandy to despair?"

Jude smiled. "I didn't date much, actually."

"Twenty-three and never been kissed?"

"As near as makes no difference."

After Molly's death, Jude had refused even to talk to Jerry Crawford for several months, hanging up each time he phoned and sidestepping him in the corridors at school. He reminded her too much of his best friend, Ace Kilgore. Maybe Ace hadn't killed Molly with his own hands, but he had certainly played a role in her death, like some evil incubus.

Finally, Jude agreed to go to the movies with Jerry one night, and on her doorstep afterward, he insisted on reclaiming the yardage he'd already gained, running his hands under her sweater and pushing his tongue through her lips. She realized she'd actually missed him, especially the animal comfort of a warm body against her own. She relaxed against his chest and tentatively caressed with her fingertips the ridges of muscle that formed the valley down his spine.

That night, she first dreamed of Molly—skull scalped and stitched with catgut, tubes snaking from her nostrils, face purple like a smashed plum. *"Listen to me, Jude,"* she insisted. *"Don't let this happen to you."* Ever since, whenever Jude had felt stirrings of desire for someone, Molly had appeared in this Medusa mode, mouthing warnings.

At Vanderbilt, Jude had been pinned for three years to a KA named Bradley Caldwell, a fair-haired Ashley Wilkes type whose parents owned an antebellum mansion in Natchez that was always included on the spring garden-club tours. When Jude visited, they housed her in a remodeled slave cabin. Bradley always treated her with a respect bordering on reverence, which even Molly didn't seem to find alarming. He wanted to marry a virgin, and he wanted that virgin to be Jude. So their definition of virginity had become as complex as a Catholic priest's definition of celibacy.

But the strain of being Bradley's beloved had finally become too great. Jude had called the whole thing off and caught the next train to New York. Bradley, however, who was working at a bank in Charlotte, was currently threatening to arrange a transfer to New York.

"They must be blind, is all I can say," said Sandy, sipping his tea.

"Thank you, Sandy. You may have rejected the South, but you're stuck with the gallantry."

"Don't worry. We'll find you a gallant Yankee."

"Isn't that an oxymoron? Everyone seems so rushed and rude up here."

"Oh, there are a few gallants left. But they're mostly from Tennessee. Speaking of gallant young men, whatever happened to Ace Kilgore?"

"He joined the marines. He's in Vietnam right now."

"So he finally gets to kill some Commies. Apparently, there is a God."

"Jerry Crawford is in his platoon. They're fighting side by side, like Achilles and Patroclus."

Sandy grinned.

"Did you hear that Jerry married Noreen after high school? She's head of the Welcome Wagon now."

Sandy started laughing.

The outside door hurtled open again, and a woman in knee-high mahogany boots with spike heels clattered into the room like a show horse. Her jeans were so tight that she must have needed a shoehorn to fit them over her buttocks. Her hennaed hair was shaved on one side of her head and chin length on the other.

"Mona, meet Jude," said Sandy, jumping to his feet like a good southern boy.

"Enchanted," she said distractedly, extending to Jude a clammy hand with sharp plum nails before vanishing down the hallway.

"Who's Mona?" asked Jude as Sandy sank back into his chair.

"One of my roommates. She does makeup at the Met."

"Tell me about the others."

"Simon, you met. Then there's Earl, who's a dancer from Cincinnati. And Tony, who's a set carpenter at the Met."

"Do you all eat meals together?"

"Hardly ever. Everyone's so busy and on different schedules. But sometimes we have group parties or holiday feasts. It's a nice mix of independence and companionship. Besides, it's all any of us can afford right now. How's your dad, by the way?"

"He's fine. After you left, my grandmother died of a heart attack—on a cruise of the South Sea Islands. They had to store her in the freezer until they reached land."

"My mother told me. I'm really sorry. She was a great lady."

"Thanks." They sat in silence for a moment, remembering the elegant old woman in her silk suits and spike heels, with her own unique version of the War Between the States, in which the South lost not because it had no gunpowder factories at secession but because the Yankees were not true gentlemen. Jude finally owned her Francis I silverware and her graduated pink pearls, but it definitely wasn't a fair swap.

"So we moved into her house," Jude said. "Dad and Audrey have four children now."

"That must be weird for you."

"He's happy, so I'm glad for him."

"It's your old friend Sandy here, Jude. You don't have to be so careful." He set his teacup on the tray and lay back in his chair with his legs extended.

"Well, I guess I did resent Audrey's trying to take my mother's place. But since Dad had her, it was easier on me when I left for Vanderbilt. What about you, Sandy?"

"What about me?" He clasped his hands behind his curly blond head, elbows out.

"What do you do for fun around here? Do you have a girlfriend, for example?"

He blushed just as he used to as a boy, crimson rising like the gauge on a thermometer from his throat, up his freckled face, and across his forehead. It was nice to know some things never changed.

"I'm too busy working."

"At the Met?"

He nodded. "I'm a stage manager. I know that sounds like a big deal, but there are dozens of us."

"How did you get from astrophysics at RPI to opera?"

"Physics was too pure for me. I like some meat on my bones."

"Were your parents upset when you dropped out of RPI?"

"Not really. You know they dote on me. Besides, the opera is an honorable institution."

"I wouldn't know. I've never been." She drained the last of her tea, which had cooled to lukewarm and was thick and sweet with honey.

"I'll take you one night."

"Okay, but I should remind you of how much I despised 'The Firestone Hour' on television when we were kids."

He laughed. "You'll like it. Trust me. Opera is almost as surreal as reality itself."

"S O   WHAT   DID   Y O U   do today, dear?" asked Jude's maternal grandmother as she served something that looked like bean stew from a gray pottery bowl painted with dark blue cornflowers.

"I went to visit a boy I grew up with who lives on Riverside Drive now. I hadn't seen him in eight years, and he's turned into a man. It was quite a shock."

"Then you understand how it is for us to see you," murmured her grandfather as he poured some red wine into her glass. Wine at their table seemed to flow as freely as iced tea back home.

Jude glanced back and forth between the grandparents she'd known mostly through Christmas and birthday cards and presents— her grandfather, tall and distinguished-looking, with a full head of silver hair and piercing raisin eyes; her grandmother, in gold pince-nez, with an elaborate bun of salt-and-pepper hair that sat on her head like a puffy cushion. A couple of times, they'd stopped off to see her en route to Florida vacations, and they'd often invited her to visit them, but she'd never accepted before. She had the impression her father and they didn't like one another. When they had picked her up at Grand Central with their driver the previous night, she had told them in the car en route to their apartment that her father sent his love (which wasn't true). They had merely thanked her, without inquiring about him.

Jude glanced around the dining room, with its walnut wainscoting and leaded glass windows and cabinet doors, determined to locate a subject for conversation. All they had in common was a woman who had died nearly two decades earlier, but her name hadn't yet been spoken. "How long have you lived here?" she asked her grandfather, who was carefully unfolding his linen napkin and placing it in his lap.

"Let's see, we bought this place after I got back from the war," he said. "In 1919, I suppose. Nearly fifty years ago. All the buildings on this block were built at the turn of the century by a group of Europeans who wanted a neighborhood. Some Alsatian friends of my father's got us involved. We used to call this street New York's Alsatian ghetto. I guess you could say we were an early commune." He smiled at her in the candlelight, but his dark eyes looked remote and unhappy. He was still wearing the three-piece pinstriped suit she'd seen him in early that morning as he departed with his uniformed driver for his office on Wall Street, where he negotiated international grain deals.

"So my mother grew up here?" asked Jude, risking the unmentionable.

Her grandfather grimaced, as though with heartburn.

Her grandmother nodded. "Her bedroom was the one you're staying in now."

"Where did she go to school?" Jude continued mercilessly. She'd picked Columbia for her Ph.D. and agreed to stay with her grandparents partly because she wanted to get to know them and, through them, her mother. None of this would happen if she pussy-footed around the topic as she always had with her father. Her father was all wrapped up in his new family now. Her mother had no one except Jude to bear her memory into the future. Therefore, Jude needed to remember what her memories of her were. Jude had gone to Paris her junior year at Vanderbilt with some vague notion of learning about her mother, whose parents were mostly French by origin. Many of the women she'd passed in the streets had had her mother's diminutive build and dark beauty. But she'd returned home with only an increased sense of her mother's absence.

"She went to a private school on the East Side. Your grandfather dropped her off every morning on the way to his office and our driver picked her up—until she was old enough to walk across the park with her friends."

"What was she like?"

Jude's grandmother glanced at her husband, but he was concentrating on his stew. Then she surveyed the room as though searching for an escape hatch. She drew a deep breath and exhaled it. Then she looked at Jude helplessly, as though asking to be let off the hook.

"She was very . . . definite," she finally replied. "She knew what she wanted, and nothing could dissuade her from having it."

Jude's grandfather didn't show by so much as a twitch whether or not he agreed. They sat for a while in silence, Jude uncertain of whether her grandmother's description was meant to be approving or not. One of the things Jude's mother had insisted on having was Jude's father. She poked at her stew—of beans, bacon, sausage, and pork in a tomato sauce. It was pleasant not to be eating country ham and corn bread. "This is delicious," she finally said. "What is it?"

"Cassoulet," her grandfather replied. "From *southern* France. To help you feel at home." He smiled.

"Please," said Jude with a laugh. "I'm so sick of southern food, I could scream—fried chicken and corn bread, barbecue and biscuits. It's a wonder I can still digest at all."

As the maid removed the dessert plates, Jude's grandmother stood up and walked over to a dark, glossy armoire. Pointing out some wooden pegs, she explained to Jude how her Huguenot forebears had collapsed the chest to carry it with them when they fled France in the seventeenth century. She was genealogist for the National Huguenot Society, and Jude gathered that she spent most of her time poring over passenger lists of ships that had left European ports after the revocation of the Edict of Nantes.

Extracting a fat, ivory-colored candle from the armoire, Jude's grandmother set it on the dining table and lit it with a taper from the silver candelabra. "Today is St. Bartholomew's Day," she explained.

"Good God, Rose," muttered her grandfather, "we've got company." Tossing his napkin on the table, he pushed back his chair.

"My dear," said Jude's grandmother, "your lack of interest doesn't alter the fact that on this day in 1572 your ancestors butchered mine."

"But not enough of them, darling, because here you are." He glanced at Jude with a faint smile.

"You can mock me all you like, Christophe. It won't bring back the hundred thousand that your forebears slaughtered like cattle in an abattoir."

"A hundred thousand is a mere drop in the bucket, my love," he said, rising to his feet, silver mane reflecting the candlelight. "A hundred *million* have died from man-made violence in the twentieth century."

"But not at the hands of the very people who had invited them to a wedding of their own kinsman."

"Stalin killed twenty million of his own people. So did Mao."

Jude studied her genteelly embattled grandparents, who seemed envigorated by this ancient religious enmity as they hadn't been by her mention of their lost daughter. Her suave grandfather was tossing off grim statistics of disaster as though dealing with so many sacks of grain.

"Go away, Christophe," her grandmother said, "before I add you to the body count."

Laughing, he exited.

But Jude stayed, to be polite, and listened to her grandmother's account, which sounded as ritualistic as an Icelandic saga. Howling Catholic mobs burst into Huguenot homes in Paris, stabbing the occupants, shooting them, hurling them from high windows to the pavement below. They tossed babies screaming for their murdered parents into the Seine to drown. Carts piled high with corpses left pathways of blood that led to a Louvre courtyard, where flies swarmed around stacks of mutilated bodies that lay festering under a hot summer sun. Giggling ladies from court inspected the genitals of a dead man suspected of impotence.

As she listened, Jude studied a medallion at her grandmother's throat—a Maltese cross, with fleurs-de-lis in each corner. A tiny golden dove in downward flight was hanging from the bottom arm. Her grandmother, in her billowy bun and gold pince-nez, had seemed so reticent discussing her daughter earlier in the evening but was now describing with relish the rivers of France—so clogged with bloated corpses that people refused to eat fish for months afterward —and the wolves that crept down out of the forests to feast on the bodies that washed ashore. Jude settled comfortably into her side chair and sipped her wine, feeling at home already in the heart of New York City.

Following her recitative, Jude's grandmother blew out the candles, kissed Jude good night, and vanished up the stairs and into her bedroom, separate from that of her husband. Jude went into the paneled den and turned on the television. Unable to find anything of interest, she switched it off. Studying the walls, she noticed Audubon prints, but no photos, no school diplomas, nothing that would testify to her mother's existence.

She strolled into the living room, which was two stories high and had dark walnut paneling and beams. At the second-floor level, there was a balcony off which the bedrooms opened. Wandering around the shadowy room, she tried to imagine the games her mother must have played there as a child. In the dim lamplight, she noticed that the wine-colored Oriental carpet had a paisley pattern like footprints. Carefully fitting her feet into the protozoan outlines, she walked across it splayfooted. Then she turned around and jumped back across it in the opposite direction, alternating feet, sometimes landing on both, playing hopscotch.

Reaching the leaded glass windows along one wall, she studied the window seat, which was cushioned with burgundy velvet. Upon lifting the lid, she discovered an empty space within. Climbing into it, she lay down, lowered the lid, and pretended she was in a coffin. She remembered lying like this in the sunken grave back home, trapped by the Commie Killers. For a few moments, it seemed easier to continue lying there while her grandparents ransacked the apartment in search of her than to emerge and have to set up an entirely new life.

As she climbed back out of the window seat, her grandmother's voice overhead said, "That's exactly what your mother used to do."

Looking up, Jude saw her standing in the shadows on the balcony. "Sorry, Grandma. I was just poking around."

"No need to apologize, my dear. Our home is your home now."

But Jude detected a note of tightly controlled agitation in her voice.

JUDE WRAPPED HER ARMS around Molly's waist as the car fishtailed crazily. Then it plunged down a cliff and began to roll. As Jude clung to her, Molly was slowly dragged out the window. Sweat broke out on Jude's forehead as she struggled to pull Molly back inside. Losing her grip, she clawed frantically at the sticky red-clay bank outside. . . .

". . . I've hungered for your touch a long lonely time," wailed the Righteous Brothers from the clock radio. "Time goes by so slowly, and time can do so much. . . ."

Jude opened one eye and saw the gold wallpaper striped with Prussian blue in her new bedroom at her grandparents' apartment. The buzzer on the alarm went off.

Shutting it off, she scooted up to lean against the headboard of the mahogany sleigh bed in which her mother had slept as a girl. She blotted the sweat off her forehead with her pajama sleeve and tried to calm her jagged breathing.

Just as Molly used to insist that stars were actually tears in the night sky through which the light behind it streamed, so Jude had concluded that everyday reality was just a period of each day allotted for attending to the needs of the body so it could continue to host the dreams that constituted the *real* reality. Some nights, she relived this car wreck that never ended. Other nights, she lay trapped by the Commie Killers in a sunken grave, Molly's skeletal arms dragging her down into the center of the earth.

But sometimes she and Molly sat in their cave playing Over the Moon, as the indigo Smokies outside the cave mouth vanished and reappeared in swirling autumn mists. Or they galloped their horses beside the churning river, as mauve clouds collided overhead and cast dark racing shadows on the valley floor. Or they lay in each other's arms on a raft in the ocher river, rocking with the current, while dancing rays of summer sun licked their flesh like a thousand tiny tongues.

The buzzer on her alarm went off again. She had to go to Columbia to register for fall courses. Lying still, she listened to the city come to life around her, like a curtain lifting on a stage set. At dawn back home, lone roosters crowed one by one until the sun popped up from behind the mountains and the bird chorus commenced its concerto to daybreak. Here, a solitary siren first broke the silence, followed by a car horn, then the whirring of a truck digesting garbage in the street below. Then more sirens, the roar of a bus, schoolchildren shrieking, a helicopter pucking overhead, dogs barking on their way to Central Park. Finally, the urban oratorio at full blast.

WAITING IN THE CAVERNOUS GYM in a line of history students who also wanted the seminar on the French Revolution, Jude inspected her new classmates, a scruffy bunch in their jeans and overalls, T-shirts and work shirts, paratrooper boots and basketball shoes, especially in contrast to the cashmered coeds and tweedy fraternity boys at Vanderbilt. Several exuded the musky odor of sweat mixed with marijuana smoke. A sorority sister at Vanderbilt, whose boyfriend played Dobro in a country-and-western band, used to sneak the joints he gave her into the Kappa house, where Jude lived. They smoked them sitting on the gabled roof. The effect on Jude had always been negligible, although a few times the antics of the birds in flight over the campus had seemed more engaging than usual.

She started thinking about her grandmother's version of the St. Bartholomew's Day Massacre the previous night—the marriage turned massacre, the wolves feasting on the bloated corpses. Like the evening news, everything Jude had studied in her career as a history major had focused on wars, assassinations, famines, and epidemics. No doubt

the guillotine would be the star of this seminar on the French Revolution. But surely sometime, somewhere, people had merely tilled the
soil and harvested their crops, year after year, until they died quietly
in their own beds, bored to death, surrounded by those who loved
them.

SANDY HAD PLACED A STRAIGHT-BACK chair amid a rigging of
ropes and pulleys behind the maroon velvet curtains, from which Jude
could see most of the stage. He was sitting at a switchboard behind
her, watching the stage on a TV screen and following the music in a
bound score. He wore headphones with an attached mouthpiece
through which he was receiving reports and issuing instructions to
technicians stationed all around the hall.

Jude, meanwhile, was bewildered by the plot. The young Count
Octavian, played by a woman, was lying in bed singing sweet nothings
to the *Marschallin*, whose husband was out of town. While the count
disguised himself as a chambermaid so as to conceal their affair from
the *Marschallin*'s approaching cousin, the *Marschallin* sang an aria be-
moaning her knowledge that the count would eventually leave her for
someone younger and more beautiful. Then the cousin, a man, became
enamored of the young count-turned-chambermaid.

At intermission, Jude remained in her chair, watching as the huge
platform carrying a Viennese drawing room rolled out from the wings,
escorted by a team of muscled young men in T-shirts and blue jeans,
with pouched leather carpenter belts around their hips and pirate-style
bandannas around their heads. One with a brown ponytail and a gold
hoop through his earlobe was Sandy's roommate Tony.

During the last act, Jude tiptoed to the switchboard and stood
behind Sandy, watching him turn the pages of his score. The *Marschallin*, aware that her young count had indeed fallen in love with a woman
his own age, was struggling with herself to let him go. Finally giving

him her hand to kiss for one last time, she swept bravely from the room.

Inexplicably, Jude found herself wanting to stroke Sandy's blond hair where it curled up around his collar. She touched a curl with her fingertip. Sandy turned his head, catching a glimpse of her finger as she withdrew it. Raising his eyes to hers, he smiled.

Walking back to Jude's grandparents' apartment through the cool night air, Sandy and Jude savored the sudden silence, broken only by an occasional passing car or a siren down Broadway. Sandy began humming the *Marschallin*'s aria during which she realized that the count would leave her.

"That was really beautiful," said Jude.

Sandy began singing it softly in German.

"What do the words mean?"

He thought for a moment. " 'With a light heart and a light hand, we must hold and take, hold and let go. If not, life will punish us and God will have no pity.' Something like that."

"Do you know German?"

Sandy nodded.

"What else?"

"Just the opera languages—Italian, French, a little Spanish."

"And East Tennesseean."

He smiled. "Yes, and British. From Simon."

They walked for a couple of blocks in companionable silence, pursued, overtaken, and abandoned by their own shadows as they passed through the patches of illumination laid down by the street-lights.

Finally, Sandy said, "Late at night, these side streets by the park are almost as quiet as Tidewater Estates."

"We might just as well never have left."

"That's the *only* similarity."

"Why did you never come back home, by the way?"

"Why would I go back? I was miserable down there. And after Molly died, even you turned into a zombie."

"I turned into a zombie?"

"Suddenly, you were perfect in every way. Those Villager shirt-waists you used to wear, pressed as carefully as altar cloths. Student council secretary. Baptist Youth Group. Hospital volunteer. Citizen-ship award. First in your class. Endlessly baby-sitting your siblings. And when I'd look in your eyes, there was no one home."

Jude studied her tassled loafers as they moved along the sidewalk through some tattered leaves that were giving off the dusty scent she would always associate with the Wildwoods in autumn, where wisps of smoke from fires in the farmers' curing sheds had drifted past like morning mist.

"There's still no one home, if you ask me."

Jude said nothing, amazed to learn that she'd projected such torpor when her heart had felt like Pompeii during the lava flow. After Molly died, she'd spent her free time racing Flame along the river, howling into the wind. She'd slide off him on the ridge where she and Molly had planned to build their cabin and pound the carpet of rotting leaves with her fists.

"I guess I'm just a faithful kind of gal," she murmured.

Sandy shrugged. "I used to envy you and Molly. You were like twin space aliens. When you were playing, you'd move in concert, without words, like birds in flight. But you've paid a very high price."

"I'm all right."

"So you say. But I knew you before, and I see you now."

"I'm not a child anymore."

"Yes, you are. You're off in Never-Never Land with Molly Pan."

Jude looked at him quickly. This was the closest anyone had ever come to guessing about her vivid night life with Molly. It felt threatening, even if it was only Sandy doing the guessing.

"I remember you at the Colonial Cotillion spring break of my senior year at Exeter, waltzing in your hoop skirt and satin heels, with kid gloves to your biceps and that ridiculous Marie Antoinette hairdo. You looked like a Stepford wife."

"You were supposed to be busy waltzing with Kitty Fairchild."

"But I was watching you. I always watched you, Jude. Around the neighborhood from the telescope in my tree house. You worried me. Your mother dead. Your father working all the time. Your grandmother off on her trips. Clementine struggling to raise you in addition to her own kids. The Commie Killers torturing you. I wanted to protect you, but I didn't know how."

"But you did, Sandy. You were wonderful. You were like my older brother."

"When Molly came along, I was relieved to have reinforcements. But I was also jealous. Because I thought of myself as more than just your big brother."

Jude looked at him, surprised. "Why did you never tell me?"

"What was the point? First there was Molly. Then that goon from the football team—Jerry. You two were like Beauty and the Beast."

Jude smiled, remembering Jerry's hard, muscled body and matching brain. But his brain was the organ that had interested her least.

Beneath the doorway to her grandparents' building, which was decorated with stone oak leaves, acorns, and squirrels, Sandy leaned over and kissed her cheek. Then he walked away fast.

As Jude undressed and hung her clothes in the closet, she thought about the kiss, as awkward as their first attempt beneath the heating ducts in Molly's basement during Spin the Bottle. Basically, Sandy had said he loved her. She loved him, too—as a brother, as a friend. Seeing him now was bringing it all back—his kindness and courage on her behalf. She felt at home with him as with no one else. Because of their shared childhood. Because they knew each other's families. Because he'd known Molly. Because he'd known *her* when she was with Molly.

She realized she was humming the *Marschallin*'s aria. "With a light heart and a light hand, we must hold and take, hold and let go. If not, life will punish us and God will have no pity." She had held on tightly to Molly. She was still holding on tightly. But if you could take love lightly, was what you were feeling love? Or was it just indifference?

Still, Molly was dead, and Jude was only twenty-three years old. Sometimes she envied the abandon with which her peers dated and dumped one another and hopped in and out of bed, foot soldiers for the sexual revolution. Maybe she and Sandy could go out some and see if anything more exotic developed. He'd said he didn't have a girlfriend. And he was attractive, sweet, smart, fun. Besides, if Bradley arrived from Charlotte as threatened, it would be helpful to have a new boyfriend already in place to stave off his adoration. What he adored wasn't her complicated and contradictory self, in any case. It was some ideal of purity that existed only within his addled antebellum brain.

Climbing into her mother's sleigh bed, she switched out the light.

As she drifted off to sleep, Molly was there waiting for her, tubes snaking from her nostrils, bloodshot blue eyes flaring.

"Forget about it, Jude!" she screamed as they raced their horses along the river. *"You belong to me. Besides, Sandy is going to hurt you."*

"Sandy wouldn't hurt a flea. You know that."

"Everyone ends up hurting each other. It's the law of the jungle."

"Nobody could ever hurt me as much as you did, Molly."

"It wasn't on purpose."

"You could have fooled me."

Molly lowered her head, hair writhing around her contused face like snarled blacksnakes. *"So Sandy is your revenge for Ace Kilgore?"*

"No, Sandy is my chance for a normal life."

CHAPTER

9

"AS SMOKE IS DRIVEN AWAY, so drive them away," the black-cassocked priest chanted in French.

"As wax melts before the fire," responded the congregation, "so let the wicked perish at the presence of God."

These were the same psalms, reflected Jude as she stood beside her grandmother before a carved oak pew, that had sustained the Huguenot guerrillas in the eighteenth century in their caves in the Cévennes as the Sun King's troops chased them down like wild game.

Behind the priest was an altar covered with a white cloth, on which sat two silver vases of white lilies and two white candles in plain silver holders. The wall in back of the altar was of opaque leaded glass. Right in the center was a Huguenot cross with a descending dove, identical to the one at her grandmother's throat, in indigo, ruby, and gold stained glass.

The tiny church with its polished oak beams was the epitome of austere good taste, as was the service. And the parishioners were dressed accordingly, as though for the funeral of a Fortune 500 executive. Over half a million of their ancestors had been tortured, butchered, and exiled simply because they didn't want to clutter up their altars with crucifixes. This had been especially unfortunate for France because it left behind only those citizens whose idea of beauty was Versailles. Jude felt unworthy of such forebears. If someone had so much as mentioned thumbscrews to her, she'd have let them put anything they wanted on her altar.

Around the walls near the ceiling hung the coats of arms of Huguenot families who had escaped the two centuries of slaughter to settle in New York City—Cresson, Robert, Runyon, Bayard, Jay, Maupin, Delancey, Perrin, three dozen others. The Sauvage coat of arms of Jude's ancestors featured four golden manticores—human heads, lion bodies, and dragon tails—on a scarlet background. There was no motto. Jude decided it should have been: "When in doubt, get the hell out."

Jude pondered all the torment these people had endured to worship as they pleased, whereas she had always spent a lot of time trying to get out of going to church at all. Earlier that morning, she had wanted to stay in bed with her memories of Molly instead of crossing Central Park in the cold January air to listen to French that she couldn't always understand. She had come along only from a wish to be amiable to her grandmother and to chat some more about her mother in the absence of her grandfather. Her grandmother had gradually become more forthcoming and now seemed even to enjoy reminiscing about her daughter, but Jude's grandfather still preferred to suffer in silence.

On the walk over, beneath trees iced silver in the night, Jude asked, "Did my mother used to come to this church with you?"

"Sometimes. Especially when she was too young to refuse."

"Could she speak French?"

"Enough to follow the service. Your grandfather and I spoke it at home with our Alsatian neighbors. And she had a tutor."

The pale winter sun hung suspended above the apartment buildings along Fifth Avenue like a blob of luminescent sugar cookie dough.

"Frankly," her grandmother admitted in a strained voice, "your mother was never very enthusiastic about her Huguenot heritage. All she wanted was to buy beautiful clothes and go out on dates. Of course, that's what you're supposed to want when you're young. But she made her father very unhappy by insisting on being a model."

"Why?"

"He thought it was tawdry. He wanted her to go to Barnard and become a classics professor. He'd groomed her for this all her life, helping her with her homework and hiring tutors. But that wasn't who she was. In any case, he had also always encouraged her to look beautiful. He gave her all the money she wanted for clothes and makeup and hairdos. He even advised her himself on the art of flirtation and seduction."

Jude glanced at her as she fell silent. She sounded jealous of her daughter's relationship to her husband. The idea of a daughter being more important to a father than his wife was a novel one for Jude.

"Thank you for at least pretending to be interested in my Huguenots," she added.

Interrupting Jude's protest, she said, "No, I know that this is something one gets interested in when one is older and is trying to figure out the point of it all. Young people are content to follow the dictates of their hormones."

"Don't forget, I'm a history major," said Jude. Although she didn't say it, it also seemed possible that her hormones were less insistent than those of her peers. How else could she have endured Bradley's regime for reestablishing her lost virginity?

"So you are," said her grandmother, who then proceeded to drill her on the ten Presidents of Huguenot descent, the famous writers, the Revolutionary War heros, the abolitionists and pioneers and suffragettes. And Jude had to admit that it was an impressive list. Apparently, there was nothing like terror to turn out high achievers.

As Jude stood to sing the recessional, she counted up the generations of her mother's family on her fingers as though saying a rosary. She realized that only two of her grandmother's thirty-two thrice-great-grandparents had been Huguenot. Several had been Dutch, for instance. Yet these distant Huguenots were the grit around which her grandmother's pearl of selfhood had coalesced. Similarly, only one of Jude's father's eight great-grandparents had been Cherokee. Yet to hear him tell it, you'd have thought he'd grown up in a tepee chipping arrowheads. They had both grabbed hold of only one thread of their DNA, clinging to it like a lifeline in a typhoon. Like Jude's Tidewater grandmother, both mourned some lost golden age. They all lived in a dream, a mythical time long since past.

But Jude knew she'd been doing the same thing, freeze-drying Molly in her memory. And she had decided it was time to recover from this crippling family malady. So she had accepted Sandy's invitation to move into a room in his Riverside Drive apartment. Molly was livid. Every night for weeks, she'd performed her Medusa act. Until Jude had finally realized that, like the Wizard of Oz, Molly was all bluster.

Walking home past the jammed skating rink, her grandmother's gloved hand holding her arm, Jude said, "By the way, Grandma, I've been thinking maybe it's time for me to move out."

Her grandmother looked up at her quickly. "I hope you're not unhappy with us, my dear."

"Not at all. You've been wonderful to me. But I guess I'd like my own place. After all, I'm twenty-four years old."

They walked on in silence alongside the Sheep Meadow, the huge apartment buildings of Central Park West stacked before them like a child's blocks under the sullen winter sky.

"I know it must have been lonely for you. Your grandfather and I aren't very much fun."

Jude smiled. "I feel very comfortable with *you*, Grandma. But I'm afraid I haven't really gotten to know Grandpa yet."

All she'd succeeded in eliciting from him were the facts: His father and four brothers had fled Alsace in 1870 to avoid fighting in the German army against the French. Having owned a gristmill in a country town, they opened another mill when they reached upstate New York. Jude's grandfather had parlayed his boyhood experience with the grain trade into a successful career on the commodities exchange.

"Well," said her grandmother as they passed some horse-drawn carriages waiting in front of the Tavern on the Green, "you may not realize it, but you remind us of your mother. Your grandfather was devastated when she moved south with your father. Frankly, I think he was half in love with her himself. He avoids you because it's painful for him to remember her. I'm very sorry. I know that you need to hear whatever he could tell you about her right now. But he just can't do it. I'm sure it would be wonderful for him if he could. It has been for me."

"Why do I remind him of her?" Jude asked. "Do I look like her?"

"You're taller, of course, but your faces are similar. Though you have your father's eyes. Her eyes were blue. I'd say you're a blend of the two."

Jude smiled. Her father had always denied any resemblance. "Why doesn't Grandpa like my father?"

Her face clouded. "It's not that he doesn't like him. We just didn't consider him appropriate for your mother."

"Why not?"

She laughed uneasily. "Well, let's just say that we were snobs. Your father was from Appalachia. He was part Cherokee. We wished him well, but we didn't want him in our family. I'm ashamed to admit that your grandfather used to refer to him as 'the hillbilly.' "

Jude smiled, thinking about the reality of her father's life—his mother's huge white house and voyages around the world, his medical degree from Cornell. L'il Abner he was not.

"Also, your father was absolutely relentless in his pursuit of your mother, practically camping out on our doorstep and trailing her around the city whenever she went out. Your grandfather felt that he didn't leave your mother any choice in the matter. After she married him, your grandfather wouldn't have anything to do with her, although I continued to see her while they were still living in New York and to write her in Tennessee.

"But once you were born, your grandfather agreed to visit on our way to Florida. When your father went to France during the war, your grandfather invited your mother to move back home with you until his return. But your mother refused, which estranged them once again. And then she died, and it was too late for another reconciliation. It's a sad and silly story. We were wrong. After all, we had struggled similarly with our own parents because I was Protestant and your grandfather was Catholic. Every generation seems to fight its own battles and then lapse into complacent bigotry." She sighed. "By the way, have you talked to your father about living alone?"

"I wasn't thinking of living alone. There's an extra room in my friend Sandy's apartment. It's closer to Columbia, too."

"You want to live with a man?" Her hand tightened on Jude's arm.

"It's one of those huge old places on Riverside Drive. He has four other roommates. One is a woman. Dad says since it's Sandy, it's okay. I've known him since we were babies. He's like my brother."

For the past several months, she'd seen a lot of Sandy. There seemed nothing they couldn't say to each other. Often they lay like a long-married couple on his mattress on the floor, watching old movies on television in their sock feet. Or else he studied opera scores while she marked up her history texts with yellow Magic Marker. Occasionally, they fell asleep side by side, but Jude always had to dash out into the night to take a taxi back to her grandparents so they wouldn't worry. If her room was just down the hall, life would be much simpler.

As Jude hung their coats in the hall closet, her grandmother said, "Before you leave, though, Jude, I want to give you something." She vanished into the dining room, returning with a flask about a foot high that had lion-head handles. On it was painted a scene in misty blues and golds of Atalanta, the unvanquished, stooping to pick up a golden ball just dropped by her competitor Melanion. He was sprinting past her, backed by trees and mountains. A hovering cherub, holding the victor's laurel wreath, appeared to be trying to persuade Atalanta not to be duped by these silly golden balls into losing her first race.

"I gave this to your mother," her grandmother said, handing it carefully to Jude, "but she never liked it. She didn't even take it to Tennessee. It was made by one of our Huguenot ancestors in Nevers, just before they fled France at the end of the seventeenth century. It's almost a museum piece, so take good care of it. It was given to me by *my* grandmother. It seems to be true that interest in these things alternates generations."

"I love it, Grandma. Thank you."

"Thank *you*, as I said, my dear, for being interested. I had thought my poor Huguenots would end with me and be forgotten. The dead depend on the living to carry on their memory."

"So I gather," said Jude a bit grimly.

Her grandfather came out of his study and looked down from the balcony. "What's going on?"

"Jude is leaving us, I'm afraid, dear."

"So soon? Where to?" Jude was pleased to note that he sounded distressed.

"To a room in her friend Sandy's apartment."

"Ah, a young man. Then I know there is nothing I can say to persuade her to stay."

"No."

Jude felt strange being discussed in the third person, as though she'd already left. "But I'll be only twenty blocks away, Grandpa. I'll stop by all the time. You'll never get rid of me." She felt guilty, however, as though she'd relentlessly extracted from them what she needed and was now moving on.

"I hope not," her grandfather replied in a fatigued voice. He turned around and shuffled back toward his study, shoulders bowed, an unhappy old man who had never recovered from losing the daughter he'd loved too much. This was the dark side to graveyard love. The *Marschallin* might be right after all: Maybe the proper conduct of life required the ability to let go of love when the time came.

JUDE SAT IN HER CHAIR behind the curtains, watching Samson, draped in chains, strangle a snotty Philistine prince in front of a pagan temple while a golden idol spewed flames in the background. As De-lilah awaited Samson in her bedchamber, Jude sneaked over to Sandy at his switchboard, resting her hand on his shoulder while he turned the pages of his score and spoke quietly into his mouthpiece.

Samson finally arrived, wearing a leather tunic that revealed his hairy barrel chest and tree-trunk legs.

Delilah began weaving around him in a transparent peignoir, singing in French, ". . . my heart opens to your voice as a flower to the dawn. . . . Respond to my tenderness; fill me with ecstasy. . . ."

Falling to his knees and burying his face in her silky gown, Samson joined in with his deep baritone: ". . . the blossom trembles in the gentle breeze. So does my heart tremble, longing for your voice. . . ."

Glancing down at Sandy, Jude saw that he was mouthing Delilah's lines. And tears had flooded his eyes behind his octagonal glasses. Suddenly, Jude understood his fascination with opera. The plots often embodied this perennial dream of tenderness taming savagery. And even when deceit and blood lust won out, the murdered actors stood up afterward for their curtain calls. On the playground back home, the Commie Killers had tormented Sandy for preferring chess and opera to football and rock 'n' roll. He had endured it all without protest. But on stage at the opera, the Commie Killers were vanquished. She absently stroked his blond curls with her hand.

Looking up, he reached for her hand and knitted his fingers with hers. A jolt shot up Jude's arm, so powerful that her hand shook. Sandy's sweetness moved her as no other man ever had. And because of it, Jude was beginning to want to give him everything. It wasn't that she was looking for the intensity of her experience with Molly that night on the raft. Although it remained vivid in her memory, the way a flashbulb leaves its imprint on a piece of unexposed film, she had written it off to unstable adolescent hormones. All she wanted now was some cozy companionship and physical affection with someone she cared about.

After the pagan temple had crashed down around everyone's shoulders, the painted cardboard blocks swinging from invisible ropes inches above the singers' heads, the curtain descended and the crowd erupted into bravos as though at a bullfight.

On the walk back to the apartment, Jude and Sandy murmured a few appreciative words about the performance before falling silent. And unlike their usual silences, this one was uncomfortable. Something was waiting to be said, but neither was willing to take the risk of saying it.

Entering the apartment, they found the living room empty of people. But some beer bottles, an ashtray full of cigarette butts, and a cardboard pizza box sat on the carpet by the armchairs. The odor of marijuana smoke and pizza filled the air. The only thing Jude really missed about her grandparents' apartment was their French cook. In a matter of months, she'd moved from ham hocks to cassoulet to Chinese takeout, and she was suffering from gastronomic culture shock.

Sandy and she walked down the shadowy hallway to their bedrooms. Outside Jude's door, they paused. Jude tried to decide whether to invite him in. It should be simple, something both had no doubt done before with other people. Yet neither made a move. Not only had the hand-holding during *Samson and Delilah* not broken the ice, but it seemed as well to have introduced some new awkwardness that Jude couldn't fathom. Finally, Sandy leaned down and pecked her cheek. "Sleep tight," he said as he turned to walk to his own door, tennis shoes squeaking on the wood floor.

Lying in bed, Jude could hear Mona next door, thrashing and gasping with her latest lover. Once they really got going, the bedsprings began to shriek like an entire pen of pigs being slaughtered. This often recurred sporadically throughout the night. Jude was awed by Mona's stamina. In the morning, she sometimes ran into the men in the bathroom, standing bare-chested in unzipped jeans, gazing at themselves in the mirror, eyes fatigued, faces gray and haggard, as though trying to figure out what disaster had just befallen them. Mona didn't usually appear until noon, wandering down the hall in a hot-pink chenille robe, lips chapped and swollen but smiling, mascara smudged around her eye sockets. Humming tunes like "The Impossible Dream," "My Way," and "I Gotta Be Me," she mixed ghastly concoctions in the blender that involved raw eggs and brewer's yeast, no doubt the source of her potency.

Jude wrapped the pillow around her head, but she could still hear the bedsprings pounding like a printing press. She wondered whether she should just get up and go to Sandy in his bed. She was pretty sure he wouldn't send her away. But they were both Southerners: He was the man; therefore, he was supposed to do the pursuing. Sliding a hand between her legs, she gripped it tightly with her thighs and directed all her mental energies toward him, willing him to appear by her bedside.

The next thing she knew, it was morning and she was late for class. Jumping up and throwing on her jeans and turtleneck, she raced down the hallway and into the living room. Earl, who danced in chorus lines for Broadway shows, had one heel propped on the windowsill, head resting on his knee. Dressed in a sweat suit, he looked like a soft sculpture. "Morning, Earl," she called as she hurried past. But he was so shy that there was no reply.

In the kitchen, Sandy was sitting at the table with half a dozen cereal boxes before him. When he was a boy, his mother insisted on buying only one box at a time, finishing it before buying the next. Now that he was on his own, Sandy bought a dozen different brands at once and sampled several every morning. It seemed a harmless-enough form of rebellion, when his peers were dumping blood on draft records at recruitment centers all across town.

He looked up at her and smiled. "Morning, Jude. Sleep well?"
"Yes, thanks. And you?"
Gazing at her with a perplexed frown, he said, "Not so great."
"No?"
"No." He lowered his eyes.
"I'm late," she said, grabbing a glass and pouring some orange juice.
"There's a good movie tonight at ten," he called as she tossed down the juice and dashed out the door. "Don't be late."

JUDE AND SANDY LAY on his bed drinking red wine, eating pretzels, and watching the movie. A man and a woman, married to other people, had met by chance in a train station and fallen in love. It was what Sandy and Simon called a "chick flick," in contrast to "dick flicks," which involved car chases, war, and violent crime.

Jude could tell that Sandy wasn't really paying attention, and neither was she. They had carefully avoided touching all evening. And they were now lying with the width of a sidewalk between them, arms crossed over their chests like funerary statues.

Sandy set his empty glass and the wadded pretzel bag on the rug beside the mattress, so Jude put her glass down, too. Both stared straight ahead at the TV screen while the couple struggled endlessly with their guilt toward their spouses over their platonic love for each other.

Sandy uncrossed his arms and stretched them awkwardly alongside his body, fists clenched, the muscles of his lower arms flexing and unflexing like a pulsing heart. As Jude watched from the corner of her eye, his hand unclenched, stirred, and crept a few inches into the no-man's-land between them. So Jude uncrossed her arms, too, and placed them on the bed beside her.

The couple had arranged to be alone together in a friend's apartment to consummate their love. As they fell into each other's arms, the friend arrived home early from work.

Jude scratched her head, then let that hand fall a foot away from her side. Sandy put his hand to his mouth to cover a yawn and returned it to the mattress within inches of Jude's hand.

Anguished, the couple parted in the train station where they'd first met, the man en route to South Africa with his family so he and the woman need never encounter each other again. Sandy's hand twitched where it lay, seeming to want to take Jude's but not daring to. She had watched it so carefully that she was sure its pattern of branching veins, like a turquoise road map, was now etched indelibly into her gray matter.

"Well," murmured Sandy as the credits rolled, "they always say the only love that lasts is unrequited love."

"Who does?" asked Jude irritably. There was a time for caution and a time for getting the show on the road. What was he waiting for?

The door flew open, and in strode Simon in his brown leather jacket and Greek fisherman's cap. Sandy shoved his hand under his thigh, like a crab scuttling away from a squid.

"Hope I'm not interrupting?" asked Simon, taking off his jacket and cap and dropping them on the floor.

He studied the *tableau vivant* on the bed for a long moment. "Now that you're living here, Jude, we should fill you in on the drill: I read Sandy a bedtime story every night."

Crawling up the mattress, he settled himself between them. Then he extracted a newspaper clipping from his pocket and read about a Japanese fisherman who put his wife in a net and dragged her behind his boat as shark bait.

Jude and Sandy smiled politely.

Simon read a second clipping concerning an Australian cyclist who had been attacked by a 350-pound ostrich, which she had managed to strangle with her bare hands.

Sandy lay there in silence while Jude tried to figure out what was going on.

"I was riding the IRT at rush hour this afternoon," Sandy said, "and this guy in a leather cap who was crushed up against me whispered in my ear, 'Drop dead, faggot.' "

"And what did you say?" asked Simon, studying him with interest.

"Nothing."

"Why would he say that?" asked Jude. All her life, people had been calling poor Sandy a faggot. She'd spent a lot of time defending his honor in high school.

Simon turned his stunning green eyes on Jude, saying, "Go on, mate. Tell her."

Sandy said nothing.

Jude leaned forward to look at him. His face was the color of a cooked lobster.

"I guess you don't need to," she said, rolling off the bed. "Sweet dreams, boys." She closed the door behind her.

Jude lay in bed, struggling to sleep so that she wouldn't have to feel so stupid. So the rumors about Sandy in high school had been true. And she had been the only one naïve enough not to believe them. And he had played on her naïveté, urging her to move in, leading her to think that a romance was possible between them. But why? Probably so that he could have the cover of respectability.

As she wept into her pillow in the dark, Mona's bed began to squeak rhythmically. Mona started to gasp in spasms. It was like a jazz ensemble. Soon the man would add his grunts to the improvisation, and then Mona would alternate her gasps with shrieks and moans.

Jude rolled over and pounded on the wall with her fist. "For God's sake, shut up!" she screamed.

The squeaking ceased abruptly and there was a long silence. Finally, it started up again, slowly and tentatively at first but rapidly gaining confidence and momentum. Jude decided to move back to her grandparents' in the morning.

JUDE WAS WRAPPING HER Atalanta flask in a sweatshirt when someone knocked at her door.

"Come in," she said glumly.

The door opened, and Sandy stood there in his bleached overalls, face and neck bright red, bangs splayed out around his cowlick as though he'd been standing in the funnel of a tornado. "Jude, I guess we need to talk," he said.

"What's there to say?" She placed the flask in her suitcase.

"Well, that I'm sorry, for one thing."

She stopped packing to give him a look. "I thought we could tell each other anything. So why didn't you tell me this?"

"I guess I was afraid you'd be appalled. And I can see that I was right."

"I'm not exactly appalled."

"What are you, then?"

"Confused, I suppose. What was that Dance of the Mating Hands all about?"

He grimaced. "I guess I hoped something might work out between us."

"And where would that have left Simon?" she asked angrily.

"All I know is what I felt. And feel. Life outside of Tidewater Estates can sometimes be complicated."

"Your life certainly seems to be," snapped Jude. She turned her back on him to stare out the window at the Ferris wheel in the amusement park across the river. She'd miss this madcap view of roller coasters and sailing yachts and garish sunsets.

"Please try to understand, Jude. Simon is my Molly. But that doesn't prevent me from loving you as well."

"So who does that make me? Ace Kilgore?" As she turned back around to study his earnest scarlet face, she softened. What he'd said was true. A current of connection that was almost palpable flowed between them. She had felt this with no one else but Molly. If it wasn't love, what was it? All the hours and days spent with Jerry and Bradley and a couple of others, in bed and out, talking and laughing and fooling around—that had been something else, often very pleasant, occasionally exciting, sometimes boring or annoying, but not love.

"There are different kinds of love," Sandy said, looking at the floor, "and different ways of expressing them. We can find a way, Jude. Please don't go. You and I have never been normal. Why should we start now?"

Jude smiled at his logic. Perhaps she could model herself after the *Marschallin*, who had vowed to love her count enough so that she could love even his love for someone else. It seemed a superhuman feat, but Jude knew from her years with Molly that real love involved more than just generating friction between various body parts, as though human beings were nothing more than cicadas droning in the waning summer dusk. And real love, if you found it, seemed the only thing that mattered. The rest was just passing the time until death claimed you.

Removing the flask from her suitcase, she unwrapped it and returned it to its spot on her windowsill. "Okay," she said.

Sandy grinned.

ONE WALL OF THE PENTHOUSE was glass, and through it Jude could see the lights of lower Manhattan spread out below her like a carpet of glowworms. A Marlboro man, a state trooper, and a tutued ballerina with thick ankles were passing a joint beside tubs of blue-gray junipers on the balcony.

The living room was packed. Sandy, wearing a white-net strapless gown with a hoop skirt, a black bouffant wig, and elbow-length gloves, was Scarlett O'Hara. Simon, in a Confederate army uniform, with a sword in a silver scabbard and black boots to his knees, was Ashley Wilkes. They planned to trade costumes the next Halloween.

Jude was wearing a swirling baby-blue chiffon Loretta Young hostess gown, a merry widow with Kotex stuffed into the too-ample cups, stiletto heels, rhinestone jewelry, white gloves, and a blond Dolly Parton wig. And she had on more makeup than an embalmed

corpse. Wiggling her way to the doorway of the cleared-out dining
room, she watched the dancers writhing shoulder-to-shoulder, drinks
sloshing, heads ducking the swaying crystal chandelier, elbows pumping like pistons.

Jude felt something cold and wet between her shoulder blades.
A deep voice whispered in her ear, "I'd like to crawl up under that
skirt, darling, and suck that stiff piece of meat between your legs."

Jude turned her head and met the glazed gray eyes of Mae West.
They scrutinized hers, turning suddenly bewildered. "Wait a minute,"
he said. "You're not a man."

"Sorry," said Jude.

Removing his glass from between her shoulders, he flounced off
with a toss of his blond fall.

Jude felt guilty even being at the party, since she was straight.
"Don't worry," Sandy had said as she made him up in the bathroom
at home. "There are always a few hets at these things, trying to 'pass.'
Besides, maybe you'll meet a nice woman." He grinned with his
cherry red lips.

"I'm afraid I'm not that kind of girl," she said, carefully dotting
a beauty spot on his cheek with her eyeliner.

"And what kind of girl are you, my dear?" asked Simon, leaning
in the bathroom doorway, twirling his waxed mustache tip like Simon
Legree. (Jude had just read that Harriet Beecher Stowe's model for
Simon Legree had been a Huguenot. She was trying to decide whether
to break the bad news to her grandmother.)

"A fag hag, apparently," said Jude, rubbing rouge into Sandy's
cheekbone.

Her struggle to love Sandy enough to love even his love for
Simon had consumed quite a few months. She had watched with misery as the two tumbled and tussled on Sandy's bed, cuddling and
cosseting each other. And she couldn't help thinking that if only her

anatomy had been male, she could have been in Simon's place. She didn't covet a penis per se, but she wouldn't have minded having one in order to have access to those who did covet them.

Some nights after Jude had gone to bed, Simon and Sandy departed for their sublife of bars, bathhouses, piers on the Hudson, and seedy movie theaters. Occasionally, it involved costumes, such as Sandy's yellow hard hat and grease monkey coveralls and Simon's fringed chaps and leather vest. And it often involved drugs with nicknames Jude couldn't keep straight, poppers and angel dust and black beauties, which they traded with their friends like marbles or baseball cards. Sometimes Jude heard them come crawling home in the dawn like mauled tomcats. This bad-boy act was a facet to Sandy that she'd never seen before. It seemed to clash with the daylight choirboy she knew so well.

"So how's it going, Jude?" yelled Sandy over the Jefferson Airplane, putting his arm around her and hauling her to his side so that his hoop skirt lurched upward, revealing lace garters and knobby knees.

Arranging the blond corkscrew curls around her face, Jude said, "This guy in drag got annoyed with me because I'm not a man. I'm getting confused." She was also getting drunk. The room was beginning to sway along with the dancers.

As Sandy was swept away by a tide of revelers, Joan of Arc appeared before Jude, wearing chain mail, dark tights, and shiny metal shin guards. All Jude could see of the face behind the visored helmet were the eyes, which were lapis lazuli in the shadows, just like Molly's. For a moment, she couldn't remember if she was awake or asleep. Her heart lurched unsteadily.

"Molly?" she said.

"Excuse me?" said Joan of Arc.

"Sorry. I thought you were someone else."

"I *am* someone else," she said, eyes crinkling with amusement. Jude laughed.

As the stunning blue eyes probed hers, Jude felt her flesh prickle.

"You make a beautiful woman," murmured Joan of Arc, one hand holding a staff with an attached blue banner studded with white fleurs-de-lis.

"I *am* a woman," said Jude.

"Obviously. And a most attractive one, too."

Joan was dragged off by a crowd of revelers pressing toward the dance floor, where the Jefferson Airplane were shouting, "Don't you want somebody to love? Don't you need somebody to love? Wouldn't you love somebody to love? You've got to find somebody to love! . . ."

William, the host, loomed in front of Jude. He was dressed as a Roman senator, in a white toga with a wreath on his head. A labor lawyer by day, he was pale and pudgy, like a pregnant ghost. His lover, Sid, was dressed as a gladiator, in some crossed leather straps, sandals, and a pouch for his genitals. But since he was a stevedore, he had the build to carry it off.

"Having fun, my pet?" asked William, repositioning his wreath.

"It's a wonderful party, William. Who's the woman dressed as Joan of Arc, by the way?"

He wrinkled his shiny bulbous nose. "Her name is Anna Olsen. She's a poet and a teacher. But forget about her, Jude. She's bad news."

"I wasn't thinking of her like that."

"No, certainly not," said William sternly. "I forgot. Our divine Jude is most regrettably het-ero-sex-ual." He enunciated each syllable with deep, mocking respect.

"Why is she bad news?" demanded Jude, smiling tolerantly.

William drifted away toward the plate-glass window like a blowfish in an overpopulated aquarium. Jude called after him, "William, why is she bad news?"

SANDY, SIMON, AND JUDE stumbled up the sidewalk, raincoats over their costumes. No taxi would stop for them because they looked both demented and drunk. So they were trudging north from the Village en route to Riverside Drive. Sandy and Jude had removed the spike heels from their blistered feet and were limping along in tattered stockings. Sandy's skirt was dragging the dirty sidewalk like a flaccid peacock tail. Jude was walking in the middle, arms linked through theirs, still a bit shaken by mistaking Joan of Arc for Molly. Was Molly now going to start invading her waking hours as well?

"Sandy, you look like Scarlett in the turnip patch after the burning of Atlanta," she observed.

"I know. And my hair—I can't do a thing with it." He yanked off his black wig and tossed it into a trash basket.

Giggling, they passed some young men who were standing by the entrance to the Port Authority. One in a leather cap and motorcycle boots called to Sandy, "Come over here, faggot. Give me a blow job, will you, darling?" His friends laughed and punched his tattooed biceps.

The man followed them up the sidewalk, stroking the crotch of his tight jeans and murmuring, "I got something here I could shove between those pretty red lips of yours." His friends ambled along behind him, making obscene sucking sounds.

Jude tightened her grip on Simon's trembling arm to prevent him from turning around and saying something that would get them all killed.

The men finally got bored and went away.

"I always get bussed at the bus," Sandy said with a sigh.

"Very funny," growled Simon.

"I suppose we asked for that," said Sandy. "Swishing around the streets in these getups."

"I thought this was the land of the free?" said Simon.

"Free if you're normal. Perverts must pay. You know what? I'm pretty sure that's the same guy who called me a faggot on the IRT the other day. They both had leather caps and blind right eyes."

"Bloody hell," said Simon.

A taxi finally stopped for them, and they rode back to the apartment in silence, Sandy's net skirt filling the backseat like foam in a beer mug.

Outside Sandy's room, Jude kissed them both on the cheek and headed down the hall.

"Jude," called Sandy.

She stopped and looked back at him. His face was scarlet beneath his smudged makeup.

"We'd love for you to stay with us tonight if you want to."

Simon nodded, hand absently stroking his filigreed sword handle.

Jude looked back and forth between them, Scarlett O'Hara and Ashley Wilkes in the wake of Sherman's March to the Sea. After the hatred she had just witnessed in the street, it would be reassuring to reassert the power of love.

"Uh, could you do that? I mean . . . I thought . . . aren't you . . ."

"We have both been known to make exceptions for irresistibly lovely women," murmured Simon, smiling gently beneath his drooping mustache, neon eyes glowing in the shadowy hallway.

Jude was astonished to find herself seriously considering the idea. She'd come a long way since the Virginia Club Colonial Cotillion.

"I'm afraid it would be too kinky for a simple Huguenot girl from Tennessee," she finally concluded. "But thank you for the sweet invitation."

"Just say the word if you change your mind," said Sandy. He looked relieved.

"We would have fun," Simon assured her.

Jude smiled. "I'll let you know, boys." Chiffon skirt swirling, she swept down the hallway, élan restored.

Lying in bed, she became intrigued by the mechanics of it all— how to keep track of two penises in various stages of tumescence. One was complicated enough. She would probably feel as frantic as someone in a straitjacket with a case of poison ivy. But it certainly seemed the most interesting way to resolve their triangle.

She fell asleep for a while. When she woke up, she found that she had in fact changed her mind. She got out of bed, slipped on her robe, and tiptoed down the hallway to Sandy's door. Placing her ear against it, she heard nothing. Either they'd gone out or they were asleep. She had no idea what time it was. Maybe she could just crawl in between them and see what happened. After all, they had issued her a standing invitation.

Slowly she turned the handle and opened the door. Across the room, she saw them, naked in the moonlight through the window. Sandy was bent over, legs planted well apart, gripping the windowsill with his hands and his teeth. Simon, standing behind him, grasped Sandy's hips with both hands. He was rocking back and forth against him, murmuring things Jude couldn't distinguish, while Sandy gasped and moaned and gnawed the windowsill.

Seeing the light from the cracked door fall across Sandy's back, Simon froze. He looked back at her—and it wasn't Simon. For a moment, Jude thought it was the young man with the blind eye from the bus station. But then she wasn't sure.

Sucking air through clenched teeth, Sandy snarled in a voice like the growl of a cornered beast, "Jesus Christ, Jude, get the fuck out of here!"

Backing into the hallway, Jude closed the door and leaned against the wall, mortified and afraid—and aroused. Shivering violently, she returned to her room and climbed back into bed, where she lay perfectly still, breathing heavily.

SANDY AND JUDE WERE STROLLING down Columbus Avenue inspecting the Roosevelt, where her father had been an intern. For several years, he had ridden the yelping ambulances into alleys where no one sane would venture on foot. The hospital was looking seedy, with newspapers and fast-food wrappers blown up in sodden heaps against the redbrick walls. Across Fifty-eighth Street was a Renaissance Revival apartment building from the turn of the century, with arched windows, and designs formed by blue-and-gold tiles inlaid among the red bricks. The windows were boarded up, and antiwar graffiti was spray-painted across the plywood—peace symbols and YANKS OUT OF NAM and MAKE LOVE NOT WAR. A sign on the door announced that the building was slated for demolition.

"My parents lived on the fifth floor of that building after they got married," said Jude as a sharp wind off the Hudson came swirling down the street. She and Sandy were being very careful with each other this morning, keeping things light and polite, as though by not acknowledging the events of the previous night they'd dissolve.

"It's sad to see a noble old place like that on its last legs," said Sandy. "When you think about all the lives that were lived in there. The joy and the sorrow those walls must have absorbed."

"My God," said Jude, "I just realized: I must have been conceived in there. When they headed south, my mother was pregnant with me."

"Ha!" said Sandy. "So you're actually a Yankee!"

"Thank God my Virginia grandmother isn't around to hear this."

"Imagine that," said Sandy, wrapping his arms around himself for warmth. "You've returned to the site of your inception. Like a salmon swimming upstream to her primordial spawning grounds."

"Let's not get carried away," suggested Jude. "Where do you think you were conceived?" They headed back uptown to meet Jude's grandparents for brunch at Café des Artistes.

"Right there in Tidewater Estates, I imagine. On a Saturday morning in midwinter. Saturday mornings were the only time they ever did it, as far as I could tell. My father would hand me a bowl of Cheerios and lock me in the playroom with my erector set. They didn't appear until lunchtime, and they remained in a haze of well-being for the rest of the weekend. I always waited until Saturday afternoon to ask for things they might object to."

"But maybe they were on a vacation somewhere more exotic?"

"Not bloody likely. Even their vacations were humdrum. Gatlinburg or Ruby Falls or Rock City."

"So where did all your evil genius come from?" asked Jude.

"Someone somewhere along the line must have cut loose with a hired hand."

"By the way," said Jude, unable to endure this charade any longer, "I'm sorry about last night."

Sandy blushed violently. "I'm sorry I was . . . otherwise engaged. Please try me again sometime."

Jude said nothing for a while. Finally, she replied, "I don't think so, Sandy. You're out of my league."

"So I gather you're shocked?"

"Who was he?"

"Who knows?"

"Where was Simon?"

"Who knows?"

"Do you really think this is wise?"

"Wisdom has nothing to do with it," said Sandy curtly.

"Clearly."

The truth was, Jude realized as Sandy opened the restaurant door for her, that she was afraid of him now, as though he were the carrier of some dark, brute force brought home from the docks, about which she knew little and wanted to know less. And the knowledge that a succession of strangers apparently wandered around their apartment in the middle of the night left her very uneasy. But it was, after all, Sandy's apartment. And she was unable to deny that the sight of him and the stranger grappling in the moonlight had excited her.

"WE USED TO BRING your mother here for Sunday lunch," Jude's grandfather said to Jude as he trimmed the fat off his sirloin. "In the days before that dreadful word *brunch* was ever invented."

Naked nymphets were cavorting on the walls all around them, behind forests of healthy indoor plants.

"I remember Jude's mother pretty well," said Sandy as he ripped apart a piece of baguette. "She used to give me a butterscotch candy whenever she saw me on the sidewalk in Tidewater Estates. So I started going over there all the time. She asked me to teach Jude to ride her new tricycle. Jude's legs were so short that her feet kept slipping off and spinning the pedals. And she thought that was so neat that she couldn't be bothered to try anything else."

Everyone laughed.

"Once she caught on, though," Sandy added, "she was a demon. She'd race down the block toward the highway before anyone realized she was gone. Her mother used to bribe me with candies to keep up with her."

"And here I thought you just liked me," said Jude. She hadn't seen him in a jacket and tie since he was at Exeter. He looked deceptively respectable.

"I must have, because I kept at it even after your mother died."

"Well, Jude tells us you are like a brother to her," said Jude's grandmother in her navy wool suit, Huguenot cross at her throat. "That makes you our grandson, and I want you to know that you will always be welcome in our home."

"Thank you very much," said Sandy. "I'm honored."

Jude studied her honorary brother as he bewitched her grandparents. If only Sandy weren't who he was, she and he would have made the perfect couple. But he was who he was, whoever that might be, and he would never be hers. The time had come to find a lover she could actually have, Jude had concluded, one who approximated the man she'd imagined Sandy to be. She'd been thinking about offering the position to Craig, a fellow Ph.D. candidate with whom she often discussed the Franco-Prussian War over cups of coffee at the West End Bar. Recently, he'd begun to touch her forearm as they talked and to press her knee with his beneath the table. He was too thin and he reeked of sandalwood incense, but otherwise he filled the bill.

"I remember the day Jude's father came home from the war," Sandy was saying.

Jude looked at her grandfather, who was listening to Sandy with attention. He seemed to have relaxed around the subject of Jude's mother. Maybe hearing Jude and her grandmother discuss her so much had desensitized him.

"The whole town went down to the train station and waved little American flags on sticks. The high school band was playing this god-awful mess that was supposed to be 'Stars and Stripes Forever.' Jude's mother was carrying Jude on her hip. Her father climbed off the train in his uniform, and I thought he was the most handsome man

I'd ever seen. Jude, who hadn't seen him since she was an infant, took one look at him, smiled coyly, reached out her arms, and cooed, 'Daddy!' And everybody laughed and cheered."

Jude watched her grandparents smile sadly as the busboy removed their plates.

"He was always a fine-looking man," agreed her grandfather.

Jude and her grandmother glanced at him, then at each other.

"Tall and lean and broad-shouldered," continued her grandfather. "With that copper skin and those mink-brown eyes."

Jude's grandmother shot her an astonished smile.

"I imagine y'all don't remember meeting me at the funeral," said Sandy, "but I remember you. Because you were the first Yankees I'd ever seen, and I was disappointed that you looked so normal."

"What were you expecting?" asked Jude's grandfather. "Horns and cloven feet?"

"Something like that," said Sandy. "But the only sinister thing about you was the dead fox around your wife's neck."

"I remember that fox," said Jude. "It had beady orange eyes."

"But I'm not even a Yankee," said her grandfather. "My family was in Alsace during your civil war."

Sandy smiled. "To Southerners, every American who isn't a Southerner is a Yankee."

By the time Jude and Sandy left her grandparents beneath the Tiffany light above their doorway, Sandy had promised them a free box at the opera. Jude's grandmother had written down his address so she could put him on the mailing list for the National Huguenot Society's newsletter, and her grandfather had noted his phone number so he could call him for a game of squash at the New York Athletic Club.

"My God, what a love feast," said Jude as they walked down 67th Street beneath the bare trees.

"Can I help it if I'm irresistible?" asked Sandy.

"Probably," said Jude. "But don't stop. It's so charming. Wait just a minute—you don't even know how to play squash."

Sandy grinned. "No. But I like locker rooms."

"With my *grandfather?*"

"He's very attractive, with all that steel-gray hair and that gunslinger jaw."

"You're sick," said Jude.

"I thought you said I was charming?"

"You're both. That's what makes you so dangerous." She was only half-kidding. How would she ever be able to integrate his daylight and moonlight selves?

"I like being perceived as dangerous," he admitted. "I was always such a Boy Scout back home."

"Well, you seem to be making up for lost time," murmured Jude.

Sandy glanced at her. "And you don't like it?"

"Not much," Jude replied hesitantly, appalled by the excitement she still felt when she pictured the faceless stranger thrusting into him.

"Well, let's see if I can defend myself to you, Jude. For years and years, I tried to be a good boy. For instance, I never touched you, however much I might have wanted to. You would have been shocked, but I don't think you'd have turned me down."

Jude thought for a moment, then shook her head no. "Maybe I wish you had, Sandy," she said, wondering if she had returned his love for her at that time whether his desire for men would have emerged nonetheless. Probably.

"Well, maybe I wish that, too. But I didn't. Instead, I bottled up my libido for years and years. When I got to London and started going to gay bars, I met hundreds of former Eagle Scouts just like myself. And we gave each other what we'd been doing without for all those years. Without having to say I love you, or to ask each other to go steady, or even to know each other's names. It was dangerous and mysterious and exciting. And it still is.''

Jude reached over for his hand. Knitting fingers, they walked along Broadway in silence. What would happen, Jude wondered, if they should ever both want each other at the same time?

"But surely this is something you understand, Jude?"

"Why do you say that?"

"Well, you were always a bit of a Girl Scout back home yourself. You must have had to confront your own shadow side by now—the part of you that longs for your dutiful everyday self to be obliterated by some all-consuming passion?"

Jude looked at him mutely, not knowing the answer to such an alarming question. Her everyday self had been obliterated only once —that night on the raft with Molly. And it had been overwhelming. But she didn't expect it to happen ever again. And she couldn't have said that she wanted it to.

LATER THAT WEEK AFTER a study session at the Columbia library, Jude and Craig ran the gauntlet of antiwar protesters who, waving Chippendale chair legs, defended the captured administration building. Back at Jude's apartment, she sneaked him down the hallway and into her bedroom. The night that ensued was uninspired, since it was sparked by only lukewarm affection and respect. But Jude made as much noise as possible within the bounds of credibility, as retaliation against Mona and Sandy.

In the sunny kitchen the next morning, Sandy's face was grim. He practically bumped chests with Craig, like rival seals. Taking the hint, Craig departed quickly.

"You could have at least been civil," Jude said to Sandy after letting Craig out the door.

"I don't have to be civil to any old scum you happen to drag in off the street," he snapped, grabbing several cereal boxes from the shelf.

"What about the scum *you* drag home? Besides, Craig's not scum. He's very sweet and bright." She hacked off a slice of bread and thrust it into the toaster.

"What would your father say?" He grabbed a bowl and slammed it down on the table.

Jude laughed incredulously. "Sandy, snap out of it."

"Out of what?"

"I think you're jealous." She studied him with gratified amusement.

"Oh, sure. Right. A gay man jealous of a straight woman."

"What's your problem then?" The toast popped up. She buttered it and spread it with raspberry jam.

He said nothing for a long time, pouring and mixing several cereals, hurling flakes around the room. Then he smiled sheepishly. "My problem is that I'm jealous."

"There. That's better," said Jude, patting his shoulder.

"Don't ever do that to me again," he said, looking up at her through bloodshot eyes.

"I'll do whatever I please." She headed out the door, carrying her toast.

"Yes, I know," he said, sadly munching his flakes. "You always have."

SIMON AND JUDE WERE SITTING propped up on Sandy's bed splitting a pepperoni pizza from a cardboard box and drinking V-8 juice. They'd tried to wait for Sandy, but hunger had won out. Scattered across the spread were pages from a manuscript Simon was editing on the Freedom Riders, mixed up with a rough draft of Jude's dissertation proposal. She'd decided to write about the perennial French phenomenon of a small group that defined itself as the "saving remnant," which everyone else then tried to murder as painfully as possible, using as case studies the Cathars, the Huguenots, the Jacobins, and the Resistance. Her delighted grandmother had been stuffing information down her throat like a mother bird feeding worms to her fledgling.

She had just interviewed a French friend of her grandfather's, who had fought with the Resistance after a Jewish shopkeeper in his village in the Alps had been crucified upside down by the SS, his mouth packed with cow manure. The man described partisans from his village mining a tunnel through the mountains with explosives to slow down the German advance. The plot was betrayed by a local farmer, and all the conspirators who were caught were forced to march into the tunnel themselves, where they were buried alive by their own trap.

As usual, Jude was actually trying to figure out the difference between people like Ace Kilgore, whose goal in life was to harm and destroy, and those like her father and grandfather and Sandy, who tried instead to defend and heal. She had concluded that it had something to do with Ace's eyes, two dead, black holes that neither reflected light from without nor projected it from within. Since he himself was cut off from the light, he was wounded and vengeful and determined to spread his contagion of rage, like some kind of spiritual rabies. It gratified him to plunge others into darkness, to prove that it was more powerful than the light that had shunned him.

But the real mystery was why ordinary people like Jerry Crawford and the Panther Twins had followed him into this void. Once while they were dating, she'd asked Jerry what he saw in Ace. He replied, "He's so strong. He's not afraid of anything." But Jude had come to suspect since that Ace was actually afraid of everything. His was the fake strength that reverted to violence under pressure.

Meanwhile, she had been delivering a discourse to an uninterested Simon on V-8 juice—why it had tasted awful to her as a child but was now delicious. Simon kept interrupting to discuss Marmite on toast. The evening news was playing on the television at the foot of the bed, the commentary a soft murmur as an American soldier incinerated a peasant hut with a flamethrower.

The phone rang. Groping for it on the floor, Simon picked up the receiver, listened, then said in his most winning voice, "Speaking!"

Holding out the receiver, he studied it and shrugged. "Funny. He hung up."

"Who was it?" asked Jude.

"Some guy asking to speak to the lady of the house."

As Jude laughed, Sandy walked through the door from the hallway, looking grim.

"Hard day at the office, dear?" called Simon from the bed.

"Hard day in the subway," he said.

"What happened?" asked Jude, alarmed by his voice, which sounded numb.

"It's not important."

"You can't come in here looking and sounding like Marilyn Monroe after her suicide and not tell us why," said Simon. He bounced off the bed and padded in his sweat socks over to Sandy. As Simon put his arms around him, Sandy started to cry angrily. Simon led him to the bed, and they sat down on the edge.

"Sorry," said Sandy, blotting his tears on the sleeve of his work shirt.

"What's wrong, love?" asked Simon, stroking the red-blond hair out of Sandy's eyes.

"When I got off the IRT just now, that same guy who harassed us at the Port Authority last Halloween, the one with the leather cap and the blind eye, was getting off with three of his friends. We were alone in the tunnel to the stairway, and he said, 'Well, well, if it isn't our friendly neighborhood homo searching for an asshole to fuck.' I turned around and gave him a look, and he said, 'And he isn't going to find one, either, because he's so fuckin' ugly.' And one of the others said, 'Maybe we should just put him out of his fuckin' fairy misery and kick his fuckin' faggot brains in.' I'd been working back-stage all day during the dress rehearsal for *Aida*, and I was so tired and so scared that I just opened my mouth and hit a high C. It bounced back and forth off those tile walls. They looked at me as though I was a crackpot and ran up the steps as fast as they could.''

Sandy smiled weakly, waiting for them to laugh, but they didn't. ''I just feel so helpless.''

''Bloody hell, Sandy, please be careful,'' said Simon.

''What can I do?'' he asked softly.

''What about telling the police?'' asked Jude. Her eyes strayed to his windowsill, on which she could see the indentations of his teeth. Could a taste for danger, like a pact with Satan, actually attract it in ways you hadn't bargained on? She wanted to protect him as he had her, but how?

The two men laughed bitterly.

''They probably *are* the police,'' said Sandy.

''Walk,'' said Jude. ''Take a bus. A taxi even. It's cheaper than a funeral.''

''So the cops tried to herd them into a paddy wagon,'' Sid was saying to the dozen people sitting around the cluttered dining table in Sandy's apartment, ''and they refused. Those motherfucking queens staged a riot like those fascist pigs had never dreamed of in their worst nightmares. Bopping them with their handbags. Stabbing them with their nails. Stomping them with their spike heels. Falsetto screams. And then a bunch of dykes and motorcycle dudes joined in, throwing bottles and swinging bike chains and hefting tire irons. And soon the whole damn block was in chaos. So the cops shoved their badass nightsticks back into their holsters and split.''

Everyone erupted into cheers, except Mona, who looked deeply bored to be in a roomful of men who never looked twice at her.

"Out of the closets and into the streets!" yelled Simon, standing up and raising his beer bottle in a toast.

Jude clicked her wineglass against Sandy's. He was smiling ironically at Simon's sudden ascent to the barricades.

"No more Mr. Nice Guy!" cried Earl, which was practically the first thing Jude had ever heard him say.

"Oh, gracious, watch out, homophobes!" said William. "Earl is on a rampage!"

Earl leapt up from his chair and began to whirl around the room in his sweatpants in a graceful frenzy, like something out of *Le Sacre du Printemps.*

Sandy handed Jude the joint that was circling the table. She drew on it and passed it to Tony in his pirate head scarf. Exhaling, she whispered to Sandy, "I don't know why I bother. This stuff has never worked for me."

Getting up, Sandy stood behind Jude and began to massage her scalp as they watched Earl's war dance, which the others were accompanying by clashing together their dirty cutlery. Tony was striking the empty and half-empty wine bottles with his knife, creating a discordant melody. Eventually, like the Pied Piper, Earl led everyone but Sandy and Jude in a bunny-hopping conga line out the door, en route to the carnival that had filled the Village streets ever since the riot.

Jude, meanwhile, was going out of her mind as Sandy continued to knead her scalp and her neck. Her only wish was that he never stop. He began to run his fingers around the folds of her ears and in and out of the passageways. Abruptly, she turned her head to one side and sucked his index finger into her mouth. He drew a sharp breath.

Jude pushed up from her chair. She turned and they faced each other, startled and afraid. They moved into each other's arms like horseshoe magnets. Their mouths joined.

Eventually, Jude turned her head aside to gasp, "We'd better wait for Simon."

"I don't want to wait anymore, Jude," Sandy said. "I've been waiting for you since I was a boy."

Jude just stood there, paralyzed by the ethics of the situation, feeling Sandy's erection against her abdomen.

"Please, Jude. Just once and never again. It will get it out of our systems."

"Or infect us like a wasting disease." Her breathing was turning jagged.

Smiling down at her whimsically, he said, "You always did think too much, brainchild."

At the sound of Molly's nickname for her, pronounced in the identical soft mountain drawl, she let him lead her down the hallway to his room.

"I WAS WRONG," she murmured to Sandy later as they lay among the tangled clothing that littered his bed and carpet. A breeze through the open window was drying their sweat and chilling them.

"What about?" He reached for her shirt and draped it languidly over her chest and abdomen.

"I'm crazy about you as a bad boy."

He smiled lazily as a boat horn blared on the river. "In matters such as these, there's no bad or good. Only love and the courage to live it. Or not.''

''Don't worry about it, Jude. It's cool,'' said Simon the next evening as they sat in the breeze wafting through Sandy's window, sharing a joint and watching pleasure craft glide down the Hudson in the twilight. ''Just as long as I get equal time one of these days.''

''It could happen,'' she said, studying her friendly rival with his dark curls and his Fu Manchu mustache. Since the stated goal of their generation was to ''smash monogamy,'' he had no choice but to appear blasé. But he seemed really not to mind. Yet if he knew what had gone on between Sandy and herself the previous evening, he would have minded a great deal. It hadn't been that conditioned reflex you could have alone or with anyone else, of spasming muscles pumping blood through swollen tissue. It had been another order of experience altogether, parallel to that night with Molly on the raft, but even more moving, if that was possible, because they had both been wide awake and unafraid and unashamed. Afterward, they had cried—from astonishment to have shared such an unlooked-for moment. From sorrow that it was over and might never recur. What she couldn't tell Simon was that she now had no wish to give him equal time or even to share Sandy with him anymore. The only person she wanted was Sandy, as soon as possible, as often as possible, for as long as possible.

Even so, she wished she hadn't drunk all that wine and smoked all that dope, so she could have avoided such delirium. Because she and Sandy and Simon were now headed down some gloomy labyrinth in which at least one of them would lose the way. Probably herself, since, as Clementine used to say, leopards didn't change their spots. Especially if they were happy leopards. Why hadn't she left well enough alone?

Sandy looked as tense and miserable as Jude felt when he arrived in the doorway and spotted her and Simon sitting together by the window. From a car radio in the street below, Janis Joplin was begging someone to take, and break, a piece of her heart.

Simon looked up at Sandy through shrewd green eyes. "Don't worry, mate. I know you love her. I love her, too. These things happen. They'll happen again. Maybe for me next time, if I get lucky."

"It's not that," said Sandy, walking in and sitting down on his mattress. He propped his elbows on his knees and buried his face in his hands.

"What's wrong, Sandy?" demanded Simon.

Sandy drew a deep breath, then exhaled. "I was standing on the subway platform just now. It was rush hour, so it was really crowded. That guy with the blind eye turned up right beside me. As he pushed past me, he snarled, 'Out of my way, queer boy.'

"I don't know what came over me, but all of a sudden I just couldn't take it anymore. So I said in a really loud voice, 'This man is a fascist!' I stood on tiptoe and pointed him out as he dodged through the crowd, trying to get away. 'He follows me around threatening me and calling me names!' I yelled.

"Most of the people ignored me, but a few looked at me sympathetically or studied him as he fought his way to the exit. On the steps, he turned around and looked at me as though I were a cockroach he was about to squash."

WHEN SANDY DIDN'T COME HOME from work the next night, Simon phoned all the hospitals in the city, finally locating him in intensive care at the Roosevelt. Someone had found him unconscious in an alley near the Port Authority.

Jude walked into his hospital room. He was tucked tightly into a narrow white bed, his face black and purple, tubes snaking from his nostril and hand. As he gasped for air, she noticed that several of his teeth were missing.

Sitting down beside him, she laid her head on his bedside and closed her eyes. People in serious accidents reported having their lives flash before their eyes. But at that moment, Jude experienced just such a retrospective of Sandy's life. Like a slide show, she saw him as a fair-haired little boy in socks and sandals. She saw him in his tree house, writing his novel, his cowlicked hair scrambled like a rat's nest. And playing chess by the brick wall on the playground at school. And throwing passes to her halfway down the football field as boys twice his size closed in on him. Sandy in a tweed jacket chattering charmingly to her grandparents, and sitting at his switchboard at the opera, overseeing dozens of workers and technicians. Sandy lying beneath her, eyes closed, languorous smile playing across his lips, hands stroking her buttocks as she braced her fists against the wall and moved up and down on him, slowly, slowly, trembling and sweating, struggling to make a finite moment last forever.

She could feel him ebbing away. She reached over and grabbed his hand to try to make him stay, but it was limp and dry and cold.

The next night while Jude ate a grim and silent dinner with Sandy's parents, who had just arrived from Tennessee, Sandy died from a blood clot to his brain while Simon dozed in the chair by his bed.

When Jude and Simon reached home after midnight, Simon followed her to her room. "Please may I stay with you tonight?" he asked.

They lay in each other's arms on her bed. Periodically, Simon cried while Jude stroked his back and blotted his tears with the sheet. She knew this drill by heart. First came the numbness, the way the stump of a newly severed limb didn't bleed. Then the fury, when you lashed out at anyone who got in your way. And finally the memories that wouldn't quit. But maybe expecting the joy of communion without the pain of its loss was like wanting to eat candy without getting cavities.

Toward dawn, Simon said in a hoarse voice, "You were the last person he made love to. I turned him down the other night. I guess I was punishing him for you. I said it was okay. But it wasn't. His tricks were one thing. Sexual encounters with men he'd never see again. But he really loved you. Eventually, he'd have left me for you."

"No, Simon. It was nothing. We were drunk. Stoned. It should never have happened. I'm sorry it did," she lied.

"Don't apologize. It was inevitable. He loved you, Jude, all his life."

"But not as much as he did you. You were the soul mate he'd always wanted and never found."

Their mouths abruptly undertook an urgent exploration of each other's faces and necks. Jude could taste the salt of Simon's tears. As he entered her, their bodies shuddered, fumbled for a rhythm, and finally moved together. And since each was fantasizing that the other was Sandy, for a moment it seemed he really was there, hovering over them, blessing their clumsy union with his whimsical smile.

PART THREE

ANNA

A WOMAN IN A LONG, burgundy wool overcoat stood in the doorway of Jude's office, smiling and frowning, both at once. Jude smiled back from her cluttered desk. She felt she should know the woman but was unable to place her. She sported a glossy, dark, flapper hairdo and mauve lipstick.

The woman snapped her fingers. "Dolly Parton!"

Jude smiled politely. "Excuse me?"

"That Halloween party a few years ago. You were Dolly Parton. And I was Joan of Arc."

The eyes. Now Jude remembered the eyes, which had been shadowed by the visor of her helmet as she stood before Jude in her chain mail and shin guards. At the moment, the eyes were sapphire blue against cheeks flushed from the cold, and they were framed by dark crescent eyebrows and long lashes.

"I'm Anna Olsen. Simon sent me. I just ran into him on his way out. He said maybe you'd have a minute to listen to my book idea."

"Come in," said Jude, standing up to clear a stack of manuscripts and page proofs off her tweed love seat. "How do you know Simon?"

"I don't very well. We have some mutual friends—the men who gave that party." She perched on the edge of the love seat.

"William and Sid?" Jude returned to her swivel chair.

Anna nodded.

"You have quite a memory," said Jude. She herself did not, however, because something was nibbling away at the edge of her awareness, something disturbing William had said that she couldn't quite recall.

"For memorable events, I do." She unbuttoned her coat, revealing a large wool scarf in shades of blue and purple.

Jude looked at her with a half smile, having just remembered Anna's telling her that night that she made a beautiful woman. She was quite the flirt. Too bad she was barking up a dead tree. "So what's your book idea?"

Anna, a poet, taught creative-writing workshops in the city high schools. She was proposing an anthology of pieces by her students, who represented more than a dozen nationalities. She was intrigued by the ways in which they adapted their cultural inheritances to the American mainstream, or failed to. America wasn't a melting pot, she maintained; it was a stockpot, full of intact lumps.

Jude nodded, hands clasped before her chin. It was what America was supposed to be all about—a haven for those who needed a fresh start, freed from ancient traditions and taboos, yet no doubt bearers of them nonetheless.

"I'll talk to Simon," said Jude, having difficulty removing her eyes from Anna's, which were now turquoise in the zebra shafts of light through the slatted blinds, like deep seawater penetrated by sun-beams. "It sounds like an interesting idea. Leave me your number and I'll give you a call."

"I'll call *you*," Anna said quickly. "When would be good?"

"Early next week?"

After seeing Anna to the elevator by the reception desk, Jude returned to her office and sat back down at her desk, swiveling her chair around to watch the woman at her keyboard in the glass building across the street. When the blinds were up, they sometimes waved to each other like next-door neighbors. Jude admired her wardrobe —a seemingly endless parade of tailored suits and silk blouses such as Jude aspired to once she could afford them.

Simon had hired Jude as his assistant when she dropped out of Columbia. After Sandy's death, everything seemed pointless, especially the study of history. She no longer wished to know about the idiotic atrocities committed by the human race since the dawn of time. So she'd been mindlessly typing and filing, fielding phone calls and visi-tors, and ransacking reviews for favorable quotes to use in ads. She planned to remain an assistant forever. But Anna's book idea interested her.

She kept thinking about Anna's eyes, how similar they were to Molly's—the same shifting shades of blue, like a mood ring. The same way of narrowing with skepticism and sparkling with amusement. They were Molly's eyes in a different face. Anna's physique, however, was tall and slender.

Turning back to her desk, Jude typed a memo to Simon rec-ommending Anna's project. Clipping it to her outline and samples, she took the package next door and laid it on his black Formica ta-bletop, on which sat several dozen paperweights—a bronze penis with a happy-face head, an Empire State Building with a removable King Kong. Jude selected what Simon claimed was the varnished hoof of

Secretariat to secure her memo. Also on the tabletop sat a photo of Sandy in a silver frame. He was smiling into the camera, wearing a white undershirt that displayed his well-cut biceps and pecs, a grassy Cape Cod dune looming behind him.

In the years since his death, Jude and Simon had both been on a tear. Simon roamed the streets at night with a switchblade at the ready in the pocket of his leather jacket, searching for the young thug with the blind eye he was convinced had killed Sandy. Despite the fact that Sandy's missing wallet made robbery the apparent motive. Often he came home to their apartment bruised and bloodied from fights he'd picked with bewildered hoodlums. Periodically, Jude removed the switchblade from his pocket and threw it in a trash basket on her way to work. But he always bought another.

Jude herself had become a bedroom guerrilla, ambushing half a dozen young men, leading them on, then leaving them high and dry and humiliated, while they phoned and fumed and leapt from tall buildings. Occasionally, she and Simon sought relief from their fury in each other's arms. But apart from the night of Sandy's death, Simon made it clear that it was just a diversion. "Rearranging the hormones," he called it. And in the morning, he was brisk and distant, as though they hadn't been lying together panting like marathon runners a few hours earlier. Sometimes Jude wasn't even sure if it had really happened or if she'd dreamed it. She had never told him about the intensity of the interchange between Sandy and herself, and she never would. Simon had referred a few times to "your little fling with Sandy." It was clear that he needed to think of it as nothing more than what she and he experienced together—some warmth in the night with friendly flesh.

But Jude had recently become disgusted with herself as a conquistador. She'd realized that she was wounding innocent civilians in her war of attrition. And she sometimes longed for a comrade-in-arms with whom she could lay down her weapons and find peace. But at other times, she concluded that she was finished with love. It hurt too much. Since she seemed incapable of taking it lightly, her only recourse was to jettison it.

Dreams were currently her sole consolation. During the weeks of numb disbelief following Sandy's death, Molly appeared for the first time since Jude had moved in with him.

"I told you he was going to hurt you," she said, briskly dealing hands for Over the Moon on the pine needles that cushioned the floor of their cave in the Wildwoods.

"Bravo. Right again," said Jude. "I thought I'd gotten rid of you."

"Dream on. You'll never get rid of me, sweetheart. So you might as well learn to listen to me."

"I do listen to you, Molly. I just don't always agree." Jude swept her cards together, picked them up, and fanned them out.

Molly shrugged and threw down the jack of spades. "Falling in love with a fag was probably just your way of staying faithful to me."

"Stop calling Sandy a fag," snapped Jude, tossing down the ten of hearts.

Molly grinned. "Poor little Jude. Forever in love with phantoms."

JUDE'S PHONE BUZZED. It was Simon, asking her to come next door. He was sitting behind his table in his striped dress shirt and Jackson Pollock tie, curly black hair pulled back into a ponytail, studying Jude's memo with his limpid green eyes. "Since you like Anna's idea so much, I think you should handle it." He wound up a green plastic *Tyrannosaurus rex* and they watched it lumber across his desktop on duck feet, red eyes flashing. "It can be your first solo flight. We'll do a small printing and see how it goes."

"Fantastic," said Jude from his doorway. "Thanks, Simon."

Back at her desk, Jude felt frustrated that she couldn't call Anna
with the good news. Why had she been so weird about giving out her
number?

JUDE MUNCHED A BREAD STICK while Anna fished the olive out
of her second martini with her plastic swizzle stick. She was wearing
a suit of very fine wool in a subtle plaid of mauve and forest green
with some gold lines through it. Looped loosely around her throat
was a scarf that repeated the mauve and gold in bold swirls.

"I can give you the names of some agents if you want," said
Jude like a policewoman reciting her rights to a detainee. The waiter,
who wore a tux even though it was only lunchtime, set their chicken
Marengo before them with a flourish, then poured Pouilly-Fuissé into
their glasses.

The decor of the midtown restaurant, which Simon maintained
was run by gangsters, centered around the apricot of the marble walls
and floors. She and Anna were sitting side by side on a cushioned
banquette, looking out across the nearly empty room. On their table
was an exotic lily with a mauve and yellow center that harmonized
with Anna's suit. This was Jude's first expense-account lunch, and she
had decided that she didn't want it to be her last.

"That won't be necessary," said Anna. "I trust you to treat me
fairly."

"Thank you," said Jude. "I'll try not to betray your trust." As
she cut her chicken, she suddenly recalled what William had said—
that Anna was bad news. She looked up from her plate. Anna met
her gaze with smiling cool-blue eyes. She certainly didn't look like
bad news.

As they sipped their cappuccinos, Jude went over the various
clauses in the contract. Afterward, on the sidewalk outside, while the

irate drivers of a line of taxis honked and swore at a vacant double-parked delivery truck, Anna and Jude agreed to meet every other Wednesday afternoon after Anna's writing workshop at Julia Richmond High School.

"SO HOW DID IT GO, JUDE?" called Simon as Jude passed his door.

She paused in his doorway. He was sprawled on his carpet in his sock feet, eating a sandwich. "A struggling writer could have eaten for a month on what that lunch cost," she replied.

"True," he said, looking up. "But think about it: A writer gets to sit home all day in Levis, telling himself amusing stories. Whereas we have to get dressed up, and ride the subway downtown, and hassle with printers and page proofs. We do all the dirty work, and they get interviewed by Dick Cavett. So we deserve a nice lunch from time to time."

Jude smiled. "Very feeble."

"Struggle is good for writers," insisted Simon. "If their lives are miserable, they have more of an incentive to create a fantasy world."

Jude laughed.

"Anna is very attractive, isn't she?"

"Is she? I didn't notice."

Simon smiled.

"What?"

"Oh, nothing," he said, biting into his corned beef.

"William once told me she was bad news. Why, do you think?"

"William has very little use for women. Especially sexy ones."

"You find Anna sexy?"

"Don't you?"

"I wouldn't know. I'm not that kind of girl."

"Neither am I," said Simon, "but I know it when I see it."

"I'M AFRAID IT'S TOO ABSTRACT," Anna was saying about one student poem.

She and Jude were walking across Central Park to the West Side as the wan winter sun sank behind the luxury apartment buildings along Central Park West. The black tree branches were making curlicue patterns like wrought ironwork against the darkening sky. The paths were mostly deserted, except for a few solitary dog walkers hunched against the cold. But Jude was so engaged by the conversation that she wasn't feeling the cold. "That may be the whole point," she said. "He's from Martinique. His culture is French, and French culture tends toward abstraction."

"I think it's just bad poetry," said Anna, who was wearing a tall mink Cossack hat. Her glossy hair framed her face like the wing tips of a raven.

"Bad, good—those categories are culture-bound. Americans are practical people, so we prefer concreteness."

"You're no help." Anna laughed, squeezing Jude's upper arm with a gloved hand. "I thought you were supposed to give me some answers, not raise more questions."

"But this one is crucial," insisted Jude. "Do we include pieces we think are good or pieces that would be regarded as good within the students' cultures of origin? And if the latter, how do we determine which those are? Because to do the former is a form of cultural imperialism." The problems Anna's project posed mirrored those within Jude's own head, where the conflicting claims of a dozen different groups clamored for primacy—Yankee and southern, Baptist and Huguenot and Catholic, Dutch and Alsatian and French, Cherokee and Scottish and English. Sometimes she envied the simple ethnic clarity of the Hitler Youth.

Emerging from the park, they strolled down Jude's grandparents' block past the Café des Artistes. This part of New York had come to feel as familiar as Tidewater Estates to Jude by now. She had walked its sidewalks almost every day for six years—through dirty slush and sodden leaves, beneath trees feathered chartreuse with bursting buds, or bare and blasted by icy winds. She often dropped by to see her grandparents when they weren't at the retirement house they'd bought on Captiva. Her friends and colleagues lived all around her.

Jude's mother had once walked these sidewalks herself, ridden horses along the paths in the park, and posed for photographers on benches and street corners. She had fallen in love with Jude's father in the cafés and restaurants and made love to him in his tiny apartment across from the Roosevelt. Jude could imagine her shock when she found herself stranded on that plateau in Tennessee, surrounded by mile after mile of forested mountain peaks and coves. By the time she was Jude's age, she was buried in a grave of sticky red clay atop that same plateau. In some odd way, Jude felt she was living out the unfinished portion of her mother's life, making the opposite choices —not marrying, not having a baby, not going back to the South, pursuing a career, sidestepping romantic commitments.

Upon reaching Broadway, Anna and Jude went into a diner that was tiled in black and white and trimmed with stainless steel. They perused the glass case that held the cakes and pies, then sat down at a table topped with black-flecked granite. After ordering tea and scones from a woman in a starched white cap that looked as though it belonged on a Victorian nurse, Anna pulled a piece of paper from her handbag and read the poem in question, which rhymed *beauty* with *duty* and *truth* with *youth*.

Jude buried her face in her hands. "I'm afraid you're right. It's just bad poetry."

"But to him, it's good. He's very proud of it. I hate my job."

"I hate mine, too. At the office, I read the manuscripts that come in unsolicited. The slush pile, it's called. I know that each one is *War and Peace* to the person who wrote it. But many of them are frankly unreadable."

"Maybe we should call this whole thing off," said Anna. "Clearly we're too tenderhearted."

"Fine," said Jude, "if you'd like to pay back your advance."

"Oh, well, I guess I'm not that tenderhearted."

As they parted on the sidewalk, Anna leaned forward to kiss Jude good-bye just as Jude extended her hand for a shake. Both stepped back. Then Jude leaned forward for a kiss, into Anna's outstretched hand. Laughing, they came together for a hug. Then they held each other at arm's length and exchanged a smile. Anna's eyes were almost indigo in the rapidly descending dusk. Jude was surprised to discover that she and Anna were the same height, a rare event for someone as tall as she.

Jude watched Anna for a moment as she strode south in her long burgundy overcoat and mink Cossack hat, looking like a guard at the Kremlin. Then Jude turned around and headed uptown toward home.

This soon became a ritual. Anna came to Jude's office building from Julia Richmond and waited in the lobby for Jude to descend with her usual satchel of manuscripts and galleys. They crossed the park, the air warming and softening with the arrival of spring. As the weeks passed, magnolia, crab apple, apple, and Japanese cherry trees, one after another, extruded their fragrant blossoms and then shed them on the pavement. While the two women walked, Anna recited in a mesmeric alto voice the poems she was considering for the book, and

Jude commented on them. At the Broadway diner, they drank tea, ate pastries, and debated possible book titles involving melting pots and rainbows. Then they embraced gingerly and each headed home.

Although they discussed the book in all its aspects—content, format, jacket, title, publicity—they rarely discussed their personal lives. Jude had managed to piece together that Anna had grown up in Chicago with a Swedish Lutheran father and an Italian mother who was devoutly Catholic. Thus, she shared Jude's cultural cacophony, which was probably why she was interested in editing such a book. She'd come to New York to do her doctorate in comparative literature at NYU, writing her dissertation on the French Symbolist poets. Now she taught workshops and wrote poetry. And she lived somewhere downtown. With whom, if anyone, Jude had no idea. There was no wedding band on her left hand. And Jude had first encountered her in a roomful of homosexuals. Occasionally, Jude recalled William's warning that Anna was bad news. But she had concluded that there was some private rancor between them. Once she knew Anna well enough, she'd ask her.

Simon was so impressed by the unprecedented diligence Jude was bringing to Anna's book that he hired a new assistant and began giving Jude manuscripts of history books to edit. At first, she insisted that the deadly antics of the human race no longer interested her. But Simon doubled her salary and persuaded her to benefit the firm with her academic training.

One afternoon in early fall, shortly before the manuscript was scheduled to go to press, Jude and Anna sat sipping iced coffee in "their" café on Broadway. "I'll miss these meetings, Jude," said Anna. "They've been lots of fun."

Jude stirred more sugar into her coffee in silence. It hadn't really occurred to her that they wouldn't go on seeing each other. In Ten-

nessee, only death interrupted a relationship, if that. But it was true
that she was Anna's editor, not her friend. Once the book was finished,
there would be no basis for further contact.

"Could we still meet for a walk now and then?" asked Anna.
She seemed agitated.

"Definitely," said Jude.

"Good. I wasn't sure if this was just another book to you."
Anna broke their gaze to glance out the window at a young man
passing by wearing a Comanche headdress and little else.

"I like you, Anna, as an author and as a person."

Anna returned her eyes to Jude's. "I like you, too. You know
what intrigues me most about you?"

"What?" Jude realized this was the most intimate conversation
they'd ever had.

"Your transparency. With you, what one sees is what one gets."

Jude shrugged. "Isn't that usually the case?"

Anna smiled sardonically. "In my experience, most people are
a house of mirrors."

As Jude walked uptown, she tried to decide whether it was a
compliment to be called transparent. Its opposite, opaque, implied
mystery and subtlety. Transparency suggested naïveté. Was it corny
to be naïve, or did it indicate authenticity and integrity?

A couple of weeks later, Anna didn't show up outside the entrance to Jude's building at the usual hour. Jude paced the marble
lobby for a long time before heading home, surprised to notice how
disappointed she was.

That night, she and Simon split some Chinese takeout in front
of the electric heater in their dingy living room. After Sandy's death,
as normal attrition claimed their roommates, they hadn't bothered to
replace them, lacking the energy. Besides, they could afford not to

have roommates now. So she and Simon lived alone in the echoing apartment with its constant reminders of Sandy. The same battered Danish-modern armchairs that had been there the day Jude first visited were still the only furniture in the living room. One night, Simon, in a seizure of grief, had started ripping the opera posters off the walls. Since he hadn't completed the job, they were still hanging there in tattered strips that flapped in the breezes off the river.

"One of these days we should fix this place up," said Simon, opening a white cardboard container of moo goo gai pan. "Paint and paper it. Buy some new rugs and furniture. Now that we're high-powered publishing executives."

"Good idea," said Jude. "It does look like the day after Woodstock in here. By the way, do you have Anna Olsen's phone number?"

"I don't really know her." He paused with his chopsticks in midair, dribbling rice onto his plate. "I've just seen her a few times at William and Sid's."

"Alone?"

He grinned, green eyes flashing. "Sandy would be so proud."

"What?" she asked irritably.

"What's it to you, darling, whether she was alone or not?"

"I need to reach her about her book, but for some reason, she's never given me her number. That's all, okay?"

"Yes. Alone." He was struggling not to smile. "All alone. Utterly alone. Gloriously alone."

Flouncing down the hallway to her bedroom to escape Simon's lurid implications, Jude turned in at Sandy's room, closing the door behind her. In the moonlight shining through the window, she surveyed the TV on which they'd watched so many chick flicks. And the phone on the rug that would never again ring for him. And the closet with its door ajar, in which a few deserted shirts swayed in the current of air under the door. And the stripped mattress on the floor, on which she and Sandy had experienced together something remarkable that still eluded her capacity for definition.

Standing there on other nights, Jude had sometimes pretended that she could feel Sandy's presence. But it wasn't true. This was an empty room with dust balls in the corner. Molly occasionally turned up in her dreams. But Sandy had vanished without a trace, leaving behind only Simon's and her memories of him, which they served up to each other from time to time like soggy leftovers from some distant bacchanal.

Anna called Jude the next morning at work to apologize for standing her up and to say that she couldn't see her until the following week.

"But I have a new title idea and I need your opinion," said Jude, doodling a mountain range across her notepad. Which, she abruptly realized, looked like the profile of a naked woman lying on her back, knees in the air.

"Okay, shoot."

"But I have to show you some roughs for a new jacket, if you like the new title," said Jude, suddenly desperate to see her, and startled by the desperation. "We don't have much time. They were about to print the jacket when I stopped them."

"I'll meet you at that café at seven."

When Anna appeared in the doorway in a belted khaki trench coat, she was wearing sunglasses, even though it was almost dusk. Sitting down, she removed the coat but not the glasses.

"Greta Garbo, I presume," said Jude, reaching for them. She wanted to see those eyes.

Anna jerked her head aside. "I'm having trouble with my vision. My doctor told me to wear these."

Jude watched her own reflection in the dark lenses as she told

Anna about her new Baptist-bred title, *Precious in His Sight.* Anna thought she preferred it to their previous choice. While studying the sketches for a new jacket, she swept off the glasses to see them better. One of her eyes, ringed with royal purple flesh, was thickly powdered and nearly swollen shut, as though she'd been stung by several bees. Realizing what she'd done, she touched it self-consciously with her fingertips, explaining, "I ran into a cupboard door."

Jude studied her, saying nothing. "Is there some way I can help?" she finally asked.

"You do help, Jude. Much more than you realize."

"I'd like to strangle whoever did this to you." Jude reached across to touch the swelling with her fingertips.

Anna laughed weakly, taking Jude's hand in both hers and holding it on the tabletop. "You'd better not. He's much bigger than you."

"Who is?"

"My husband."

Jude looked at her. "I didn't realize you were married." She glanced down at Anna's hand. It was still ringless.

"It hasn't been a real marriage for years. We just stay together for our children." She squeezed Jude's hand, then released it. Jude removed it to her lap. It lay there on her thigh, tingling.

Jude's head fell forward, so her chin rested on her chest. She gazed at her napoleon, which was oozing custard. "Children?" she murmured.

"Two, a boy and a girl. They're at prep school."

Jude looked up from her pastry to Anna's face. That probably meant Anna was over forty. At least a dozen years between them. Practically a different generation. She studied Anna's swollen eye. "Why do you stay with him if he treats you like this?"

"He didn't mean to."

"They never do," said Jude. "But is that any excuse?"

"He has many other nice qualities."

"I'm sure even Hitler had his moments," replied Jude.

"Besides, I provoked him. He gets very jealous. Yesterday, he got jealous over you, as a matter of fact. That's why I stood you up."

"Over me? Why?"

Anna lowered her head as though consulting her tea leaves for guidance. "Well," she said slowly, "I guess he feels we spend a lot of time together. And maybe I've mentioned your name a few too many times."

"But is it a crime to have a new friend?"

Anna looked up, eyes clouded with anxiety. "Not if she remains just a friend."

"So what's the problem then?" Jude glanced nervously around the diner, all the occupants of which seemed to be eavesdropping on Anna and herself.

Anna smiled brightly. "There is no problem." She scribbled a number on her paper napkin and handed it to Jude. "It's best to call me in late afternoon," she said, "before Jim gets home."

As Jude walked north toward Riverside Drive, her brain was as chaotic as the stock exchange after the crash. She kept picturing Anna's swollen face. She wanted to protect her from this man, whoever he was. But he was her husband. And he was jealous of Jude? Was this why William felt Anna was bad news? She was too passive to extract herself from an abusive marriage? But Jude had been seeing her for months, and this was the first time she'd noticed any bruises. Maybe it would be best just to back off and give it all a rest. But, oh God, those eyes that shifted like the waters of the sea, from cerulean to indigo to turquoise. Having watched them all these months, how could she give them up?

When Jude woke up the next morning, she discovered a feeling of dread in the pit of her stomach. As she gazed past her Atalanta flask to the drifting gray waters of the Hudson, she remembered Anna's bruised eye and her own wish to protect her. But Jude wasn't a home-breaker. And Anna was her author. It was unprofessional to get involved in her private life. She would make a point of not phoning. And if Anna phoned her, she vowed to keep it brief and focused on the book, in compliance with her family motto: "When in doubt, get the hell out."

Simon appeared in her office doorway toward lunchtime that day, carrying a disheveled manuscript. "Here. A present." Giving her his most winning smile, he plopped it on her desk.

Picking up the first few pages, Jude skimmed them. It was a scholarly history of lesbianism from the Middle Ages to the present. Looking up, she said, "Please don't do this to me, Simon."

"Do what?"

"I've got too much on my plate right now as it is," she temporized.

"But you're the only one who can edit it, Jude. You're a history Ph.D. manqué. Besides, everyone else is about to go to St. Thomas for the sales conference." He backed out of her office, grinning.

That night, Jude sat by her phone for a long time, the new manuscript lying unread on her bed, inspecting the number Anna had scribbled on the paper napkin. It had four 4s in it. Four was Jude's favorite number.

Finally forcing herself to start the manuscript, she read into the night about women who lived alone being burned as witches. About women being tortured and hanged for dressing as men. About women being stoned for refusing to marry. About women killing their female lovers to prevent them from marrying men. The manuscript needed a lot of work. The stilted language made the horrors sound almost bland, and each page was half-filled with arcane footnotes. She scribbled suggestions to the author all over the pages.

The next day at work, Jude jumped each time her phone rang. When she answered and discovered that it wasn't Anna, she became irritated and snapped at whoever it was. And when she hung up, she wracked her brain for some detail about the anthology that required Anna's opinion. She was worried about her. She wanted to be sure she was okay. But the manuscript was already at the printer's and everything was regrettably under control. And besides, she had taken a vow to let Anna resolve her marital masochism alone.

Jude walked home up Columbus Avenue, looking into shop windows, wondering whether she should buy a new fall outfit. Anna rarely wore the same clothes twice. Whereas Jude usually paid very little attention to her own appearance. But it might be nice to give Anna something fresh to look at when they next met.

Beside a display window in which she'd been studying shoes, Jude spotted a doorway she'd never noticed before. It opened on a staircase that led, according to a small hand-printed sign, to: MADAME TOUSSAINT, VOODOO SPELLS AND TAROT READINGS. On a whim, Jude climbed the dirty linoleum-covered steps. At the first landing was a battered steel door with a buzzer beside it. A card underneath read: MADAME TOUSSAINT. Jude buzzed. The door buzzed back and Jude pushed it open.

She was assaulted by the scent of patchouli oil. The walls and ceiling of the room were draped with gold-patterned Indian bedspreads that billowed like spinnakers in the draft from the door. Soft music sounding like reggae Gregorian chants floated down from two speakers near the ceiling. Large cushions covered in Prussian blue velvet lay on the floor around a brass tray on bamboo legs.

The strands of colored beads in the far doorway parted, and the largest black woman Jude had ever seen squeezed through the door frame. She was wearing an African-print muumuu and matching pillbox headgear in shades of orange and brown. Extending her hand, she murmured, "Welcome. I am Madame Toussaint. How may I help you this afternoon?"

Jude studied the face. The eyes were surrounded by so much flesh that they seemed to be squinting. Chins were stacked one atop another like the overlapping ranges of the Smokies. "I'd like a reading," Jude said, astonished at herself.

Madame Toussaint gestured to a cushion by the tray. Jude plopped down, sending up a cloud of dust. Madame Toussaint sank down on her cushion with a grace Jude would have thought impossible in someone so large. Watching Jude with her tiny bright eyes, she shuffled the cards, an ordinary deck with DELTA AIRLINES printed on their backs. Jude cut them. The woman dealt some out on the brass tray. Then she studied them for a long time, occasionally glancing at Jude, while voices from the speakers near the ceiling chanted softly about rivers flowing red with the blood of white oppressors.

Finally, Madame Toussaint closed her eyes and started talking in a listless monotone. About money and success that were headed Jude's way. About the spirits of departed loved ones who were whispering messages for Jude into Madame Toussaint's ear. About a past life as a courtesan on Atlantis, where Jude had been faithless in love, for which she was now doing atonement. Jude listened with growing indignation. Clearly this was a scam.

"A new love is moving toward you very fast," Madame Toussaint intoned, rocking rhythmically with her eyes closed. "With someone older than yourself. Someone who is troubled. Someone you can help. Someone who will help you."

Jude had snapped to rigid attention.

"This relationship will be deep and lasting and very important for both women," continued Madame Toussaint.

Jude shuddered. "Women?" she echoed faintly.

Madame Toussaint nodded slowly, still rocking. "A water sign. A creative person. An artist of some sort."

Anna was a poet and a Pisces.

Who was this storefront charlatan? Jude jumped up.

Madame Toussaint opened her eyes and watched calmly as Jude fluttered around the room. After her panic had subsided a bit, Madame Toussaint murmured, "Twenty dollars, please."

Reaching into her shoulder bag, Jude thrust a bill at her and headed for the doorway.

As Jude gripped the doorknob like an activated hand grenade, Madame Toussaint added for free, "There are worse things in this world than a woman who loves you."

Jude rushed out the door and down the steps. In the street, she discovered that she had a four-aspirin headache.

SINCE SIMON AND ALL the top brass had departed for the sales conference in St. Thomas, Jude decided to stay at her apartment the next day so she could edit without interruption the manuscript on the history of lesbianism. She asked her assistant to forward her phone calls. Then she assembled the manuscript, some pencils, and a cup of coffee on the low table in the living room. She put some records on the turntable to drown out the din from Riverside Drive. Then she sat down and went to work on the turgid prose, crossing out and rewriting all morning long. She found a certain satisfaction in locating the nugget of meaning hidden in the dross of a paragraph and restating it in one succinct sentence.

Also included with the text were some photographs of the handful of famous lesbians from the past who had managed not to be murdered or incarcerated in loony bins. One featured two women in Victorian gowns with pinched waists and bustles. They had their arms around each other and were gazing into each other's eyes with un-masked adoration. As she studied them, Jude wondered if she and Molly had been lesbians. They had loved each other deeply, and both were female. They had explored each other's bodies to a certain extent and had experienced some sort of orgasm together that night on the raft. But labeling their interaction so clinically robbed it of its wonder. In any case, Jude had been with half a dozen men since. So did that make her bisexual? But she had never loved a man and a woman both at once. And none of the men had engaged her as Molly had, not even Sandy. Although he might have if he'd lived. But she and Molly had shared years of peace and passion, whereas she and Sandy had just begun. Most people she knew didn't fit into these pigeonholes anyway.

Jude realized that the last song on the last record in the stack was repeating time after time. Sipping her cold coffee, she concentrated on the lyrics:

Every night you sit and watch the TV screen,
And the life you live is only in your dreams.
But I think I know what it is on your mind.
Yes, I think I know what you're thinking 'bout all the time.
You want to be loved.
You want to know somebody somewhere cares. . . .

Lying back in her chair, she listened to these lines again and again, debating their accuracy vis-à-vis herself. She had been convinced that she didn't want to be loved anymore.

Abruptly, she recalled Anna's remark that her husband didn't mind if Anna had a new friend so long as "she remains just a friend." Jude realized she'd been deliberately obtuse during that conversation. Anna had raised a topic that they needed to deal with, yet Jude had sidestepped it. Sitting up, she switched off the record player, picked up the phone, and dialed Anna's number.

After a dozen rings, Jude hung up. Jumping up, she grabbed her jacket and left the apartment. Taking the bus through the park to the East Side, she walked downtown until she came to Julia Richmond High. Going into a coffee shop across the street, she sat at a table by the plate-glass window and ordered a grilled cheese sandwich. She didn't even like grilled cheese sandwiches, but they were Anna's favorite. As she chewed the greasy cardboard bread, she watched the school doorway. It wasn't Anna's usual day there, but who knew? In any case, Jude had no idea where downtown she lived, so this was her only chance of finding her.

After waiting for an hour and a half, nursing a cup of coffee under the scowl of the gum-chewing waitress, Jude went out into the street. Striding to the park, she followed the route back to the West Side that she and Anna usually took, discussing with Anna in her head how they should defuse the attraction that was undeniably building between them.

Upon reaching Columbus Avenue, Jude ducked into a bookshop. Going directly to the poetry section, she extracted from the shelves volumes by Rimbaud, Baudelaire, and Mallarmé. Anna had written her thesis on them, but Jude could remember very little from her poetry course at the Sorbonne. She wanted to reread them so she could discuss them intelligently with Anna. Their exchanges about literature and history were the most crucial part of their relationship. Maybe if they emphasized them more, the physical attraction would simply wither away from lack of encouragement.

As she headed toward the cash register, she spotted a rack of magazines. On it sat a road atlas. Picking it up, she looked up Illinois. Locating the inset showing the streets of Chicago, she studied it closely. She'd never been to Chicago, so she tried to imagine the tall

apartment buildings along Lake Michigan and the quaint ethnic neigh-
borhoods inland that Anna had once described to her. This was Anna's
hometown. She wondered what street she had lived on, what games
she and her friends had played, where she'd gone to school, whether
she'd had a pet. She'd have to ask her when she next saw her. Which
would be in eleven days now, she calculated on her fingers.

Returning the atlas to its shelf, Jude noticed a stack of *Vogues*.
Grabbing one, she added it to her pile of poetry books, hoping it
might give her some ideas for the new outfit she wanted to assemble
in time for this next meeting with Anna.

En route to her apartment, Jude turned in at her local liquor
store and bought a bottle of Pouilly-Fuissé. This was the wine Anna
had suggested for the chicken Marengo at their first lunch together.
Jude recalled that she herself had drunk only one glass, trying to keep
her wits about her for the discussion of the book contract. Anna had
polished off the rest of the bottle alone. Jude admired her gusto. She
ate pastries and grilled cheese sandwiches and washed them down with
wine or beer or Irish coffee. Jude wondered whether she might have
a thyroid condition, because she stayed so slim.

Plopping down in the armchair before the coffee table, the manuscript lying in stacks all across the carpet, Jude opened the wine and
poured herself a glass. Sipping it, she read Baudelaire out loud, de-
spairing over her French accent, which had gone to hell in her years
since Paris.

When the bottle was half empty, Jude came to a poem entitled
"*Femmes Damnées*." "Have we then committed such a strange act?"
Hippolyta demanded of her lover, Delphine. "Explain if you can my
turmoil and my terror. I shiver with fear when you call me 'my angel.'
But I feel my mouth drawn to yours."

Jude paused to finish the wine in her glass and refill it. "Far
from the living, condemned wanderers, prowl through the wastelands

like wolves,'' suggested Baudelaire to the distressed women. "Fashion your own destiny, muddled souls. And flee the divine spark that you carry within you.''

Drawing a deep breath, Jude let the book fall into her lap. She couldn't detect within herself the shame she was apparently supposed to feel over her love for Molly. She personally had no problem with prowling wastelands like a wolf. She liked wastelands. After all, she'd grown up in one. She'd also grown up regarding herself as a wolf child on the fringes of the forest, longing for her wilderness home. Sometimes her thimbleful of Cherokee blood came in handy.

Heart thudding, she grabbed the phone off the floor and dialed Anna, sitting there in terror as the phone rang time after time.

"Hello?'' said a pleasant male voice.

"Is Anna there?''

"Who is this?'' The voice had turned gruff and suspicious.

Jude hesitated, wondering whether she should just hang up. "Allison,'' she ad-libbed.

"Allison who?''

"Allison Marks.''

"I guess we haven't met.''

"I work with Anna at Julia Richmond.''

"Well, she isn't here right now. Shall I have her call you back?''

"Never mind. It's not urgent. I'll see her next week at school.''

Jude slammed down the receiver and lay back in her chair, rattled to have made first contact with the enemy, annoyed to have resorted to a pseudonym. She reached over and turned on the record player to the song from that morning. Time after time, she listened to the soppy lines, heart beginning to feel like a piece of wrung-out laundry: "You want to be loved. You want to know somebody somewhere cares. . . .'' Reaching for the bottle of Pouilly-Fuissé, she guzzled the remaining two inches, while the frenzied singer wailed about wanting to know that somebody somewhere cares.

WHEN JUDE WOKE UP toward noon the next day, she found herself sprawled in the armchair in the living room, her manuscript scattered all around the room. She felt as though someone had buried a hatchet in her forehead, and her mouth tasted as though she'd gargled with old zinnia water. Standing up, she felt nauseous. Not having eaten anything since the grilled cheese sandwich, she went into the kitchen, picked the mold off some stale bread, and toasted the slices. After three cups of black coffee and two aspirin, she showered and changed her clothes. Then she returned to the living room and tackled the manuscript anew, struggling all afternoon to pare down the footnotes that threatened like a cancer to eclipse the text.

As the sun sank behind the high-rises of Fort Lee, Jude took a tea break. Picking up *Vogue*, she carefully studied the latest fashions draped on the contorted frames of the mutant models. Then she came to the horoscopes. Hers read: "Planetary forces are conspiring right now, Arians, to shake up the stability you've so painstakingly constructed for yourself. The more you fight your need for transformation, the stronger it will grow, like the monster in a fairy tale. So accept the inevitable, and be grateful for the new wisdom it will bring you."

Frowning, she read Anna's forecast: "New seas await you, Pisces. If you plunge in, you will locate the treasures of the deep. But if you wish safety, then remain on the shore."

Jude let the magazine flutter to the carpet like a shot duck. Leaning her head against the chair back, she speculated on whether Anna wanted treasures or safety. And if she should decide to plunge in, would she change her mind and climb back out again as Molly had done, leaving Jude to flounder alone?

Jude realized she was starving and there was nothing in the kitchen, so she threw on her blazer and headed out the door. When she reached Broadway, she bought a hot dog from a street vendor. Leaving a Hansel and Gretel trail of oozing mustard and catsup, she headed south. With all these planetary forces ganging up on them, maybe she'd run into Anna if she wandered around the Village.

Stalking the four miles in record time, Jude paced the narrow, winding streets one after another, watching brave women holding hands, watching women alone as they eyed her eying them. But always she was on the lookout for Anna's tall, slender frame and her glossy black cap of hair.

Passing a movie theater, she noticed a placard planted on the sidewalk out front, bearing an enlarged review from the *Times*. She discovered that the movie inside, called *Dark Desire*, concerned a love affair between two women. The review was a rave, and a show was about to start.

Sitting in the dark with her head in her hands, Jude tried to get a grip. She didn't believe in planetary forces or hypothyroidal psychics or astrological mumbo jumbo. She didn't even believe in love any-more, and certainly not love with a married mother. So what was happening to her?

The plot concerned a university teacher named Deirdre who was in love with a younger student named Karen. Flattered, Karen also fell in love with her. Unfortunately, Karen was married and had three children. After about two minutes of excitement and happiness, the problems began. Karen's children failed at school, and cried them-selves to sleep at night, and were rejected by their playmates, and became pyromaniacs and shoplifters. Karen's husband, Jason, a prince among men, who did the dishes after meals and took his own clothes to the cleaners, demanded a divorce. He remarried an adorable doormat who was a gourmet cook and who liked to fall to her knees and give him blow jobs whenever he walked through the door. They sued Karen for custody of the basket-case children. Karen, meanwhile, had had to drop out of college to support herself as a laundromat attendant. Deirdre, weary of hanging around all the time with a grumpy laundromat attendant, deserted her for a woman in silver full leathers who raced a Harley around London for an express message service. In the end, Karen hanged herself in Deirdre's bedroom, above the bed on which they'd first so blissfully made love.

Stumbling out into the street, Jude wandered along it searching for a taxi, profoundly demoralized to see the direction in which she and Anna were headed if they didn't do something fast. Maybe she should ask Simon for a transfer to the London office? She could vanish without leaving a forwarding address. In the short run, they'd suffer, but they'd be spared even greater future suffering.

Looking up, Jude saw flashing above her head like a UFO some neon palm trees and the words: THE OASIS. The sign hung above the doorway into a bar. Through the front window, she spotted a mural that featured camels and sand dunes and shapely veiled figures with clay jugs on their heads. The room was packed with women. Two were kissing on the mouth in a corner.

What the hell, decided Jude, if the gods needed for her to be a lesbian, at least let it be with a woman who wasn't someone else's wife. She marched through the door like John Wayne into a saloon infested with desperadoes. All across the room, heads turned to inspect her. Bellying up to the bar, she ordered a glass of white wine, feeling her stomach turn queasy in protest. After a few sips, she summoned the courage to glance around at the other women. The one standing beside her met her gaze with a smile. She had a lean face with high cheekbones and a pointed chin. Tiny silver Scottie dogs hung like Monopoly pieces from her earlobes.

"I like your jacket," she said, nodding at Jude's blazer, a loose-weave plaid in shades of gray and blue.

"Thanks," said Jude. She sipped her wine, elbow propped casually on the bar. "Do you come here often?"

"Every now and then. And you?"

"From time to time."

"I think it's really the nicest women's club in New York. It's cozy. More like a neighborhood pub. Less like a meat market."

Jude nodded as though she, too, were a jaded habituée of the lesbian meat markets of New York. They sipped their drinks. The other woman was drinking scotch. Her flannel shirt was a Macdonald plaid.

"Would you like to sit down?" asked the woman. "I see a table over there in the corner."

They sat. The woman introduced herself, explaining that her nickname was Scottie because she raised Scotties in Bayonne, New Jersey. Each bought the other a drink. A couple of times, they gyrated to the throbbing disco music. The second time, they stayed on the floor for a slow dance. Scottie was as tall as Anna, and their bodies fit together well as they swayed to the languid beat, each with an upper thigh stroking the other's pubic area.

When they sat back down, Scottie said, "Jude, there's something I want to ask you." She looked off across the room. "I hope I'm not out of line."

"Go ahead," said Jude, heart beating fast. This was it. It wasn't love, but it would take her mind off Anna and safeguard Anna's marriage.

"No, never mind," said Scottie, suddenly embarrassed.

"Please. I want you to."

"I can't," mumbled Scottie.

"But that's why I'm here."

"Huh?"

"Just tell me."

"Okay. Here goes." Scottie took a deep breath. "I was wondering if you'd be willing to make a donation to my fund for breeding my championship bitch to last year's Best in Show at Westminster?"

Sighing with relief, Jude handed her a twenty and headed home.

SIMON RETURNED FROM ST. THOMAS the next afternoon with a stunning tan, a new straw hat, and a planter's punch hangover. "You look like shit," he informed her when he found her guzzling Pouilly-Fuissé in the living room while an hysteric on the record player shrieked about wanting to be loved. A manuscript was strewn around the floor. "What's wrong?"

"This damn book you assigned me," she snarled. "It's a fucking mess."

"Sorry I asked," he said, heading down the hallway with his suitcase. "I need a nap."

After a few minutes, Jude trailed him to his room. He'd lowered the shades, dropped his Hawaiian shirt on the floor, and crawled under the covers. Jude stepped out of her jeans, threw off her T-shirt, and climbed in beside him. His back was turned, but she could tell by his breathing that he was only pretending to be asleep. "Pretty please, Simon?"

"I'm sorry, Jude, but I'm hung over."

She reached across his back and began to touch him in ways he usually found irresistible. "I've got a headache," he whimpered like a frigid wife.

"Look, we both know you use me shamelessly whenever you don't have the time or energy to find a man. So now it's my turn."

"Do I have to?"

"Yes," she said, gratified to have produced a halfhearted hard-on.

He rolled on top of her without enthusiasm. "I'm not the one you should be fucking."

"Just shut up," she snapped, a hand on each of his hips, pulling him into herself.

When he finally collapsed in a sweaty heap, she moaned, "God, Simon, don't stop yet."

"Get a goddamn dildo," he snarled. As he rolled off her, he said, "Call the woman, Jude."

"Who?"

"For God's sake, stop acting like you've never been around the block!"

"What if her husband answers?"

"Tell him you're in love with his wife."

"I'm not in love with her," Jude insisted.

"Tell him you want to rip off all her clothes and do unspeakable things to her body."

"You're no help."

"God helps those who help themselves."

"Obviously I'm no lesbian," she said reasonably. "Considering what I've just been doing with you."

"Give me a break. Go see a therapist. I need to sleep."

Jude jumped up, grabbed her clothes, and stalked back to her own room. Sitting down on her bed, shivering from the chill, she picked up the receiver and dialed the first five digits of Anna's number, finger lingering hopefully over her lucky 4s. Then she slammed it down and returned naked to the living room to polish off the Pouilly-Fuissé.

AS JUDE WALKED INTO her office the next morning, the phone on her desk was ringing. She lunged for it as though for the brass ring on a merry-go-round.

"All right, I give up," said Anna's alto voice. "You win. When can I see you?"

"How about right now?" asked Jude, elated, watching her resolutions for a sane and happy life fly out the window.

"This is not a good idea," said Jude as they strolled through Central Park, a warm breeze swirling cherry blossoms all around them like fluffy pink eiderdown.

"I agree," said Anna.

"I don't want this in my life," said Jude, feeling happier than she had in years.

"Nor do I. So how do we stop it?"

They halted and turned to face each other. Jude studied Anna's eye. The swelling had subsided and her bruise was fading to the turquoise of her irises. "Tell me about your husband," she requested. "That might help."

Anna put her arm around Jude, and they resumed walking. "We have so little time," she said, "and I don't want to spend it talking about him. Or my children. They have nothing to do with you and me. They're my responsibility, and I'll deal with them. But you're my escape from all that. I don't need to be your lover, but I want you as my friend."

"You already have my friendship. You know that."

"And the other?" she asked without looking at Jude.

Jude hesitated, struggling. "I love you, Anna. But not like that." She remembered Molly's saying these same words to her.

Anna's face fell. "Well, never mind," she said. "The one who is able to set limits loves less. But I accept that. I just want to spend time with you, Jude, in whatever way is possible."

"Maybe the one who sets limits loves more," said Jude. "Maybe she doesn't want to endanger something that has become absolutely vital to her happiness."

Anna's smile was like the sun coming out from behind a cloud. "Why would developing a new facet to our relationship doom it? It could very well deepen it."

Jude remained silent. She had just understood that because of her losses, she had learned to equate love with longing. But what if the longing should cease and the love should bring fulfillment instead?

JUDE PROWLED HER LIVING ROOM, which she and Simon had refurbished with ivory grass cloth on the walls, tweed sofas and arm-chairs, and thick plum-colored wall-to-wall carpeting. Having so care-fully preserved all traces of Sandy, Simon now wanted them completely obliterated. Manic from a new love affair of his own, he had also bought a house on Cape Cod, where he was spending the weekend with a lawyer named Marvin, who was as brunette as Sandy had been blond.

Anna was supposed to be arriving at any moment to discuss yet again why their love had to remain platonic. This had been going on for several weeks, to Simon's sardonic amusement. He referred to their maneuverings as the Dyke Dramarama. But for him, sex was about as complicated as blowing his nose—and about as meaningful.

There were, after all, many issues to consider: Anna's husband and children. The age difference. The fact that Anna could lose her teaching job. The fact that they could both be murdered in the street, as Sandy had been, as women had been throughout history. And Jude had additional fears she hadn't yet voiced. Anna had acknowledged being with other women. Would she be disappointed by Jude's in-experience? Hopefully Anna could lead, but could Jude follow? Most of all, though, Jude was terrified. Her mother, Molly, and Sandy had died. What if loving Anna meant losing her as well?

Anna walked in and kissed the air beside Jude's cheek. Jude helped her out of her new royal-purple silk windbreaker and hung it in the closet. Both had been investing small fortunes in new clothes and personal grooming, providing each other with a kind of visual potlach.

Sinking into Simon's new couch in a tight skirt that rode halfway up her thighs, Anna said, "So, Jude, what compelling new reason do you have tonight for why we should keep our hands to ourselves?"

She sounded irritated. In the beginning, Jude's compunctions had touched her, but she seemed to be getting fed up. At their most recent session at the café on Broadway, Jude had explained that she was determined to make this startling new love of theirs last, even if preserving it required them to renounce it. Anna had studied her with disbelief before standing up and marching out the door. But she returned a few minutes later to inform Jude that she was seriously psychotic.

Jude sank down beside her on the new couch and handed her a piece of paper listing the sales figures for *Precious in His Sight*.

"Very nice," said Anna, handing it back. "But so what?"

"Simon wants us to make it an annual thing, with contests and awards and scholarships."

Anna smiled. "But that's fabulous!"

Jude went into the kitchen and returned with a chilled bottle of champagne. They toasted their new series.

"But what does this have to do with our personal relationship?" asked Anna as she sipped her champagne, legs carefully crossed so that Jude could see her finely turned ankle, exquisitely fitting Italian shoe, and the seam up the back of her dark silk stocking that led into the shadowy realm between her legs. Jude's fingers twitched, longing to straighten the seam.

"Well, once the book came out, I was no longer your editor, so we were free to pursue whatever connection we wanted. But now I'm back to being your editor. And it would be unethical for me to have an affair with an author. Like a lawyer romancing a client."

"That's too bad." Anna sighed. "Because I've just written you an incredibly romantic poem. I guess I'll have to read it to someone else." She studied her carefully trimmed nails.

"What's it called?"

"Leda and the Swan Song."

"All right, let's hear it," said Jude with a half smile.

She removed a piece of paper from her handbag and began reading. The early stanzas acknowledged the chagrin of past loves lost. The middle ones dwelt on the delights of new love, despite an awareness that it must one day fade.

In closing, Anna looked up right at Jude and recited from memory:

> *I'll touch you so gently tonight, my friend,*
> *That you'll scarcely recall all that gall*
> *You'll cry as before, but this time for joy,*
> *In the red through the window at dawn.*
>
> *Stay with me tonight.*
> *Hand me your pain.*
> *Look in my eyes.*
> *Let love live again.*

They sat there in silence, each stroking with her eyes the planes and hollows of the other's face.

Jude set her champagne glass on Simon's antique oak end table. Leaning over, she placed a hand on either side of Anna's head and looked into her eyes, which were flaring in the lamplight like cool, blue flames. After several prim kisses, their mouths opened, and the debate was concluded. They lay in each other's arms for a long time as desire swept over them in waves, too weak from its pummeling to undertake anything more exotic. Out the window at the foot of the couch, the Ferris wheel across the Hudson was a spinning hoop of sparks.

CHAPTER

1 2

A S THEY STROLLED UP BROADWAY, Anna was telling Jude about the son of the French poet Stéphane Mallarmé, Anatole, who had died of rheumatism at age eight after many months of horrible suffering. Stéphane had struggled to master his grief by writing poems about the experience.

Anna began to recite in French some of the fragments he'd composed before admitting defeat: " 'What has sought refuge, your future in me, becomes my purity throughout life, which I shall not sully. . . .' "

Anna's French was rhythmical and almost unaccented to Jude's American ear. She wasn't listening too closely for the meaning because the sound of the sorrowful words alone was so haunting.

" 'We have learned through you a better part of ourselves,

which often evades us,' " continued Anna, " 'but shall now reside within us. . . .' "

The closer they got to Jude's apartment, the faster they walked, until they were nearly trotting, eager to fall onto Jude's bed and feel the blood course through each other's veins. Anna was the Florence Nightingale of sex. With her, Jude had been experiencing a passion she'd never guessed was possible—hours of long, slow arousal involving every limb, digit, fold, and recess of flesh, until each cell in both bodies was vibrating with a tension that screamed for release.

With Sandy, there had been a searing incandescence from hard, silky, swollen flesh pounding like a pestle into her slippery secret passages. And a thundering through their flesh like the hooves of wild horses as they fought and bucked and reared and plunged. Whereas with Anna, there was rather the faint, salty scent of a sea marsh at dawn. And tongues that delicately teased and tested and tuned, sending ripples of desire radiating outward like dragonflies skimming the surface of a glassy pond. And moist velvet walls that opened and pulsed and clung like bivalves. And the sound of the surf swirling in tiny sucking whirlpools.

It was the difference between galloping across a plain under a white-hot sun at high noon and diving deep beneath the sea. If the French were correct to call orgasm *la petite mort*, Sandy had provided death by auto-da-fé, and Anna, death by drowning. Either seemed worth planning the rest of your life around. But Jude's single episodes with Molly and Sandy had sizzled her like stray bolts of lightning, whereas Anna seemed to be rewiring her circuits for an ongoing supply of high-voltage power. She was a high priestess of passion, approaching lovemaking as a ritual, one that had to be respected and revered, one that could be replicated indefinitely by observing the established rites.

As in any religion, some of the regalia were flowers, candles, incense, and wine. Others were perfume, new sheets, massage oil, and assorted hors d'oeuvres on a tray by the bed. And she liked very slow music that sounded like the spheres revolving in outer space, and icicles shattering on lunar rocks, and winds howling across the tundra. Her variety of holy communion required that all the senses be activated and focused, then fused, and finally obliterated, before the dove of peace could make its descent.

Jude wandered through her workdays in a haze of exhausted arousal, accomplishing almost nothing, waiting for the night. Fortunately, Simon was in a similar coma over Marvin, so he didn't notice. Both mooned around the office, gazing out windows with dumb, dazed grins while their company's sales figures plummeted to new lows. Their coworkers were humoring them, like the parents of children with chicken pox who wait for the fever to break and pray that their own immunity hasn't worn off.

The afternoon after her first session with Anna, Jude had found herself buying out the lingerie shop next door to her office building. Molly and Sandy would have preferred her to be a boy. But in a matter of hours, Anna had erased all that, leaving Jude grateful to be female, and the more female, the better. Anna liked to lie on Jude's bed and watch her remove the silk camisoles and satin teddies—not like a strip show but like an actual flesh-and-blood woman undressing in the flickering shadows cast by the candle flames. She reminded Jude of herself as a little girl when she used to watch her mother dress for parties, worshiping at her altar in a hushed silence, intoxicated by her perfume, which mixed with a strange musky odor that seemed to emanate through her pores from somewhere deep inside her body. Now Jude understood what that exciting, frightening fragrance had been—the scent of a woman in love. It filled the room now when she and Anna were together and permeated the sheets where they had lain. One time, Anna left behind a cashmere sweater, which Jude had decided not to return. On the nights when they weren't together,

Jude buried her face in it while she slept, breathing in the blend of Anna's Opium, her sweat, and that unmistakable scent that proved to Jude beyond any words or deeds that Anna desired her. If that scent should vanish, Jude knew it would be a warning that their passion was languishing.

" 'The ultimate goal,' " recited Anna as the elevator ascended to Jude's apartment, " 'was nothing but to leave life pure. . . . You accomplished this ahead of your time. . . .' "

Unable to wait any longer, Jude forced her knee between Anna's knees and buried her face in Anna's neck, breathing deeply of her Opium. With one hand, she pressed the red stop button.

"Jude," gasped Anna as Jude's other hand slid up her thigh and beneath her skirt, "what if someone's waiting for the elevator?"

"Tough luck," said Jude, watching Anna's gorgeous blue eyes go bleary and flutter shut as her thighs parted and her head fell back against the wall. Jude's role in Anna's religion of love was that of the heretic who defied and flouted the creed. Like the good Catholic girl she had once been, Anna was turned on by transgression.

When they at last reached Jude's floor, Anna was still breathing spasmodically as she straightened out her clothing. The door slid open. Simon and Marvin were standing there looking deeply annoyed. Simon glanced from Jude to Anna. "I think the girls have discovered your elevator stunt, Marvin."

"Aren't these young studs remarkable?" Anna asked him smoothly, patting her black hair into place.

Although he smiled, Jude suddenly suspected that Simon didn't like Anna. She wasn't sure why not. In the beginning, he had egged Jude on. Surely he wasn't jealous, since he had a new love of his own?

"TELL ME SOME MORE POEMS," murmured Jude, lying amid her mangled sheets later that evening. Her entire body felt sated and fatigued, and her mind was glazed and dull, as though Anna's Opium were ether.

Anna began languidly to recite Baudelaire while Jude watched the waters of the Hudson reflect the flickering lights from the amusement park in wavering, golden party streamers. She recalled the similar safe feeling of lying on a mattress of pine needles in the cave back home, watching the sunset reflected in the river and listening to Molly describe their future cabin on the clifftop while dozing mourning doves cooed from their coves in the Wildwoods.

As though echoing her thoughts, Anna murmured, " 'Mais le vert paradis des amours enfantines. / Les courses, les chansons, les baisers, les bouquets, / Les violons vibrant derrière les collines. . . .' "

"The green paradise of childhood love, the races, the songs, the kisses, the flowers, the violins trembling behind the hills. . . ." Anna's and her raft was this bed, and the Hudson had replaced the Holston. But everything else was the same now as then. The long arc of lonely hours had finally come full circle, and Jude had recreated with Anna the happiness she had once known with Molly, a closeness and contentment she thought she'd lost forever. The green paradise of childhood love was alive again here in this New York City apartment.

"You're crying," murmured Anna, pausing in mid-Baudelaire. "Why are you crying, my love?"

Jude began to sob. She rolled over against Anna's long, lean body and laid her head on her lovely breasts. When she finally calmed down enough to look up through puffy red eyes, she discovered that Anna was watching her, her blue eyes suffused with a tenderness Jude had never before experienced. She shut her own eyes and felt her heart ascend to her throat so that she almost choked from happiness.

"So tell me, sweetheart," said Anna, stroking Jude's hair, "are you crying because you're happy or because you're sad?"

"Both," wailed Jude, starting to cry all over again.

Sitting up to blot her eyes and blow her nose, she told Anna for the first time in any detail about Molly and Sandy and their deaths, about her own loneliness and grief and rage.

After listening for a long time, Anna concluded, "So now, with me, you've been given another chance."

Jude started crying again. She felt as vulnerable as a hermit crab that had left behind its old shell but hadn't yet located a new one.

Anna pulled her back down alongside her own body and held her close, kneading the quivering muscles of her back. After a while, she began softly singing a lullaby of popular songs from her youth— "Sha Boom," "*Qué Sera Sera*," "Glow, Little Glowworm," "Mr. Sandman," "Three Coins in a Fountain," "Don't Let the Stars Get in Your Eyes."

On and on she sang, each tune worse than the last, until Jude began to laugh, begging her to stop. "What was wrong with you teenagers in the fifties?" she demanded. "Those are the worst songs I've ever heard!"

Anna shrugged. "We were romantics. 'If you can't be with the one you love, love the one you're with.' You call that a love song?"

JUDE WAS LYING ON the living room couch in her sock feet, reading a manuscript about the Knights Templars that Simon had just assigned her. The inquisitors sent by the Pope to examine the London Templars had just returned home to France in disgust, complaining that no one in England knew how to torture properly. Their recommendation was that the English Templars be shipped to France, where torture was state of the art. As usual, Jude was trying to figure out the difference between the torturers and the nontorturers.

The doorbell buzzed. Jude wasn't expecting anyone. Anna was at the opera with Jim, and Simon was on the prowl down in the Village, having thrown over poor, baffled Marvin. Every month or two, he was madly in love with some new man, whom he portrayed as perfect in every regard. A few weeks later, he had evolved a list of irremedial faults that required him to dump the man in question and plunge into a depression, swearing he would never love again. It was his version of graveyard love. No real person could ever measure up to the ideal of Sandy that he carried in his heart, flashing it like a silver sheriff's star at anyone who got too close. Jude understood. It was easier to love the dead. They rarely talked back.

Getting up, she padded to the door in her jeans and turtleneck. Through the peephole, she saw Anna in her sealskin coat, glossy dark hair framing her face.

Opening the door, Jude asked with a delighted smile, "What are you doing here?"

Anna pushed her into the entryway, slammed the door, grabbed her hand, and dragged her into the living room. "Quick!" she said. "I have to meet Jim at the opera in forty minutes."

Accepting the challenge, Jude removed Anna's fur coat, silk dress, and elaborate undergarments like a sailor unrigging a luxury yacht. They rolled around the plum carpet like the Marx brothers in a car chase, Jude fully clothed. Afterward, Jude rerigged her and sent her out the door with something to think about if *La Traviata* turned boring.

Plopping back down on the couch with a smile still on her face, Jude reflected that the only thing that bothered her about this delirious love was that Anna would never spend an entire night. She always rolled out of Jude's arms at some point to throw on her clothes and race home to Jim. But when Jude had complained, Anna replied, "You don't want to be married to me, Jude. Marriage kills off any tenderness you ever felt for someone. I'm older than you and I've had more experience, so you'll just have to take my word for it."

There was plenty Jude had to take her word for, because Anna

was running the show. Most days, she phoned Jude at the office whenever Jim wasn't around. A few times a week, if she had several hours
free, she proposed that they meet—for a walk, a meal, a museum,
or a nap. Anna was determined that Jim know nothing of their liaison
lest he destroy it, as she claimed he had others in her past. Since Jim
kept a professor's unpredictable hours, Jude never knew when Anna
would phone, so she had rearranged her life to be eternally available.
All she did now was work and wait for Anna. She made a point of
rarely being far from a phone for which Anna had the number. And
when she was with Anna, she often glanced at her watch to see how
much time was left before Anna would go away and she'd have to
start waiting again.

Having this affair with Anna was like being an undercover agent.
But sometimes she thought she wouldn't want to bring it out into the
open even if Anna would allow it. All their intrigue, some of it a bit
exaggerated, was exciting. And because Anna always left her hungering
for more, the yearning that Jude had learned as a child to label *love*
was never quenched, so she never found out the answer to her original
question of what might remain after satiation.

When she wasn't with Anna, however, Jude's imagination sometimes went into overdrive. Did Anna still see the women she had
loved before Jude? Did Jude measure up, or did Anna pretend that
Jude was someone else while they were making love? She pictured
Anna at the Oasis Bar in the Village, picking up attractive young dog
trainers from New Jersey, taking them back to her house near Washington Square (which she had never let Jude visit). She imagined Anna
doing to them all the lascivious things Jude knew she was capable of.

But often when her thoughts took this gruesome turn, the doorbell would ring and Anna would be standing there with her arms full
of lilacs. Or Jude's phone would ring during an editorial meeting at
work and Anna would be on the other end, impersonating an obscene

phone caller with a thick Polish accent, describing in lurid detail all the things she planned to do to Jude if Jude could manage to escape to her apartment within the next hour. This had gone on for over two years now, and Jude's only requirement was that it never end.

Simon, however, seemed eager for it to end. He kept proposing business trips he maintained were essential for Jude's career advancement. She always replied that she didn't want to leave town. Finally, he insisted that she go with him to the Frankfurt Book Fair. "Ten thousand publishers from all over the world, Jude. It's the most important publishing event of the year. You need to be there to make contacts for selling the foreign rights to your books. It's not fair to your authors not to go."

"Thanks, but I have all the contacts I want," she said from her desk chair as he lounged in her doorway at work.

"You have contact with me and with Anna. That's it. You'll never become a world-class editor by lying in bed day after day with the same person."

"But I don't want to be a world-class editor," she replied. "All I want is to be Anna's love slave."

Simon laughed, despite his disapproval. "Please say you'll go with me to Germany for a week, Jude. If you do, I'll send you and Anna to the National Conference for the Teachers of English in Boston next month. To promote Anna's handbook."

Jude instantly accepted this bribe. Anna had done a workbook to help secondary school English teachers establish student-poetry contests and anthologies on a local level, as she had done in New York City. If they went to this conference, they could at last spend an entire night together. Two nights, in fact—in a strange hotel room with a king-size bed and room service.

Jude sulked her way through the Frankfurt Book Fair, hanging around her company's stand in the vast exposition hall while Simon met with a different publisher every half hour. In the evening, they went to elaborate cocktail parties and dinners with hosts of fascinating people, but Jude merely waited sullenly for the moment when she could rush back to her room at the Intercontinental and phone Anna in New York. Anna went to Jude's apartment at the end of each afternoon to receive this call. If she didn't answer, it meant she'd gotten tied up, and then they had to wait another twenty-four hours for their next hit of sweet nothings. After each call, Jude felt calmed and soothed, as though Anna's voice had injected her with heroin.

The only thing in Frankfurt that made any impression on Jude, other than the exorbitant price of phone calls to the United States, was a publisher from Paris named Jasmine, a friend of Simon's since childhood, whose father had fought with his during the war. The three of them dined one night in a brasserie near the train station. Jasmine was one of those elegant women Jude used to spot in the streets of Paris, as petite as Jude's mother, but with a presence as formidable as that of Charles de Gaulle. She was wearing huge, pale rose gemstones at her ears and on one finger, as well as a beaten-silver Indian belt etched with intricate arabesques of fruit and flowers.

Simon ordered the three of them a dark German beer he found superior. As they sipped it, Jasmine studied Jude so intently with her dark eyes that Jude felt like bacillus under a microscope. But her eyes weren't critical, just curious.

Simon and Jasmine exchanged news about their respective families. Then they traded tips about the books being hawked and hyped at the fair.

"Tell Jasmine about your titles, Jude," Simon instructed.

Jude described Anna's student-poetry anthologies and the new handbook. Jasmine seemed interested although dubious about whether such a self-help concept would float in France, given its centralized educational bureaucracy. Then Jude mentioned her history of the Knights Templars, due to appear the following spring, which seemed to leave Jasmine cold.

"And I edited *Forbidden Fruits*," continued Jude. "It's a scholarly history of lesbianism from the Middle Ages to the present. It came out a year ago, to very good reviews. The paperback rights went for six figures, and so far we've sold rights to Holland, England, Sweden, and Germany."

Jasmine nodded, exhaling a stream of cigarette smoke. "Ah, yes. I have heard good things about it from our scout in New York."

She was still studying Jude carefully. Jude wondered whether she could read from her face that her only real interest in life was making love to another woman. If so, did this disgust her?

"Would you be so kind as to send me a copy?" asked Jasmine. "Though I am not certain such a book would sell in France. We prefer not to categorize our romantic behavior quite so succinctly as the Anglo-Saxons."

Simon laughed and said, "But, Jasmine, many of the events in the book took place in Paris."

"But this is not our fault," she replied. "Repressed Protestants from all over the world flock to Paris to enjoy our supposed sexual license. These are the people you read about, debauching themselves on the Left Bank. But there is no specific word in the French language that means 'to have sex.' We only 'make love.' And true Parisians are the most austere race you will ever encounter. The quality of an interaction is all that interests us, not frequency or quantity."

"Garbage!" snapped Simon.

"But this is true," insisted Jasmine. "Take those pastries as an example."

Simon and Jude looked at the plate of exquisite apricot and marzipan tarts that they'd both been devouring with their coffee. But Jasmine hadn't taken even one. Simon guiltily held out the plate to her.

"But this is my point," she said, fending them off with one hand. "I have been enjoying their scent of apricot and almond, mixed with the odor of the coffee. Mixed also with your aftershave, Simon. And with Jude's marvelous perfume. And with the tobacco of our cigarettes. I enjoy looking at them there, dark orange on the blue plate, topped with ivory slivers of almond. With that pot of yellow and orange narcissus behind them. I have eaten hundreds of similar tarts in my life, so I can taste in my mouth right now the contrast between the acid and the sugar. I feel on my tongue the stickiness of the fruit, the graininess of the marzipan, the crunch of the almonds beneath my teeth. So I have no need to eat one. The experience is complete as it stands."

"But, Jasmine, tarts are made to be eaten," retorted Simon. "That's their function."

"Be my guest," said Jasmine. "But if you eat one, you have destroyed it. And since the hunger for sweetness always returns, why not stop short of destroying the tarts and learn to enjoy instead the hunger that they stimulate."

Simon and Jude looked at each other blankly.

"You know something, Jasmine?" said Simon. "You're a bleeding lunatic. I always suspected it, but now I know for sure."

She laughed, and then she and he exchanged some witty, sophisticated double-talk in which it was impossible for Jude to tell what either was actually saying. Suddenly, Jude found herself wondering if Jasmine didn't perhaps share her taste for women. There had been a certain shrewd candor in her eyes as she so frankly inspected Jude— which you didn't often find in women who were primarily interested in how they might be appearing to whatever men were in the immediate vicinity.

For the first time since she'd gotten involved with Anna, Jude had actually listened to a conversation that didn't directly concern Anna. Nor had she excused herself to go to the ladies' room so she could close her eyes and picture Anna's face and whisper her name. Nor had she once consulted her watch to discover when she could return to the hotel and phone Anna. Realizing this, she felt guilty, as though she'd been somehow unfaithful.

As Jude and Simon strolled back to their hotel through the dark streets strewn with international publishers at play, Jude asked, "Is Jasmine a lesbian?"

"I don't really know. I've wondered the same thing. She has a husband somewhere, but I've never met him."

"As we know, that means nothing."

"I think the French are schizophrenic," confided Simon. "They have a public self and a private self, and there's often an unbreachable chasm between the two. They veil their private selves behind a persiflage of charm and theorizing. But once a Frenchman reveals himself to you, you have a friend for life. In contrast to an American, who's your best friend after twenty minutes and then you never see him again."

"And what about the English?" asked Jude. She was intrigued by the ease with which Simon and his European colleagues spoke in terms of national characteristics.

"We use our famous rapier wit to make sure that no one ever gets close enough to be a friend in the first place."

"But that's not true," said Jude with a laugh. "You're a wonderful friend to me, Simon."

"But I emigrated, didn't I?"

JUDE WAS SITTING DOWN front in the ballroom of a hotel near the Boston Public Gardens, where Anna was delivering a pitch for her handbook to the assembled high school English teachers. She had warned Jude that she wasn't going to look at her from the podium lest she smile or blush. Jude, however, was looking at Anna, who was wearing the same mauve and forest-green wool suit from their first lunch. And she was recalling the marvels that lay just beneath that fabric of fine wool. She pictured Anna naked on the carpet in their room earlier that morning, hips swiveling lubriciously against Jude's thigh. And Anna sprawled in an armchair in the morning sun, robe fallen open, moaning softly like a purring cat, hands gripping Jude's head, which was buried between her thighs. It amused Jude to think that many of the teachers who were listening so admiringly to Anna's excellent presentation would be mortified to know how she'd passed the hour just prior to coming down here to speak to them on educating the youth of America. But how many among them, Jude wondered as she searched their attentive faces, *wouldn't* be mortified?

Jude's company had a stand in the adjoining hall, along with eighty other publishers. Each featured titles of interest to high school English teachers. An editor from her firm's textbook division was in charge of their display. Jude's only responsibility, Simon had informed her with a tiny, indulgent smile at last week's marketing meeting, was to keep Anna content. The promotion department had set up interviews for her after lunch and the next morning. Otherwise, they planned to remain in their room, working on Anna's contentment, pausing only long enough to tip the waiters from room service.

Jude woke up that night in the unfamiliar bed and reached over for Anna. But Anna's side of the bed was cold and empty. She waited for her to return from the bathroom, but she didn't. "Anna?" she called. There was no response.

Sitting up, she switched on the light. The clock on the bedside table read 1:30 A.M. She climbed out of bed and padded into the bathroom. Still no Anna. Her plaid suit had vanished, but every-thing else remained. Jude paced the room, wondering what to do. She phoned the front desk, but the night clerk had seen no one matching Anna's description. Finally, she started putting on her underwear.

A key scratched around the lock. The door swung open and Anna walked in.

"Where have you been?" asked Jude, sitting on the bedside with a stocking half on.

Anna's expression turned furtive. "I had to find a phone."

"How come?"

"I told Jim I'd call."

"At one in the morning?"

"He stays up late."

"But there's a phone right here." Jude frowned, wondering what Anna had to say to Jim that Jude couldn't hear.

"I didn't want to wake you."

"I wish you had. I've been worried."

"I'm a big girl, Jude. I can take care of myself." She sounded irritated.

Anna undressed in silence. For a moment, Jude wondered whether she'd met some alluring English teacher as she autographed books after her talk and had gone to her room for an assignation. Then she dismissed this as too ridiculous, with herself right there, ready to satisfy Anna's slightest whim. But maybe Anna missed the challenge of someone she wasn't sure she could have.

"Did you really have to call him right in the middle of our time alone together?" murmured Jude, sitting immobile on the bedside as she stared at the print on the wall of Paul Revere racing his horse across Concord Bridge.

"He's my husband, darling. He still has a few rights."

"Yes, but he has you to himself most of the time."

"If we're going to start complaining about the ghosts of loves past, what about that wax museum you carry in your heart? Sandy and Molly and God knows how many others."

"You know perfectly well that my waxworks had a meltdown the night we first made love," said Jude, smiling.

Anna smiled back and said in a softer voice, "Once the children are in college, I'll be all yours, my love." She slid under the covers and reached for Jude. "You already have me in a way that Jim doesn't," she added as she unhooked Jude's bra and slipped the straps off her arms. "I don't make love with him anymore."

As she pulled Jude down beside her, Jude was swept with relief. She'd often wondered about this but had felt she couldn't ask, since she was the new kid on Anna's block. As Jude shuddered with desire and subsided into Anna's embrace, she thought she smelled alcohol. But they had split a bottle of wine with dinner.

As ANNA DID HER FINAL magazine interview in their room the next morning, Jude went to the front desk to settle their account. On the invoice, she noticed a charge for half a dozen drinks in the Ironsides Lounge, where she and Anna had never set foot.

"I'm afraid I've been charged for someone else's drinks," she told the cashier.

He rifled through some slips and handed her a bill dated the previous day and signed by Anna. Shaken, Jude wrote her name on the credit-card slip. Anna must have gone to the lounge last night when Jude couldn't find her. She had signed for six drinks, so someone else must have been with her. But who? And why had she lied about it?

On the way back to the room, Jude tried to decide whether to confront Anna. Did she think Jude wouldn't notice the extra drinks, or had she done it on purpose, as a declaration of independence here in Freedom City?

The reporter had left, and Anna was packing for home. Jude didn't want their last hours together to be spent arguing, so she decided to put her ugly suspicions on ice. She knew Anna loved her. What more did she need to know?

As she packed, sick with misery that their time together was ending, and ending for her on a sour note, Jude had a sudden inspiration. "Listen, Anna," she said urgently, "call Jim and tell him you have to stay for another night . . . to do some interviews in the morning. We'll drive to the Cape. Stay at Simon's house. Rent horses and ride them on the beach."

"It sounds wonderful," she said as she closed and latched her suitcase, "but I've got to get back."

"Please, Anna. Who knows when we'll have another night together?"

Anna finally did as Jude asked, phoning Jim. Listening to her lie so smoothly to him about the importance of tomorrow's fictitious interview, Jude felt suddenly uneasy. If Anna sometimes lied to her, she wouldn't be able to tell the difference any more than Jim could right now.

Later, they settled in at Simon's glass-and-beam house among the dunes. Driving to Provincetown in their rented Cutlass, they bought jeans, sweatshirts, and tennis shoes. Then they went to a stable on the outskirts of town and hired two horses. The horses weren't happy to have their fall vacation interrupted. They plodded resentfully among the grassy dunes toward the beach, snorting and shaking their heads time after time in protest. But once they reached the hard-packed sand by the sea, they caught some of Jude's and Anna's enthusiasm and began prancing through the foam along the water's edge as though tiptoeing across hot coals.

Jude slackened her reins and her horse took off, shooting down the beach like an arrow from a bow, careening through the surf, hooves hurling up a spray of salt water mixed with flying sand. For a moment, she worried that Anna might not be able to handle such speed, since she said she'd learned to ride in a ring at summer camp. But looking back, Jude saw her lying low along her horse's arching neck, a grin on her face.

When the horses finally gave out and slowed to a jouncing trot, Jude headed hers toward the dunes, Anna's following. Sliding off the horses, the women looped their reins around a jagged branch of driftwood. Then they scrambled up a dune and sat down in the sand. As they surveyed the ocean, the horses stamped and whinnied below. On the horizon, several shiny black whales were surfacing and spouting with a sound like an erupting geyser, then diving beneath the waves again.

ANNA AND JUDE WALKED into Simon's kitchen. Anna had been silent and sullen on the ride home from the grocery store, shrugging off Jude's attempts at conversation.

"Is something wrong?" Jude finally asked as they set the bags on the counter.

"I'm just tired," said Anna in a lackluster voice. "All those dumb interviews. I'm not used to being with other people day and night."

"Why don't you sit on the deck with a gin and tonic while I make supper?"

"That would be marvelous. Do you mind?"

"No, that's why I offered. Simon told me that my assignment is to keep you content."

Anna smiled wearily. "Well done, my good and faithful servant."

As she peeled and deveined shrimp in the sink, Jude watched Anna lying in a deck chair, languidly squeezing the slice of lime into her drink. In repose, her face looked its age, as it never did in motion. Her jowls sagged slightly and her cheekbones were becoming more pronounced as the flesh began to fall. There were a couple of folds of loose skin at her throat and a network of fine wrinkles that stretched like a rigging from the outer corners of her eyes. Her ink-black hair had developed a few silver highlights. Recently, she'd had some hot flashes, and her menstrual periods had become as unpredictable as a two-year-old's tantrums. Jude felt she was watching in Anna the unfolding of her own future. The baby fat of youth was being replaced by bones and wrinkles. This was the first time Jude had ever seen her so moody. Since they normally got together by appointment only, each made sure to be at her most charming. They saved their sulks for the lucky men they lived with.

By the time Jude set their supper on the glass-topped table on the deck, Anna had downed three gin and tonics and seemed more cheery. She filled their glasses with Sancerre while Jude served rice and topped it with the shrimp, which she'd sautéed with tomatoes, garlic, sherry, scallions, and parsley.

"Where did you learn to cook so well?" asked Anna after sampling the dish.

"If you can read, you can cook," replied Jude.

"That's not true. I'm a terrible cook. And not from lack of reading. If it hadn't been for Shake 'n Bake, my kids would have been regulars at the soup kitchen around the corner. When we live together, you do the cooking and I'll shop and clean."

"It's a deal," said Jude. "Where shall we live—your place or mine?"

"How about Paris?"

"God, I'd love to live with you in Paris, Anna."

"We will," Anna assured her. "At least for a year. If professors can take sabbaticals, why can't we? We'll have an apartment in Montmartre, overlooking all of Paris. You'll cook me perfect little meals like this one, and I'll devote myself to your sexual fulfillment."

Jude smiled. "You're on. Someday, though, I want to show you the Smokies."

"With pleasure. They sound spectacular."

"They are. Especially if you don't have to live there."

"I thought that was your plan. To build a cabin and stay there forever with Saint Molly?"

"Ah, Molly . . . That's another story. If Molly had lived, you and I would never have met. There I'd be right now, in my Tennessee mountain home."

"Maybe you and I should build that cabin," mused Anna.

Jude grinned. "You'd better wait and see if you like the place first."

Jude passed Anna the salad and refilled their wineglasses, while the surf crashed and the breeze off the ocean toyed with their hair.

"I wish we didn't have to go back," said Jude. "I wish we could stay right here like this forever."

"I doubt if you'd love me if you saw me all the time," said Anna in a strange voice.

"Of course I would."

"I can be very unpleasant. You have no idea."

"I doubt that," said Jude.

"Trust me on this, darling."

CHAPTER

13

STANDING BEFORE THE TEAL DOOR of Anna's tiny town house in a cobblestoned mews near Washington Square, Jude seized Simon's hand so that they would look the part of a young couple about town. She'd had to beg him to come along in the first place. Jim had finally figured out that Anna was having an affair. But he didn't yet know with whom, so Anna wanted to cover her tracks. Simon was appalled by such intrigue, but Jude was prepared to do anything to placate Anna.

Although placating her had become quite a challenge now that Jude was traveling so much. Simon had laid it on the line: He'd stuck his neck out for her by making her an editor when she had no experience. If she didn't work out, it was his head that would roll. Therefore, she had to shake herself out of her stupor of lust and start doing her job. So Jude was now supposed to go each year not only to Frankfurt but also to the ABA, the MLA, and the AHA, depending on what books she had to promote. And twice a year, she went to Los Angeles to peddle film rights.

The end result was that Jude was away from New York now as much as two months a year. And often on weekends, she went to Simon's beach house on the Cape to help entertain authors or publishers from abroad. When she returned from these trips and weekends, Anna was usually sullen and withdrawn, like a child punishing a parent for an absence. This annoyed Jude, because before she started this regimen, Anna had sometimes allowed as much time as such a trip required to elapse between their encounters. It was as though she wanted Jude always on tap, even if she didn't have time to see her.

In any case, Anna was almost always tied up with Jim on weekends. She spent much of the summer with him and her children at their cottage on the Jersey shore, and at Christmas their whole family went skiing in Colorado. Was it possible to have an affair, Jude wondered, with someone you never saw? Or was that precisely why it had lasted so long? As though each relationship had a certain amount of capital you could draw on, and the less you withdrew, the longer it could endure.

Once, when Jude tried to discuss all this, Anna broke down in tears on Jude's couch, saying, "I feel as though you're moving on, Jude. In the beginning, we were in this thing together. My anthology was the first book for both of us. But here I am, still teaching my workshops, while you fly around the world meeting exciting new people."

"No one will ever excite me as much as you do, Anna," Jude replied, taking Anna's hand in both hers.

She laughed bitterly, extracting her hand. "But for how much longer? I'm turning into a boring old failure, but you're a rising star."

Jude sat in silence, recalling various offers Anna had turned down that would have resulted by now in a flourishing career as an educational consultant. Jude had been forced to realize that Anna was actually a bit lazy. Her children were away at school. She had a housekeeper who cleaned and shopped and cooked. She taught two workshops a week and sometimes wrote poetry. What did she do all day? For a brief panicked moment, Jude wondered whether she had another lover. Or two.

"I did it for you," Jude maintained, realizing this wasn't entirely true. She'd done it partly for Simon. "I thought you'd find me more interesting if I was successful. And the extra money I'm earning can finance our year in Paris. Or our cabin in the Smokies."

"Ah, Jude, my love," she murmured, planting a kiss on her mouth. "My eternal touching innocent. You always believe what other people tell you."

"What's that supposed to mean?"

ANNA OPENED HER DOOR. She was wearing gray-green silk hostess pajamas and dangling earrings of silver filigree, like tiny frosted spiderwebs. "How nice to see you both," she said with her most charming smile. "Jim, these are my publishers. Simon and Jude, this is my husband, Jim."

Anna ran her arm through Jim's as he shook hands with them both and murmured a welcome. He looked every inch the suave professor in his tweed jacket with suede elbow patches. His long salt-and-pepper sideburns matched his bushy eyebrows. Jude was shocked to realize that he was her father's age. It was the same old story: He'd been Anna's thesis adviser. They'd fallen in love over Mallarmé. He'd left his wife and children to marry her and produce a second batch of children. The passage of time having banked their fires, he now had affairs with students who seemed younger with each passing term.

Fingering his lapel, Anna said anxiously, "Jim has a new jacket from Scotland. Isn't it handsome? Doesn't he look elegant?"

Jude had never seen Anna so coy.

As he turned to walk away, Jim said under his breath, "Screw you, Anna."

Acting as though she hadn't heard, Anna ushered Jude and Simon into the living room, which was packed with drink-sipping, canapé-munching students and faculty. French doors opened onto an enclosed garden with ivy-drenched walls. The room itself was lined with books. Four plush sofas formed a conversation pit around a huge, square coffee table with an ivory marble top. After fixing a scotch for them both, Anna departed to pass hors d'oeuvres and introduce strangers. Across the room, Jim was holding forth on Rimbaud to a young woman in a miniskirt the size of a dish towel.

Jude watched Simon study Anna in her clinging silk hostess pajamas. She was weaving a bit as she walked. Getting drunk at your own party seemed a bad idea, but the crowd looked so dreary that Jude was downing her drink too quickly, as well.

"You don't like her, do you?" she asked Simon.

"I never said that."

"You don't need to."

He hesitated, then drew a deep breath. "It's not that I don't like her, Jude. I just don't think she's right for you."

"Why not?" asked Jude. Because she had made Jude want to quit her job and spend all day in bed? "In the beginning, you were our biggest fan."

"I asked William about her awhile back. I wish I hadn't, because I haven't been able to decide whether to tell you what he said."

"What, for God's sake?"

"He said her husband has affairs with young women, so Anna does, too. She likes the stimulation of the chase."

"Don't we all?"

"Yes, we do. But it ends there for her. Once the woman is really hooked, Anna dumps her and rushes back home to Jim for solace. And he does the same. Apparently, they've both left corpses scattered all over town. It's the glue that holds them together."

"Well, it's not like that with us," Jude snapped. "Anna loves me. She says she's finally met her match. We're both intelligent and well educated. We adore lovemaking. We have fun together when we go out. She and Jim aren't lovers anymore, and they're going to split once their children are out of school. And then she'll move in with me or get a place nearby. We're going to live in Paris for a while. Maybe build a cabin in the Smokies. You have to understand, Simon —I love Anna more than I've ever loved anyone else in my entire life."

He shook his head, awed to have triggered such a diatribe of devotion. "I hope you're right, Jude. Please forgive me for meddling."

"Of course, I forgive you, Simon. It means you care about me."

"I just don't want to see you demolished again. Sometimes you don't seem to know how to protect yourself."

"In this case I don't need to protect myself."

As Simon wandered off in search of more scotch, Jude thought it over irritably and decided he was mistaken. Although their time together was more limited than in the beginning, she and Anna still ate delicious meals together. They attended concerts and operas and painting exhibitions. At the movies, they sat there stroking each other's palms with their fingertips and then rushed back home to Jude's bed. They exchanged cards and flowers and candy. They saved up their brightest thoughts and funniest jokes. Jude continued to serve as Anna's demon lover, making the rest of her dreary life bearable. And

Anna remained Jude's tour guide through the previously uncharted realms of her own passions.

Whereas Anna and Jim got to argue over picking up the cleaning, the ring around the bathtub, and how much to tip the plumber.

Given the scotch, Simon's remarks, and jet lag, Jude realized she was feeling awful. She was just back from a week in London at a new biennial Feminist Book Fair. As it turned out, the event had had very little to do with books and a lot to do with feminism. Everywhere you looked, some outraged special-interest group was caucusing. The women of color were angry at the white women. The working-class women were angry at the middle-class women. The non-English-speaking women were angry at the Anglophones. The lesbians were angry at the heterosexuals. The heterosexuals were angry at the lesbians. And everybody was angry at men.

The high point of the conference for Jude was her dinner with Jasmine at a carvery on the Strand that featured huge, dripping roasts of ham, beef, lamb, and pork upended on spikes, from which the waiters hacked slabs. A Baptist God might have created just such a place in the hereafter—as punishment for evil vegetarians. Jasmine, who turned out to be a food snob, insisted that the only way to avoid gastronomic catastrophe in England was to stick to such unadorned meat and potatoes.

As they consumed enough animal flesh to have nourished a pride of lions for a week, they discussed the funnels of rage that were swirling like twisters through the conference hall. Jasmine described the rival feminist factions in Paris, one of which had bombed another's printing press and hounded its leader into exile on the Canary Islands. She explained her theory of the dynamics of minority political movements, learned at her father's knee during the French Resistance: External injustices generated anger. When it seemed impossible to right the wrongs, the stalled anger pooled within the oppressed group, causing it to split into warring factions, which then destroyed one another, completing the tyrant's task for him. The only way to avoid this disintegration, Jasmine maintained, was to move beyond the anger, using it to fuel efforts to change specific conditions without allowing yourself to become attached to the results.

Jude wandered up to Anna's second floor, searching for a bathroom whose medicine chest might contain an aspirin. It was odd to be in the house where Anna had lived with Jim and their children for close to two decades. It was a warm and welcoming place, with lots of carpets, cushions, and curtains.

Passing a door that was ajar, Jude glanced in. It was a bedroom. And kneeling on the carpet was Anna, with Jim standing over her.

". . . and I know I'm disgusting," she was moaning. "And I know if I weren't so disgusting, darling, you wouldn't need to sleep with all these other women." She embraced his knees. "I didn't mean to drink so much this time, Jim."

Jim was gazing out the window into the bare branches of a scrawny maple tree in the garden, apparently uninterested.

"Please forgive me," begged Anna.

Jim refused even to look at her.

Anna reached up and began fumbling for his zipper. "I know what you like, darling, and I can do it better than any sophomore you will ever meet."

Still staring out the window, Jim grabbed her wrist. Gradually, he tightened his grip, until she was whimpering. He wrenched her arm sharply to one side so that she fell to the floor.

She lay there crying and gasping, "You hate me, Jim. I know you hate me. I don't blame you. I'm disgusting."

Jude stood there mortified, wanting to rush to the rescue but paralyzed by disbelief. Jim hauled Anna back up to her knees before him and began unbuckling his belt.

Jude ran along the hallway and down the stairs. Grabbing coats from the closet, she dragged a startled Simon into the street.

"What's wrong?" he asked, still carrying his sloshing plastic cup of scotch.

"Nothing."

Simon raised his eyebrows. "Tell me, Jude. Let me help."

"You already have."

". . . SO I WAS UPSTAIRS in the bathroom," Anna was saying as she and Jude walked down the street from Jude's office toward the park, "and when I came back down, you and Simon had vanished."

Jude said nothing. There was a bruise around Anna's wrist like a wide purple shackle. It matched the dark circles under Jude's eyes from her past two nights of insomnia. As she lay wide awake in the dark, she kept asking herself if it had been a setup. Not that Anna had planned for Jude to witness this exact scene with Jim, but that she had planned for *something* to happen to shake Jude up. But did she want to shake Jude up in order to end the relationship or in order to revitalize it? Whichever, she had certainly succeeded. Jude was a wreck.

"Is something the matter?" asked Anna.

After a long pause, Jude said, "I thought you didn't make love with Jim anymore."

Anna looked suddenly secretive. "Why do you ask?"

Drawing a deep breath, Jude described what she'd seen. The two stopped and faced one another in the middle of the sidewalk, so the other pedestrians had to detour irritably around them.

"Well, I guess I was pretty drunk," admitted Anna. "But what's a blow job between friends?"

Jude grimaced. Anna wasn't usually so crude. She realized that the blow job wasn't the entire issue. Taking Anna's hand, she stroked the ugly bruise with her fingertips. "Anna, no one should treat you like that. You have to leave him. Or take him to a therapist. Or do *something.*"

Jude was being forced to realize that Anna might be terminally passive. When they were first together, she had said she'd leave Jim when their children were in college. Now her timetable for departure required them to be *out* of college.

Anna gave her a look. "How can I leave him when I have no money?"

For the first time, it occurred to Jude that someone who taught a few workshops and wrote mostly unpublished poetry wasn't self-supporting, even with the royalties from the anthologies. The odd blow job was probably a small price to pay for the clothes and restaurants and concert tickets Anna invested in with such insouciance.

"Move in with Simon and me," said Jude. "I'll help you out. You can look for a job."

"Who'd want to hire a middle-aged mother who can't type?" she asked. "What am I supposed to do? Wait on tables?"

"Why not? It's honest work. More honest than blow jobs for men you no longer love."

"So my hillbilly honey has finally reverted to type. Miss Southern Baptist has never done it with someone she didn't love."

Jude had never heard this sarcastic tone of voice from Anna before. She was appalled. "Yes, of course I have, Anna. That's not the point."

"The green paradise of childhood love, bullshit. It's time you grew up, little girl."

"Anna, don't." Jude felt as though Anna had just socked her in the solar plexus.

"Welcome to the black pit of adult lust, my darling."

Who was this woman? Jude wondered. Certainly not her tender

lover of last week. Studying her contorted red face, Jude noticed that she was swaying as she stood there, like a skyscraper in an earthquake. She was drunk.

A FEW NIGHTS LATER, Anna arrived at Jude's apartment building in a taxi with a couple of cardboard boxes of belongings. She acted as though the ugly scene between them on the sidewalk hadn't happened, so Jude did, too. But every cell in her body was hanging back, watching, fearing a reappearance of Anna's evil twin. She'd been telling herself that if you opened the Pandora's box of passions, they all came out, not just the pleasant ones. But an occasional moment of unpleasantness was worth all the happiness.

Jude stashed the boxes in Sandy's old room, pending a discussion with Simon as to which free room could be Anna's. Elated by this evidence of movement on Anna's part, she let Anna lead her down the hallway to her own bedroom. In the full moon through the window, she began to remove Anna's rayon jumpsuit. And she discovered a dark splotch across her hip and thigh.

Turning on the lamp by the bed, Jude inspected the moist purple contusion with her fingertips.

"I fell in the bathtub," said Anna.

"Please stay here tonight," Jude replied. "Simon and I will go to your house tomorrow and get your stuff."

"I've decided to come live with you, Jude. But not tonight."

"When then?"

"Tomorrow night," she said, turning off the lamp and taking Jude's hand. Sinking onto the mattress, she pulled Jude down beside her. Succumbing, against her better judgment, Jude maneuvered Anna onto her back and began to kiss her breast.

"Bite it," said Anna.

"What?"

"Bite my nipple. Hard."

Jude looked up at her.

"Please."

"But I don't want to hurt you."

Grabbing a handful of Jude's hair, Anna wrenched her head back down to her breast. "I said bite it, goddamn it!"

Seizing Anna's bruised wrist, Jude struggled to free her hair. They wrestled ferociously across the mattress like jungle cats, straining and struggling, crashing against the wall. Anna finally let go of Jude's hair. With her free hand, she reached over and grabbed the Atalanta flask from Jude's windowsill. She hurled it across the room, where it fell to the floor and shattered into a dozen pieces.

"Goddamn you to hell, Anna!" screamed Jude, a flash of fury scrambling her brain. She hauled back her fist to slug her. Then she froze with her hand in midair, teeth bared, muscles shaking and quivering. Anna cringed away and sank back down on the bed.

Scalp throbbing, Jude leapt off the bed, careened across the room, and slammed her fist into the wall. Anna rolled over into a fetal position and began to rock back and forth, whimpering like a wounded animal.

Eyeing the shards of her cherished flask, Jude sat back down on the bedside, breathing heavily. She began to pat Anna's back, trying to calm her as she would have a spooked horse. "I'm sorry, Anna," she murmured. "I didn't mean to yell at you." Leaning over to kiss her shoulder, she discovered that Anna was gnawing her own knee.

"Anna, don't."

Anna looked up, eyes wild. She'd chewed through her skin, like a frenzied vampire queen, and her mouth and knee were dripping blood in the moonlight.

"You've got to get some help," Jude finally said. "Something's gone wrong."

"Mind your own damn business," muttered Anna, rolling off the bed.

"It is my business. Because I love you."

"If you really loved me," said Anna as she fastened her bra and stepped into her jumpsuit, "you'd do what I ask. You don't love me. You love your *idea* of me. You've assigned me a role in this lesbian 'Little House on the Prairie' that goes on inside your head. But it's got nothing to do with what I might want or need. You keep telling me how marvelous I am, but you don't know the first thing about me."

Jude sat in a stunned silence. Could this be true?

Upon reaching the door, Anna turned to say, "Well, we can't sink much lower than this. So I'm going to do you a favor, Jude, and not see you anymore. Please don't try to get in touch with me."

Jude looked up at her incredulously. "Just like that?"

"Just like that." Anna walked out.

Sitting on the edge of her bed, rubbing her bruised hand, Jude relived that endless moment when her fist had been cocked to beat the shit out of Anna. For the first time in her life, she understood the phrase *to see red*. She had seen red, bloodred. And she had nearly reproduced this vision in red by battering Anna to bits right there on the white sheets. She could feel even now the visceral satisfaction it would have brought her to bury her fists time after time in Anna's cowering flesh. Anna was right: Jude couldn't sink much lower than this. After a lifetime of deploring it in others, she had caught a glimpse of her own capacity for violence and of the intoxicating erotic charge it could carry.

As she squatted down and collected the shards of her grandmother's flask, Jude realized that Anna was right not to stay with someone who had come within a hairsbreadth of beating her up. Yet her departure was actually a sexist act, since she'd stayed for years with a *man* who beat her up. Picturing Anna's mouth dripping blood in the moonlight, Jude felt a certain reluctant comprehension of Jim's behavior. Yes, he sometimes injured her. But apparently if someone else wouldn't do it for her, she'd do it herself. Dazed, Jude tried to analyze the steps by which she'd started out trying not to hurt Anna, only to end up wanting to kill her.

Jude remembered Anna's telling her in the beginning that most people were a house of mirrors. If she'd paid attention then, she could have spared herself a lot of agony. But now she was lost inside the fun house.

Before descending into an exhausted sleep, she vowed to cut her losses. She'd obey Anna and not contact her. If Anna needed someone to punish her for their bouts of illicit pleasure, like the flagellation of depraved medieval monks, it wasn't going to be Jude. Jim could do it.

For the next few days, Jude wandered around the office in a haze of misery, unable to eat or sleep. Several times, she caught Simon watching her with concern. Finally, she went into his office to announce, "You were right about Anna."

He looked up from a pile of papers. "What's happened?"

"She's dumped me without a backward glance."

He grimaced. "I'm sorry. If it's any help, I love you."

"It helps. But not much."

He smiled sadly.

"Simon," ventured Jude, "when you and Sandy used to go down to the docks in your chaps—what was that all about?"

He gave her a look. "What do you think it was all about? Lust."

"Weren't you afraid?"

"My dear child, that's the whole point. The terror of the chase.

The wild beast that may rip you to shreds once you corner him.''

"Well, in the end, that may be what turns Anna on—pain and fear.''

Simon raised his eyebrows. "The difference is that no one on the docks pretends it has anything to do with love.''

"I wonder if there's a workshop I could take to win her back. 'Hurt Your Way to Happiness.' If only I could behave as badly as her husband, she might leave him to be with me.''

Simon didn't smile.

"Yes, I know you tried to warn me," she said. "So did William.''

Upon leaving her office that afternoon, Jude decided to stop by Madame Toussaint's for a sixty-thousand-mile checkup. After all, she had helped lure Jude into this quagmire with Anna in the first place. Maybe she could advise her on how to climb back out again, or at least tell her what was in store for her around the next bend in this enchanting cosmic tunnel of love.

But when she reached the block where Madame Toussaint's lair had been, she couldn't find it. She couldn't even find the doorway or the staircase, much less the little hand-printed sign. She searched up and down five blocks in either direction, along both sides of the street. Then she went into several shops to inquire about a large tarot-reading psychic. But no one had ever heard of Madame Toussaint.

THAT NIGHT, JUDE DISCOVERED that her index finger had a life of its own. Like Lassie to the rescue, it dialed Anna's number, despite feeble protests from her benumbed brain.

Anna answered.

"It's Jude. I have to talk to you.''

"I'm afraid I can't right now. Jim's here." Her voice was calm and pleasant.

"When then?"

"Soon. Don't be so impatient, my darling," she murmured. "We'll have the rest of our lives together in our cabin in the mountains."

Jude held the receiver away from her ear to stare at it. Had she gotten a wrong number?

Jim shouted in the background, "Did you hear me, bitch?"

"Got to go," Anna whispered. "He's angry."

"Get the fuck over here!" he yelled.

"Anna, I'm coming to get you right now," said Jude. "Be ready."

"No, Jude, don't. . . ." Her phone clicked off.

Jude dashed from her building and grabbed a cab to the Village. Instructing the driver to wait at the end of the mews, she ran to Anna's house. When she pounded on the front door, no one came. Trying the handle, she found it unlocked. She pushed the door open and raced in. Like a bloodhound on the trail of an escaped convict, she scurried around the living room and kitchen.

Anna and Jim were sitting on a black leather couch in the den at the back of the house, watching the local news on a television set built into a wall of wooden shelves and cabinets, which were crammed with stereo equipment, books, and objets d'art. Both were holding lowball glasses full of ice cubes and a milky liquid. Anna, who was wearing a scarlet caftan, looked up at Jude through barely focused blue eyes. Her sleek hair stood on end at the crown, like a kiwi bird's head feathers. Jim had risen unsteadily to his feet, his flushed face webbed with broken veins.

"Who the hell are you?" he asked.

"Don't you remember Jude from our party last month, dear?" asked Anna, the perfect hostess. "She's my editor."

"What the fuck are you doing in my house?"

Jude tried to decide. "I've come to take Anna back to my apartment."

"What are you—a nut or something?"

"I've seen her bruises, Jim. I know you beat her up. And it's going to stop."

"What business is it of yours?"

"It's my business because I love Anna," Jude was alarmed to hear herself confess.

Anna dropped her glass, spilling her drink all down the front of her caftan.

"Get out of my house," Jim said calmly, face turning purple.

"Not without Anna. Come on, Anna."

Anna just looked at her with bleary distress, making no move to rise. Jim headed around the corner of the couch toward Jude.

"I'm calling the police," said Jude as she edged toward the doorway.

"Call whomever you like," said Jim, fists clenching. "This is my house and my wife. And you're trespassing on private property."

In the taxi on the way home, Jude felt like a fool. Anna had made no move on her own behalf or in support of Jude. Jude had felt as helpless as she must have as a toddler, trying to rescue her mother from the stranger in the army uniform who everyone claimed was her father. As she had the afternoon she tried to persuade Molly not to go on the Baptist retreat with Ace Kilgore. As she had the night she saw Sandy coupling with the stranger in the moonlight. Why was she always drawn to people who wanted to slow-dance with danger? She was like a moth who flitted around a candle flame while her fellow moths immolated themselves in it.

But danger you could find anywhere. It was kindness when she came across it that lured her like a flame. She remembered standing in her grandfather's backyard as a toddler, holding a large rock above her head, about to drop it on a toad just to see what would happen. As she let it fall, her grandfather appeared from nowhere and caught it in midair. He squatted down and picked up the toad, whose throat was pulsing repulsively. It sat on his palm, ugly eyes bulging.

"Jude," said her grandfather, stroking the horrible warty back with his fingertip, "our job is to protect and provide for other creatures. That's the minimum requirement for being human. It's what the word *love* means. Many people behave like rabid dogs, but that's no reason to join them."

CROSSING THE MARBLE LOBBY of her office building the next afternoon, Jude spotted Anna waiting for her by the door for their usual Wednesday stroll. Baffled, Jude kissed her cheek. As she backed away, she noticed that the whites around Anna's cornflower blue irises were faintly tinged with yellow. There was also a sore on her neck, which she'd powdered and tried to conceal with a dashing white aviator scarf.

"What's this?" asked Jude, touching the sore.

"A spider bite," she said. Her lips were trembling.

All of a sudden, the pieces fell into place for Jude: She'd learned enough from her years with her father to recognize jaundice when she saw it. They walked toward the park in silence, Jude trying to figure out what to do with this new suspicion.

"Is everything okay?" asked Anna anxiously.

Jude looked at her with disbelief. Did she not even remember breaking up with Jude? Or Jude's failed rescue attempt the previous night?

"Anna," she finally replied, "I don't know how to say this, but I'm worried about your drinking."

Anna looked startled, then stealthy.

"I think you're overdoing it."

"If you had a husband who slept with every coed in town, you'd probably overdo it, too. And children who flunk out of every college in the Northeast. And students who expect you to solve the ghastly problems of their decaying cultures and dysfunctional families. And a lover who thinks that life is an episode from 'The Waltons.' Believe me, I have good reason to overdo it."

"Who doesn't have reason?" snapped Jude. "Having reason is no reason."

At Broadway, they headed uptown for Jude's apartment. And Jude was forced to confront the fact that she was as much of a masochist as Anna. Any healthy person would have sent Anna home to her own fate. But by now, Jude's fate seemed irretrievably merged with Anna's.

After making love as tenderly as in the beginning, they held each other and listened to thunder rolling in from the Poconos. Jude knew that no matter what was happening to them, she herself wouldn't be able to end it—even if that was what was best for them both. But it would mean more for her than just the death of their relationship. It would be the death of her dream that happiness with another person was possible in this life.

During their lovemaking, Jude had discovered more "spider bites" on Anna's arms and back, and her abdomen had seemed faintly distended. She made a mental note to phone her father and find out what this meant.

"Anna, I can't bear to lose you," she murmured.

"You're not going to lose me, Jude. You know I love you. I'll never leave you."

As Jude watched rainwater flow in torrents down the window-panes, she tried to figure out which was the real Anna—the snarling beast who ripped apart her own flesh with her bared teeth, or the woman who lay beside her right now, stroking her hair and running her tongue around the folds of her ear and talking about the apartment they'd rent in Montmartre once she divorced Jim.

"You know I'm going to Australia for a few days on Friday?"

Anna sat up abruptly. "How could I know when you don't tell me?"

"I did tell you, Anna. A couple of times."

"No, you didn't," she insisted.

"Well, maybe not," said Jude, deciding it wasn't worth an argument. "But anyway, I am."

"Why?"

"I have to speak on a panel about feminist editing."

"Will that woman be there?"

"Which woman?"

"That French friend of Simon's."

"Jasmine. Yes. She's one of the organizers."

Anna said nothing for a long time. Jude began to feel guilty without having anything to feel guilty about.

"Please don't go," Anna said.

"I'm sorry, my love, but I have to. They're counting on me. But I'll be back before you know I'm gone."

"If you stay here, you could help me move some things into your apartment."

Jude turned her head to look at her. Was this really true, or was it just a ploy?

"What if something terrible happens while you're gone?"

"Jesus, Anna, please don't do this to me," Jude moaned. "You'll be fine for a few days. It'll give you time to see a doctor and find out about these sores. Then when I get back, we can move you into my apartment. Okay?"

"Okay," she finally said.

"Promise me you'll see a doctor while I'm gone."

"I promise."

JUDE AND JASMINE TOOK a local bus to the seaside south of Adelaide as a remedy for their jet lag. As they strolled along the deserted white beach under a searing sun, they discussed ideas for the panel. Would women, free from the pressures of the marketplace, write differently from men? What were these pressures, and how did they distort women's writing? What role did fiction play in challenging or confirming the dominant stereotypes of women in Western culture? Was it possible to run a successful publishing house in a capitalist economy without a hierarchy among the employees and a star system among the authors?

As she and Jasmine wrangled over these issues and others, Jude felt herself becoming more energized than she'd been in months. The deadly struggles with Anna faded from her mind, and she felt her tensed muscles relax and her breath start to flow freely again. They sat down at a green metal table beneath some eucalyptus trees, alongside a roadhouse with a metal roof. As the sun sank into the ocean, they sipped Australian beer and discussed Simon's inability to find a love that lasted longer than three weeks.

"Yet three weeks of pleasure is not nothing," said Jasmine.

Even on safari in the outback, she was impeccable, in spotless white cotton pedal pushers and a loose silk shirt in shades of orange and red that coordinated with the sunset. Under the open shirt, she was wearing a lacy white camisole, and she had a gold herringbone chain at her throat.

"No, but I think he longs for what he had with his friend Sandy. But he'll never find that again, because Sandy was a very unusual person." Jude was studying the ash-gray bark of the trunk tree beside her, which was mottled with impetigolike patches of rust and black. They reminded her of Anna's scabs. She hoped Anna would go to the doctor as she had promised. But often these days, she seemed not to remember what she said from one moment to the next.

"I never met Sandy. But he was also your friend, was he not?" asked Jasmine, watching the golden sea shining like molten ore in the setting sun.

"That's right. We grew up together. He was like a brother to me."

"But more than a brother?"

Jude looked at her quickly. "Simon told you that?"

Jasmine nodded.

"Did he also tell you I've been with a woman for the past several years?"

She nodded again. "Sometimes our dear friend Simon talks too much. I hope you do not mind. Because I am supportive of you in this regard."

Jude blushed. "No, I don't mind. And thanks for your support." But was Jasmine saying that she also loved women? Jude couldn't tell, but she couldn't ask, either. Jasmine's manner discouraged familiarity.

Also speaking on their panel were editors from England, Holland, and Australia. The five women sat at a long table beneath a huge white-canvas tent and discussed women's writing among themselves and with the large and lively audience. Afterward, the panel members dined with the festival officials at an Indian restaurant in downtown Adelaide and everyone agreed that the event had been very successful.

In the hotel lobby, before ascending to their rooms on different floors, Jasmine, who was departing at dawn for Paris, said to Jude, "I must say good-bye to you now. But I will look forward to our next meeting. At the ABA in Atlanta, no?"

"Yes. In May. I look forward to it, too. And meanwhile, take good care of yourself, Jasmine."

Jasmine smiled and gazed into her eyes. Placing her hands firmly on Jude's shoulders, she leaned forward and kissed each of her cheeks in decisive slow motion.

The attentive stewardesses on Jude's endless flight back to the United States on Singapore Airlines the next day had the same fragile build and carefully kempt dark beauty as Jasmine. Unlike Jasmine, though, they seemed submissive and eager to please. Jude realized that what impressed her most about Jasmine was that she was in charge of her own life. She ran a successful publishing company. She traveled around the world. In contrast to Anna, whose lifetime of laziness was coming home to roost, limiting her options in ways that were punishing Jude as well.

She remembered how she and Anna used to debate literature and philosophy and art in their early days together. Anna recited her poems and Jude made suggestions. Anna read the books Jude was editing and they discussed them. But now all they talked about was their next meal. It was as though the intensity of their physical exchanges had extinguished all their more subtle forms of intercourse. She vowed that when she got home she would once again initiate with Anna the kind of conversations she had just enjoyed in Adelaide. Maybe it wasn't too late.

When the plane finally landed in Los Angeles, Jude was disturbed to realize that she'd thought more about Jasmine as she hurtled across the Pacific than she had about Anna. But it was a new experience for her to be able *not* to think about Anna. For years, her first thought upon waking and her last before sleeping had been of Anna. And throughout each day, she had replayed every word that they had exchanged the previous day. Anna's name had echoed continuously through her brain, like a Moslem on a pilgrimage to Mecca chanting, *"La illaha illa Allah."*

Stumbling through the international arrival gate at JFK after thirty-two hours in transit, Jude was astonished to find Anna waiting for her. This was a first. All around them, reunited lovers, relatives, and friends were embracing, so Jude and Anna tried to parody the friendly welcoming hug of long-lost sisters.

"Do you have any idea," Anna whispered in her ear, "how much I want to bury my tongue deep inside you?"

Jude stroked her cheek and gazed into her eyes, but she was thinking that the only thing she wanted deep inside her right then was some hot coffee.

Anna grabbed her bag and led her to the exit door. They waited at the curb for a bus to town. A van from the Hilton pulled up. As Anna climbed aboard with the suitcase, Jude called, "Wait a minute, Anna. This isn't us."

Gesturing frantically for her to get on, Anna whispered, "I've rented us a room for the day."

Jude smiled, but her heart sank. She was exhausted and she had a million things to do. Back at her office and apartment, a hundred phone messages and several days of mail awaited her.

Anna had stopped off at the room on her way to the airport. It was as crammed with yellow tulips as a Dutch wake, and a bottle of sparkling cider was packed in melting ice in the sink. Anna phoned room service and ordered chicken salad and toast points.

All Jude wanted was to sleep. Instead, she drank cider while Anna informed her that she was absolutely right: She used to have a drinking problem. But no longer. She'd sworn off alcohol for good.

"What about the sores?" asked Jude as they sat at the linen-shrouded table rolled in by the waiter from room service. "Did you go to the doctor?"

"He said it was an allergic reaction," said Anna. "To some sleeping pills I was taking."

"And?" Jude eyed her suspiciously, having no idea anymore what was truth and what was fabrication.

"And now that I'm not taking them, the sores will go away."

"That's a relief," said Jude, picking up a piece of toast and tackling the chicken salad, her sixth meal since Hawaii.

"So did you sleep with her?"

"With whom?"

"With Jasmine."

"Of course not. Did you think I would?"

"Yes."

"Did you care?"

"Very much. I've been miserable."

"So now you're relieved?"

"Temporarily."

"Don't worry," said Jude without enough forethought. "She's married."

Anna regarded her ironically. "But that's what turns you on, isn't it? The primal triangle? Stealing Mommy from Daddy?"

Jude paused with the toast point halfway to her mouth. "Is that how you see it?"

"And once you succeed," Anna continued blandly, "Mommy seems very boring."

Jude thought this over. "Maybe so," she finally conceded, not even caring enough to argue. Though she actually thought that her waning interest in Anna had more to do with not knowing from one moment to the next whether she'd be dealing with a tender Madonna or an avenging destroyer. Loving Anna had become like trying to love Kali. Finally, you just gave up.

Anna insisted that they take a bath together, slithering around on each other like minnows in a hatchery. Afterward, she dried Jude with a large, fluffy towel. Then she basted her like a turkey with lotion and massaged her on the bed until she was groaning with fatigue. Stripping off her own robe, Anna lay down beside her. Jude stroked her belly, which seemed even more puffy than before. "What did the doctor say about your bloating?"

"It's menopause," she said. "Water retention. I've put myself on a diet and exercise plan to regain my girlish figure. In a couple of months, you won't recognize me. I want it to be like it used to be for us, Jude."

"So do I."

Lying in the giant bed later that afternoon, nearly delirious with exhaustion, Anna asleep beside her, Jude recalled their first hotel room, at the conference in Boston several years earlier, and her own anxiety at waking up in the middle of the night and finding Anna gone. Something had happened between them since then. Who knew what. The worm had turned. The wind had shifted. Now it was Anna who waited for Jude, Anna who felt anxiety over being left behind.

She had good reason to, Jude reluctantly acknowledged. Their luxurious afternoon in bed had felt to Jude like just another chore, one among many that had to be dealt with upon her return. To generate enough energy for lovemaking, so that they could get this reunion over with and go home, Jude had found herself visualizing that walk along the white sand with Jasmine and their talks that had stimulated so many exciting new ideas. There was a whole world out there, full of people Jude had never met, people with horrible problems that they didn't expect Jude to solve.

Holding the sleeping Anna in her arms, Jude was swept with sadness. Anna was right: Jude was moving on. She would have stayed put if she could have, but she was like a flailing swimmer being carried out to sea on a riptide. She had no plans to leave Anna, but emotionally she was already gone. She thought about Molly with new sympathy, because this time it was Jude who had stopped loving first and who would feel the guilt for the rest of her life. Her throat tight, she kissed Anna's closed eyelids. Anna smiled in her sleep and snuggled closer.

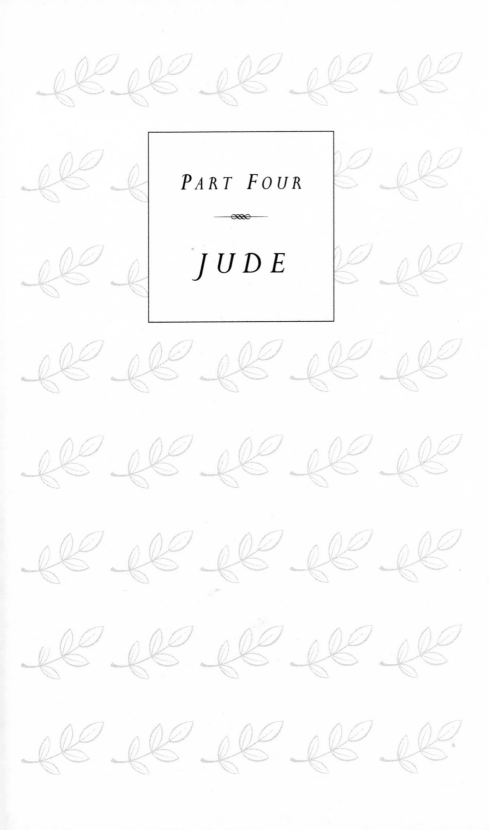

PART FOUR

JUDE

CHAPTER
1 4

BALANCING A GLASS OF CHAMPAGNE, Jude wandered across the closely cropped lawn of Jasmine's seventeenth-century stone town house, wondering how it had escaped being torched during the Revolution. After winding along the tourist-crammed side streets near St. Germain des Prés, she had passed through black iron doors in a high stucco wall and discovered this lawn strewn with wrought-iron furniture and shaded by horse-chestnut trees full of ivory obelisks. Jasmine, who had a spiky new frosted waif hairdo, kissed her on both cheeks. Then she tucked her arm through Jude's to conduct her to the champagne table, where she cast her adrift on a sea of bright Ungaro sails.

Although Jude knew that she was presentable in her raw-silk trousers and coral linen blazer, she had always felt like Godzilla in Paris, possessing as she did the long, lean mountaineer build of her father and his father—in contrast to her urban mother, who had reportedly had wrists the size of a broomstick.

Jasmine was talking to a young woman in a black silk jumpsuit who had draped a silver-studded black leather carbine belt diagonally across her chest. The woman was studying Jude's breasts. Slowly, her kohl-ringed eyes rose up Jude's chest. When their gazes met, the woman smiled faintly, as though to indicate anything was possible. Jude recognized *le regard*, the famous French technique for seducing one another and unnerving visitors. She smiled back, struggling to feel playful despite her chagrin at looming like Gulliver over everyone else on the lawn.

The woman arrived by her side. "You are new here, yes?"

Looking down from her heights, Jude nodded.

"From America?"

The kohl was making the woman's dark eyes look huge and appealing. "From New York."

"On holiday?"

"No, I'm going to work for Jasmine."

"How fortunate for us."

Jude smiled. "Thank you. For me, too."

"I am Martine. I also work for Jasmine."

"Delighted to meet you. I'm Jude."

As Jude sipped her champagne, the woman continued her inspection of Jude. In Tennessee, people wooed with words. Strangers who looked too intently at someone they didn't know were considered either rude or insane. But for the French, the eyes were the initial erogenous zone.

Across the lawn, Jude spotted Jasmine by the champagne table, talking sotto voce with the young man Jude recognized from that night on Simon's deck, when she had first offered Jude a job. Jasmine looked up, right at Jude, and seemed to give her a small nod, as though of encouragement. Was a flirtation with Martine the initiation rite that would usher Jude into Jasmine's inner circle?

Drawing a deep breath, Jude returned her attention to Martine. She hadn't flirted in years. While Anna was alive, she lacked the interest. Now that Anna was dead, she lacked the energy. She wasn't sure she remembered what to do anymore. With an uneasy sideways glance, she studied the small firm breasts that formed the valley down which Martine's carbine belt meandered. She remembered lying with Anna while out the window the lights from Palisades Amusement Park wavered like party streamers on the drifting waters of the Hudson. She remembered cradling Anna's beautiful breast in her palm, its nipple caressing her heart line. . . .

Abruptly, Jude understood that all she wanted at that moment was to go back to her new apartment on the butte of Montmartre, and watch through the curly iron grillwork as the sun set bloodred behind the parkland to the west, and review her final evening with Anna. Not even this attractive woman in her high-fashion carbine belt could erase that image of Anna in her hospital bed, hands bound with gauze so that she couldn't scratch the scabs off her sores.

"What is the matter?" demanded Jasmine as Jude bent over to peck her cheeks and murmur thanks for the party. "You don't like Martine?"

"I like her fine, but I don't feel very well tonight." Jude realized too late that she'd been rude to rush away like that, leaving Martine alone on the lawn in the dusk with swallows swooping through the shadows cast by the giant looming chestnut trees.

"But you are perhaps lonely and would like a lovely companion?"

"She is lovely, but I'm hung up on someone in New York."

"But you would nevertheless like a small adventure when you are away from home?"

"I guess not."

Jasmine shook her head. "I will never understand Americans. But perhaps you will have dinner with me soon and explain yourself?"

Searching for a taxi by the Seine, Jude reflected that if this was *l'amour*, it bore little resemblance to what she knew of love. But then again, that wasn't much.

THE FOLLOWING WEEK, as raindrops bounced off the cobblestones in Jasmine's courtyard, Jude gazed up at the muscled granite torsos of two Greek gods who supported the front balcony on their shoulders. Across the balcony stretched arabesques of wrought iron indistinguishable from real vines, leaves, and grape clusters. She wondered who had first decided to try to make metal look like vines, and why.

"Tonight is my night for recreation," announced Jasmine as she hung Jude's damp raincoat in the closet. "Everyone else is at my house in Picardy. So we can say and do whatever we like."

Jude glanced at her. She had expected a dinner party. But Jasmine was wearing casual trousers and a black T-shirt with shoulder pads, and there was no evidence of other guests. Jasmine steered her by the elbow into a high-ceilinged room filled with Louis-the-something settees and armchairs as maladapted to the human form as the wrought-iron furniture on her lawn the night of her garden party. Wine velvet drapes shut out the dripping twilight, and crusaders in tunics emblazoned with red Maltese crosses glared down from splendidly caparisoned horses in gilt frames on the walls. These crusaders in their fish-scale chain mail and steel skullcaps had Jasmine's hooded eyelids and dark, intense gaze.

Observing Jude's interest, Jasmine nodded at one. "He fought with Simon de Montfort at Minerve in 1210. One hundred and forty Cathars were burned at the stake for heresy."

"Neat," said Jude, noticing that the painted toenails in Jasmine's open-toed, high-heeled mules matched the mauve on her eyelids.

Jasmine inclined her head toward a bottle of Jack Daniel's on the coffee table. "And this is how *your* people pass their time, *n'est-ce pas?*"

Jude smiled. "Yes. How kind of you to help me feel at home."

She poured bourbon and Perrier into two tumblers, adding an ice cube to Jude's. "I believe all Americans like ice?"

Toasting Jude's new job, they sipped the amber liquid. Jude could feel it creeping down her esophagus like a grass fire.

"You are enjoying Paris?"

"Yes, very much. It reminds me a bit of the American South, as a matter of fact."

"Oh? In what way?"

"The overfeminized women. Scarlett O'Hara must have been part French." Jude laughed.

"Why do you laugh?" Jasmine was smiling politely.

"I had a grandmother who compared every foreign country she visited to Virginia. And I just realized I was doing the same."

"You find French women overfeminized?" Jasmine settled back against the wine brocade cushions.

"Compared to American women. But your heritage is courtly love. Ours is survival on the frontier. Your ancestors were fighting boredom. Ours, extinction."

"You are still fighting extinction, no? With all your bombs and missiles."

"And you, boredom, with all your elaborations on daily necessity."

Jasmine said nothing. For a moment, Jude wondered if she'd been rude without realizing it, or whether Jasmine was just reluctant to acknowledge that accessories could be optional. On the coffee table, she noticed a large silver bowl that contained packs of every conceivable brand of cigar and cigarette. "What was the heresy in Minerve?" she asked.

"*La liberté*," replied Jasmine. "They wanted to rule their own kingdom."

"We tried that in the South, too. It was a big mistake."

"Southerners should never cross swords with Northerners."

Jude smiled. "Sometimes you leave us no choice. Submit or die, so we march to our deaths, heads held high."

"Courageous, but not very smart."

"Southerners have never been noted for intelligence. We're simple country people."

"Yes, as simple as a Moorish screen," Jasmine observed with a wry smile. "Shall we move to the table?"

Two places were set on a blue paisley cloth with enough crystal, silver, and burnt-sienna bone china for a complete trousseau. As Jasmine exited into the kitchen, Jude studied her fork handle, encrusted with the omnipresent vines and leaves. She didn't recognize the pattern, despite having memorized all the most popular ones during Charm Class in junior high.

Jude's own pattern, which she'd selected at age six under the tutelage of her grandmother, was Francis I, which she'd loved because it had twenty-eight pieces of fruit on the knife handles. Every Christmas and birthday, she'd received pieces from her grandmother, who didn't allow herself to die until Jude possessed twelve complete place settings. Inheriting her grandmother's twelve settings, Jude then owned twenty-four. Molly's pattern, forced on her by her mother in the face of her total indifference, had been Burgundy, which was similar to Francis I but without the fruit. After Molly's death, her mother insisted Jude take Molly's seven and a half settings as a memento. Jude's thirty-one and a half place settings of unused flatware were now tarnishing in Simon's attic on Cape Cod, waiting for her to hostess a banquet. Her father used to say that men struggled to pass on their genes, and women their silverware.

Jasmine returned with two scalloped grapefruit shells mounded high with avocado slices, grapefruit sections, and prawns. She poured white wine into one set of glasses, Evian into another. Jude watched to see which fork she'd use before committing herself. Once upon a time, she'd known them all—the dinner fork, the salad fork, the shrimp fork, the ice cream fork, the lobster fork, the lemon fork, the olive fork, the half-olive fork, the pickle fork, the tomato fork.

"This is marvelous," said Jude, tasting a hint of garlic mayonnaise and feeling a stab of nostalgia for the French cook at her grandparents' apartment when she first moved to New York. "I didn't know you could cook."

"I have a wonderful woman from Corsica who left this meal for us. Tonight is her night off."

Removing the empty grapefruit shells, Jasmine returned with medallions of lamb in a plum sauce that matched her toenails, parsley-flecked new potatoes glistening with butter, and embryonic peas and carrots with a faint scent of mint. She poured some red wine from a bottle that had evidently been breathing on the mahogany Empire sideboard as they sipped their Jack Daniel's.

Raising her crystal goblet, Jasmine gazed into the wine, murmuring, "When one drinks wine in France, one engages all the senses."

Jude nodded politely.

"First, we observe the deep burgundy blood of the grape."

Jude raised her glass and looked down into her grape blood.

Chopping up a cherry Popsicle in a Dixie cup, Anna watching her from the blood-flecked sheets, the whites of her eyes a urine yellow, her lips gray and cracked.

"Jude, I'm not afraid to die," she said, "but I don't want to die alone."

"I will be here," Jude replied numbly. "Wait for me." Looking up from the crushed Popsicle into Anna's weary lapis lazuli eyes that used to dance and sparkle just like Molly's.

Putting her nose into her glass, Jasmine inhaled deeply and held it, as though smoking a joint. Then she exhaled. "Next, we allow the bouquet to ascend our nostrils, to the pleasure center of the brain."

Jude sniffed her wine obligingly, but her pleasure center was unfortunately sealed.

Jasmine took a sip and swirled it around her mouth, studying Jude with her intense crusader eyes. She swallowed. "Then we taste the wine, which of course engages the taste buds. But also the sense of touch, as the wine caresses the tongue and the moist cavities of the mouth."

Meeting her gaze, Jude obediently sipped and rinsed as though at the dentist's. But her senses were unengaged, and she intended to keep them that way.

"Well," said Jude, "that covers four out of five. And how about hearing?"

Lowering her eyes, Jasmine said nothing for a while. "Hearing has been involved all along," she finally replied. "You have been listening to my voice, no?"

"Oh. Yes. Right you are."

Abruptly, Jasmine put down her glass and picked up a knife and fork. They ate in silence.

"And how is your apartment?" Jasmine eventually asked.

"It's fine, thanks. I have a wonderful view of Paris. You'll have to come see."

"I rarely go out. People come to me here." She sounded annoyed. Jude felt anxiety prickle the hairs at the back of her neck. "And your work? Is everyone at the office helping you get started?"

"Yes, everyone's been wonderful."

"You know, if you are going to get along here, you should at least pretend to play." She looked Jude in the eye, but with *la réprimande*, not *le regard*.

"But if you pretend," said Jude, "then you're playing." She

toyed with her ivory knife rest. This was, after all, her new boss, and bosses had to be placated. But she'd spent her years in New York trying to learn to be straightforward. A challenge, since in the South directness had been second only to bad hair on the list of deadly sins.

"Exactly."

"So don't you all ever stop playing?"

"What is the alternative? Boredom, followed by death."

"Childhood is for playing. Then life becomes serious."

"And did you play as a child? *Ah, non.* Children are earnest in all that they do. Only adults can really play, because we have learned that life is a game in any case. One that will soon be over."

"Well, I guess I'm not feeling very playful these days." Jude laid her knife and fork parallel on her plate to indicate that she was finished. But did this gesture symbolize the same thing in France?

"Ah, yes. You have said that you are—how do you say, carrying the torch? And this person in New York does not desire you?"

"She's dead."

"She was your lover?"

"Yes."

"Someone new would perhaps help you to forget her."

"I don't want to forget Anna."

Jasmine studied Jude, then said gently, "But she is dead. And you are not."

Jude looked down at the black geometric pattern across her burnt sienna plate.

"Americans are so sincere." Shaking her head, Jasmine passed Jude the cut-glass salad bowl. "It is touching."

"Well, as corny as it may sound, I'm afraid I can only make love to people I love," Jude muttered, realizing as she served herself some romaine and chopped escarole that this wasn't entirely true.

Jasmine smiled. "But one can love for a single night, no? Or for a week.

A love does not have to endure into the next century in order to be love.''

"Children in the South play a kissing game called Five Minutes in Heaven. But once you become an adult, you're supposed to graduate to what we call graveyard love.''

"And this is what—your graveyard love?''

"Graveyard love is a love that lasts until both people are dead and buried in the graveyard.''

"Oh, I see. As in Shakespeare. 'Love is not love which alters when it alteration finds.' ''

Jude nodded, impressed that Jasmine should know the English classics in addition to her own.

Jasmine shook her head. "And they say that Americans are not romantic.''

"Who does?''

"I believe Europeans think of Americans as Puritans. Practical and efficient. And somewhat naïve to believe that the world operates like that.''

"But graveyard love isn't American; it's southern. The South was settled by broken-down cavaliers, not religious fanatics. It's the Citadel of the Lost Cause.''

Jasmine carried out the salad plates, Jude's mostly untouched. She returned with a marble slab holding several cheeses—cubes and wheels and wedges, dark orange, pale yellow, white coated with black pepper or flecked with blue-green. She might have poured another wine or two, but the grape blood was all as one to Jude by now.

"General de Gaulle once asked how he could be expected to govern a nation that made three hundred and forty-six varieties of cheese,'' said Jasmine.

Jude smiled. "Yes, but they all begin with milk and end with mold. Just like people. So that simplifies things a bit.''

Jasmine regarded Jude thoughtfully, opened her mouth, then closed it without saying anything.

The meal concluded with balls of sherbet, passion fruit and citron, in scalloped silver bowls, accompanied by disks of fragile dark chocolate lace.

They moved back to the living room for coffee. The thick, bitter espresso held out the promise of eventual sobriety, followed by terminal insomnia.

"Would you like to smoke?" Jasmine nodded toward the bowl of cigarette packs.

Jude extracted a Dunhill and lit up, sinking back into the cushions. Jasmine picked up an embossed leather album from the coffee table and showed Jude photos of her other houses—an ancient family château in Picardy, a modern glass-and-timber structure on Martinique. Clearly there would be many fringe benefits to Jude's job. If she managed to keep it, given her reluctance to play. At the back of the album were photos of people—one of Jasmine as a teenager, attired in a riding habit, seated on a horse in the middle of a flying change.

"Do you still ride?" asked Jude.

"Not in years."

"I used to ride, too. But I never did dressage. In fact, we never used saddles. We just jumped on and took off."

Jasmine eyed her speculatively, a Hun at the city gates. While returning the album to the coffee table, she scooted closer on the couch, until her thigh barely touched Jude's. A scent close to chrysanthemums mixed with coriander seemed to be emanating from her flesh, ascending Jude's nostrils to waft around the barred portals of her pleasure center.

Sitting by Anna's bedside at the Roosevelt, dabbing with a cotton ball soaked in witch hazel at an oozing sore that wouldn't clot. Anna's seersucker robe had fallen open. The pale breast she had begged Jude to bite was lying there like a poached egg. A nurse entered and unpinned the urine-soaked diaper. The sad, gray, sour-smelling genitals, the matted pubic hair, the sagging belly whose unused muscles had turned to flab . . .

Jude turned her head away from Jasmine to deflect the spicy scent. Jasmine murmured concern that she seemed chilled.

Jude found herself rising to her feet. "I have to go now." The part of her that had once leapt like a brazier with Anna was now frozen solid. Jasmine was right: Jude was chilled. Permanently.

Jasmine looked startled. "But it is early."

"I'm really tired. Also a bit drunk."

"If you would like to stay," she said, "my driver can take you back to Montmartre when he returns from Picardy later tonight."

"Thanks, but I'd better go home and sleep it off."

Jasmine shrugged, looking somewhat pleased. As she retrieved Jude's coat from the closet, Jude suddenly understood that to refuse to play was to play. The only way not to play was to stay, thereby short-circuiting the game. But she didn't love Jasmine. Besides, she was confused. She had thought it was Martine that Jasmine had lined up for her. Or were these overtones of seduction just hospitality as usual in Paris?

"Jasmine?" she murmured. In New York, she could have asked someone outright what was going on. But with Jasmine, she always felt tongue-tied unless they were discussing abstractions.

Jasmine looked at her. Her hooded eyes with their hint of mauve seemed to convey disappointment at Jude's possible change of strategy. Would she have been able to believe that Jude had no strategy?

"I just realized," said Jude, "that in English the word *love* is close to *live*. Whereas in French, *l'amour* is close to *la mort*. What do you think that means?"

Jasmine studied Jude as she held out her coat.

JUDE SAT BY HER OPEN DOORS watching the lights of Paris flicker and sweep and flare like heat lightning on a hot southern night. Some fans were conducting a séance in the shed in Jude's courtyard, trying to summon the shade of Dalida, a famous French singer who had recently committed suicide in her house at the end of the block. Jude could see the flicker of candles and hear voices softly chanting Dalida's greatest hits. Jude's inebriation was turning into a migraine, one sensation Jasmine hadn't included in her catalog of the delights of wine drinking in France.

The phone rang. Picking it up, she heard Simon's BBC voice from New York, where it was late afternoon. He was still at work. Jude pictured him with his long legs stretched out beneath his huge black Formica desk, hands toying with one of his bizarre paperweights.

"So how's it going over there, Jude?"

"Not too bad, thank you. It's fascinating trying to figure out the tastes of the French reading public. But socially, I'm a flop."

"I refuse to believe it."

"Alas, it's true. They're playing Hearts and I'm playing Old Maid."

"I think you should learn to play Hearts again."

"Five minutes in heaven and a lifetime of pain. No, thank you."

"I know how you feel, Jude. But it's the only game in town."

"Some of us learn life's little lessons."

"I do understand. Part of you died with Anna. But you have to plunge back into the swim."

"Why?"

"Because you're a V-eight engine who's sparking on only two cylinders."

"You're mixing your metaphors."

"Stop changing the subject."

"But I'm an editor, Simon. I'm paid to notice these things. Anyway, don't worry. Jasmine is doing her best to provide me with romantic interludes."

"She's just trying to help."

"You've discussed me with her? Is that why she invited me to Paris?"

Simon hesitated. "We spoke about you at the ABA. I'm sorry if you feel betrayed. She cares about you. So do I. We hate seeing you so devastated."

"Simon, you're such a busybody. Maybe I just need to lick my wounds alone in my lair."

"No, I'm with Jasmine on this one, Jude. The City of Light on midsummer night. What could be bad?"

After hanging up, Jude sat counting the bridges over the Seine, along which cars were crawling like lightning bugs on parade. Was Simon right? When Sandy died, Simon lay sobbing in Jude's arms all night long. For months afterward, he wandered New York like the soul of an unburied corpse, losing so much weight that he belted his jeans with an extension cord. Yet now, plump and jolly, he danced in Provincetown bars until dawn with handsome men, each younger and blonder than the last. He claimed he'd become a New Testament scholar, studying Matthew, Mark, Luke, and John at every opportunity.

She switched on the television to a movie featuring two French journalists, a man and a woman, in Naples to cover the drug trial of a mafioso. While threats were made against their lives, they gave each other *le regard* in every bistro in town, even though they were married to each other's cousins back in Paris. Every time one said, "This is impossible," they fell into each other's arms in a sixteenth-century pension and made mad passionate love while hit men lurked in the street below. But whenever one said, "I love you and want to spend the rest of my life with you," both leapt up, packed their bags, and raced out the door in opposite directions. In the end, the woman, a cool blonde who seemed the picture of wholesome propriety, turned out to be in league with the hit men. Dying from a gunshot wound as a result of her betrayal, the male reporter whispered to her with his last breath that he had never loved her so much as he did at that moment.

As the credits rolled, Jude realized that there was much that she didn't yet understand about her reading public.

CHAPTER

1 5

RIBBONS OF SUNLIGHT were weaving through a grid of holes in the white domed ceiling. The round table was crammed with salads, charcuterie, cheeses, baguettes, and bottles of mineral water. Jude was studying Martine, who was insisting to their assembled co-workers that desire by definition implied lack and therefore to consummate it was to destroy it. So appealing when Jude first saw her crossing Jasmine's lawn in her black silk jumpsuit and studded carbine belt, Martine was currently wearing a tiny navy-blue double-breasted pinstriped suit with a scarlet pocket handkerchief and wing-tip shoes.

Cecile, the new editor, who wore red-framed eyeglasses with tinted lenses the size of teacups, replied to Martine that no one truly possessed another. Even the merging during lovemaking was temporary and illusory. The unattainable, of necessity, always remained unattainable. So long as a single breath was left in the body, one was doomed to a desire without fulfillment. Or at least that seemed to be her line. Jude's grasp of French was modest even when someone wasn't speaking as fast as a tobacco auctioneer and with an intensity appropriate to the final stages of labor.

Martine curled her upper lip like Elvis Presley and called Cecile the French equivalent of scumbag of the Western world. If they'd been Southerners, Cecile would have pulled out a handgun and shot Martine at this point. Yet no one but Jude seemed alarmed, including Cecile herself. In fact, they all smiled faintly and ripped off chunks of baguette with renewed appetite, hurling crumbs around the room.

Jude tried to think of something supportive of Cecile to say in her fumbling French, having no idea whether she agreed with her or not. But Cecile was a newcomer, and this episode from the Spanish Inquisition seemed an unacceptable welcome.

Martine began talking about the role of the father in rupturing the mother-child fusion and his introduction of the child into the compensatory realm of the symbolic, in which fantasized images could substitute for the original lost love object. Although it sounded very much like the story of her own life, Jude realized that she had reached the outer limits of her French vocabulary. So she sat back and observed Martine's body language, which involved a stabbing index finger, karate chops with the side of her hand, pursed lips, and elaborate shoulder shrugs.

Simon had always presided over their work lunches in New York with his dry British wit, joking and gossiping and punning, humoring those gauche enough to argue until they stopped it. But the women in this office seemed to have elaborated argument into an art form. Jude was impressed, having herself been trained to be pleasant at any cost. "Smile, girls, smile!" Miss Melrose used to shriek, fluttering her Minnie Mouse eyelashes. "And if you don't feel it, fake it. The only thing a southern woman must never fake is her pearls."

Martine was now slashing and lunging at Cecile like Cyrano de
Bergerac over something to do with the role of the Other as a tool
for honing self-definition. She seemed to feel that you knew who you
were by identifying who you weren't. Her dark eyes were blazing and
her head was tossing like a horse on too tight a rein. She was gorgeous,
even with a mouth like an Uzi. But she'd been avoiding Jude ever
since Jude walked away from her on Jasmine's lawn, leaving rooms
when Jude entered and pretending not to see her when they passed
in the corridor. Jude wondered if she was supposed to be feeling *le
manque*, which in a normal French person would apparently engender
le désir.

Abruptly, the dispute concluded. Cecile and Martine appeared
to have called a truce rather than reaching agreement. Cecile took a
tiny mirror from her handbag and carefully applied enough scarlet
lipstick to frost a cake. Everyone else lit a cigarette and relaxed
into her chair, as though after inspired lovemaking. Martine offered
Cecile a Gauloise, gazing into her eyes over the lighter. Cecile was
now one of the gang. Jude's colleagues glanced at her, a deaf-mute
cowboy Other with whom they were saddled because of some whim
of Jasmine's.

"Alors, la premiere phase . . ." said Martine, exhaling a cloud of
blue smoke. And everyone proceeded to deconstruct her argument
with Cecile, like the instant replay of a football game.

Stubbing out their cigarettes, they stood up, dusted baguette
crumbs off their laps, and headed for their offices, crunching across
the carpet of crumbs as though over a plague of locusts. Martine
glanced behind her as she exited in her fetching suit. To be sure that
Jude was noticing that she wasn't noticing her? Jude did notice, but
she found it irritating rather than alluring. Although she was beginning
to wonder if the more unpleasant Martine was to her the more it
meant that she liked her. Because the French seemed to thrive

on contradiction. The oldest bridge in town was called the Pont
Neuf.

Entering her office, Jude looked out the window and down an
alley to the tumbled stone ruins of the Roman baths, sacked and
burned by the barbarians in the third century. History Ph.D. manquée
that she was, this city enchanted her. It was a *feuilleté* of superimposed
civilizations—Gallic, Roman, Hun, Norman, Frank. Since her job required her to develop an understanding of French culture so that she
would know which books to choose for translation, she'd hung a map
of Paris the size of a bedspread across one wall. Accustomed to the
rectangular blocks of New York City, she initially found a round city
disturbing. But in time, she realized that there were thirty-six gates
around the circumference. She decided to slice the *feuilleté*, hiking
from one gate to its opposite in eighteen diameters, reading her guidebook before whatever landmarks she encountered, stopping at cafés
for coffee when she got tired. She'd done this twice already, marking
her meandering routes on the giant map with a red felt-tip pen. Each
trip requiring a full afternoon, she'd put herself on a regimen of one
per week. As a grand finale, she planned to walk the circumference
of the city, then the smaller circles within, where previous town walls
had stood. In six months' time, this map would resemble a giant red
spiderweb.

Upon hearing Jude's plan, Jasmine had cocked her frosted head
quizzically and said, "But this is insanity." She was probably right,
but at least it was well-organized insanity.

Next door, Jude could hear Martine growling and snapping in a
staccato phone conversation. Then a heavy object crashed against her
wall. Jude got up and went to her doorway. Martine dashed out,
slamming her door so hard that the entire wall shuddered.

The woman across the hall, a pleasant copper-haired secretary
named Giselle, was also standing in her doorway, watching Martine

careen down the corridor and out the entrance in her pinstriped suit, screaming, *"Merde!"*

Jude looked questioningly at Giselle.

"Her lover left her last month," Giselle explained. "Martine had a nervous breakdown and tried to kill herself. She is still very upset."

Jude returned to her desk feeling apologetic toward Martine. They had both just lost their lovers. No wonder their interactions with each other were so befuddled. She vowed to make more of an effort with her.

Since much of Jude's job involved reading manuscripts at her apartment or meeting with scouts and agents, she came and went as she pleased. As it was a beautiful sunny afternoon, she decided to undertake that week's requisite trek across Paris. This fieldwork was, after all, an important part of her job. So she took the Métro to Porte de Charenton and walked over to Porte de Bercy. From there, she headed up the Seine in the direction of Porte de Champerret, past docks and cranes, with a forest of glass-and-steel high-rises on her right and a jammed highway on her left, a panorama decidedly different from the ancient ruined splendor most people thought of as Paris.

As she walked, Jude pondered the notion of an encounter with the Other as a route to self-definition. It seemed pretty flimsy to know who you were only by knowing who you weren't. What would you do if you were alone in a cave?

Crossing the Pont Sully to Ile St. Louis, Jude strolled down a quiet street lined with elegant seventeenth-century stone town houses. Arriving at an ice cream parlor, she sat down in the sunshine at an outside table and ordered a dish of chocolate chip. As she waited, she read in her guidebook that this island had served as a medieval dueling field. And across the bridge in front of her was the house where Abélard had been castrated for love of Héloïse.

While she ate her ice cream, Jude gazed at Notre Dame, which crouched before her like a giant horned insect with flying-buttress limbs and compound eyes of stained glass. She kept glancing back and forth between the barbed spires straining toward heaven and the grotesque stone gargoyles, half dog and half dragon, that vomited rainwater off the roofs.

After paying her bill, Jude crossed the Pont St. Louis and wandered down the Quai aux Fleurs. As she passed the Tour de l'Horloge, from which a bell signaling the St. Bartholomew's Day Massacre had been rung, she paused to lean on the stone parapet of the Pont au Change, where hundreds of the butchered had been dumped into the Seine to drift downriver past the Louvre, trailing wakes of blood.

Jude arrived at the park at the tip of Ile de la Cité. Caressing couples sprawled on the benches and reclined along the stones shelves that sloped down to the river. Sitting on a green slatted bench, she tilted her head back and closed her eyes, the sunshine warming her face. Thrushes were chattering among the bushes of red roses, which were filling the air with their cloying sweetness. On the far shore, two dreadlocked black men were playing reggae on steel drums, while a *bateau mouche* swarming with camera-clicking tourists plowed the gray waters and doused the torrid lovers lying along the banks. As Jude watched them, she realized that she'd never before felt so lonely as here in this city where she and Anna had planned to commence their life together.

JUDE SANK DOWN in the chair by Anna's bedside and took one of her twitching hands. Earlier that week, Anna had slipped into a coma. Dusk was descending beyond the bouquets along the window ledge. Anna's room at the Roosevelt was on the fifth floor. Directly across the street was the condemned apartment building where Jude's parents had lived during her father's residency, its arched windows boarded up with warped plywood.

Turning from the window, Jude studied Anna's yellow face with its crescent eyebrows and cap of dark hair. She looked as though she was merely asleep and would wake up like Sleeping Beauty if Jude kissed her. Was Anna's collapse actually her fault, Jude wondered, for having ceased to love her? Had she felt Jude's withdrawal and gone on a terminal binge? But to be in such bad shape now, she must have been marinating herself for decades. All those nights when she had rolled out of Jude's arms to go home to Jim, she had actually been going home to her only real love—Smirnoff. But why? What secret pain did she carry inside herself that had to be so brutally anesthetized? What ancient horror was she trying to externalize by remaining with a man who beat her up and by trying to provoke a woman who adored her into doing the same? Jude searched the waxen mask of Anna's face as though it belonged to a stranger.

The door opened and Jim walked in, followed by a middle-aged man and woman Jude had never seen before. The woman had Anna's crescent eyebrows and raven hair. Jim, florid-faced and reeking of alcohol, looked at Jude with a flicker of recognition as she placed Anna's hand on the bedside and stood up.

"Hello," she said. "I'm Jude."

"Yes, I know," he said without enthusiasm. He gestured to the couple. "Stanley and Muriel Rivers. From Chicago. Muriel is Anna's sister." To them, he said, "This is Anna's editor."

Jude gazed at him coolly, wondering whether to wrangle with him over something that was drawing to a close in any case. "And her best friend," she added, feeling childish. But what she wanted to say was, "Listen, asshole, I've experienced aspects to Anna that you don't even know exist."

Grabbing her coat, she murmured, "I was just leaving." She watched Jim closely as he moved to Anna's bedside and looked down at her, swaying unsteadily. His salt-and-pepper hair was scrambled and his bushy sideburns needed a trim. She felt a certain reluctant kinship with him: Anna had been cheating on them both all these years, coupling with a lover with whose charms neither could ever have hoped to compete.

Suddenly, Jim buried his face in his hands and started sobbing. Muriel raced to his side and put her arms around him. As Jude watched, she felt her hands clench into fists, eager to wrap themselves around his throat. Was he upset because now he had no punching bag? He could move right into the role of grieving widower, and no one but Jude would know what a farce it was.

Out in the street, Jude stalked north up Broadway, gripped by rage—rage against Jim, but also rage against Anna and herself. Why had they lived a lie for so many years?

Entering the diner where she and Anna used to discuss Anna's anthology, she sat down at their usual granite-topped table by the window and ordered their usual Earl Grey tea. As she sipped it, she forced herself to confront the complications of what she'd imagined was her green paradise of childhood love revisited—the ways in which she'd blinded herself to Anna's desperate situation. The warning signals she had missed or ignored. Anna's complicity in Jim's cruelty; his, in her drinking; Jude's, in their ghastly marriage. Anna's and Jude's final months together had been like slicing open a fragrant pineapple from the tropics, only to find it dark brown and putrid at the core.

The apartment was dark and empty when Jude reached home. Simon was at his house on the Cape with two Dutch publishers. After hanging up her coat, Jude sat down on the living room couch. She remembered lying on that couch with Anna the first night they ever kissed, after weeks of titillating indecision. Apparently, this was the price you paid for a clandestine affair. When it was over, there was no one to turn to in your grief, no one to burden with all your touching memories. Simon, William, Sid, and a few others were the only ones who knew about Anna and herself. Everyone else regarded Simon and her as a couple, since they lived together. And Jude had arranged her life to exclude other confidants. She worked and spent time with Anna. That was all. She grabbed the phone.

"You sound awful, Jude," Aunt Audrey yelled while children fought in the background. "What's wrong, honey?"

"A friend of mine is very sick. Is my father there?"

When she described Anna's current condition, her father sighed and said, "I wish I could give you some hope, baby, but I can't."

"So she's dying?"

"I'm afraid so. And it's a horrible death. Especially for those who have to watch it."

Jude went completely numb. She felt no anger, no sadness, nothing at all.

"You and Anna are very close, aren't you?"

"Very." This was as near as she'd ever come to acknowledging the relationship to him. She wondered whether he got the picture. He'd met Anna only once, on a trip to New York to show Aunt Audrey and the children the sights. Jude had brought Anna to a chaotic family dinner at Mamma Leone's. Her father and Anna had had a chance to exchange very few words as the baby bopped Danny on the head with an asparagus spear, but Jude noticed them glancing at each other throughout the meal. Afterward, Anna said that she'd been impressed by his combination of kindness and strength. Kind men were often weak and strong men cruel, she said, but he seemed to combine the best qualities of both sexes. "He's what a man is supposed to be." At the time, Jude hadn't thought to wonder why, if Anna knew this, she stayed with a weak, cruel man.

"She seems like a lovely person."

"She is. I love her, Dad."

"Yes, I know," he said. "I'm sorry, baby. Life can be very unfair sometimes."

"Did I tell you she's at the Roosevelt?"

"No kidding."

"Her windows look out at the fifth floor of that apartment building where you and Mother used to live."

"My God," he said. "It's so strange, the way things recycle."

"Which apartment was yours?"

There was a long pause, during which Jude wondered whether he was upset or simply unable to remember. "The fifth, sixth, and seventh windows from the left," he replied in a strained voice. "Please give them my best regards."

A few nights later, Jude was sitting by Anna's bedside holding her hand, which had been bound to a splint with gauze so that she couldn't rip the scabs off her sores. The night nurse had apologetically explained that Anna was very willful about picking her scabs, even while unconscious, and that her wounds would barely clot now. Her sheets became blood-soaked and had to be changed constantly. Jude hated the idea of giving the already overextended nurses more work, but the splints appalled her and she was considering removing them. They reminded her of the metal mittens Victorian parents had put on their children's hands to prevent them from masturbating.

As she debated this issue, Jude studied Anna's face, still remarkably beautiful despite the puffiness and the mustard tint to the skin. It was so familiar. Jude's fingers and tongue must have stroked each ridge and hollow a thousand times.

Her mind finally relinquished its ethical struggle over the splints. Gradually, it quieted and cleared—until it felt like a high mountain lake reflecting the sky. And in that moment, Jude sensed the presence of Anna, as though Anna's heart had suddenly yawned open to receive her and enfold her in an embrace. And Jude knew in that instant that their love for each other hadn't vanished after all. It had just transformed itself, like water evaporating into mist. Apparently, there were detours to union that bypassed the flesh.

As this fugitive taste of connection faded, Jude sat there watching this woman she loved, this woman she now realized she would always love. But if Anna weren't dying, would she have been able to feel this? Jude wondered. Before Anna's collapse, they'd reached a dead end with each other. Was the essential ingredient for a graveyard love the grave?

Later that evening, as Jude sat by Anna's bedside marking a manuscript for the printers, she asked absently, "Would you like a Popsicle, my love?"

"Yes, please."

Jude looked at her. Her eyes were closed. Her body was still. "Anna, can you hear me?"

There was no response.

"If you can hear me, move your hand."

Not a muscle moved, except for Anna's mouth, which pursed to receive the Popsicle, like a newborn's mouth searching for the nipple.

"Anna," said Jude, just in case, "I want you to know that our time together has been the happiest in my life. And although I don't see right now how to go on without you, I don't regret a moment of it."

Anna's hand crept to her breast and used its splint to scrape off a scab. Blood welled up and ran like a freshet down her side, pooling inside her robe and soaking through to the clean white sheets.

"Goddamn it, Anna, stop that!" screamed Jude, grabbing the hand. She burst into tears. "Please talk to me. For one last time before you go."

Anna's eyes remained closed, her lips puckered for more Popsicle.

Jude pictured Sandy, inert in his hospital bed, his teeth shattered. And Molly on her stretcher, head stitched like a softball, face the purple of a smashed plum. And herself at her mother's bedside all those years ago, singing "Rise, Shine, Give God His Glory." When her mother refused to wake up, Jude began yelling the lyrics right into her ear—until her father had to pick her up and carry her into the hallway as she still sobbed that stupid, hopeless hymn.

CHAPTER 16

JASMINE'S OFFICE was furnished very differently from her antiques-crammed, crusader-haunted living quarters several blocks away. The house was dark and muffled, but the office featured gleaming chrome, black leather upholstery, and the latest in office equipment. Jude had been describing an American novel she thought Jasmine should buy, concerning a love affair between two nurses.

"Ordinary women living ordinary lives, women who happen to love each other," said Jude, semireclining before Jasmine's desk in a designer dental chair.

"But it is too long," said Jasmine. "And it would increase a third in translation. And it is too boring—going to work, shopping, cooking dinner, helping children with schoolwork. Our readers are interested in the chase, not the collapse into tedium that follows."

"But that's life."

"Your life perhaps. Because you do not know how to play."

Jude smiled. She hadn't picked a book yet that appealed to Jasmine. She couldn't imagine why Jasmine continued to pay her salary.

Jasmine's door hurtled open and a young man marched in without knocking. He had a handsome, pouty face with high cheekbones, a wide forehead, and a navy-blue five o'clock shadow.

"Ah, Robert," said Jasmine, half-rising, evidently taken aback.

Robert glared at her, then at Jude. He was wearing baggy pleated trousers, a long-sleeved rayon shirt buttoned at the throat, and pointy-toed basket-weave shoes. Fag shoes, Simon would have called them. His black hair was spiky on top and long in back, and a tiny gold hoop was dangling from one earlobe. Without taking his dark, wounded eyes off Jasmine, he sank uninvited into a chrome-and-leather chair, hands resting on his knees.

They sat in silence, Jude waiting for Jasmine to introduce her. He was young. Could he be her son? Jude had no idea how old Jasmine was or if she even had children. She had the beginnings of that parenthesis people got around their mouths as they approached fifty, which made their chins look hinged like Charlie McCarthy's. But if she'd had a face-lift, this process would have been forestalled. Yet her body was as taut and shapely as a thirty-year-old's.

Robert was furious with Jasmine, his eyebrows meeting in the center in a deep frown. And it was clear that he didn't care for Jude, either. What wasn't clear was why not, since he'd never before laid eyes on her, so far as she knew.

Maybe he was Jasmine's lover. Despite Simon's belief that she had a husband stashed away somewhere, Jude had concluded that Jasmine liked women, having mostly seen her surrounded by devoted female employees. Yet if Jasmine had in fact come on to her that night when Jude dined with her—which she wouldn't have sworn to—Jude had turned her down. She was no threat to Robert. So why was he glaring at her as though she'd opened the oven on his soufflé?

"Do you work in publishing, too?" Jude finally asked him.

"Don't ask me what work I do. All Americans ask that."

"What should I ask instead?"

He sighed. "Why not ask, for example, if I am *sportif?*"

"Okay. Are you sportif, Robert?"

Jasmine smiled.

Robert spat air through loose lips. "I am not obliged to answer such a stupid question."

Jude shrugged. She had merely been trying to stave off homicide. She sat in silence, staring at a yellowed photo of a young man with Jasmine's hooded eyelids that was in an antique silver frame on the bookshelf. Jasmine's friends and colleagues displayed the most intriguing mix of impeccable manners and breathtaking rudeness. She wished she was back in New York playing "Indiana Jones and the Lost Temple of Atlantis" on her computer at work.

Finally, Robert stood up and strode from the room without looking back.

"So who's Robert?" Jude asked.

Jasmine waved her multiringed hand as though shooing an annoying fly. Once Jude had finally summoned the courage to ask her some personal questions, she had discovered that Jasmine never answered them, anyway.

Jasmine resumed her discussion of why nurse novels wouldn't sell in Paris. Jude was getting the impression that her readers regarded life as a cross between a Greek tragedy and a Harlequin romance— all storm and betrayal and suffering. Probably Jude would have, too, if she'd grown up in a country that had been invaded by marauders from every direction throughout recorded history, instead of one founded by madcap dreamers who believed you could pack up your sorrows and hop the next ship for the promised land.

Her eyes kept returning to the photo on Jasmine's desk. The young man looked a lot like Jasmine.

"My brother," she said, noticing that Jude wasn't paying attention to her discourse on the limitations of realism in fiction.

"You look very much alike."

"So I'm told. But he is dead now. Tortured and shot by the Germans. He was a messenger for the Resistance. Fifteen years old. I was ten. I thought I would die, too, because I adored him so much. But I didn't."

Jude looked at her with new interest. This might be the first real thing Jasmine had ever said to her. She seemed embarrassed, exhaling a cloud of cigarette smoke like an octopus spewing ink in a predator's face.

Quickly, Jasmine asked about Anna's poetry anthologies. She had decided to try one for French schoolgirls, feeling they might take themselves more seriously as writers if they received that kind of confirmation at an age before hormones fogged their brains. Jude agreed to organize one but expressed doubt about whether her French was up to the job of dealing with the schools.

"Martine can help you."

Jude nodded cautiously.

"It will give you a chance to get to know her," she said, looking at Jude from beneath her hooded eyelids. "She is a marvelous lover."

"I'm sure she is," muttered Jude, wondering how Jasmine knew this. "But I'm not really interested in a new lover right now."

"What *are* you interested in?" asked Jasmine irritably, a repeatedly thwarted Aphrodite.

"My job. Paris. The French."

"If you wish to understand the French, you must take a French lover. It would expand your vocabulary as well."

Jude laughed. "You make it sound like a self-improvement course."

"It would be, I assure you."

The door opened again, and Martine walked in carrying a shopping bag that was almost dragging the floor. Her shiny, chin-length auburn hair was parted in the middle and layered at the nape of her neck. Her huge dark eyes, like licorice throat lozenges, were ringed with kohl, giving her a bruised urchin look. Beneath her navy-blue silk suit, she wore an ivory silk blouse, which was unbuttoned to reveal a lacy camisole.

It was a Saturday, so Jude was wearing blue jeans, a Big Apple T-shirt, and cowboy boots with silver toe guards. She hadn't expected anyone to be at the office when she stopped by to leave off some memos en route to a hike across Paris. Already weary of the daily fashion parade at the office, whose corridors functioned like a couturier's runway, she cherished her collapse into dishabille on weekends.

"Ah, Martine," said Jasmine. "We were just speaking of you."

Martine nodded to Jude, but her eyes never left Jasmine's.

"Did you know that Martine also writes poetry?" Jasmine asked Jude.

Jude shook her head no.

"Martine, get your last book off my shelf and sign it for Jude."

Martine did so. Then she handed Jude the book, still not looking at her. Flipping it open, Jude read an obscure inscription about secrets between them that awaited revelation.

"Merci beaucoup," she said to Martine, who nodded, still looking at Jasmine.

"So what have you bought?" Jasmine asked her.

"A skirt," she replied in a small voice. "And a blazer. A dress and some boots."

"Very good. But you must try them on for us."

Martine disappeared into the next room.

"She is a very gifted poet," said Jasmine.

"I look forward to reading her book," said Jude, in fact dreading it because all poetry reminded her of Anna.

"They are love poems. To her last lover, who has now left her."

Jasmine gave Jude a look loaded with meaning. But what meaning? She wished Jasmine would just back off and let her pick her own poison. She couldn't love on command.

Martine reappeared in a mauve chiffon skirt, the silk blouse, and the camisole. Watching her, Jude wondered how she'd tried to kill herself. There were no scars on her wrists or rope burns at her throat. Pills probably. Someone as fastidious as Martine wouldn't use anything so messy as a gun or a knife. Jude was impressed by the purity of her response to lost love.

Jasmine was studying Martine's flawless physique. "Yes, lovely. But the blouse—no. Take it off."

Martine unbuttoned the silk shirt and let it waft to the floor like an apple blossom on a spring zephyr. She stood there in the camisole, her shoulders and upper chest goose-bumped, whether from cold or excitement Jude couldn't have said.

"And now the blazer," said Jasmine in a low voice.

Martine picked up the cream-colored cashmere blazer and slipped it on over the camisole.

"No," announced Jasmine. "*Absolument pas*. Not with the camisole. Take it off."

Martine removed the jacket and folded it carefully across the back of a chair. Then she shrugged off the camisole, revealing high, firm breasts with small, stiffening nipples. Putting the jacket back on, she buttoned it, leaving a pale canyon of flesh down the middle of her torso, breasts rising up on either side like rounded mesas.

"Magnificent," murmured Jasmine, eyes locked with Martine's. "But now try the dress."

Martine glided into the next room. While they watched, she let her skirt drop slowly to the floor. Then she bent over to remove the boots from their box, and Jude glimpsed in the grid of shadows cast by the blinds smooth black-silk bikini briefs, a garter belt, and black-stockinged legs in high-heeled pumps.

Martine kicked off her shoes and drew on the boots, which had spike heels and rose up above her knees. After letting the black knit dress fall down over her admirable lingerie, she walked toward Jude and Jasmine, a slit up the front of the ankle-length skirt displaying and then concealing the high black boots and dark-stockinged thighs.

Jude realized that Jasmine was now watching her. Evidently, the next move in this game was up to her, but she didn't know what it was supposed to be. Martine still hadn't looked her way. She continued to gaze at Jasmine. She seemed afraid. Jasmine had been exercising some sort of dressage on her, and on Jude—spurring their desire, then reining it in. Should she leave? Jude wondered. Were Martine and Jasmine lovers? If so, what did Jasmine want Jude's role to be? What did Martine want? She recalled Jasmine's attitude toward the apricot tarts in Frankfurt. Was Martine the dessert du jour that one savored without touching? Jude was a guest wandering in this foreign land. She wanted to do the appropriate thing, but what was it?

"Where did you buy them?" Jude finally asked.

There was a long silence.

"It is not important," murmured Martine, finally looking at Jude, irritated.

Jasmine sighed like a teacher with a slow pupil.

Jude recalled that she was an orphan raised by wolves. Her family coat-of-arms read: "When in doubt, get the hell out." She struggled up from her chrome-and-leather reclining chair.

"I'd better get going," said Jude, pulling on her Levi's jacket. "Miles to go before I sleep and all that."

Jasmine smiled, perhaps challenged by Jude's seeming indifference. Maybe she imagined that Jude was finally learning to play. But all Jude really knew how to do when faced with a situation that smacked of sadism was to flee, as her forebears had. One day, maybe she'd stick around to explore her own capacity for the dark, but at the moment all she wanted was a cheeseburger.

As the Métro clattered toward Porte des Lilas, Jude contemplated the concept of lovemaking as blood sport. Anna and she had approached it as a mystic rite. They had ascended from this vale of tears for hours at a time. The stimulation of the hunt, or spiritual transfiguration—which was its proper goal?

At the far end of the car, Jude heard a man singing an interesting jazz version of "Desperado" in a Georgia accent, accompanied by a guitar and harmonica. Leaning forward, she saw that the ponytailed young man wore a Stetson and cowboy boots. His harmonica was fastened to a frame around his neck so that he could alternate between it and his voice. As he strolled up the aisle collecting change, she handed him some centimes. The car pulled into a station and the door hissed open.

"Have un bon weekend, y'all," he called to the passengers as he stepped onto the platform. Noticing Jude's silver toe guards, he pointed to them, then gave her a thumbs-up signal. Two southern cowboys riding the Paris range. Jude smiled at him as the door slid shut and the car whisked her out of his life, presumably forever.

Getting out at Porte des Lilas, Jude walked west until she came to a Burger King disguised as a bistro. Inside, she ordered a Whopper with cheese, fries, and a Coke, sop to her sudden homesickness. When the man behind the counter handed her the tray, he said, "Bon appetit, madame!"

As she munched her greasy fries under the awning along the pavement, Jude pictured Martine in her camisole, flesh riddled with goose bumps, eyes riveted on Jasmine's. What had that been all about, anyway? Martine had been trying to please Jasmine, who was her boss and maybe her lover. Jude had been trying to keep her job and be a polite guest. But what had Jasmine been doing? She appeared to be teasing Jude—or testing her. Did she want to help Jude and Martine in their grief or merely manipulate them for her own inscrutable purposes? Or was it all a friendly romp, intended to welcome the new kid to the neighborhood? She realized she was bowling out of her league with these complicated women.

Back in Montmartre, Jude went into her neighborhood patisserie to buy herself a reward for the completion of walk number four.

"I would like a tart," she told the man behind the counter in French, rhyming *tarte* with *rat* and clearing her throat in the middle to indicate the *r*. She'd been practicing this alone in her apartment and felt she'd finally mastered it.

"*Une quoi?*" asked the man, looking at her as though she were a litter box that needed cleaning.

"*Une tarte,*" she repeated, drawing back the corners of her mouth as though playing an oboe and exaggerating the gurgle.

"*Ah,*" he said, "*une tarte?*"

To Jude, this sounded identical to what she'd just said. "*Oui, une tarte.*"

"*Mais, bien sûr. Une tarte.*" His *r* was the growl of a puppy at play. "What kind of tart?"

"*Poire,*" she growled back.

"*Poire,*" he corrected.

She had wanted a tart, not a language lesson. "*S'il vous plaît,*" she said, accepting defeat.

Exhausted, Jude dragged herself up the six spiral flights of steps to her apartment. Throwing open the glass doors, she gasped the fresh air, free of exhaust fumes that high up. It was starting to rain. A sullen black cloud was almost obscuring the Eiffel Tower.

As she placed her pear tart on a plate and took a fork from the drawer, Jude decided to watch "*La Classe*" on television. Every evening, a schoolroom of famous French comics did send-ups of everything their fellow citizens held sacred. Jude plopped down on the couch and switched on the TV with the remote control. A comedian dressed as a matador was sitting on a stool, playing a guitar and singing a mournful ballad. The refrain was, "My bull is dead./I killed him this afternoon./Now I'm alone and, oh, so blue."

Another comedian appeared, dressed in the ruffled skirt and busty peasant top of a female flamenco dancer. He began to clack his heels and castinets with dignified restraint, giving the matador smoldering over-the-shoulder glances. Gradually, both sped up, trying to outdo each other, until they were in a frenzy over the dead bull, the matador strumming frantically and the dancer whirling around the stage like a clattering Valkyrie. The teacher and the class were in hysterics.

Nuking the program with her remote control, Jude sat there holding her empty plate and realizing that that afternoon at the office, Jasmine and Martine had spread out an entire smorgasbord of sensual delights to lure her back from the graveside. But she had departed without even sampling the finger foods. She was like a starving dog who snapped at every hand that offered her food. She had been very rude, and she probably owed Jasmine an apology.

Reaching over to the end table, she picked up Martine's book. Its white paper cover bore the title *Le Coeur Sauvage* in dark red letters. Flipping it open, she reread Martine's mystifying inscription: "With the hope of one day exploring the secret passages and chambers between us that remain to be revealed."

Jude decided to invite her to lunch. Martine was beautiful and intelligent. Jude admired her wardrobe and her physique. Although they'd gotten off to a bad start, it sounded as though the interest might still be mutual. They were both in mourning. If they could just get out from under Jasmine's surveillance, maybe they could help each other rejoin the ranks of the living.

As the phone purred, Jude remembered it was Saturday night. If Martine answered, it would mean that she was as alone and lonely as Jude.

"Allo?" She sounded drunk or drugged or sleepy.

"Hi. It's Jude. From the office."

"Oui?" She sounded deeply uninterested.

"Uh, I wondered if you'd like to have lunch with me tomorrow."

There was a long silence. Jude could hear some voices in the background. But if Martine was entertaining, would she have answered the phone?

"Pourquoi pas."

"Great. When and where?"

She suggested a brasserie called Le Vrai Paris near her apartment south of the Luxembourg Gardens at about one o'clock.

"I'll look forward to it," said Jude.

"Et moi, aussi. A très bientôt."

Her voice had warmed up as the conversation progressed, and by the end she had sounded downright pleased. Jude sat back in her chair, smiling thoughtfully. Lightning had begun to lash the monuments of Paris, and thunder was rumbling in the Bois de Vincennes. God moving furniture, Molly used to say. Jude felt happy for the first time in months. She would cook Martine nice meals and serve them on the table by the window, with the lights of Paris flickering below. She would cheer Martine up, help her feel alive and attractive again. And Martine could do the same for her.

JUDE SAT IN LE VRAI PARIS watching people come and go. Martine was an hour and a half late. Jude had spilled kir on her white jeans, and her hair was kinking as last night's rain evaporated in the hot afternoon sun. She went to the bathroom and struggled hopelessly with her unwanted curls. Then she phoned Martine for the third time. But there was still no answer.

In an upstairs room, accordion renditions of French dance-hall tunes were pouring out the open windows into the street. After each number, people stamped and cheered, making Le Vrai Paris sound like a happening kind of place. But Jude had been there long enough to hear the songs recycle a couple of times and to realize that it was a tape.

Returning to her table, Jude ordered another kir from the burly barman and watched the TV above his head. A matador in Nîmes was plunging his sword into a bull's neck. The snorting bull sank slowly to his knees in the swirling Midi dust. An instant replay in slow motion showed the pass with the muleta that preceded the coup de grâce. Contorting his torso and gesturing with his arms, the commentator critiqued the angle of the matador's shoulder in relation to the horns.

The bull, soaked in blood and coated with flies, was dragged from the arena on a sledge pulled by horses. Then the next bull entered, outraged and defiant, immediately charging the waving red cape. Jude was rooting for the bull. But he was the only one in France not to realize that he didn't have a prayer. The picador leaned over from his horse to plunge his spike between the bull's shoulder blades. He worked the lance up and down like a lover.

Jude realized that not only was her hair a disaster; she'd also been stood up. But why? Paying her bill, she wandered out onto the sidewalk in her stained jeans. An American in a DON'T FOLLOW ME. I'M LOST T-shirt collared Jude to ask the way to Notre Dame, which he pronounced like the American university.

Too distressed to deal with directions, she said, *"Je ne sais pas. Je suis Cherokee."*

He looked at her and crossed the street.

Jude went into a *tabac* on the next block and bought some Marlboro Lights. Leaning in a doorway in the sun, she lit a cigarette and wondered what to do next, taking the pulse of her emotions like a doctor by a deathbed. She didn't want to go back to her empty apartment. She hadn't felt its emptiness until last night, when she had allowed herself to imagine Martine there with her. Her overzealous imagination had deformed the reality of the situation. Martine was evidently like an overcooked meringue—luscious on the surface but hard as nails beneath.

Eventually, Jude noticed half a dozen coral roses thrust through a metal ring that hung from the stone molding beside the door. Above it was a plaque that read: *"Ici est tombé le 22 juillet 1943 Pierre Beaulieu, combattant pour la liberation de la France."* The stone all around the doorway was chipped and pocked. A Resistance fighter had been gunned down where Jude was now standing. She imagined him dropping to his knees, riddled like a Gruyère with bullet holes, pavement and doorway splattered with blood. . . .

Jude stamped out her cigarette. Since her calf muscles were aching badly from yesterday's crosstown trek, she couldn't undertake another. She decided to head home. Maybe stop off at a movie or phone Simon at his house on the Cape.

Wandering across the Seine toward Montmartre, she passed the spot where the grand master of the Knights Templars had been burned at the stake after seven years of torture. She followed the route alongside the river taken by the rubbish carts that had carried Marie Antoinette and Louis XVI to the guillotine. Then she crossed the Place de la Concorde, where the vast crowds had assembled to witness the beheadings.

Strolling along the boulevard past the Madeleine, she arrived at a café with a scarlet awning: L'Élite. Pausing, she studied the customers sitting in bow-backed basket chairs at small, round tables along the pavement. They were surrounded by ancient killing fields. Yet there they sat, laughing and eating and drinking, smoking and flirting. Like Jasmine, they seemed to know how to enjoy life, despite its legacy of horror and its inevitable end.

All of a sudden, Jude understood that she had been drawn to Paris in the first place in order to learn this art. But she'd been fighting it off, like a bat who prefers the dark to the light of day, insisting on doing everything in ways that were already familiar to her. Martine was right to have stood her up today. Jude was the neophyte here. It was up to her to figure out how to fit in. It wasn't necessary that she understand what was going on in order to participate.

As she turned the corner toward l'Opéra, Jude caught a glimpse of the white domes of Sacré Coeur floating above the dance halls and leather shops of Pigalle, shimmering in the afternoon heat like a mirage of the Holy City in a desert.

THE NEXT MORNING, JUDE was awakened from a dreamless sleep by a cavalry of cooing pigeons charging across her skylight, their claws skittering down the glass. Daylight was pouring through her doors. Getting up, she threw them open. Swallows swooped and dipped in the fresh morning air all around her. The pewter rooftops of Paris, washed clean by a rainstorm in the night, were gleaming silver, rows of red-tile chimney flues stretching across them like crenellated ruins. Five women in flowing robes stood behind curly iron grilles at open doors on different floors across the courtyard, conjuring the golden ball of sun in the east like a coven of pagan priestesses.

CHAPTER

17

JUDE WAS LYING NAKED on her living-room carpet in the sunlight streaming through the open doors. Propped up on cushions like a pasha, she was smoking a miniature Dutch cigar and drinking a foamy glass of Michelob. The phone rang, destroying her fantasy that she was on the beach at Cannes, about to be discovered by a major Hollywood director.

It was Jasmine, inviting her to a strip club that night. Jude hesitated. A burlesque show seemed a questionable way for alleged feminists to spend their time. Once in New York with Sandy and Simon, she'd watched the disheartening bumping and grinding of gaunt heroin addicts, and she'd left feeling embarrassed and full of pity.

"You must come," said Jasmine. "It will amuse you."

Since she was Jude's boss and both these sentences sounded like commands, Jude accepted. Besides, her current self-imposed assignment was simply to observe the Parisians at play, like a kitten learning from a cat how to lap milk. Out her doors, she could see two pigeons balancing on either end of a television antenna, carefully seesawing up and down. Even the pigeons here knew how to have fun.

JUDE WAS STANDING on the sidewalk when Jasmine's Citroën pulled up. Jasmine climbed out, resplendent in electric-blue silk that molded her admirable curves. Behind her exited a man with lots of silver hair and piercing umber eyes.

"Jude, allow me to present my husband, Philippe," said Jasmine. "Philippe, this is my remarkable young American editor."

"Enchanted," he said, holding Jude's outstretched hand in both of his. He was wearing a cream-colored double-breasted suit, with a tie and pocket handkerchief in shades of salmon and indigo.

Jude was speechless at the appearance of yet another character from Jasmine's personal soap opera. It was getting as complicated as "The Young and the Restless." Martine and Robert had also just gotten out, both greeting her with all the enthusiasm of a woman discovering a run in her stockings. Martine was wearing a size six Hell's Angels outfit—black leather miniskirt, net stockings and ankle boots with spike heels, and a miniature motorcycle jacket with so many snaps and zippers that a team of assistants would have been required to fasten them. Behind her stood a fair, slight young man with the face of an aging altar boy. His name turned out to be Jean-Claude.

Since Martine had never mentioned their date manqué at Le Vrai Paris, Jude finally asked her one day at the office what had happened. She pursed her lips, shrugged, and said that she had run into a friend. They had stopped for an espresso. Then she found it was too late to meet Jude, so she went to visit someone else. She neither apologized nor suggested a new rendezvous, so Jude let it drop. If this was how things were done in Paris, she was now pledged to accept it without complaint. Though she couldn't help but wonder if Martine had planned to stand her up from the start to teach Jude not to trifle with her. But Jude hadn't been trifling. In fact, she'd been trying not to trifle. But maybe Martine liked trifling and had become alarmed when Jude wanted lunch as well.

Nevertheless, Martine and Jude now comprised an efficient team for dealing with nuns, headmistresses, and teachers regarding their student-poetry anthology. Although as they strolled across town to these meetings, Jude couldn't help but notice that she was the only woman in Paris whose arm Martine didn't take as she walked. She had decided that Martine wasn't avoiding and insulting her in order to provoke *le désir*. She simply didn't like her.

A tuxedoed maître d', whose brilliantined hair was combed straight back off his forehead like a mobster's, escorted them into a room with crimson wallpaper and carpeting. Jasmine alternated them boy-girl in the velvet seats circling the round table. Many others in the room appeared to be Japanese and American businessmen, with and without dates or spouses.

The waiter brought champagne in a silver ice bucket and filled their glasses as they discussed Jude's tan. Evidently, she wasn't the first in Paris to discover the delights of sunbathing on her living-room floor. There was already a ground fog of cigarette smoke in the room, so they passed out Gitanes and lit up all around.

The stage was flanked by statues of two giant female nudes. As the glittery sequined curtain between them rose, a dozen women appeared in Beefeater hats, garter belts and net stockings, black boots, and nothing else. They marched and saluted mechanically to the tune of "Rule Britannia."

From the corner of her eye, Jude watched Jasmine, with Philippe on one side and Robert on the other, as respectable-appearing as any fashionable Parisian matron. For all Jude knew, she was one. She looked amused as the women goose-stepped on their lovely long legs. Jude felt something, but it wasn't amusement. For one thing, she wasn't sure she enjoyed seeing other women objectified like this for the delectation of a roomful of horny businessmen.

The Beefeaters exited and the curtain came down. When it lifted again, clouds of orange smoke were rising like mist from the stage floor. A woman in a plumed Athena helmet with narrow gold tubing around her neck and waist performed what looked like a sacred temple dance, her feet planted and knees flexed. Her upraised arms were squared at the elbows, and her torso was swaying and whipping, like a cypress in a hurricane, to jarring, clashing sitar music.

The lights went out and when they came back on, there were four dancers in Athena helmets. Each time the stage darkened and the lights returned, there would be a different number of Athenas lashing and writhing in the swirling mists in their plumed gold helmets. Just as they began to seem interchangeable and eternal—the female essence embodied—the curtain came down.

As it rose again, a bald man in camouflage gear with a huge beer belly marched out. He had rifles, machine guns, and pistols slung all over him. In an Indiana accent, he told a very boring battle story that involved artillery fire and fighter planes, which he imitated with his mouth. Everyone in the audience began to laugh uproariously at all this testosterone run amuck, startled by the contrast to the intoxicating sensuality of the Athenas.

The curtain came crashing down like a guillotine blade on this overweight warrior. A few moments later, it lifted and a woman with a dark ponytail cascading over her shoulders was slithering like a python around a large, red, neon hoop, to the accompaniment of eerie harp music. Her pale body was bathed in swirling rainbow spotlights: long legs, finely muscled arms and shoulders, full, tight breasts, a narrow waist tapering into firm, boyish buttocks. The pulsing lights were making dizzy hallucinogenic patterns across her flesh as she wound in and out around the hoop and slowly splayed her perfect naked limbs in shifting geometric patterns across its disk.

Jude watched, transfixed. This performance was probably politically reprehensible, but it was the most erotic thing she'd ever seen. For the first time since her months of watching Anna decay in her hospital bed, Jude's palms turned clammy. Here was a woman who could teach her how to enjoy life again.

Through the shifting veils of cigarette smoke, Jude spotted Martine's hand caressing Robert's forearm. Her eyes shifted ever so slightly in Jude's direction.

Just as the entire audience was beginning to hyperventilate, the ponytailed woman vanished. And then the other women emerged from backstage, floating one by one across the stage on a conveyor belt. They wore headdresses with tresses of golden coins, and they were striking the poses of flexing Greek athletes.

To the strains of a Chopin funeral march, six of the women strode off the belt and through a poison-green neon tube out front, which was bent into the shape of a large coffin. Forming three couples along the front lip of the stage, they performed stylized love play, never touching, hands molding and caressing the air beside a breast or a buttock, hips slowly swiveling closer and closer but never meeting.

The conveyor belt continued to carry the other posing and preening women across the stage in front of the backdrop. And the neon coffin stood there changing colors, trying to assert its dominance. But it was unable to distract the audience's attention from the magnificent women out front as three of them knelt before the dark pubic triangles of their partners. Each slid an arm between her partner's legs to clasp a buttock and draw her closer. And the lights faded discreetly away.

These young women were not sad sacks like the New York

burlesque queens, Jude reflected. They were temple prostitutes, pet-
ulant goddesses, self-sufficient and aloof and unattainable. Like master
electricians, they themselves were in charge of the currents of desire
sweeping the audience, stepping up the voltage, then pulling the plug.
The lesser mortals in the audience were here to worship their beauty,
which was immortal, even if the bearers of it were not. And like true
goddesses, they were mocking the audience for giving them the homage they demanded, an homage that would never be rewarded with
anything more than amused scorn. This was a form of femininity Jude
knew nothing about, one that must have prevailed when the race
began, in the days when the female body was revered as the source
of all life.

She smiled, at last getting the sobering joke. The women were
now back on stage in their Beefeater hats. The eyes of the woman
with the dark ponytail seemed to meet Jude's for a moment, before
looking right through her. They fell into formation and tottered off-
stage like windup toys to a cacophony of "Stars and Stripes Forever,"
"God Save the Queen," and "The Marseillaise." This was their final
comment on male martiality, in pathetic bumbling contrast to their
own insolent, indolent sensuality.

Jude's group drifted up the sidewalk toward the Champs Elysées.
Jasmine was holding Martine's arm, and Philippe was stroking John-
Claude's nearly beardless cheek as he whispered something in his ear.
Robert ambled alongside Jude in silence, like a tamed bear. They sat
down around a table on the terrace of a restaurant with a front-row
view of the Arc de Triomphe. Philippe ordered more champagne and
a platter of shellfish, which arrived packed in enough crushed ice to
chill a corpse. They employed implements worthy of the Inquisition
to drag the only half-dead sea creatures from their elaborate armor.

As the others discussed the performance, Jude looked back and
forth between Jasmine and Martine. Not only were they elegant and

seductive; they were smart. Jude now understood that Paris was perhaps the last outpost of matriarchy on earth. Everywhere she went—
the Luxembourg Gardens, the Tuileries, the facade of the Hôtel de
Ville, the Place de la Concorde, l'Opéra—there were statues of
women, naked and robed, queens and goddesses, priestesses and saints.
She thought about the Provençal courts of love in the twelfth century,
where flocks of pages had devoted themselves to the grandes dames
sans merci, and the Paris salons in the eighteenth and nineteenth centuries, which had destroyed careers and toppled governments. Where
else in the world were women both outspokenly female and completely in charge?

Tuning into the conversation, Jude discovered that Robert was
accusing the strip club of nationalizing eroticism, domesticating it for
consumption by tourists, like the Hawaiian hula.

"And why not?" demanded Jean-Claude, who Jude had learned
was a medical doctor just back from a famine relief project in the sub-
Sahara. "If others are exotic to us, why should we resent being exotic
to them? We are not, after all, the master race."

The point, according to Robert, was that the tourists weren't
being exposed to the real thing. Tonight's show was like an innoculation against some deadly local plague. The tourists were being given
a minute dose of eroticism in a safe setting by indifferent professionals.
Afterward, they could go home to Iowa thinking they'd experienced
all that Paris had to offer.

Jude was discouraged to realize that she'd missed the point. But
she was still wrapped in a haze of eroticism, and it didn't feel like a
minute dose. In fact, she couldn't seem to get rid of the image of that
woman with the ponytail splaying her perfect limbs across the neon
disk in the swirls of rainbow light.

Martine had been studying Robert speculatively. Finally, she said,
"Yet you are not the first to have said this, Robert. Barthes calls such

shows 'the theater of fear.' He says we display the evils of the flesh in order to exorcise them. Not for tourists, for ourselves. We wish to convert the female body into a household property/propriety.''

Robert looked caught out, struggling with himself over whether it was less cool to have plagiarized from Barthes or to claim never to have read him.

''I believe some of us did not find the performance unmoving,'' said Jasmine. ''Me, for example. And you, Jude. What did you think of it?''

Jude struggled to translate her complicated thoughts into her rudimentary French. She ended up saying only that she had found it magnificent. She realized that she had no personality in French. No wonder Martine always acted so bored by her. She was, and who could blame her?

Philippe observed with a smile that French men were good sports to put up with their peevish female consorts, who demanded deference as their right yet mocked their men's little foibles mercilessly.

Jean-Claude remarked sotto voce that perhaps that was why he saw so many men in wedding bands at Le Trap. Jude gathered Le Trap was a gay bar, and she was beginning to suspect from the way they looked at each other that Philippe and Jean-Claude were lovers.

Jasmine said that unfortunately the cunning little foibles of the male were going to destroy life on this earth, or at least render it unbearable.

With regard to male foibles, they began discussing whether passion and domestic affection were incompatible. They reminded Jude of dragonflies, alighting on a topic for a shimmering moment, then darting off to the next, so inexplicably that she could scarcely keep up, much less join in.

''Within a marriage,'' Philippe was saying with a wry smile at Jasmine, ''lovemaking becomes an expectation and a duty. Once it is no longer a free choice, it ceases by definition to be passion. And you can be sure—"

"So you are saying," interrupted Martine, "that duty is rational and passion—"

"Yet a slave might passionately—" interjected Robert.

The three were now holding forth all at once, none listening to the others. In addition, they were speaking so fast and using so much slang that Jude couldn't follow anyone. So she looked back and forth among them in the din. Philippe was Domestic Affection for Jasmine, but who was Passion? All perhaps. Probably not Jean-Claude, but who knew?

Someone's knee was pressing hers under the table. Whether deliberately or not, she couldn't tell. She glanced at all the faces but uncovered no clues. She had no idea who was what to whom here.

Suddenly, Robert was yelling at Martine that whatever controlled restricted. And whatever restricted was tyrannical. And whatever was tyrannical was fascist. That language itself controlled and restricted and therefore was fascist.

"*Ah non,*" murmured Martine. "To label is to unmask, and to unmask is to alter."

"To label is to limit," insisted Robert, "and to limit is to destroy."

Jude suddenly had the feeling neither cared all that much about labels. They had just picked opposite sides for the pleasure of the clash.

"*Donc,* if language is fascist," replied Martine, blowing smoke in Robert's face, "you, who talk so much and all the time, are fascist, *n'est-ce pas?*"

Robert erupted into hysteria. Jude realized she was witnessing the famous *furia francese,* the French fury, the sudden frenzy that used to possess French warriors on medieval battlefields, terrifying their more laid-back Italian opponents. But Martine merely gazed at him with ennui. She would definitely have flunked Charm Class.

Behind Martine's auburn head loomed the Arc de Triomphe. Thirty years before, the aunts and mothers and grandmothers of Jude's companions at this table, their men having been slaughtered on battlefields to the north, had silently lined this sidewalk to watch the precision rape of their beautiful city. The Nazis had tromped through the Arc de Triomphe with their rifles and jeeps and tanks and horses in a shimmering haze of dust and exhaust fumes. But then, with small daily humiliations, the women of Paris had made the Germans regret that they'd ever left Prussia.

Jean-Claude had somehow managed to capture the floor, regardless of his faint voice. He was summarizing Stendhal's discourse on the different types of love and the different stages of each type. His comments had something or other to do with the relevance or irrelevance of labels in the face of a lived passion.

As Mark Twain once said about Americans and the weather, Parisians talked endlessly about *l'amour*. But did anyone ever do anything about it? Jude wondered. Because it was this relentless intercourse of ideas within their quicksilver minds that seemed to give them pleasure. And after all, only people with a profound aversion to bodily fluids could have invented the bidet.

As though reading Jude's mind, Jasmine explained to her, "Everyone in Paris talks about love, but only two hundred people actually do it."

"The rest of us prefer to watch," said Philippe.

Everyone laughed.

The others decided to go to some private club to continue their discussions. Jude declined because she was exhausted from concentrating so hard to follow the conversation. They offered to drive her home, but she said she'd walk. When Jasmine looked alarmed for her,

Jude promised to take a taxi. But she felt so safe in Paris after New York City that she foolishly went on foot wherever and whenever she pleased. The others embraced her and made kind comments about enjoying the evening.

As she walked down the Champs Elysées toward the granite obelisk at the Place de la Concorde, Jude felt happy. Her apprenticeship was apparently working. The group she'd just left seemed to like her—apart from Martine, who didn't like anyone. And Jude liked them. In fact, Jasmine and she were well on their way to a serious friendship. Her games had sometimes seemed malign to Jude in the beginning, but she now understood that they were the French version of a Maori welcome, intended to help newcomers feel included. And Jude finally did. There was no longer any doubt in her mind that the French were the world's most charming and interesting citizens, from whom she had a great deal to learn.

Jude's senses were wide open from taking in the beauty of the women onstage. And from the sonorous flow of her companions' voices, punctuated by Robert's *furia francese* like a trumpet solo in a Baroque concerto. From the prickly feeling of champagne bubbles on her tongue, the salty taste of the creatures fresh from the sea, and the swirling scent of tobacco mixed with perfume.

So stimulated did she feel, with the warm night breeze off the Seine ruffling her hair like caressing fingers, that she walked to a women's club in the Marais called Marrakesh, which someone at work had once mentioned. The outside room contained a massive oak bar surrounded with high stools. As she perched on one and sipped a kir royale, she could see an inner room for dancing, which was ringed with low tables and easy chairs. Sinuously bulging marble columns held up the ceiling.

Jude moved from the bar to the dance area and watched the room fill up with women, mostly young and casually dressed, although there were a few fifties-style butches in men's suits and ties and a couple of transvestites in blond wigs, black leather shorts, and garters. There were also a few men lurking in the shadows, watching the women with the glassy eyes of prizefighters who'd just been knocked out but hadn't yet fallen.

Eventually, the dancing began, to music that was a blend of New Age synthesizer and classical guitar, along with what sounded like a team of crickets shoveling coal in the background. It didn't seem to matter if you had a partner, because most dancers were just swaying to the music and watching themselves in the mirrored walls as the strobe lights pulsed.

As Jude began to notice that she had drunk too much, the ponytailed woman from the strip club walked in with several other women. Jude scarcely recognized her with her clothes on, but the ponytail was unmistakable, with large spit curls below her ears, like Hasidic *peisim*. She wore cordovan boots to her knees, tight, faded jeans, and a white T-shirt with some kind of bone carving on a cord around her neck. She and her friends sat down two tables away and ordered drinks. As they lit Marlboros, Jude strained to hear their voices in the breaks between the songs. But all she could catch was a word with a lot of vowel sounds, which appeared to be the ponytailed woman's name: *o-eee-ah*.

After a while, one woman seized Ponytail by the hand and dragged her to the dance floor. The two writhed back and forth in perfect synchronicity, eyes closed, only inches between them. Jude wondered why she knew how to dance so well. Maybe she was a ballet dancer waiting for a break, supporting herself by her job at the club. But she wasn't gaunt enough for ballet.

Jude sat there watching admiringly as women of all sizes and shapes and colorings laughed and talked and danced and flirted. Sometime soon, once she had completed her novitiate in the convent of pleasure, she hoped to be able to join them. After several songs, Ponytail and her group got up and left. Shortly afterward, Jude did, too.

That night, Jude dreamed about the woman. She was just standing there in her jeans and T-shirt, looking at Jude and saying nothing. Then she was gone. Jude woke up, bemused not to see her standing by the bed, so real had she seemed. She looked at the clock. It was only 3 A.M., so she turned over and went back to sleep.

A few evenings later, as she walked home from work, Jude decided to celebrate the return of her appetite for life with an early dinner at a restaurant near the Porte St. Denis, to which her *Guide to Gay Paree* had given three stars. Apart from the huge fourteenth-century stone portals from an early town wall that blocked traffic in the middle of the street, the area was dominated by luggage stores. A prostitute stood on the corner near the alley where the restaurant was located.

Inside were only a dozen tables. Grouped around two were several more prostitutes, one dressed in leather. Another wore a feather boa and a black ribbon around her neck with a crucifix dangling from it. They were chatting and laughing and eating a lot, apparently stoking up for a long night. A couple of other women in street clothes sat with them. One, Jude realized, had long black hair sweeping down from a ponytail atop her head.

Jude sat down. A pleasant woman in black leather trousers came over to describe the menu and take her order. As she sipped Sancerre and tried not to stare at the group in the corner, she wondered whether her own features were becoming as familiar to Ponytail as hers were to Jude—the long, narrow nose with a slight hook where it joined her brow, pale eyes that narrowed when she smiled, high cheekbones that were flushed even without makeup. Jude kept hearing that word with all the vowels—*o-eee-ah*.

When the hookers got up to hit the streets, so did the woman. As she reached the door, Jude heard someone call her Olivia. So at least that mystery was solved. Before exiting, Olivia turned her head Jude's way. As their glances met, Jude thought she noticed a flicker of recognition in the woman's blue-gray eyes. And then she was gone.

Having lost her appetite at the sight of those eyes, Jude rearranged the food on her plate, hiding a duck leg under a lettuce leaf. She tried to figure out if Olivia was a prostitute. But the others were in costume, whereas she was wearing just jeans and a T-shirt. But maybe that was her costume.

After paying her bill, Jude walked down the alley and turned into the street. Although she looked around for Olivia or her friends, she saw no one familiar. For a moment, she considered going back to the strip club alone, just so she could watch Olivia again. But it was too early, and Jude wasn't dressed up enough. Besides, she couldn't see going by herself and being pointed out by the waiters as a lecherous lesbian, and she didn't know any men to invite as her cover.

In any case, she could feel an obscure longing starting to stir, and she didn't want to encourage it. She planned to give herself a break and take life lightly from here on out.

For the next couple of weeks, she read through a stack of English and American novels and wrote reports for Jasmine. She sent postcards to two dozen friends in New York. She planned visits to publishers in London, Amsterdam, and Copenhagen. She organized a new address book, eliminating many Tennessee and New York City entries and adding some French ones. She also pruned her large pile of business cards, many of which she had no memory of receiving, though no doubt she'd promised letters and lunch dates. Life was like a motel, and your job was just to change the sheets and get ready for the next guest.

THE MORNING OF HER FLIGHT to London, in the taxi north through Paris toward the *périphérique*, Jude was startled to find herself scrutinizing each woman they passed for a black ponytail. Even though she hadn't seen Olivia since that night at the restaurant, she realized that she had been halfway looking for her whenever she had turned a corner. Not to be able to do this for three days in London seemed suddenly unbearable. As they approached Charles de Gaulle airport, her agitation increased.

At the departure terminal, marchers were circling, wearing signs saying that Air France mechanics were on strike. Relieved, Jude told the driver to take her back to Montmartre. As they retraced their route, Jude took a good, long look at her cacophony of emotions, and she was appalled. Was she becoming infatuated with a woman she'd never even met?

That night, she dreamed again of Olivia standing before her in blue jeans. Slowly, she smiled. Then she said in French, "If you love me, you must tell me so. Do not be afraid, because I love you, too."

Waking up the next morning, Jude recalled the dream. It was the first time she'd ever dreamed in French. What did it mean? Or was it just her solitary brain slipping its gears? It would be absurd to say that she loved a woman she'd seen only three times from across the room. Besides, she was finished with all that nonsense. She didn't want anything heavy anymore—just some good times and some tenderness.

LATE THAT NIGHT, JUDE sat at a corner table in Marrakesh, smoking a Dunhill and nursing a kir. The thrill of spending her evenings watching the Eiffel Tower until its spotlights switched off at midnight was beginning to pale. She wanted someone to watch it with her. It was past time to emerge from her widowhood. So far, she had exchanged *le regard* with three candidates, but none had clicked.

Stubbing out her cigarette, she glanced toward the doorway. And there was Olivia, alone, dressed in black stretch pants and a baggy blue sweater. As she searched the room for her friends, her face fell slightly. She sat down at a table and ordered a drink, which she sipped slowly, trying to make it last.

Once the dance floor was full, Olivia got up and moved to the center, nodding to a couple of women who called her name as she passed. Wrapping her arms around herself, she closed her eyes and swayed to the music like an underwater plant. As the tempo picked up, she ran her palms down her torso and writhed gently to the beat.

Jude considered and dismissed the idea of going out on the floor and dancing beside her. The Hully Gully she had mastered. Her Boogaloo was passable. But this New Age trance dancing escaped her.

After studying the dancers for a long time, though, Jude got up and began to copy their languid movements. Slowly, she wended her way through the swaying, twisting torsos until she reached Olivia.

Dancing beside her, Jude pretended not to notice her. Finally, she allowed herself to glance at Olivia, only to find Olivia watching her with sulky blue eyes. They held each other's gaze for nearly a minute. Then Olivia nodded once, slowly, as though coming to a decision.

They swiveled around to face each other. Eyes locked, they moved back and forth in unison, a pair of mating cobras. Then, with a contemptuous toss of her ponytail, Olivia walked away.

Mortified, Jude kept dancing, not knowing what else to do. Olivia reached across her table for her cigarettes and headed for the door. At the door, she stopped and looked back, right at Jude. For a moment, Jude couldn't breathe. Olivia inclined her head toward the street ever so slightly. Jude smiled, trying to stay calm.

Olivia smiled back. Jude started through the crowd, moving toward the door. Olivia smiled more broadly, turned, and headed for the street. Jude followed, heart pounding like Japanese drums.

Outside, Jude stood alone in the dark street, with Olivia nowhere in sight, feeling ridiculous. But then she spotted her under a streetlight at the corner, looking back for Jude.

As Jude walked toward her, Olivia turned down the cross street. When Jude reached the corner, she turned, too. And there was Olivia, waiting halfway down the block. Jude began to trot to catch up, but Olivia started running, too, ponytail lashing side to side. The full moon was bathing the narrow streets in yellow, and the buildings were casting dark shadows as though at high noon. Olivia darted in and out of the shadows like a ghost.

Running out of breath, Jude slowed down, suspecting that she was making a fool of herself by chasing this young woman through the nighttime streets of Paris. In any case, Olivia had outrun her, and now she didn't see her. She glanced up and down the street several times, but Olivia didn't reappear.

Dejected, Jude walked toward the river to find a taxi back to Montmartre. It was probably just as well.

But there by the Pont Marie stood Olivia, hand resting on the stone parapet, watching for Jude, smiling in the moonlight.

Jude caught up with her. Before she could think what to say, Olivia put an index finger to her lips and shook her head. Then she reached out and stroked Jude's flushed cheek with her fingertips. Jude shuddered. Their lips touched and Olivia's tongue caressed Jude's lower lip.

As Jude gasped, Olivia whirled around and dashed across the

bridge to Ile St. Louis, the silver Seine licking the pilings below. Turning down a tree-lined street, she paused in the doorway of a building with a huge, stone lion head above the lintel. Punching in the night code, she shoved open the heavy maroon door and entered. When Jude reached the door, breathless, it slammed shut in her face.

Bewildered, Jude crossed the street, leaned against the wall above the Seine, and looked up. It was very late, and the entire building was dark. No lights went on anywhere to indicate the location of Olivia's apartment. She began to wonder whether she'd hallucinated the whole thing. A firm grasp on reality had never been her forte. She touched the spot on her lip that Olivia's tongue had caressed. It was still tingling.

The Métro had stopped running, but Jude walked until she found a taxi by the Louvre. The driver, a woman, was wearing a gold silk shirt with lots of Afghan jewelry at her ears, throat, and wrists. She turned to look at Jude in the light from the dashboard. Her skin was olive, eyes and eyebrows dark, teeth a flashing white as she told Jude that the street she'd named didn't exist.

Jude insisted it did.

She snarled that she'd been driving a taxi in Paris for five years and had never heard of it. Therefore, it didn't exist.

"But your singer Dalida lived at the end of it. She committed suicide there."

"This is impossible," she said. "How could Dalida have committed suicide on a street that doesn't exist?"

"Look, I live there myself. I know it exists. Please just look it up in your street guide."

She shrugged in the shadows. "Why should I look it up when I already know it isn't there?"

Jude was beginning to wonder whether she had passed through a black hole when she entered Marrakesh that night and had emerged in a parallel universe. Finally, she persuaded the woman to drive her to Place des Abbesses.

After crossing the square by the Bateau Lavoir, Jude was delighted to discover that her street was still there, dozing in the moonlight. She concluded that her driver was probably accustomed to driving men who gave her large tips just for the pleasure of her profile during the ride. She hadn't wanted to waste her time on a woman, especially one who was bewitched.

CHAPTER

1 8

JUDE BEGAN TO LIVE FOR THE DARK. Leaving the office at the end of each day, she returned to her apartment, where she bathed, dressed, made herself up, and sat at her glass doors, welcoming the descent of dusk over the city. She passed the time trying to figure out which building among the thousands spread out below her was Olivia's. She could see Notre Dame. Olivia's street was somewhere to the east. Once it was late enough, she went to Marrakesh and sat at her corner table. But for the first two weeks, Olivia failed to arrive.

On the fifteenth night, Jude walked from Marrakesh to Ile St. Louis along the route they had followed in the moonlight. As a half-moon rose over her shoulder, she stood by the wall above the Seine, gazing at Olivia's darkened building. Every few minutes, a *bateau mouche* went by, illuminating her in its spotlights. But she outlasted them all, leaning against the wall until the moon peaked and began its trajectory toward dawn.

Then she hiked back to Montmartre, slept for a few hours, and went to the office, where a lunchtime debate was underway over whether the loss of Alsace-Lorraine during the Franco-Prussian War had incited French enthusiasm for a colonial empire. As she listened in the shifting ribbons of light from the pierced dome overhead, she found herself nodding off, chin on her chest.

When she awoke, she slipped from her chair and out the door. Back in her office, she grabbed the phone directory. But then she realized that she didn't know Olivia's last name. So she dialed the strip club and asked the woman who answered for Olivia's home number, explaining that she was a friend from America. The woman asked if Jude was her friend, why didn't she know her phone number? As Jude sat in silence trying to think of an answer to this trick question, the woman hung up.

Each night for the next week, Jude stood by the wall above the Seine as the moon waned, waiting for Olivia to come home. But she never did. On the seventh night, it finally occurred to her that maybe Olivia stayed at a lover's. Was one of the women she'd seen her with at the bar or the restaurant her lover? For a moment, she was limp with jealousy. Steadying herself with one hand against the rough stone wall, she tried to talk herself out of this, since she'd never even officially met the woman.

Looking down at the water, which was paved with sheets of silver light reflected from the streetlamps, she tried to figure out why she always ended up on the banks of some river—the Holston, the Hudson, now the Seine—obsessed with someone who had vanished.

The next night, she wandered through the alleys around the strip club with a handful of lavender tulips, in the company of several other flower-clutching perverts, searching for the stage entrance. After an hour stationed before a steel door they had decided was the one, they watched it swing open. As they held their collective breath, a white poodle pranced out, lifted his leg, and peed against the wall. His owner, who looked like Peter Lorre, leered at them from the doorway.

Finally, Jude decided to go back to the club as a paying customer so that she could at least see Olivia onstage again. Shopkeepers sometimes called her monsieur because of her jeans and boots and androgynous build and because many French men were themselves androgynous. So Jude went to the hairdresser's and got a spiky punk clip. Experimenting with her eyeliner pencil, she gave herself a fairly convincing five o'clock shadow. She bound her breasts with an elastic bandage. Then she put on a black T-shirt, a black silk blazer, jeans, and her cowboy boots. Just to check, she stopped in at several shops en route to the club. And for once she was pleased when everyone called her monsieur.

As she strode down the street toward the Champs Elysées, she began to swagger. It was restful no longer to be groped by men's eyes and to relax the radar that informed her of who was in her vicinity and whether anything about him suggested potential rapine. As she passed a woman in a miniskirt, she glanced at her legs, then ran her eyes up her torso to her face. The woman's eyes met hers for a moment, then flicked disdainfully away like a tango dancer's chin. Jude grinned. No wonder men didn't want to give up their erotic prerogatives.

The maître d' at the club also called her monsieur as he seated her on a banquette near the stage and brought her a scotch. But when the Beefeaters came out, Olivia wasn't among them. As Jude disconsolately watched the other women strut their stuff, she wondered whether Olivia had gone on holiday. Where would such a gorgeous creature go? Greece, Jude concluded, so that she could cavort with all the other goddesses.

MARTINE AND JUDE WERE SITTING in the conference room reviewing submissions for their anthology. Jude was struggling to say that although the New York City students had sometimes lacked a grasp of English grammar and syntax, their poems had displayed energy and invention. Whereas the French students had so far written poems that were technically perfect but full of images and insights as uninspired as if they'd been selected from a prix fixe menu. She was finding it difficult to be tactful in a language not her own. At some point, she realized that she'd been calling Martine *tu*.

Martine replied that they needed to draw up some guidelines for the teachers to assist them in encouraging their students to depart from the norms. She had a look of distaste on her face, and she was pointedly calling Jude *vous*. Jude realized that no one in all of Paris called her *tu* yet. She was still their resident Other. Yet she was intrigued to have inspired such contempt in Martine. She didn't understand why. Trying to make friends with her had been like trying to cozy up to a barracuda. Writing it off as a lost cause, Jude retreated to *vous* with an apologetic shrug.

The door opened and Jasmine walked in. She sat down at the round table and began questioning them about how many pages the anthology would be and when they expected to have a finished manuscript.

As Jasmine's and Martine's voices droned on and on, Jude found herself picturing Olivia naked beside her on cushions on her living-room carpet, sunbathing in the rays coming through the open door while swallows swooped past outside.

"Jude, can you tell us some more about this?" asked Jasmine.

Jude started. "I'm sorry. I missed the question."

"I was telling Martine about your handbook for the schools," said Jasmine, studying her quizzically.

"Oh, right." She began to describe how the handbook could help local schools set up their own programs and contests.

The door opened again, and Giselle arrived, clutching half a dozen lunchtime baguettes like a bat boy. She was followed by Cecile, Robert, and several others.

While everyone else passed food and poured mineral water, Jasmine turned to Jude and said, "This new short haircut of yours is most attractive."

"Thank you."

"Is something the matter? You do not seem well."

"I'm just tired. I was up late last night."

"Ah," said Jasmine, eying her speculatively, "you have a new friend to keep you awake?"

"No, not really." Keeping secrets was no way to fuel an evolving friendship, but Jude had no wish to tell Jasmine about Olivia or about her return alone to the strip club. Besides, what was there to tell?

"What a pity," said Jasmine with a smile. "But in that case, perhaps you would care to come to my house in Picardy this weekend? You could get some rest. I would provide you with a large curtained bedstead from the seventeenth century. Covered with fresh linen sheets and a fluffy duvet of goose down. I would fill your room with flowers from my garden and feed you pâté and champagne on a tray by your bedside."

As she talked, she was giving Jude *le regard*. Jude felt herself sinking into Jasmine's invitation as though into the goose-down duvet. But she wasn't sure exactly what she was being invited to do. Jasmine made even the most normal everyday activity sound like an episode from the *Kama Sutra*. Although she couldn't have said for sure if that was Jasmine's intent. In any case, she realized that she didn't want to leave Paris and the possibility of finally finding Olivia. All she really wanted out of life anymore was to be lying in Olivia's embrace on Ile St. Louis.

"It sounds marvelous, and I'd love to some other time," Jude replied. "But I'm afraid I'm tied up this weekend."

Jasmine studied her, trying to divine from her face what her engagement might be, but Jude struggled to offer no clues.

After Jasmine departed, Jude excused herself from the lunchtime seminar and returned to her office. Plopping down in her desk chair, she gazed up at the map of Paris spread across her wall. The red meanderings of her routes across Paris were beginning to weave themselves into a tangled web. Picking up the phone, she dialed Simon in New York.

It was early morning there, and Simon sounded bleary when he asked, "So how's New York's most tenacious graveyard lover today?"

"It's no laughing matter, Simon. I've done it again."

"Fallen in love?"

"I think so."

"Bloody hell, Jude, I can't leave you alone for a minute."

"Mock me all you like, Simon, but tell me what to do."

"Relax. Enjoy it. You're in Paris. Tell me about her."

"She has dark hair and blue eyes."

"Surprise, surprise. What does she do for work?"

"She's a dancer."

"Ballet?"

"Not exactly."

"Ballroom?"

"Burlesque."

Simon chuckled. "I see. Rough trade. So you've finally decided to take a walk on the wild side?"

"I didn't decide anything. These matters aren't rational."

"Not for you, that's for sure. Her age?"

"Young."

"Does she love you back, or is it another of your lost causes?"

"I have no idea."

"You haven't asked her?"

"I've never talked to her. I saw her dancing in a strip show. And then I saw her again at a lesbian bar. And she kissed me once on the bridge to Ile St. Louis when I was following her home."

There was a long silence. "Good Lord, Jude," said Simon. "Get a grip."

"I'm trying to. That's why I called you."

"Track her down. Get to know her. Immerse yourself in her annoying little habits. Watch her pick her teeth and chew her nails."

"I can't find her. I'm not even sure I didn't make her up."

"Jude, why don't you ask Jasmine for some time off? Come back to New York and see your friends. I think you must be alone too much over there. This sounds serious."

"Maybe I will, but first I have to find her," she said vaguely. "If she exists."

"Okay, but if you don't find her, don't panic. Call me up. I'll fly right over. Don't brood alone in stoic silence. And remember that there are many people here across the sea who adore and admire you."

After thanking Simon and bidding him good-bye, Jude hung up and left the office, marching directly to Ile St. Louis, determined to stage a showdown. Since it was afternoon, the night code was off at Olivia's building. So she buzzed herself in and crossed the mosaic courtyard. She climbed the iron staircases and walked the hallways on all five floors, studying each door. But she could detect no clue as to which might be Olivia's.

Verging on despair, Jude returned to the street and began to wander across the bridge toward Montmartre. People kept passing her, carrying their baguettes for dinner, waving and stroking them like giant phalluses. Pausing at the spot where Olivia had kissed her, if she had, Jude gazed down into the water as it swirled around the pilings. She wondered if she was losing her mind—or had already lost it.

Glancing back at Olivia's building, Jude saw her coming out the huge maroon door. She was dressed in a short skirt and a tank top, and she was carrying some books. Spinning around, Jude dashed back across the bridge. As Olivia crossed to the Left Bank and wound through the crowded side streets, Jude ran after her, trying to catch up. But Olivia was moving as fast as the shadow of a bird in flight.

Finally, in the doorway of an ancient Sorbonne lecture hall, Olivia paused and turned. Looking right at Jude, she smiled. Then she vanished into the building.

Enchanted finally to see her again, Jude decided that she had to speak with her. She couldn't sleep, and when she did, she dreamed of Olivia. Her clothes were hanging off her, limp as sails in the Sargasso Sea. She couldn't concentrate enough to read manuscripts for work. She couldn't follow the discussions at editorial meetings. Maybe if she could talk with Olivia, the spell would be broken. Maybe she'd tell Jude she was a disgusting pervert. Anything would be better than the past several weeks of living with her absence.

As Jude sat at a café sipping a *crème* and watching the door to the lecture hall, she mapped out their life together. Evidently, Olivia was a student when she wasn't busy driving other people crazy. Jude would support her while she finished school, so she could quit the club. She had seemed so vulnerable up there all alone on the stage in the swirling rainbow spotlights. Jude wanted to protect her. She didn't like the idea of all those revolting businessmen watching her dance naked. Besides, it was dangerous. What if one of them started stalking her?

They could have an apartment in Paris for Olivia and another in New York for Jude. Maybe Olivia would like Tennessee. They could build the cabin overlooking the Smokies that she'd planned with Molly and Anna. Olivia was young, so hopefully she didn't have a lot of baggage like husbands and children. Jude looked forward to being with someone long enough to grow thoroughly bored by her. She'd enjoy watching her hair go gray and her face crease and her perfect breasts sag. They'd take care of each other when they got sick, and Olivia could hold Jude's hand as she died, as Jude had Anna's.

Other students were exiting from the lecture hall, but not Olivia. Jude paid her bill and walked to the doorway. She asked a young man what the course was, and he said Anglo-American Philosophy. So Olivia was apparently a philosopher. She'd have a professor's schedule, and they'd be able to travel in the summers and at Christmas.

Olivia still hadn't emerged. Jude walked into the musty old building and poked her head into the lecture hall. It was empty, apart from some wads of paper on the floor by the lectern. Olivia must have slipped out a side door. Jude was getting irritated. Here she was planning their future, yet Olivia seemed to be evading her. The only way out of this endless nightmare seemed to be to plunge into it ever more deeply. So she returned to Ile St. Louis and stationed herself by the wall in front of Olivia's building. She would stay there for as long as it took to confront her.

For a while, she studied the wrought-iron grilles across all the windows on Olivia's block, wondering whether the bars on French jails were similarly patterned. Like snowflakes, no two designs were the same. Then she started thinking about this stale analogy. Presumably, no one had ever seen every snowflake that ever existed, so how did scientists know that no two were alike? She was willing to bet that some were.

She looked down and discovered a woman with a green Michelin guide standing before her. The woman asked in a French even worse than her own if she knew which building had been Camille Claudel's studio.

"I'm sorry," said Jude. "I don't actually know."

"I think it must be the one with the maroon door," she mused. "She went insane in there after Rodin rejected her."

"No kidding," said Jude uneasily.

After a couple of hours, her feet were hurting. She sank down to the sidewalk and sat with her back against the stone wall, studying the downspout on Olivia's building. It was gilded to resemble fish scales. At the bottom was the fish's head, with round eyes and a gaping mouth through which the rainwater from the roof would pour. Jude wondered why Olivia lived in such a fancy building. Maybe her father was a diplomat who didn't realize how his daughter earned her pocket money when he was on assignment abroad. Or maybe she was an au pair for a wealthy family by day and a goddess by night.

As the sunset faded into dusk, Jude began to feel chilled, so she buttoned the jacket of her cotton suit and turned up the collar. Then she reviewed her entire history with Olivia, from the moment she first saw her in the neon hoop at the strip club until she vanished that afternoon into the Sorbonne lecture hall: the glances they'd exchanged, her dreams, their dance at the Marrakesh, their flight to Ile St. Louis through the moonlight, Olivia's fingertips caressing her cheek on the Pont Marie, her tongue stroking Jude's lip.

At last, Jude unraveled what had happened: Olivia had revealed herself just enough for Jude to become intrigued. Then she had removed herself so that Jude would feel the lack of her. This lack was now generating Jude's crazed desire, just as Martine had insisted during that first lunch at the office.

A woman began to scream through an open window on the top floor of Olivia's building. The hair on the back of Jude's neck bristled.

Someone was being attacked. Could it be Olivia? As the screaming increased in intensity, Jude jumped up, trying desperately to think what the Paris equivalent of 911 might be. She glanced up and down the street for someone who would know what to do, but the sidewalks were empty.

But then the screams modulated into a strangulated tattoo of *oui*'s. "Oui . . . oui . . . oui . . . oui . . ." Like the fifth little piggy who couldn't find her way home. Only *l'amour* this time, Jude realized, not *la mort*. She sank back down on the sidewalk.

"*Merde, ça me fait mal . . . ,*" moaned the woman from on high. "*Plus. Plus. Plus. Oui, plus . . .*"

Jude leaned her head against the wall and closed her eyes while the woman gasped, "In the name of God, don't stop yet, you filthy swine!"

Jude drew a deep breath and tried to think about something else—the number of *bateaux mouches* that must pass that spot every day, for example. As she performed calculations in her head, the woman emitted several high-pitched shrieks, like a buzzard swooping down on a field mouse. Then she fell silent. Jude was pretty sure she'd faked her orgasm. Her own armpits were clammy.

Extending her trousered legs across the sidewalk, Jude studied her high-fashion cowboy boots with the filigreed silver toe guards. What was she doing sprawled on a Parisian sidewalk outside the apartment of an exotic dancer she'd never met? She had finally fallen into the pit. She now understood the fascination for Molly and Sandy and Anna of people who made them suffer. It was the promise of extinguishing your lonely separate self in a power you had defined as greater than your own. It was graveyard love run amok.

Her head began to nod. Finally, her chin fell forward and settled on her chest. As darkness descended, she slept.

When she next opened her eyes, the sky overhead was black,

with a faint golden tint from the city lights. And Olivia was passing beneath the stone lion head and into her building, ponytail swishing. But Jude was so shocked by the sight of her that she couldn't utter a sound.

Crazed with frustration, she continued lying against the wall and tried to figure out what to do next. The night code would be on, so she couldn't get in. Besides, she still didn't know which apartment was Olivia's. She noticed a round object on the sidewalk beside her hand. Reaching out, she touched it gingerly. It was smooth. Examining it with her fingertips, she realized that it was an apple. When she picked it up and studied it in the glow from the streetlight at the corner, she discovered that it was a perfect yellow Delicious apple. She sniffed it. What if it was poisoned like Snow White's? She thought for a moment about the rolling golden balls on her smashed Atalanta flask.

But Olivia must have left it, she realized with a stab of delight. She must have squatted down and placed it gently on the sidewalk right beside Jude's hand. Suddenly overcome with hunger and thirst, she bit into it. The juice ran all over her hand and down her chin.

As she lay there devouring the apple, a light came on behind the sheer curtains over the glass doors of a third-floor apartment facing the river. While Jude watched, the silhouette of a naked woman appeared behind the curtains. Slowly, she began to undulate to unheard music, hands caressing breasts and thighs, ponytail swirling and lashing.

The roaring of ocean breakers filled Jude's head, and a softness fluttered through her veins like the velvet wings of a thousand moths in flight. Tossing the apple core over the wall behind her, Jude wrapped her arms across her chest, gasping and shivering. The light went off and the building plunged back into darkness.

Jude lay motionless against the wall all night long, awake but stunned. A stray cat stopped by to rub up against her, purring. It smelled of spoiled fish. Occasional solitary cars passed by on hissing tires on the Right Bank. The silver Seine slapped the stone banks below like laundry snapping on a line.

As birds began to chirp in the chestnuts along the river, Jude managed to stand up in the rosy dawn and go in search of coffee. Finding a café in the Latin Quarter that was just opening, she went to the ladies' room to wash her face and hands. Looking into the mirror, she studied her own eyes, mahogany like her father's, dim with fatigue and ringed with mauve. This couldn't go on. Soon the police would arrive to cart her off to an asylum, as they had Camille Claudel. Maybe she'd better take Simon's advice and return to New York.

But after drinking a *crème* and eating a *tartine* at a table in the café, she began to feel calmer. So she bought a couple more buttered tartines and returned with them to Ile St. Louis, where she leaned in Olivia's doorway. Eventually, a man with a briefcase emerged, and she ducked through the door before it sucked shut. She climbed the iron staircase to the third floor. Calculating that the window where the silhouette had appeared was in the far-right apartment, Jude rang the bell, palms clammy, heart pounding.

Since no one came, she rang again.

Olivia opened the door on the third ring, wearing a royal purple chenille robe, ponytail undone so that her dark hair hung around her face like a mantilla. *"Oui?"* she said in a sleepy voice.

"I've brought you some breakfast." Jude pointed at the bag of *tartines.* "We need to talk."

"Excuse me, madame, but who are you?"

Shaken, Jude said, "You know who I am, Olivia. My name's Jude."

"No, I do not know who you are." She began to close the door.

"But you've seen me a dozen times," pleaded Jude.

"I am sorry, but you are mistaken."

Jude looked at her helplessly. "Well then, please excuse me, madame." She turned to leave, completely numb in order to stave off an eventual collapse into utter chagrin and despair.

"All right. Yes," she said as Jude started down the hallway. "Now I remember you. What is it that you want?"

Jude turned back around, hopeful, relieved, and angry. "What do *you* want?"

"But I want nothing," she said with a laugh. "I am not the one who is ringing a stranger's doorbell at dawn."

Jude stared at her, beginning to dislike her, afraid that it would show and that Olivia would slam the door in her face. "Then why did you want me to follow you home that night from Marrakesh? Why did you kiss me on the Pont Marie? Why did you leave me that apple last night? Why did you dance for me at your window?"

"I do not know what you are talking about. This is very annoying."

"You're damn right it is!" Jude hurled the *tartines* at her feet and stomped off down the corridor.

"Wait," she called.

Jude stopped, head lowered like a charging bull's, not turning around. It was awful, but at least it was over. She didn't even want to think about the price she would have to pay for the folly of letting herself love another phantom.

"Come back."

Jude hesitated, consulting her family motto: "When in doubt, get the hell out."

"*S'il te plaît,*" she said softly.

This was the first person in Paris to call Jude *tu*. If only she had understood that the pathway to endearment here was paved with anger, she could have saved herself a lot of fake smiles. She returned to

Olivia, who was looking down at the bag of *tartines*. Bending over, Jude picked it up and handed it to her.

"Come in," she said, standing aside.

They went down a narrow hallway to a small kitchen that reeked of stale cat food. Jude sat down at a square wooden table. They exchanged remarks concerning the strength of the coffee and Jude's wish for milk and sugar.

"So what's this all about?" Jude finally asked.

"What is what all about?" Olivia poured coffee and hot milk into two giant cups and placed the tattered *tartines* on a plate.

"Well, your performance last night by the window, for example?"

"It is whatever you care to make of it."

Jude finally understood why so many French men had gone on the Crusades—to get away from French women.

"So it was totally without meaning for you?"

"A brief fantasy between two people is pleasant, is it not?"

Jude looked at her while the words *brief* and *fantasy* sank in. But she was relieved finally to have Olivia take some responsibility for this disaster. "Perhaps," she said. "If both people know it's a fantasy. If not, someone gets hurt."

"People must watch out for their own hearts in these matters, no?"

"In America, when we love someone, we try to watch out for their hearts as well as our own."

For a long moment, Olivia studied Jude, as though she were an exotic pinned butterfly struggling not to succumb to formaldehyde. "So you have come to love me," she said matter-of-factly, as though discussing the price of mangoes in the market.

"Oh, I suppose so. Yes." Jude finally understood the rules of this game: The one who fell in love first lost. She had lost. She'd

thought that the goal was to get past the game to the substance. She
now realized that the game was all there was. There was nothing
beyond. Only a new game with someone else. Paris was one vast
Disneyland of Desire.

"But this is madness. You do not even know me."

"If I knew you, I might not even like you." Jude laughed loudly,
like the lunatic she had become.

Olivia's eyes widened with alarm. She put her hand on Jude's
forearm and scooted closer, apparently intrigued by the danger Jude
suddenly represented. Jude smiled at this notion of herself as a bar-
barian at the gate. Olivia didn't realize that she was dealing with
Cherry Ames, rural nurse, helper and healer.

"You know, Olivia," said Jude in a low voice, "you could have
made my life much easier if you'd just left me alone."

Olivia blinked, looking baffled. "But why would I wish to make
your life easy?"

"I suppose that is awfully unsophisticated of me."

"But now you are being sarcastic, and this is not nice." Standing
up, she took Jude's hand and pulled her to her feet. She led her down
the hallway and into a bedroom strewn with clothing. Glass doors
with sheer curtains looked out on the Seine.

Settling herself against her pillows, she held out her arms so that
her robe parted. "Come," she said softly.

Jude stood there looking at Olivia's perfect body in the morning
sun, at her shiny, dark hair fanned out across the white pillow.
"Shouldn't we get to know each other a bit first?"

"What better way?" asked Olivia, smiling.

Jude reminded herself of her pledge not to insist on always doing
things her own way. Olivia was offering her magnificent body, but
Jude wanted to chat first about her inner child? With trembling hands,
she removed her own clothing as gracefully as possible and then joined

Olivia on the bed, feeling like one of the Seven Dwarfs approaching Snow White.

AS SLIM FINGERS OF SUNSHINE pushed their way through the folds of the curtains across Olivia's glass doors, she gazed into Jude's eyes and moaned and murmured at all the appropriate spots. And she employed her various body parts with an admirable technical efficiency. But Jude quickly understood that her heart and her soul were elsewhere, well protected by her exquisitely arranged flesh. For Olivia, this was just another performance.

Lying there afterward with Olivia's shiny hair swirled across her chest like a swath of new-mown hay, Jude reminded herself that the first time with a new person was sometimes awkward. It took a while to learn someone else's rhythms. Besides, Olivia was young. Jude would enjoy awakening her to the pleasures available through the sense of touch, as Anna had her. There was no rush.

"And now you must go so that I can sleep," Olivia said amiably. "Because I must work late tonight."

Jude looked down into her eyes, a bleary turquoise in the sunlight, with tiny translucent rings of butterscotch around the pupils, just like Molly's. "When can I come back?"

"But this is what you came for, is it not?" She seemed perplexed. "And now you have learned that it is no more remarkable with me than with anyone else."

"Well, I agree that it wasn't that exciting," said Jude. "But never mind. We can work on it."

Olivia propped herself up on one elbow to look at Jude, eyes amused and bemused. "Why would one wish to work on something that is meant to be play?"

"Well, to make it more satisfying for both of us."

"But I am satisfied," she said. "I see that you are not. *Mais ce n'est pas grave.* It is always disappointing, is it not, compared to what one dreams will be possible?''

Jude didn't agree. ''In any case, this isn't what I came for,'' she said, feeling she was swimming out of her depth. ''I came to tell you that I love you.''

''Oh, yes. I forgot. You believe that you love me.''

''No, I know that I love you.'' But as Simon had predicted, the better she knew Olivia, the less lovable she seemed.

''If one loves, one wishes to please the beloved, *n'est-ce pas?*'' Olivia asked, drawing on her skills as a philosophy student.

Jude could see this one coming. She braced herself.

''So my wish is that you will go away now and enjoy your life and remember that you passed a pleasant hour one summer morning on Ile St. Louis with a woman who found you ravishing in every way.''

This was the most charming brush-off Jude had ever heard of. Smiling doggedly, she stood up and began pulling on her underwear. ''I should never have come.''

Olivia pursed her lips and shrugged. *''Ce n'est rien.''*

To you it is nothing, thought Jude as she stepped into her trousers and pulled on her silk T-shirt. To me, it is everything. But that's not your problem.

Olivia got up and pulled on her robe. Jude shrugged on her suit jacket and followed her down the hallway.

''I am sorry if I have disappointed you,'' she murmured as Jude walked past her out the door. ''I meant only to please. But you must understand that you are not the first to have trailed me around Paris like a hungry ghost.''

As Jude passed under the stone lion head above the doorway and out into the street, she reflected that cats at play probably didn't know how their claws felt to mice. She walked out onto the Pont Marie and stared down into the Seine for a long time. She wondered whether to jump. She would not be the first to die for the love of a beautiful dancer—although she might be the first woman. Feminism was truly a wonderful thing. She decided not to jump. It would be just her luck to land in a *bateau mouche* full of Baptist Youth from Tennessee. Besides, Simon would never forgive her for such a lapse into cliché.

She spun around and headed south, dazed like the sole survivor of a plane crash. As she skirted the Luxembourg Gardens, she tried to figure out how to get through the rest of her life now that all pleasure and purpose had gone out of it yet again, like a leaky beach ball. Olivia was very skilled at her craft, tossing out the bait, jerking the line when Jude struck so that the hook would lodge firmly, and then reeling her in. But why? Did she enjoy watching another creature flopping and gasping on dry land, with no idea how to return to the water?

Heading south down the Avenue du Général Leclerc, Jude spotted the entrance to the Catacombs. The labyrinth of ancient stone quarries stretched beneath her feet for nearly two hundred miles. In the eighteenth century, 6 million skeletons from crowded Parisian cemeteries had been transferred down there for storage.

After paying her entry fee, Jude descended the winding stone steps to a dim, damp corridor well below the sewers and the Métro. A message carved into the stone lintel read: "Stop! This is the empire of death." Jude kept going.

The passageway within was lined on either side with bones, stacked so that the ball ends protruded to form a textured wall. At chest height ran a row of skulls, lined up as neatly as coconuts at a greengrocer's. Sometimes a pillar of skulls also ran vertically from ceiling to floor, forming crosses.

Jude strolled for what felt like miles down the shadowy gravel pathway with no one else around, water dripping from the ceiling. Here and there, barred side tunnels headed off into the blackness. This place had been the headquarters of the Resistance during World War II. In Roman times, early Christians had held services down here. Smugglers had stashed contraband and criminals had hidden out from prosecution.

Carved into a stone by a doorway, Jude spotted a verse from Lamartine that Anna had once recited as they crossed Central Park:

> *Into the ocean sinks the plaintive wave.*
> *Onto the winds, the fugitive leaf.*
> *Dawn fades into evening,*
> *And man into death.*

Just beyond were skeletons from the Innocents Cemetery, where the Huguenots fished out of the Seine had been buried. Jude stopped to contemplate the stained ivory femurs and tibias of her ancient cousins. But there was nothing so unusual about their plight. Every group had its victims and its executioners.

Glancing around to be sure she was unobserved, she climbed a gate and wedged her body between the top bar and the stone ceiling. Dropping to the ground on the other side, she stood there for a moment. Once she set out, she wouldn't be able to find her way back. She'd read about men who had wandered into these tunnels and been found as skeletons centuries later.

Steadying herself with her hands against the damp carved walls of rock, she scrambled in her cowboy boots up the rubble and set out down the side passage. She walked and walked, lighting her way with the tiny flashlight on her key ring, randomly choosing one fork or another at junctures, until she had lost all sense of direction. She remembered reading about a man who had gotten lost down here and stumbled across a room piled high with cat heads and no bodies. The restaurant in the street directly overhead served as its specialty an incomparable rabbit stew.

After what seemed like hours, short of breath and calves aching, she ran headlong into a wall. Feeling all around herself with her hands, she discovered that she was in a more or less round chamber, from which there was no exit except the narrow chute by which she had just arrived.

She cleared away enough stones to make room for herself on the floor. Then she plopped down and tried to figure out what she was doing pitching camp in the empire of death. But why not? Cruelty was the law of the land above her head. Love was the only antidote, yet its pursuit led merely to more pain. Life was a boxed canyon with nowhere left to turn.

Using her pocketbook for a pillow, she stretched out on the floor and wrapped her suit jacket around herself. Surrounded by six million skeletons of people who had already made their final voyage, she tried to imagine what it was going to be like to die. Anna could have told her. But if Anna were still alive, she wouldn't have known, and Jude wouldn't have been lost in the catacombs in the first place.

ANNA'S CHILDREN, HOME from their colleges because things were looking so bad, finally departed. They had been sitting beside Anna's bed in the Roosevelt all evening, wearing jeans and rugby shirts and acting sullen.

Then one of Anna's students arrived with a flute and a music stand to play "Jesu, Joy of Man's Desiring" for Anna. The off-pitch warble filled the room like a robin being tortured. Jude watched Anna struggle to raise her splinted hands to cover her ears. Jude gently maneuvered the student out the door.

In the silence that followed, Jude took one of Anna's hands in hers. Undoing the tape, she unwound the gauze until the splint beneath it fell to the floor. Then she moved to the other side of the bed and did the same thing to the other hand. She watched Anna's fingers as they stirred to life and flexed slightly. She usually undid Anna's hands until a nurse noticed and made her bind them up again. Anna liked to move her fingers, and Jude liked to feel their warmth when she held them and to rub them with lotion, and to clip and file the nails.

She picked up the cup of crushed Popsicle and held out a spoonful to Anna just as Anna smacked her lips to signal that she wanted some. The moments of almost uncanny closeness that Jude had begun to experience with her had become more and more frequent, until now they constituted a steady state. By some instinct, Jude knew when and where to scratch her, when she wanted a Popsicle. They had finally achieved that perfect harmony possible for a couple only when one of them is in a coma.

Jude was surprised to hear herself begin to enunciate in a low, even voice a poem Anna used to recite when they walked along through the swirling apple blossoms in Central Park:

> They are not long, the weeping and the laughter,
> Love and desire and hate:
> I think they have no portion in us after
> We pass the gate.
> They are not long, the days of wine and roses.
> Out of a misty dream
> Our path emerges for a little while, then closes,
> Within a dream.

Afterward, Jude sat very still, timing her breathing to Anna's, as she used to during lovemaking. And in a quiet, matter-of-fact voice, she found herself saying, ''All right, I guess it's time now, Anna? Time for you to go. Go ahead. It's all right. I can take care of myself. Jim can take care of himself. Your students can take care of themselves. Your children can take care of themselves. We're all fine. Just go. Don't be afraid. Everything is going to be all right." For several minutes, she repeated these phrases, understanding that Anna needed to let go of her now but that she needed Jude's help in order to do so. A sob caught in her throat as she chanted the necessary phrases like a litany.

But then she jumped up abruptly, as though attacked by a swarm of bees. And all of a sudden, she was absolutely furious. She didn't want to be in this dreary hospital room any longer, watching bouquets from Anna's students wilt and shrivel and be replaced, watching the body she had loved rot. She had been here for days. Weeks. Months. Other women her age were out dancing and singing and making love. Damn it, why couldn't Anna just go ahead and die and get it over with?

Striding to the far corner, Jude threw herself down in a lounge chair. She lay back and closed her eyes, breathing unevenly.

She looked around for Molly, but Molly had deserted her years ago. So she jumped on her horse and galloped alone along the beach, salt spray drenching her shirt, hooves pounding beneath her like pistons. She slid off the heaving horse by a dune and watched the turquoise waves arc and tumble, advancing and receding, crashing and hissing, leaving lips of foam flecked with shells like tiny broken teeth.

Jude opened her eyes and watched the white sheet over Anna's chest rise and fall time after time, the bellows that was stoking her flame.

And then she realized that the sheet was still. Getting up, she walked over to the bed. Anna wasn't breathing anymore. Jude reached down and took one of her hands in both her own and stared at her composed yellow face with disbelief.

Finally, she managed to whisper, "Godspeed, Anna."

Anna drew a deep, rattling breath, leaning forward, almost sitting up, vacant lapis eyes wide open, seeming to stare at something across the room. Then she exhaled, eyes fluttering shut, and sank back into her pillows.

Jude shuddered violently, as though Anna's soul had just passed right through her own body, the force of its transit carrying her along halfway to the brink of death.

Then Jude felt elation surge up from the pit of her stomach and spread throughout her body. And she was flooded with the sudden conviction that Anna had just cast aside her scab-pocked body like a withered husk and moved on.

Jude stood there holding Anna's hand for a long time as it began to cool and stiffen, unable to make the least effort to comprehend what had been there in her body, which Jude had known so well, that now was absent. And where it had gone.

JUDE TOUCHED THE FLOOR of hewn stone with her fingertips. It was pitch-black. There was no sound except for some water dripping from the ceiling and her own heartbeat pounding in her ears. She was in the empire of death, surrounded by those who knew the answers to these questions. She had come here like a homing pigeon. Once the 6 million skeletons surrounding her had all loved and suffered in the streets above her head. Now they were here below, neatly stacked domes and cylinders of calcium, finally at rest.

Jude realized that the only thing she wanted from life anymore was to leave it. It was a Saturday, and Monday was a holiday, so no one would miss her at work until Tuesday. She tried to figure out whether the ticket takers kept track of their visitors. If one fewer emerged at closing time, would they come looking for her? If so, she needed to be dead already. She had a bottle of aspirin in her pocketbook for menstrual cramps. A sorority sister at Vanderbilt had killed herself with a bottle of Bayer aspirin.

As she planned her death, she began to feel sleepy. Deciding that she wanted to be well rested and wide awake when she made her final journey, she let herself doze for one last time, lulled by the scurrying of rats' feet like soft whispers in the velvet darkness. The dreaded empire of death was actually a peaceful place. It was in the streets up above that pain roamed and horror reigned.

Jude's mother, Molly, Sandy, Anna, and her Tennessee grandparents were planting daylilies all over the ridge where Molly and she had planned to build their cabin. The green river valley below meandered toward the misty mountains. Mockingbirds were calling from the Wildwoods, which were decked out with redbud and dogwood blossoms in shades of pink and crimson and purple and white. Jude dug all afternoon in the steaming soil under a hot spring sun.

When they had finished, the others came over, hands caked with dirt.

Anna, whole and well again, said, "Jude, we are happy here, and we want you to be happy there."

The others nodded.

"How can I be happy apart from all of you?" asked Jude.

"You have to try," said Molly.

"It's too soon for you, Jude," said Sandy with his sweet smile.

"Virginians never kill themselves," said her grandmother.

"Darling," said her mother, "once you can love without needing an object, then you are love. And you will rush to unite with love and will leave behind that strange place, so beautiful but so marred by hate."

"We are always with you, Jude," said her grandfather, gesturing to the others. "A cloud of witnesses watching over you."

One by one, they dissolved, becoming the sunlight playing on the ripples in the river, and the breeze that rustled the blossoms in the Wildwoods, and the mist that drifted down the coves and veiled the high mountain peaks and knobs.

Jude couldn't remember where she was. Someplace as dark and silent as a tomb, except for a steady dripping sound. Then she remembered that she was supposed to kill herself now with her bottle of Bayer. But now it suddenly seemed like a really dumb idea.

She sat up. She had a headache. She had no idea whether it was day or night, or how long she'd slept. She stood up, feeling dizzy and steadying herself with a hand against the wall. She grabbed her handbag from the floor. The leather strap had been gnawed through. Clutching it, she headed down the tunnel in what she thought was the direction from which she'd come, flashing the light on her key chain now and then, trying to make the battery last. It seemed unlikely that she'd find her way back. Probably she'd wander beneath the streets of Paris until her strength gave out. Then she'd sit down somewhere and await death by starvation and ravening rats. If she was ever found, no one would know that it had been a suicide by default.

After what seemed like several hours of doomed, dogged plodding, she was astonished to detect a faint light ahead. Soon she heard the hollow echoing voice of a French child telling his mother that dead people were boring.

Reaching the main corridor, she climbed back over the grating, ignoring some startled German tourists. As she ascended the long, winding staircase to the street, she was pleased to find herself still alive. Death would come soon enough. One day, this baffling life of hers would simply peel away like a bad sunburn.

She walked out the door into the amber dusk. Asking the date of a barman at a café, she learned she'd been underground for two days. From the way he looked at her, or rather tried to avoid looking at her, she realized that she was a fright in her rumpled suit and chalk-caked boots.

Getting off the Métro at Place des Abbesses, she wandered down the shopping street, dazzled like Rip van Winkle by the foodstuffs spilling from the shops—grotesque spiny creatures from the sea, slabs of shimmering neon fish, pungent cheeses in all shapes and shades; pastries oozing fruit or dribbled with chocolate or smothered in whipped cream, chickens swiveling on spits, walls of wine for every occasion, exotic fruits and vegetables from the former colonies, which she squeezed and poked as though she knew what she was doing. Suddenly, she was ravenous.

Back at her apartment, she ran a bath, pouring in some raspberry bubble bath Jasmine had given her that she'd never opened. Shedding her disgusting clothes, she studied herself in the bathroom mirror. Although she admittedly looked better with her clothes on, she wasn't so bad without them. She subsided into the foam.

Dressed in fresh jeans and a T-shirt, she set a place for herself on the table by the glass doors, complete with a single coral rose in a bud vase, a cloth mat and napkin, and a candle in a holder. In the kitchen, she alternated firm white rounds of mozzarella with thick, juicy slices of tomato on a bed of crisp romaine, then sprinkled it all with chopped basil and olive oil. She dismembered the herbed chicken, still warm from the shop spit. And she cut up a crusty demibaguette, putting the pieces in a woven basket. She set all this on a wooden tray, along with a wineglass and a chilled bottle of Sancerre, and carried them to the table.

As she sipped the wine, cold and sharp on her stale tongue, she watched the huge orange sun sink behind the Bois de Boulogne, turning the Eiffel Tower and the Panthéon and the Arc de Triomphe and the Invalides into dark silhouettes on the horizon, fronted by the black arabesques of her wrought-iron railing. Dipping a piece of baguette into the olive oil and the juice from the tomato, she tried to figure out what had come over her two days earlier when she'd been prepared to give up all this splendor in order to die in a stone cell surrounded by rats and bones.

ON HER WAY TO WORK the next morning, Jude took her usual
detour across Ile St. Louis. Standing on the sidewalk in front of
Olivia's building, she was surprised to find that everything looked just
as it had for the past several weeks, oblivious to her transfiguration in
the Catacombs—the maroon door with the lion-head lintel, the elaborate wrought-iron grilles at the windows, the gilded fish-scale downspout, the stone wall above the Seine, the relentless *bateaux mouches*
plowing the silver waters, the thrushes singing in the chestnut trees
by the river, the tourists clutching their guidebooks and searching for
Camille Claudel's studio.

Jude allowed her eyes to shift to the third floor. The glass doors
in Olivia's bedroom were slightly parted. The sheer curtains were
stirring in the breeze, fluttering like a ghost. Olivia was probably right

there behind them, asleep in her bed after a late night at the strip
club.

Every cell in Jude's body screamed out for another try. The night
code would be off by now. She could enter the maroon door and
climb the steps, ring Olivia's buzzer. Who knew, maybe Olivia would
be pleased to see her.

Using all the strength at her disposal, Jude turned away from the
building and forced herself to plod, one step at a time, toward her
office.

As she left Olivia behind, dozing in the sunlight like a lazy lion-
ess, she sent her a mental apology. Olivia had engineered a light and
charming flirtation, designed to disarm Jude's absurd passion for her
in a fashion that would have left Jude's ego intact. If only she could
have accepted it in that spirit, both would have gone through the rest
of their lives harboring a sweet memory. Instead, Jude had insisted on
turning it into *Romeo and Juliet*, crawling into her earthen vault and
petitioning Death as her witness. As she trudged up the steps to her
office, she realized that she was nothing but an uptight Anglo-Saxon
asshole.

Giselle was sitting at her desk as Jude walked past. "*Bonjour*,
Jude," she called.

Jude backed up and paused in her doorway. "*Bonjour*, Giselle,"
she replied. "How are you?"

"Fine, thank you. How was your weekend?"

Jude smiled wryly. "Fine, thank you."

"Did you go away?"

"Sort of," said Jude.

Giselle looked at her quizzically, her copper-colored pre-
Raphaelite hair framing her face.

"Not really. I just did some tourist stuff. The Catacombs."

Giselle grimaced. "Not so nice, eh?"

"I kind of liked it," said Jude. "But I wouldn't want to live there."

Giselle laughed.

Jude spent the morning at her desk extracting, adapting, and translating a series of exercises from Anna's workbook designed to help writing students find their own voices. She and Martine had decided to give them to the schools in hopes of stimulating some more original poems. She remembered when she and Anna had invented the exercises. It had been a happy time, love and work merging seamlessly. The sad thing about happiness was that while you were in it, you believed it would last forever, so you appreciated it less than you might if you realized what a rare and precious gift it was.

Jude laid down her pen and leaned forward, resting her forehead on her desk. She had just understood where she had gone wrong with Olivia. She had been captivated by Olivia's physical beauty. She had woven a fantasy around that rather than trying to get past it to the beauty of Olivia's soul. No wonder Olivia had felt insulted and vengeful.

Jude reached out for the phone. Then she remembered that she still didn't know Olivia's last name or number. Grabbing a fresh sheet of paper, she picked up her pen and began a letter of explanation and regret to Olivia. But right in the middle of assuming the blame for everything that had gone on between them, she paused. How could anyone get past Olivia's physical beauty to her spiritual beauty when she wouldn't even sit down and talk to you like a normal person? Besides, Olivia flaunted her wretched body like a baker his cream cakes. Jude ripped up her letter and let the pieces flutter into the trash can like a flock of dying moths.

Realizing that lunch hour was already under way, Jude stood up and walked down the hallway to the conference room. Half a dozen of her coworkers were sitting beneath the shifting ribbons of sunlight, sipping Evian and nibbling roast chicken. Jude nodded to everyone, sat down, ripped off a hunk of baguette, and picked up a chicken leg.

Tuning into the debate du jour, she discovered that it concerned the question of whether the modern world was sexually repressed or sexually obsessed. Cecile's team was maintaining that capitalists had seized control of sexuality via repressive laws and religion in order to divert libido into production. Martine's team was insisting that, to the contrary, contemporary societies provoked preoccupation with sexuality to drug their citizens into submission—like giving alcohol to Native Americans or heroin to ghetto blacks to prevent them from rioting in the streets.

"But at least we are agreed, are we not," inquired Cecile, removing her large red-framed glasses to peer around the table like a NATO commander, "that any discourse on the deployment of sexuality must privilege the issue of power?"

Martine thought for a moment, inspected her teammates, then nodded reluctantly. She was a woman who hated agreement.

Jude had finally figured out that the route to conversational brilliance here was to take an assumption, such as that sex shows were sexy, and contradict it. So, launching her first plunge into the waters of lunchtime controversy, she suggested haltingly that Americans were often more interested in the pleasurable sensations their bodies experienced during lovemaking than in power manipulations.

Everyone looked at her as though she were a kindergarten pupil in a graduate seminar.

"But of course Americans do not understand eroticism," said Martine. "That is why it is impossible to be attracted to them. They are too obvious." She bit off the ball end of a chicken bone and sucked at the marrow. Most of the others nodded agreement.

So she hadn't been attracted to Jude? Or was this just another come-on? Suddenly, Jude was fed up with Martine's bad manners. She had lacked the courage to open herself up to Jude. She had insisted on remaining safe behind her kinky games. She had no idea who Jude really was. Yet just like Martine herself, Jude had earned her spurs in the rodeo of *l'amour*. She had won several purple hearts on the killing fields of love. She had crawled on her belly through the trenches of despair. She had faced down death in the foxholes of failed affection. She had stripped off her armor to parade unafraid on the battlements of passion. She deserved honor and respect from her fellow combatants, not contempt.

Jude felt her own recessive French genes rear up and triumph over Charm Class, yielding a sudden fit of *furia francese*. In her stumbling French, she told her colleagues that most ancient civilizations such as India and China and Persia had an *ars erotica* that instructed people, not in how to dominate each other, but in how to cooperate to achieve mutual pleasure. That these pleasures were carefully classified, not as forbidden or permitted, but in terms of quality, intensity, duration, and spiritual significance. That forcing children, as they themselves had been forced, to confess their sexual desires as "sins" and thus teaching them to despise their bodies, was a recent local disease. That they used their endless boring debates on sex and the sexes as foreplay, like debauchees trying to flog a response from senses blocked by misuse or shame. But that elsewhere in the world people possessed ample erotic energy as a natural endowment, which they could call on as they wished without a need for tiresome gimmicks. That some people approached sex as a normal human appetite, not as a sinister plot designed to deprive them of *la liberté*. That no self-respecting American would want to attract them in any case because they were too weird, and because they ate octopus and tripe. That the world was old and France was young. That the world was large and France was small. That life outside their sacred hexagon was not necessarily as they saw it. That they should stop deconstructing everyone and everything else and deconstruct themselves.

Remorselessly, Jude vented her months of frustration with Martine and Olivia, heaping one generalization atop another, just as she had watched them do all these weeks, until she had constructed a magnificent sand castle in thin air—one that began to crumble as she realized that she'd just lost her job. Normally, someone would have interrupted her diatribe and saved her from such total self-demolition, but they must have been so astonished to hear her speak, and so ferociously at that, that everyone had remained silent.

There was a long pause, during which everyone blinked several times. Then Cecile reached over to offer Jude a Gitane, an invitation to join her platoon. Jude declined it.

Giselle thrust her baguette at Jude like a fencing foil so she could rip off a hunk if she wanted—which she didn't.

Gazing at Jude with new interest, Martine murmured, *"Mais tu as bien parlé."*

But Jude didn't care if it turned Martine on to be treated as contemptuously as she treated everyone else. Drawing on Gary Cooper in *High Noon* for inspiration, she stood up, squared her shoulders, gazed out the window into the midday sun, and marched out the door in her silver-toed cowboy boots.

Upon reaching the street, Jude had no idea what to do next. All she really wanted was to return to Ile St. Louis. And to kneel before Olivia on the pavement and beg for another chance to behave more lightheartedly. Voluntarily giving up a graveyard love while the other person still walked the earth was unheard of. Yet Jude knew that was what she had to do now if she wanted to avoid another weekend in the Catacombs.

She dodged through the ambling crowds until she reached the Luxembourg Gardens, where she strolled along the paths of pale dirt, raked into patterns overnight, past orderly ranks of marigolds, geraniums, and artemesia that stood at attention like troops on parade. Past palms and oleanders and orange trees growing in square green boxes. Past ivy trained to hang in symmetrical swags. She came to a cage containing hundreds of espaliered fruit trees, twisted and bound like heretics on the rack into the shape of minorahs, with white paper bags over their nubile fruits.

Through some lime trees, planted in rows, their tops sheared into rectangles, Jude spotted a bronze lion with a dead ostrich at her feet. And just beyond was an eight-point buck with his doe and fawn, frozen as though by a stun gun while sniffing the morning air.

Jude descended some steps guarded by two lions that had been turned to stone in midstalk. And in the center of a lawn that was clipped as closely as a putting green, poised on a high stone catafalque, stood Artemis, a quiver of arrows on her back and a young stag leaping by her side. She, too, was frozen in midstride in her flowing tunic, so that she had to stand there eternally in the summer sun and winter winds. A dozen queens of France, several resembling transvestites in their elaborate robes and crowns, gazed down at Artemis from the encircling terrace through pitiless stone eyes.

As Jude studied poor captive Artemis, goddess of the wild, a voice inside herself demanded, "What is a wolf child like you doing in this petrified forest ruled by a mob of icy granite drag queens?"

Jude walked quickly to Jasmine's house. Eying the stone gods supporting her balcony on their shoulders, she rang. The Portuguese bonne ushered Jude into the living room, where she perched on an uncomfortable Louis XVI armchair, beneath the dyspeptic gaze of Jasmine's crusader forebears.

When Jasmine finally appeared, wearing a black-satin robe patterned with magenta Art Nouveau lilies, Jude told her she was going back to New York.

"But you have just arrived," Jasmine said with a perplexed laugh. "We have been trying to help you feel welcome here. You do, I hope?"

The bonne carried in a black lacquer tray on which sat a coffeepot and some cups and saucers.

"You've been very kind."

"Then why do you wish to leave?" She set the cups on the saucers.

"I'm not really much use to you, Jasmine. You haven't published any of the books I've recommended."

"*Mais, doucement,* Jude. This will happen. You are learning. Life is long. Do not be so impatient." She carefully pushed the plunger on the coffeepot to force the grounds to the bottom. Then she filled the cups and handed one to Jude.

"And socially I'm as inept as a banjo picker in a string quartet."

"I warned you when you arrived, did I not, that you needed to learn to play?"

"I'm afraid I'm a slow learner."

"Ah." Jasmine nodded and fell silent, studying her long, mauve nails. Looking up, she said, "Simon phoned. He says you have fallen in love with someone rather inappropriate."

"Jesus Christ," snapped Jude. "Who does he think he is—my father?"

"He was very concerned about you."

"He's one to talk," muttered Jude. "His bed is as crowded as Jones Beach on the Fourth of July."

"He was worried that you might try to . . . harm yourself. I tried to phone you all weekend. I admit that I became worried myself.''

Jude said nothing as Jasmine watched her through narrowed eyes.

''This inappropriate someone does not return your love?'' she asked gently.

Jude nodded no.

''But you know that we at the office are all very fond of you?''

''Not anymore,'' said Jude, recalling her lunchtime seizure of *furia francese.*

Jasmine smiled. ''Martine phoned just before you arrived. She said everyone was most impressed by what you said at lunch—not that they agree, *naturellement.*''

''*Naturellement pas.*''

''So why not stay? You will soon find another love. Martine, for example.''

Jude gave her a look. ''I don't want another love. I want Olivia. But she doesn't want me. So I have to go. If I stayed, it would be a constant battle not to bother her.''

''Why must you be so stubborn in love?'' asked Jasmine. ''People come and people go. Only desire remains.''

Jude did her imitation of an insouciant French shrug. ''Maybe it's because I'm an Aries. Look, Jasmine, the point is that this just isn't my scene. Love as a martial art doesn't do it for me.''

Jasmine smiled. ''Of course you must do as you think best,'' she said. ''But I, for one, do not wish to lose you. Our friendship is just beginning. And who knows where it will take us?'' She gazed into Jude's eyes.

''Jasmine, just give it a rest.''

''Well, I can see that you are determined to suffer,'' she said, annoyed at Jude's refusal to carry the beat.

"I have a gift for it. I've done it all my life."

As Jude left, they kissed several times on alternate cheeks, like chickens pecking grain. They assured each other that they would write and phone and meet at book fairs just as before, but Jude wondered whether they really would. Sometimes absence made the heart grow fonder, but often what was out of sight was out of mind.

At the travel agency down the street Jude asked a handsome young man in a navy-blue uniform for a plane ticket to New York.

"But of course, madame," he said with a dazzling smile. "A plane to New York. And when do you wish to go?"

"I can go anytime. When are the flights?" She had offered to stay until Jasmine could find her replacement, but Jasmine said she'd invented the job for Jude and wouldn't be looking for someone else. Martine could complete the poetry project alone.

"Ah, but madame, there are flights from Paris to New York constantly. You have only to decide when you wish to go, and I will give you a ticket. Eh, voilà! You will be in New York City!"

"Oh," said Jude, brightening at the prospect of immediate escape. Soon she'd be on Simon's deck on the Cape, watching the waves pound the sand. She could imagine his hilarity over her haunting by the wraith of Ile St. Louis. They would do what they'd done for each other so often—laugh the pain away. "In that case, I'd like to go tomorrow afternoon."

"So," he said with his charming smile, "madame would like to go from Paris to New York tomorrow afternoon?"

"Yes, exactly. Paris to New York. Tomorrow afternoon." Suddenly, Jude was desperate to be back home, where she could cease to be the Other who had to be seduced and demolished lest she prove the bearer of new ways that might threaten to topple the old.

"Ah, but madame, I am so terribly sorry," he said with a delighted smile. "You cannot go from Paris to New York tomorrow afternoon, because there are no seats available until next Monday."

Jude burst out laughing.

He looked at her, alarmed to be alone in his office with a crackpot. "Something is the matter?"

"I'm almost sure you wouldn't understand."

THE FOLLOWING MONDAY, JUDE looked out the plane window at the massed columns of clouds below, papillae in the gullet of the sky. She reclined in her seat as drinks, meals, headsets, blankets, pillows, and duty-free purchases appeared and disappeared for her seatmate, a Vassar student returning from her junior year in Paris. Out of habit, Jude searched the wispy pillars of cloud for some trace of Molly or her mother, but she saw only a lacy pattern of ice crystals on the plane window.

As the plane plunged through the billowing white canyons, Jude suddenly understood that although those she had loved were largely illusions of her own making, the love that she had felt for them was real. Graveyard love was the love itself, not the specters who inspired it. And it belonged to her. It *was* her. It was the only thing about her that would survive if the plane crashed at that very moment. She was nothing more than a spark who yearned for the flame. And the fact of the yearning was proof of the flame.

As Jude watched her seatmate stand up and head down the aisle toward the toilet, she reflected that if Simon wouldn't give her back her editorial job she could always find work writing lyrics for Barry Manilow. A stewardess paused in the aisle to lean an elbow against the back of the seat in front of Jude. She had a braided twist of dark hair. A gold-and-scarlet scarf at her throat coordinated with her lipstick.

"But you have asked for nothing since we left Paris," she said. "Is there anything at all that I can do for you?" She studied Jude closely with her deep blue eyes.

Jude returned her gaze for a long moment. "Who knows?" she finally replied.

The woman raised one dark crescent eyebrow. *"Et pourquoi pas?"* she murmured, the ghost of a smile playing around the corners of her lips.

A C K N O W L E D G M E N T S

I am very grateful to my editor Carole DeSanti, my copy editor Carol Edwards, my publisher Elaine Koster, and my agent Gloria Loomis, for their invaluable assistance on this book. Many thanks also to my daughter Sara Alther, who, as she says, "has been in this writing thing with you from the beginning." To Francoise Gilot, for guided tours of Paris and important insights into the creative process. To Jan Hokenson, for the use of her room with The View in Montmartre. To Carey Kaplan, for her gift for titles and her incisive critiques of more drafts than she probably cares to remember. To Max and Sissy Strauss, for furthering my opera education. To Jody Crosby, Sandra Norton, Andy Senesac, Christine Tissot, Vicky Wilson, and Evan Zimroth, for careful readings and useful suggestions.

The typeface used in this book is a version of Perpetua, originally designed for Monotype in 1925 by Eric Gill (1882–1940). Gill came to type design at the urging of Stanley Morison from being a stonecutter and wood engraver. This background gave him a point of view unique among type designers—the reverse of most others, in fact, since (as he pointed out in *An Essay on Typography*) type had developed from *handwritten* versions of letters cut in *stone*; in creating Perpetua, Gill set out to return to the source. A product of the ferment in the world of crafts (including typography) in the wake of William Morris, Gill was part of an early-twentieth-century British milieu in which to be both a Catholic and a Socialist, to make art on both religious and sexual themes (sometimes in the same drawing!), to be both an artist and a craftsman were not considered contradictory.